Shinobi Life

Vol. 6

Created by
Shoko Conami

HAMBURG // LONDON // LOS ANGELES // TOKYO

Shinobi Life 6
Created by Shoko Conami

Translation - Lori Riser
English Adaptation - Ysabet Reinhardt MacFarlane
Copy Editor - Joseph Heller
Retouch and Lettering - Star Print Brokers
Production Artist - Michael Paolilli
Graphic Designer - Kenneth Chan

Editor - Lillian Diaz-Przybyl
Print Production Manager - Lucas Rivera
Managing Editor - Vy Nguyen
Senior Designer - Louis Csontos
Art Director - Al-Insan Lashley
Director of Sales and Manufacturing - Allyson De Simone
Associate Publisher - Marco F. Pavia
President and C.O.O. - John Parker
C.E.O. and Chief Creative Officer - Stu Levy

A  Manga

TOKYOPOP and 🐾 are trademarks or registered trademarks of TOKYOPOP Inc.

TOKYOPOP Inc.
5900 Wilshire Blvd. Suite 2000
Los Angeles, CA 90036

E-mail: info@TOKYOPOP.com
Come visit us online at www.TOKYOPOP.com

ISBN: 978-1-4278-1755-6

First TOKYOPOP printing: October 2010
10 9 8 7 6 5 4 3 2 1
Printed in the USA

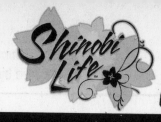

Shinobi Life™

6

SHOKO CONAMI

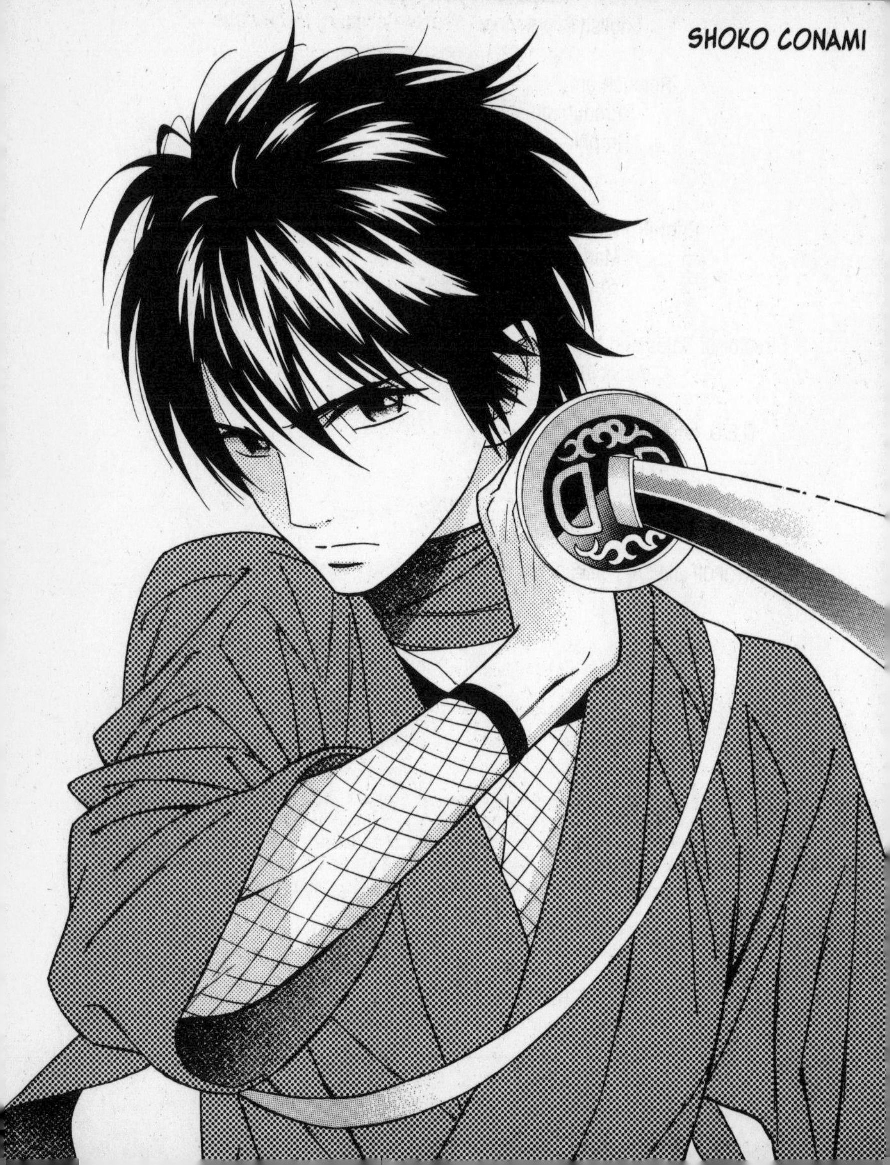

Character Introduction

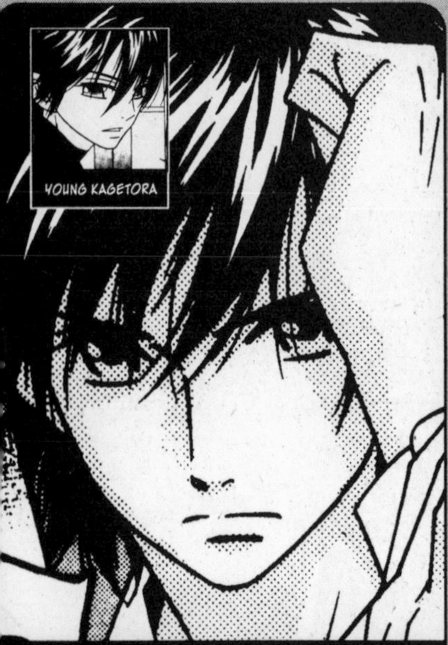
YOUNG KAGETORA

KAGETORA

A NINJA FROM THE PAST. HE'S DECIDED TO LIVE IN THE PRESENT WITH BENI.

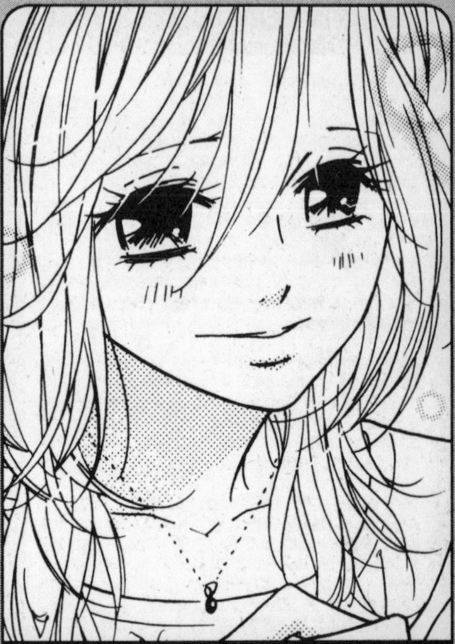

BENI FUJIWARA

A HIGH SCHOOL GIRL WHO'S STARTING TO LIKE KAGETORA (?!).

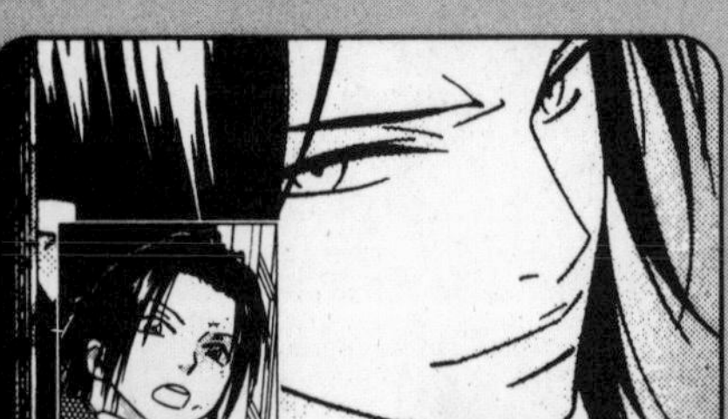
YOUNG HITAKI

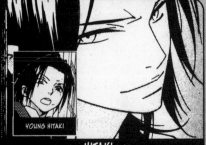

HITAKI

KAGETORA'S NINJA FRIEND. HE TRIES TO TAKE KAGETORA'S LIFE.

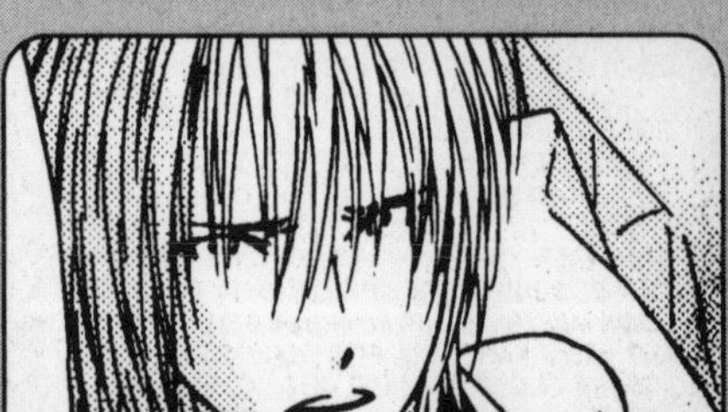

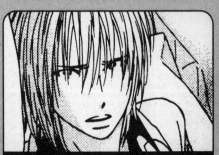

RIHITO IWATSURU

BENI'S CLASSMATE AND FIANCÉ.

BENI FUJIWARA, A HIGH SCHOOL GIRL WHO LONGS FOR DEATH AS REVENGE AGAINST HER CONTROLLING FATHER, IS UNEXPECTEDLY RESCUED ONE DAY WHEN SHE FALLS OFF A BUILDING. HER SAVIOR? A NINJA NAMED KAGETORA, WHO FALLS FROM THE SKY AT THE RIGHT MOMENT. KAGETORA CALLS BENI "BENI HIME," AND DEVOTES HIMSELF TO PROTECTING HER AT ANY COST...AT FIRST BECAUSE HE MISTAKES HER FOR HER OWN ANCESTOR, WHO LOOKED EXACTLY LIKE HER. YES, KAGETORA IS A NINJA WHO HAS TRAVELED THROUGH TIME FROM THE PAST!

AS TIME PASSES, BENI GRADUALLY BECOMES FOND OF KAGETORA AFTER HE REPEATEDLY SAVES HER FROM DANGER AND PLEDGES HIS ETERNAL LOYALTY. SHE TRIES TO PRETEND TO BE BENI HIME FOR HIM, AND THEY SLOWLY BECOME CLOSER AND CLOSER.

BUT WHEN THE PAIR UNEXPECTEDLY TRAVELS BACK TO KAGETORA'S TIME, HE RUNS INTO THE REAL BENI HIME AND REALIZES THAT THE TWO WOMEN ARE NOT THE SAME PERSON. AFTER BENI HIME TELLS KAGETORA THAT SHE WANTS TO LIVE AS A NORMAL VILLAGER, HE LOSES HIS PURPOSE IN LIFE. WHEN A FELLOW NINJA, HITAKI, BRANDS HIM A TRAITOR AND TRIES TO KILL HIM, KAGETORA DECIDES TO RETURN TO THE PRESENT WITH BENI AND LIVE WITH HER.

THINGS SEEM TO BE GOING SMOOTHLY FOR BENI AND KAGETORA'S FLEDGLING ROMANCE, BUT THAT COMES TO AN ABRUPT END WHEN BENI'S FATHER REVEALS THAT BENI ALREADY HAS A FIANCE--RIHITO IWATSURU! AND WHAT'S MORE, RIHITO SEEMS TO BE CONNECTED TO HITAKI.

BENI AND KAGETORA FLEE HER FATHER'S HOUSE TO ESCAPE HIS CONTROL AND RIHITO'S AGGRESSION. WHEN HITAKI CORNERS THEM ON A ROOFTOP, THEY DECIDE TO ESCAPE TO THE PAST...BUT ALONG THE WAY, THEY'RE SEPARATED. ALONE IN THE PAST, BENI ENCOUNTERS KAGETORA--BUT A 14-YEAR-OLD KAGETORA WHO DOESN'T KNOW HER OR BENI HIME! SHE SOON MEETS HITAKI'S YOUNGER SELF AS WELL, AND FROM KAGETORA SHE LEARNS HOW HITAKI AND HIS OLDER BROTHER WERE SEPARATED AS CHILDREN. KAGETORA, WHO HAS NO FAMILY OF HIS OWN, FEELS GUILTY FOR ENVYING HITAKI'S RELATIONSHIP WITH HIS BROTHER. BENI WISHES SHE COULD EASE SOME OF HIS LONELINESS, BUT A HUNDRED YEARS SEPARATE THEIR HEARTS...

RENKAKU

KAGETORA AND HITAKI'S GUARDIAN IN THE PAST.

HACHIKUMA

HITAKI'S GUARDIAN IN THE PAST.

TOUKICHI

CONTENTS

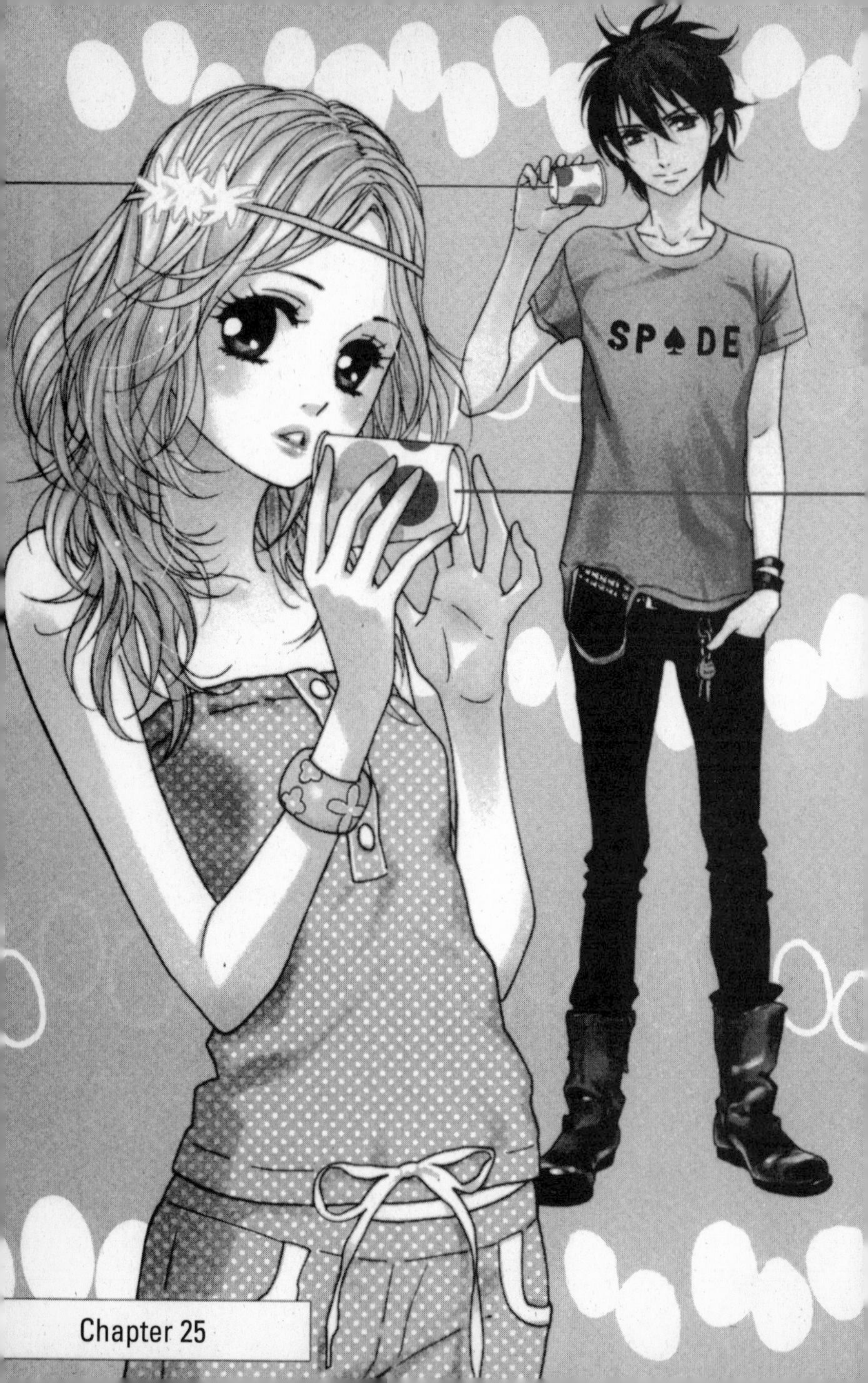
SP♠DE

Chapter 25

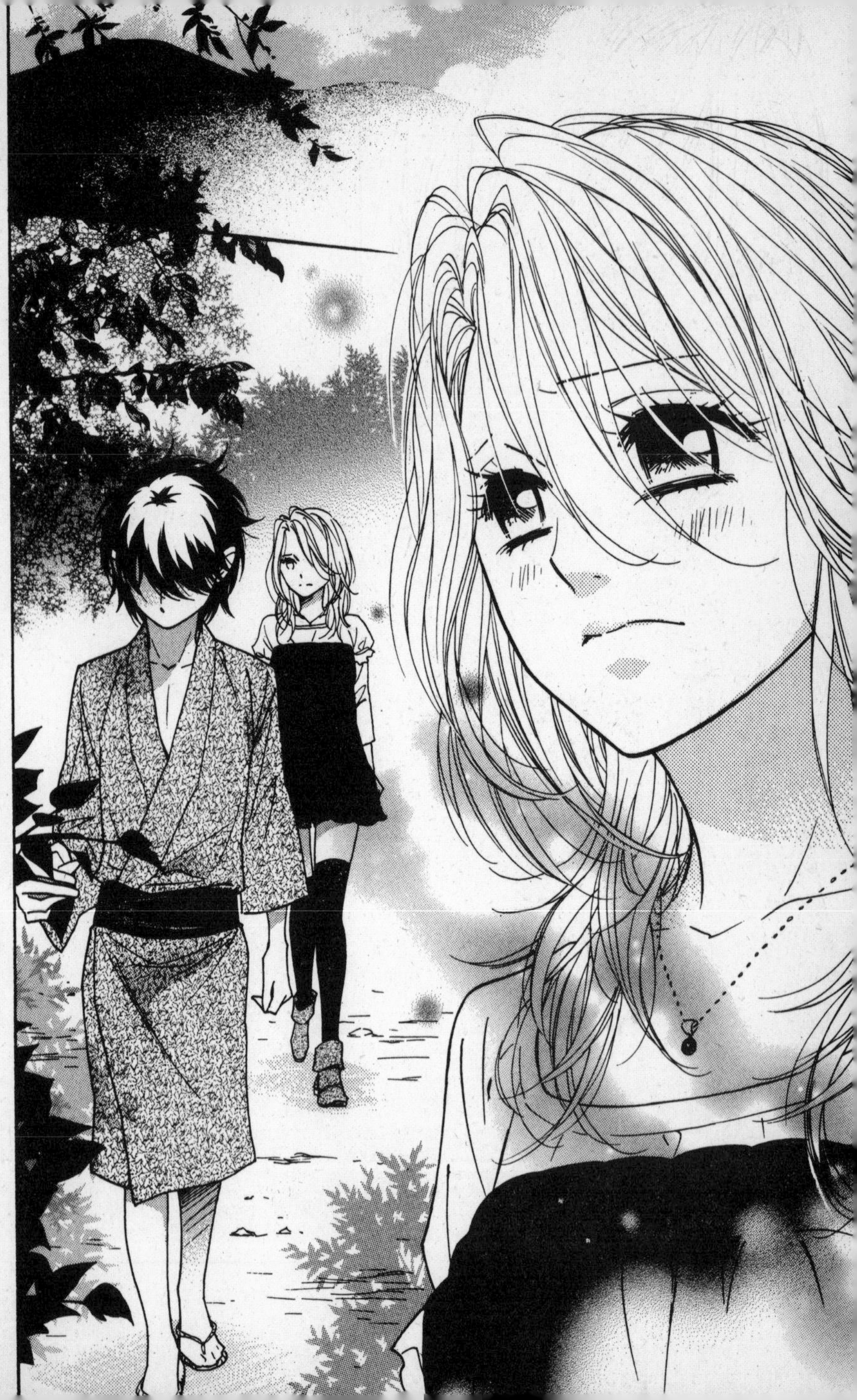

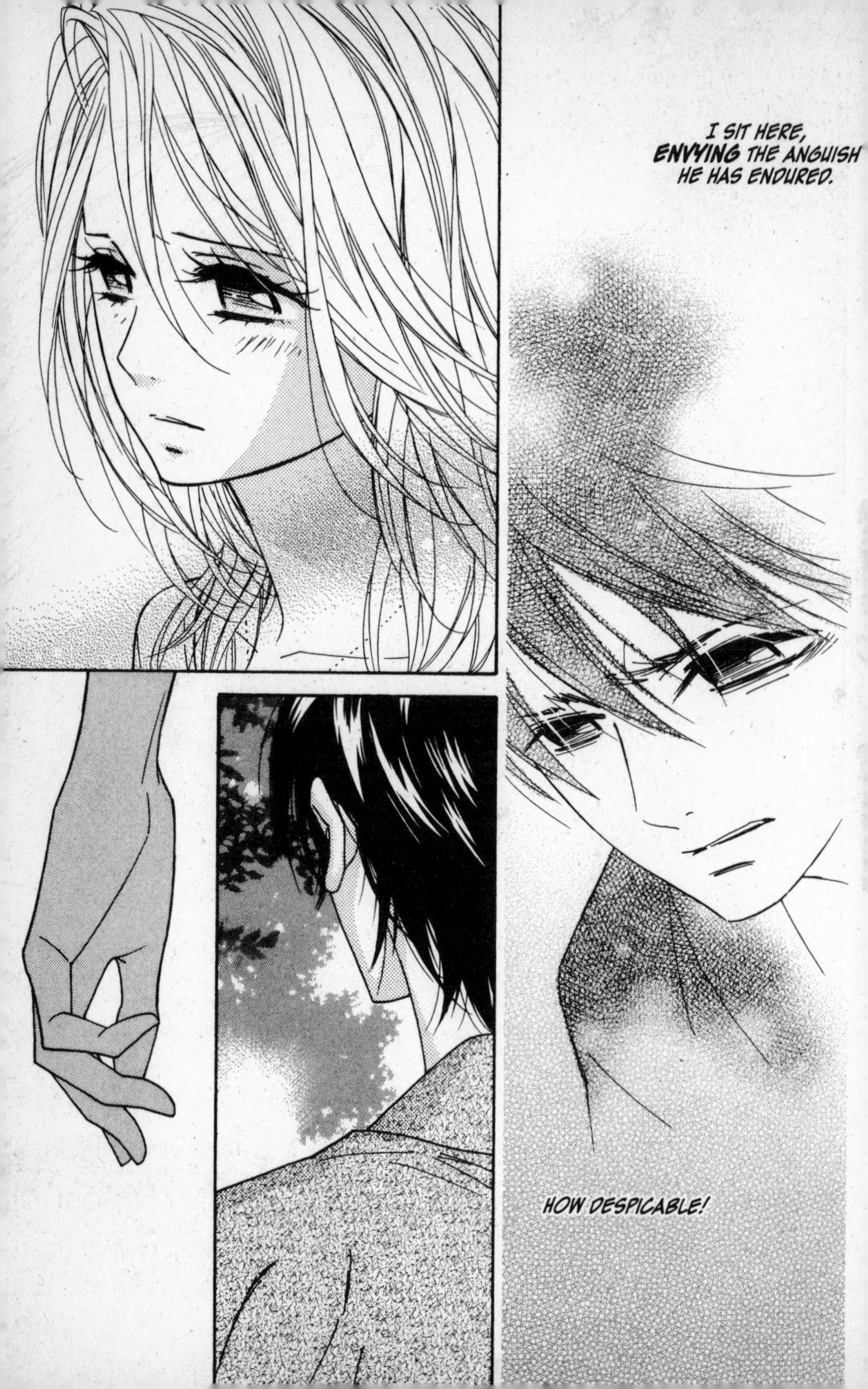
I SIT HERE, ENVYING THE ANGUISH HE HAS ENDURED.
HOW DESPICABLE!

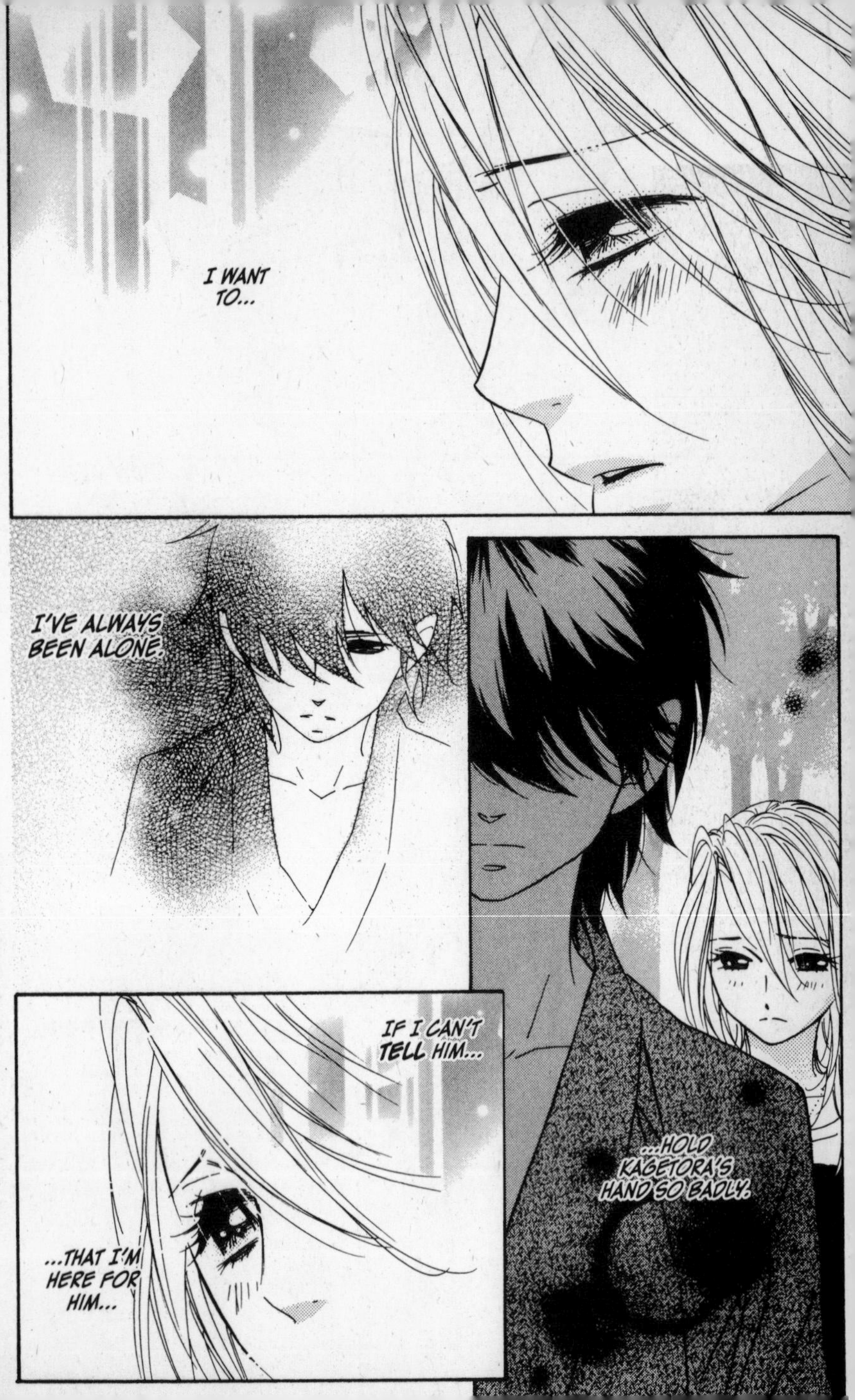
I WANT TO...
I'VE ALWAYS BEEN ALONE.
IF I CAN'T TELL HIM...
...THAT I'M HERE FOR HIM...
...HOLD KAGETORA'S HAND SO BADLY.

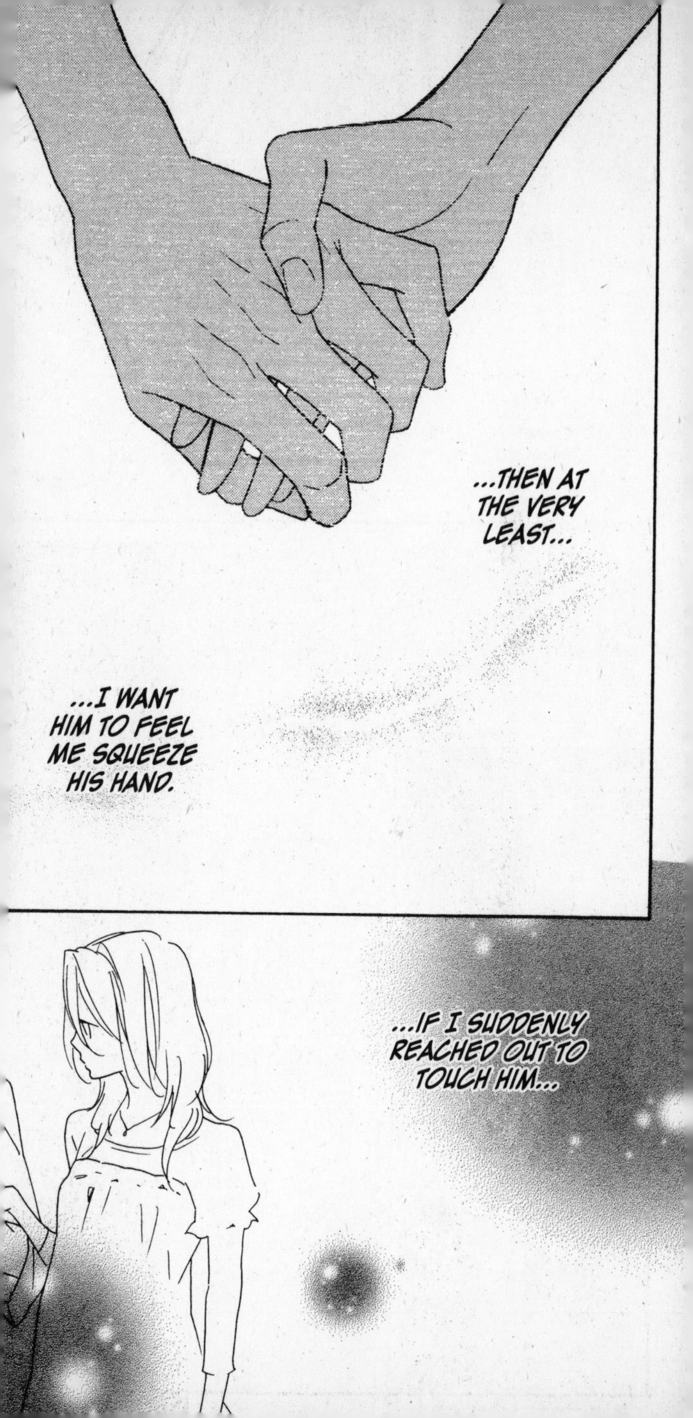
...THEN AT THE VERY LEAST...
...I WANT HIM TO FEEL ME SQUEEZE HIS HAND.
...IF I SUDDENLY REACHED OUT TO TOUCH HIM...

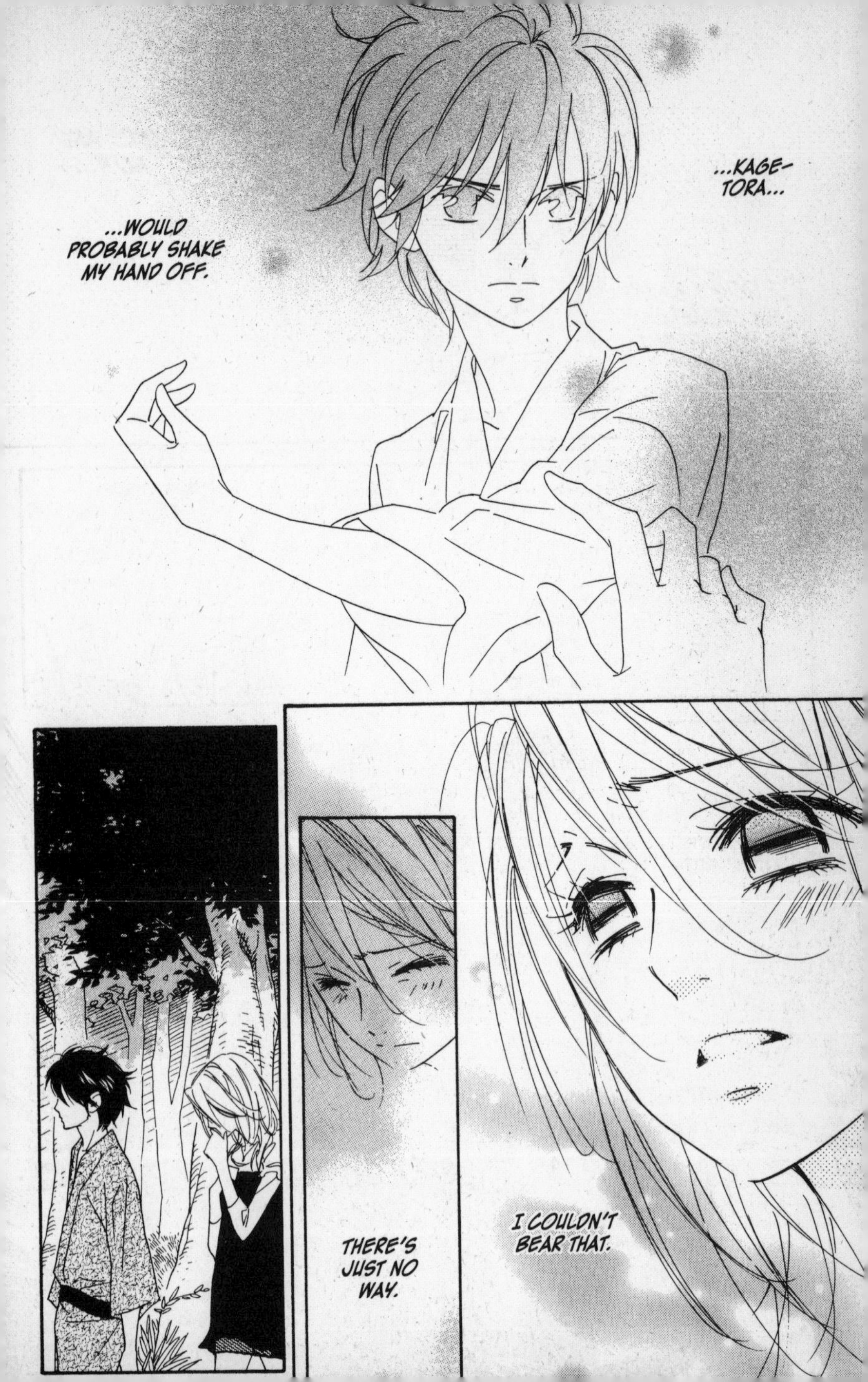
...KAGE-TORA...
...WOULD PROBABLY SHAKE MY HAND OFF.
I COULDN'T BEAR THAT.
THERE'S JUST NO WAY.

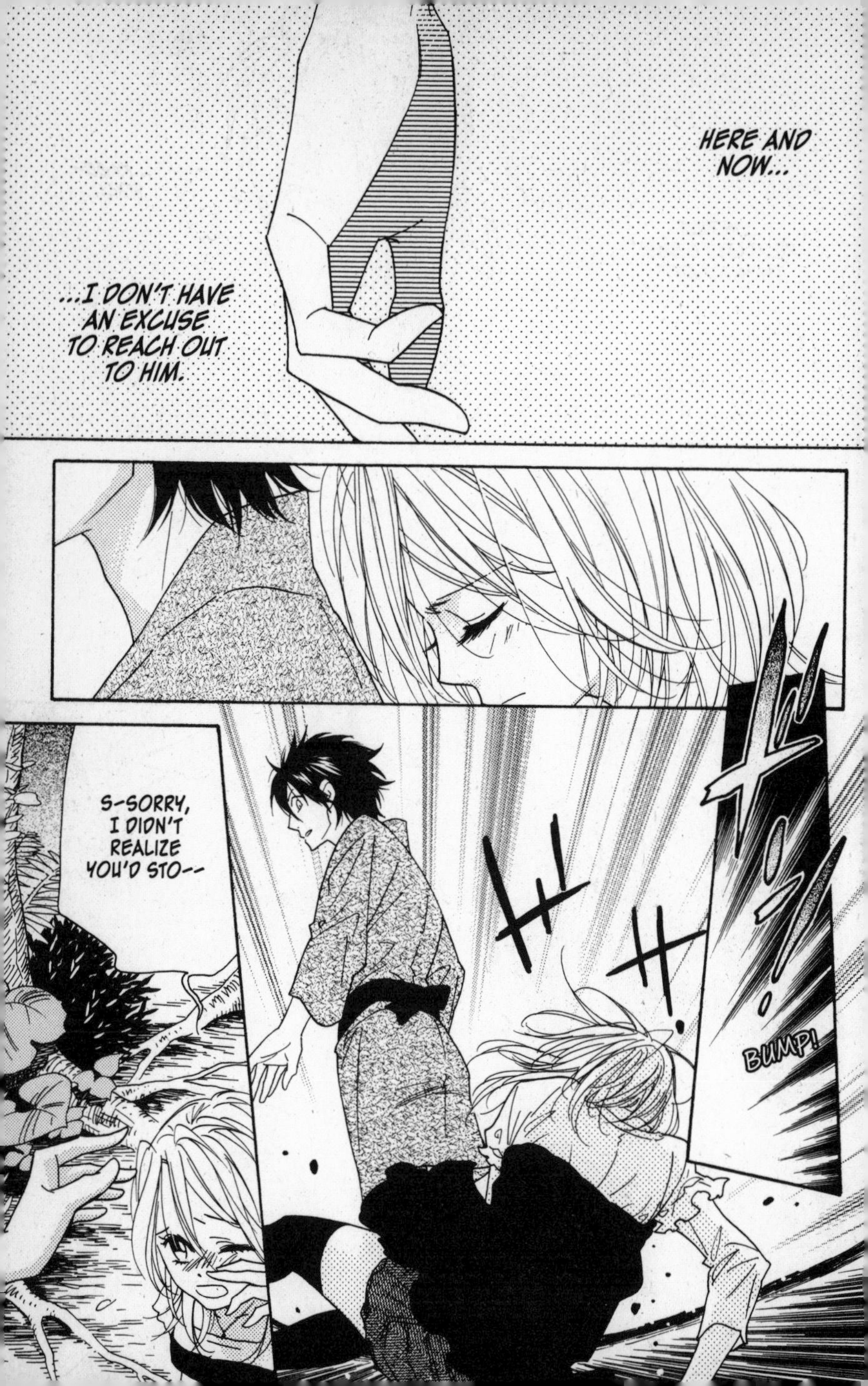
HERE AND NOW...
...I DON'T HAVE AN EXCUSE TO REACH OUT TO HIM.
BUMP!
S-SORRY, I DIDN'T REALIZE YOU'D STO--

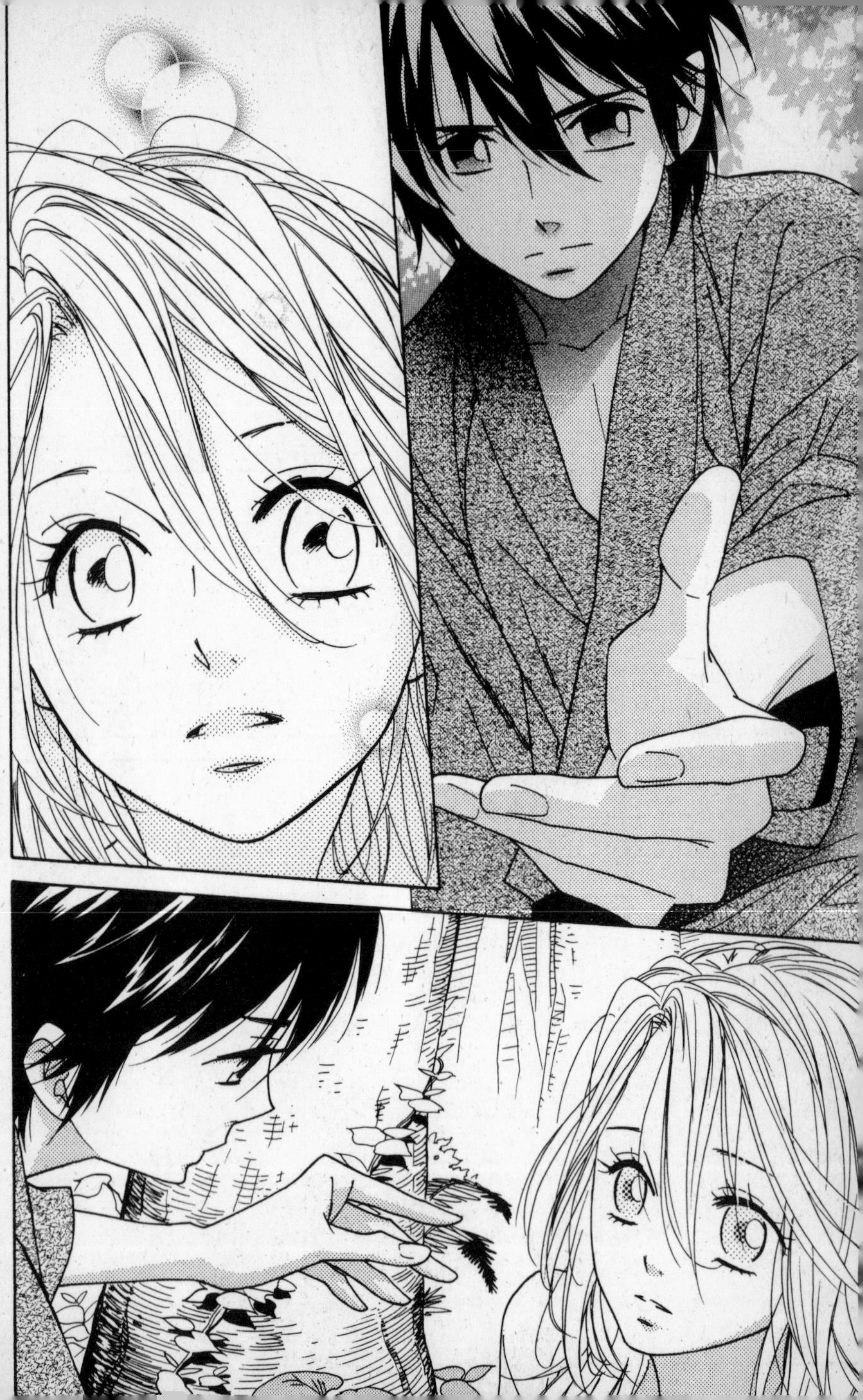

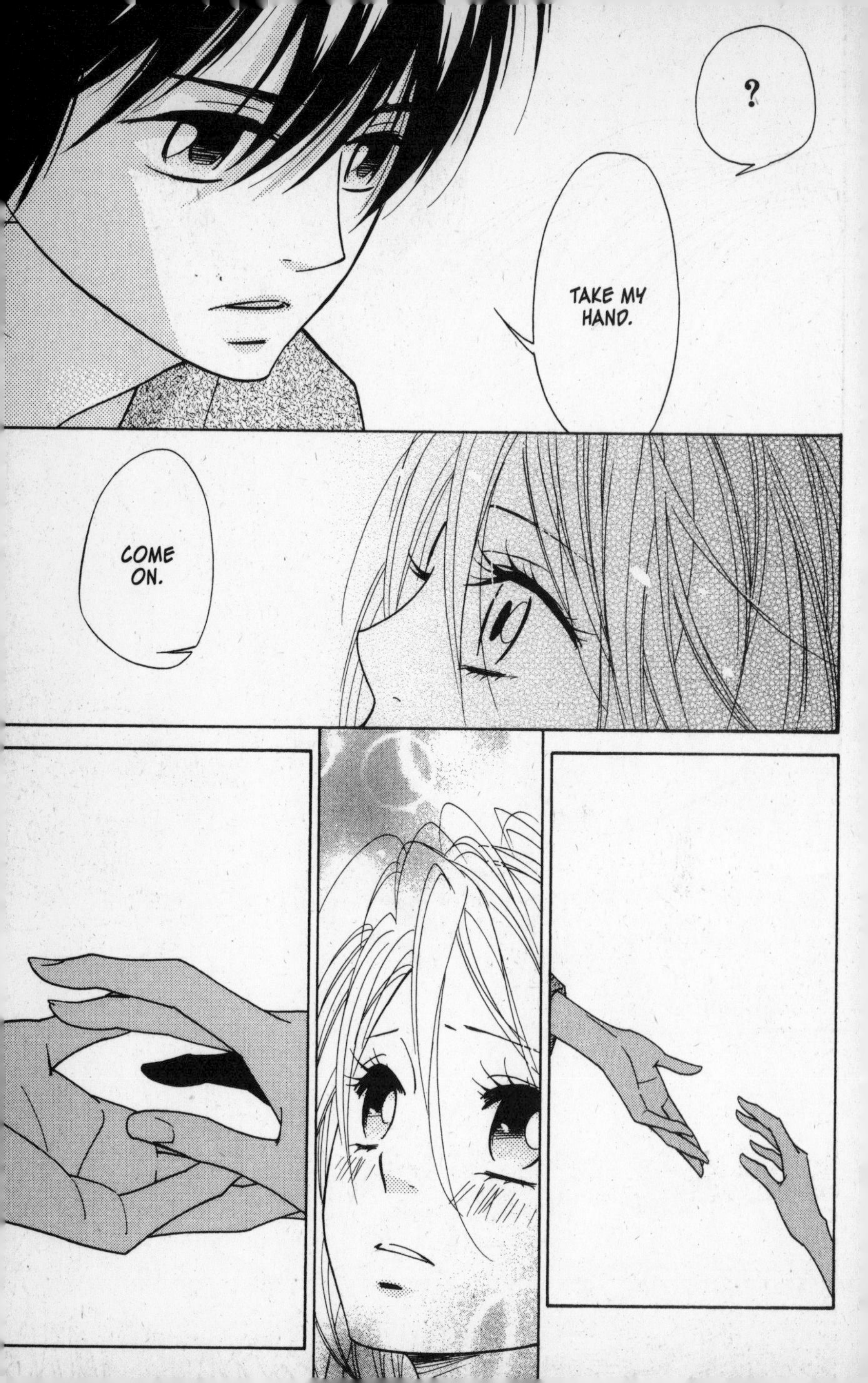
?
TAKE MY HAND.
COME ON.

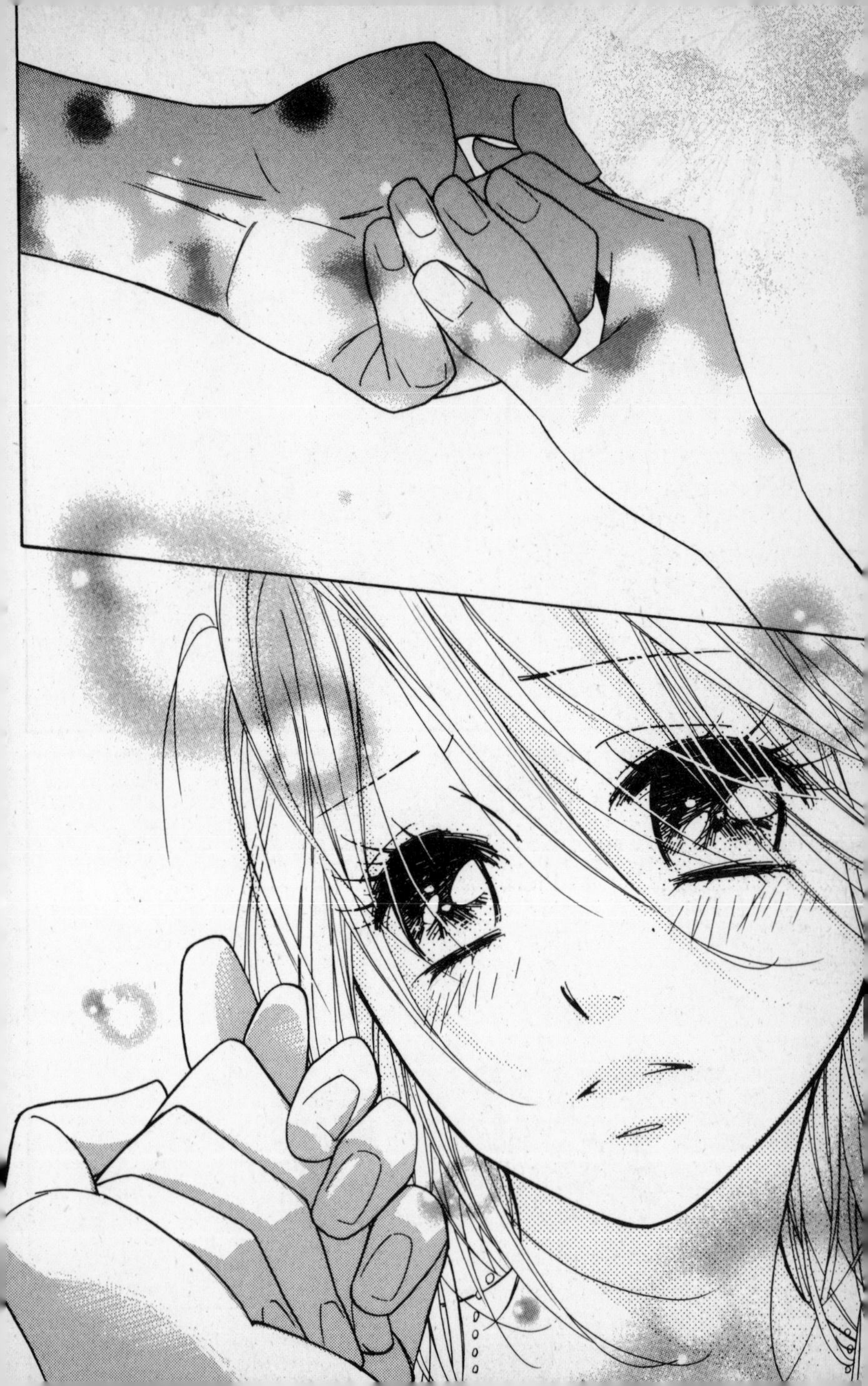

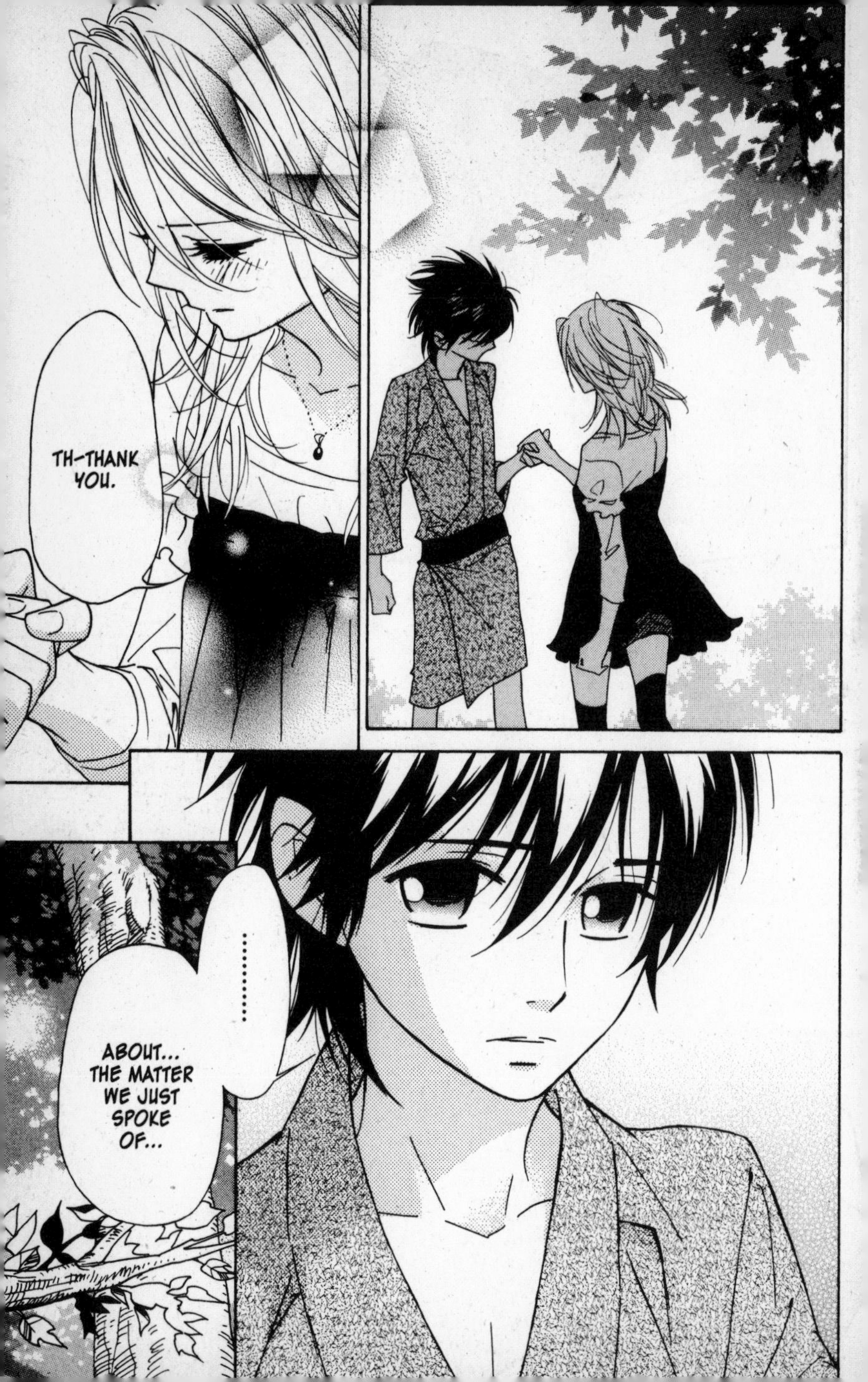

TH-THANK YOU.
......
ABOUT... THE MATTER WE JUST SPOKE OF...

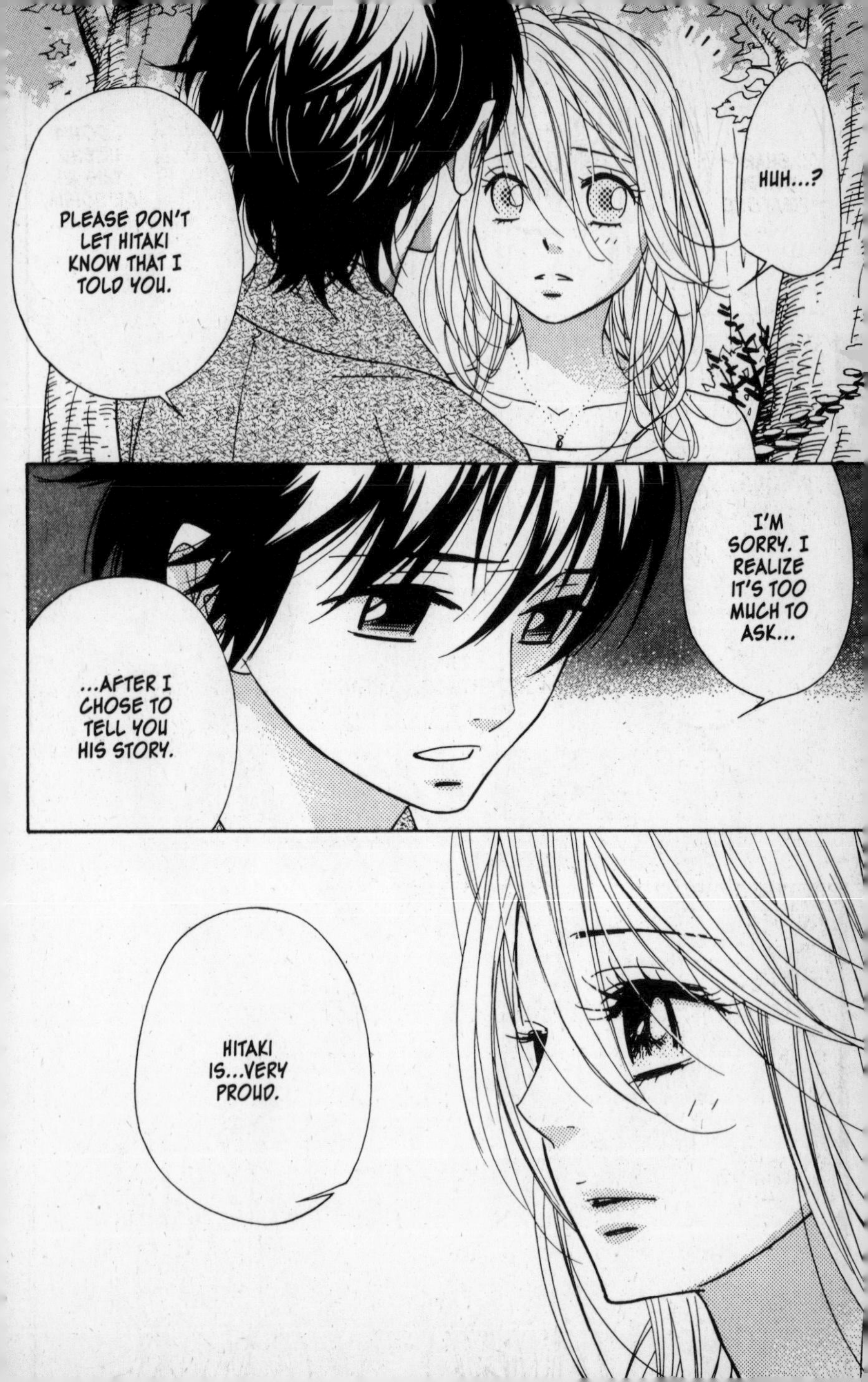
HUH...?
PLEASE DON'T LET HITAKI KNOW THAT I TOLD YOU.
I'M SORRY. I REALIZE IT'S TOO MUCH TO ASK...
...AFTER I CHOSE TO TELL YOU HIS STORY.
HITAKI IS...VERY PROUD.

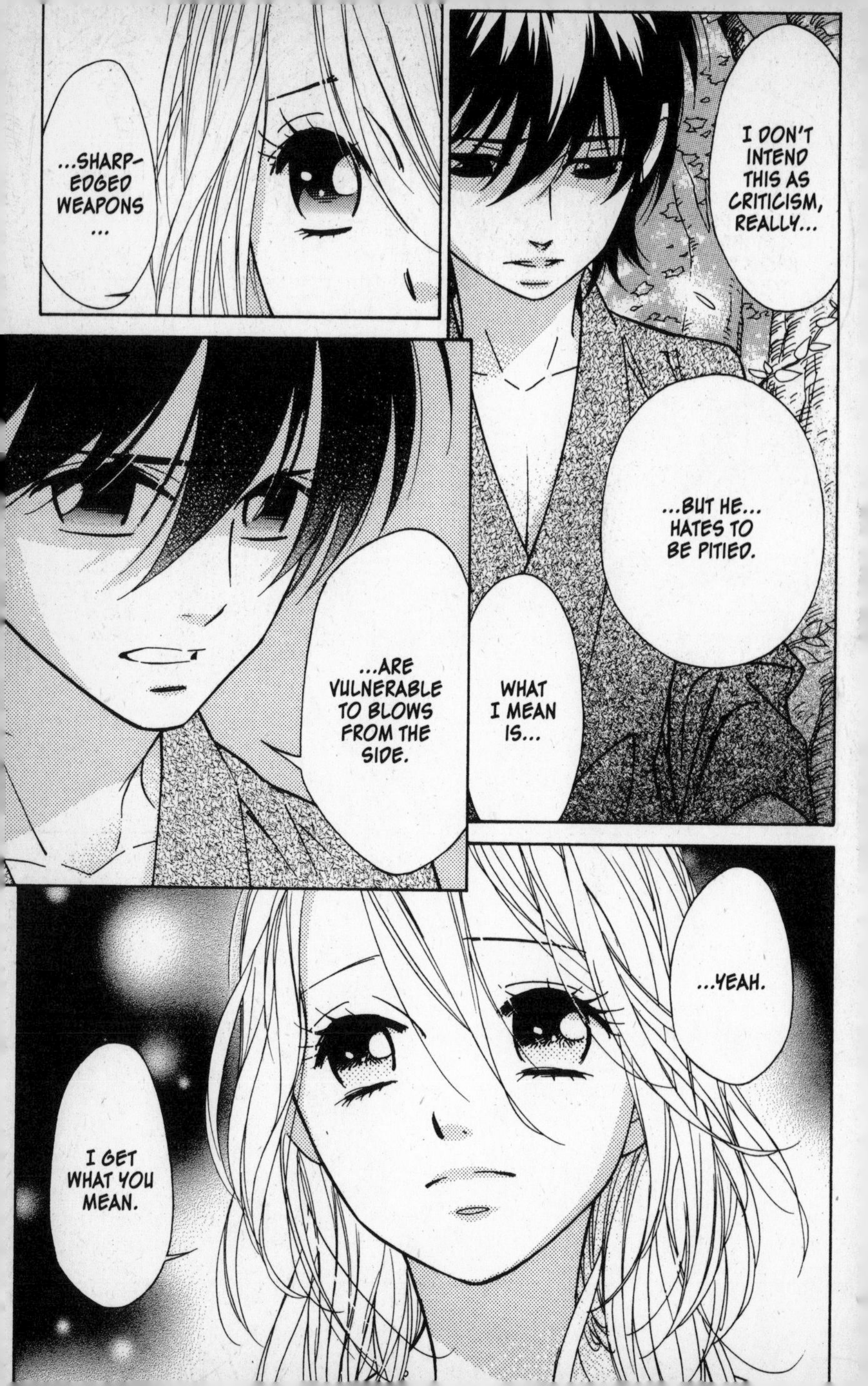
I DON'T INTEND THIS AS CRITICISM, REALLY...
...BUT HE... HATES TO BE PITIED.
WHAT I MEAN IS...
...SHARP-EDGED WEAPONS ...
...ARE VULNERABLE TO BLOWS FROM THE SIDE.
...YEAH.
I GET WHAT YOU MEAN.

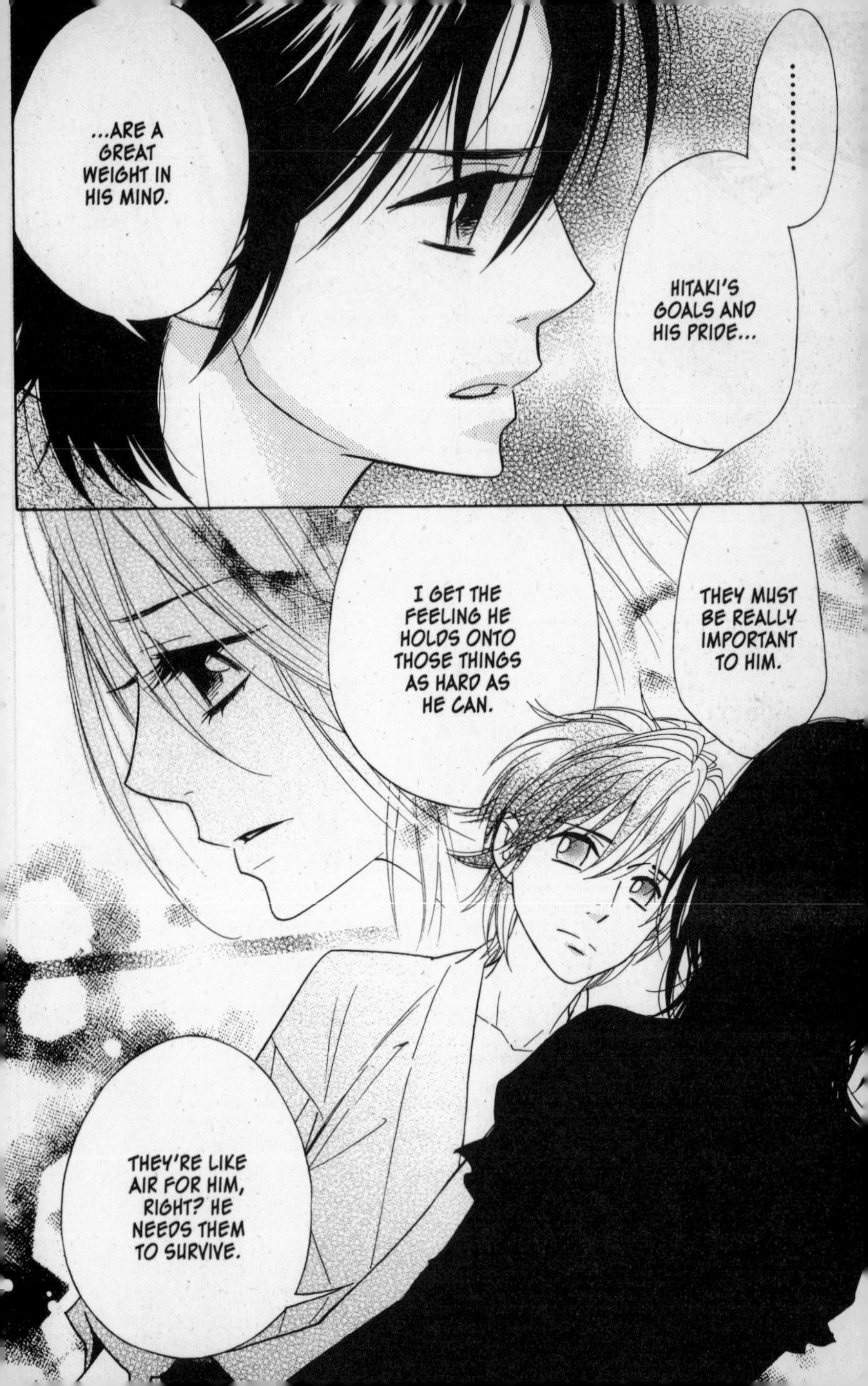
……
HITAKI'S GOALS AND HIS PRIDE...
...ARE A GREAT WEIGHT IN HIS MIND.
THEY MUST BE REALLY IMPORTANT TO HIM.
I GET THE FEELING HE HOLDS ONTO THOSE THINGS AS HARD AS HE CAN.
THEY'RE LIKE AIR FOR HIM, RIGHT? HE NEEDS THEM TO SURVIVE.

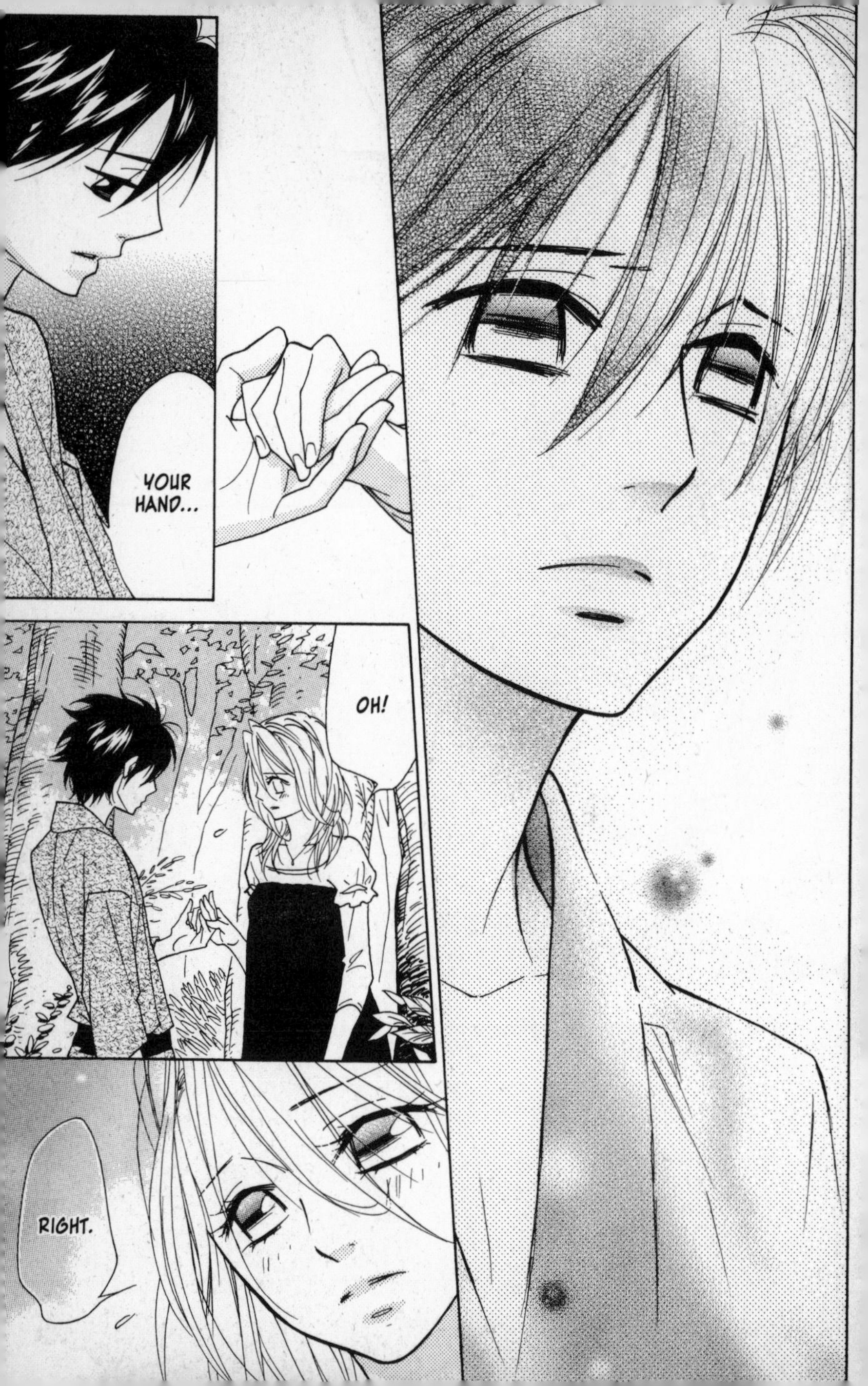
YOUR HAND...
OH!
RIGHT.

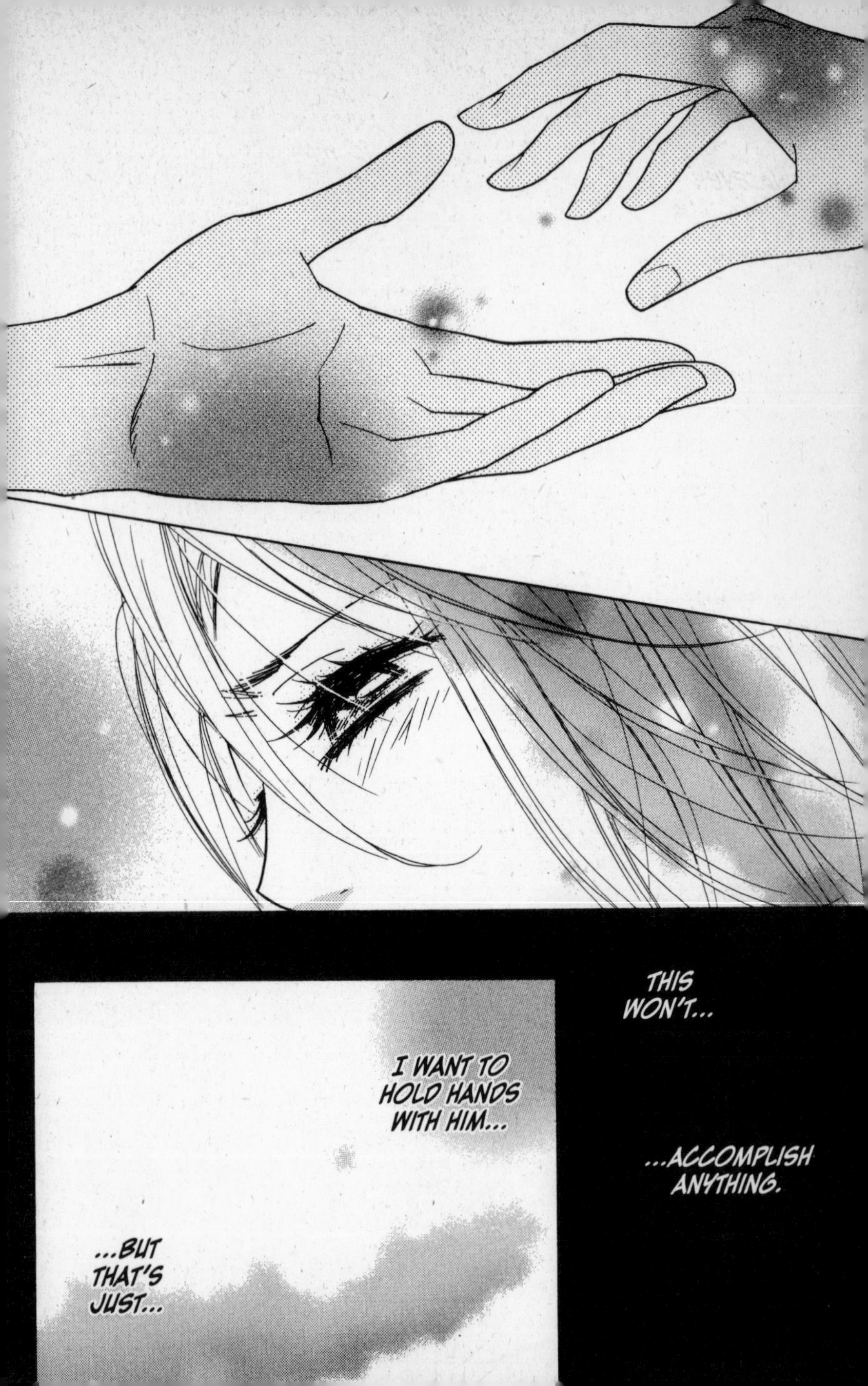
THIS WON'T...
...ACCOMPLISH ANYTHING.
I WANT TO HOLD HANDS WITH HIM...
...BUT THAT'S JUST...

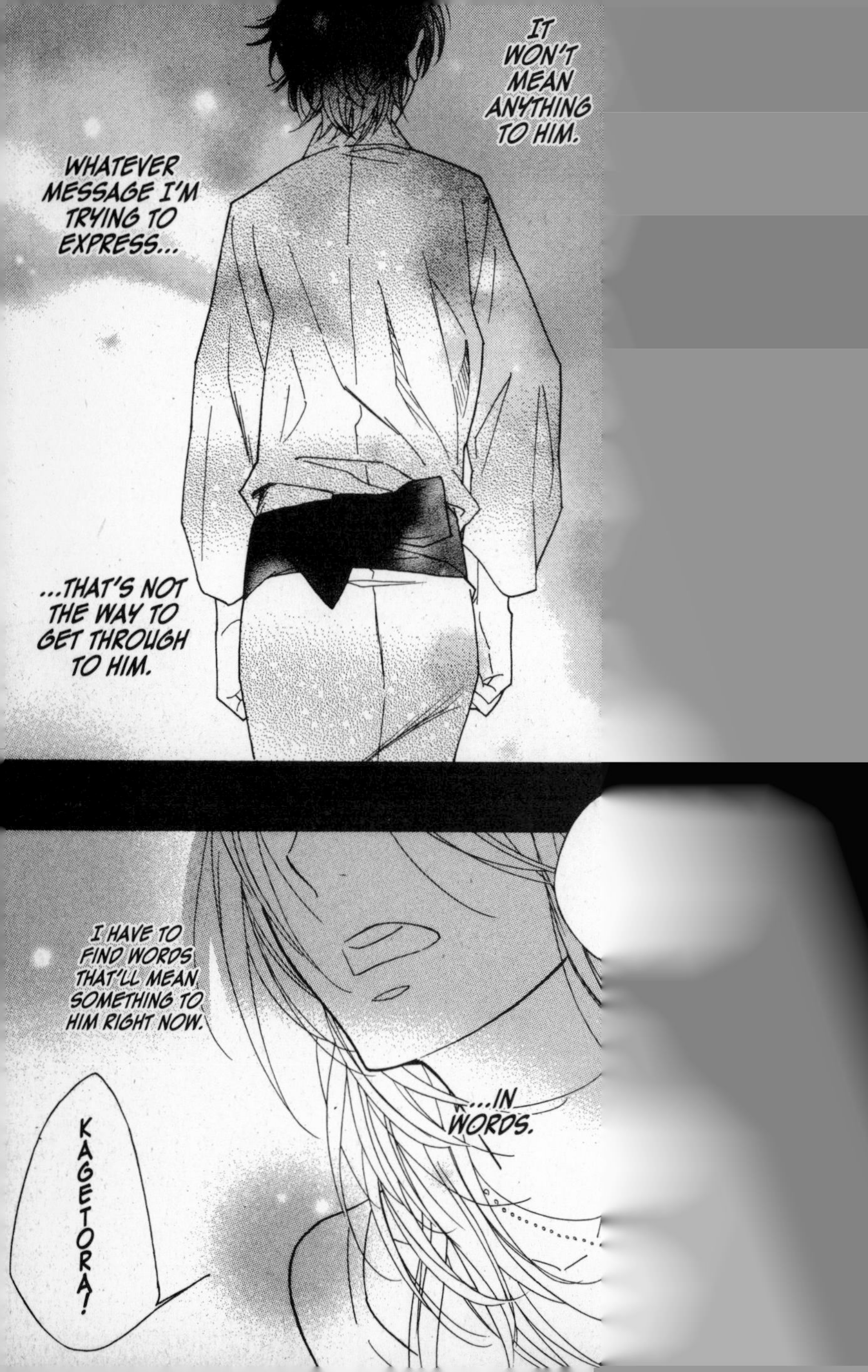
IT WON'T MEAN ANYTHING TO HIM.
WHATEVER MESSAGE I'M TRYING TO EXPRESS...
...THAT'S NOT THE WAY TO GET THROUGH TO HIM.
...IN WORDS.
I HAVE TO FIND WORDS THAT'LL MEAN SOMETHING TO HIM RIGHT NOW.
KAGETORA!

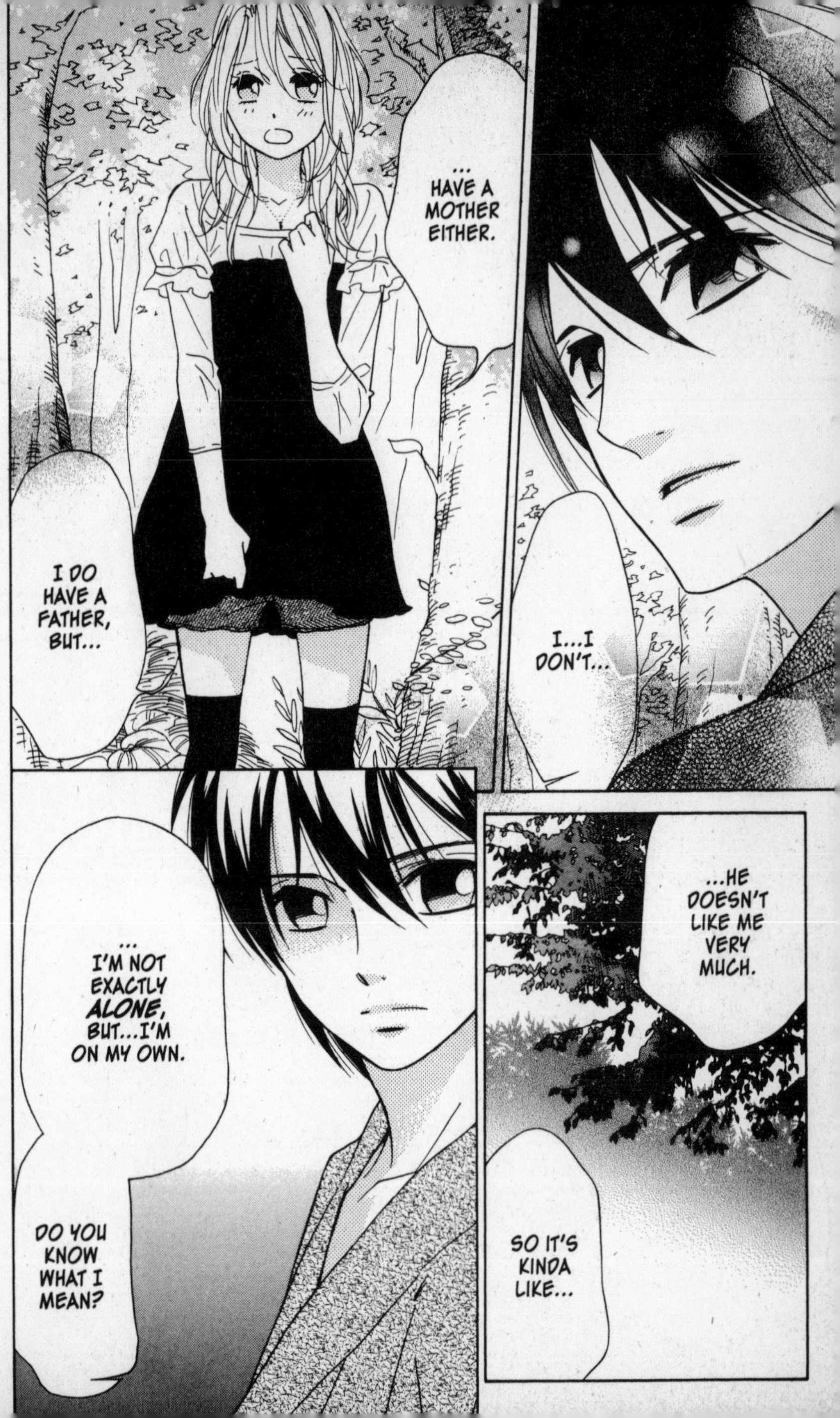

I...I DON'T...
...HAVE A MOTHER EITHER.
I DO HAVE A FATHER, BUT...
...HE DOESN'T LIKE ME VERY MUCH.
SO IT'S KINDA LIKE...
...I'M NOT EXACTLY *ALONE*, BUT...I'M ON MY OWN.
DO YOU KNOW WHAT I MEAN?

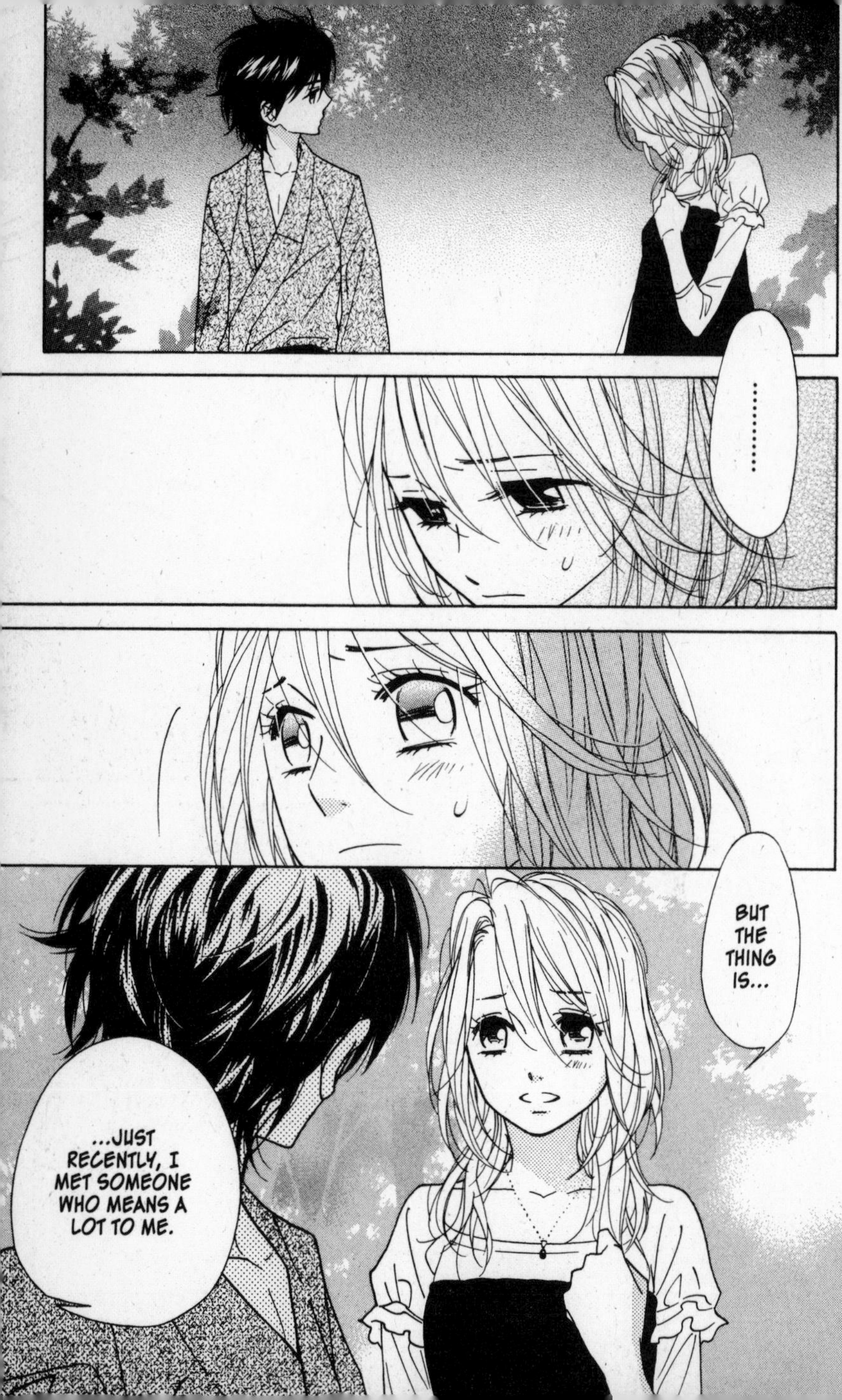
......
BUT THE THING IS...
...JUST RECENTLY, I MET SOMEONE WHO MEANS A LOT TO ME.

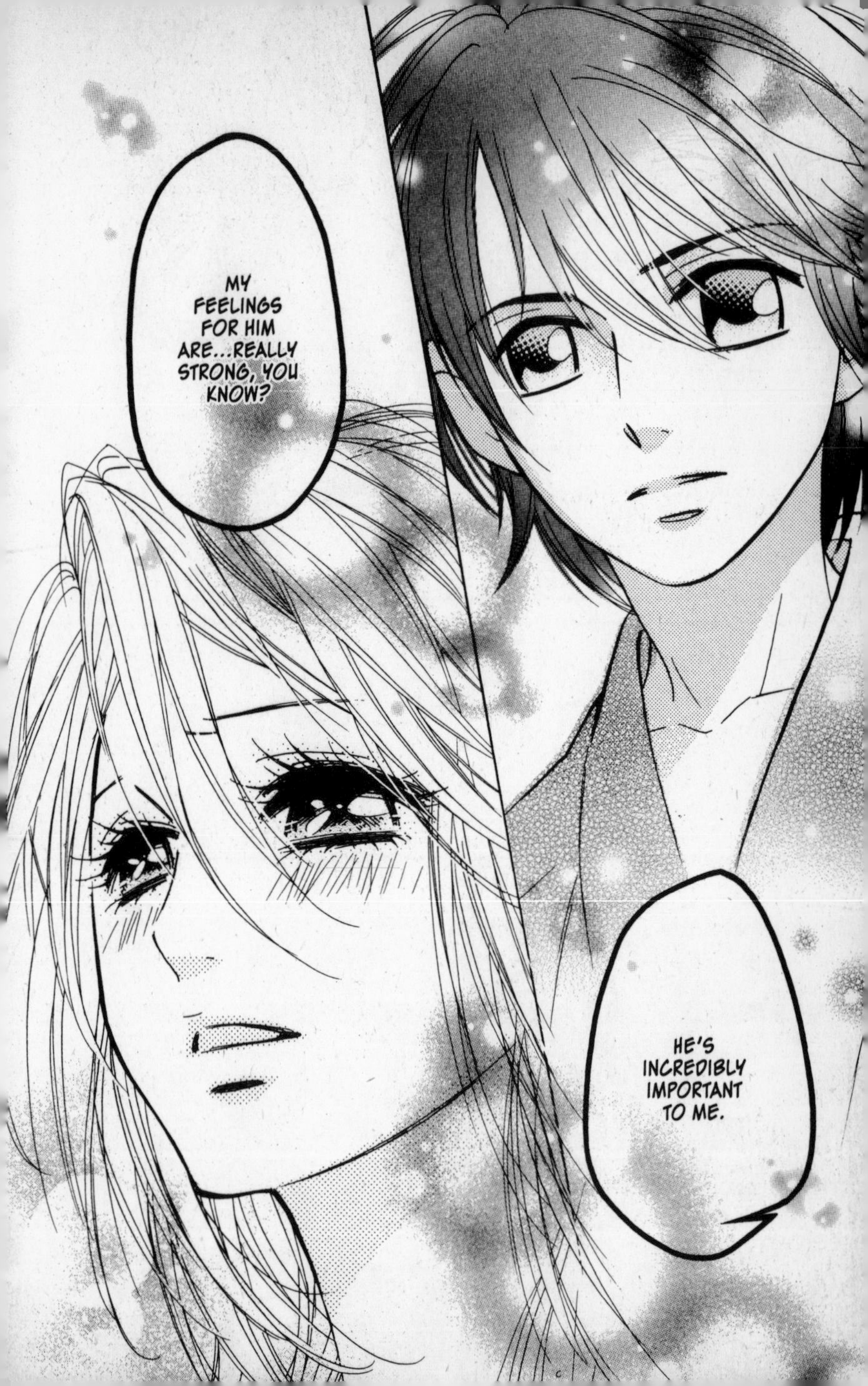
MY FEELINGS FOR HIM ARE...REALLY STRONG, YOU KNOW?
HE'S INCREDIBLY IMPORTANT TO ME.

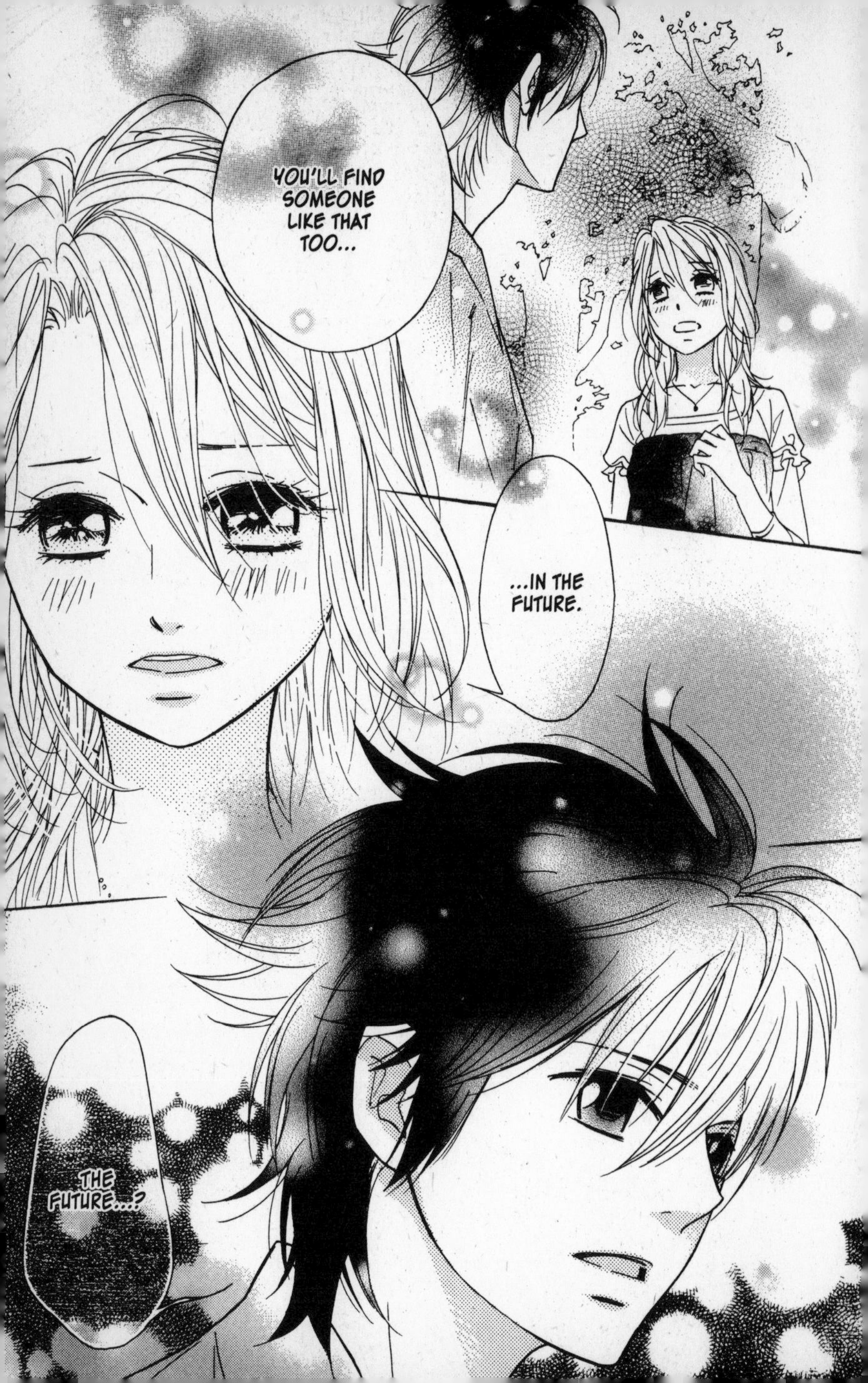
YOU'LL FIND SOMEONE LIKE THAT TOO...
...IN THE FUTURE.
THE FUTURE...?

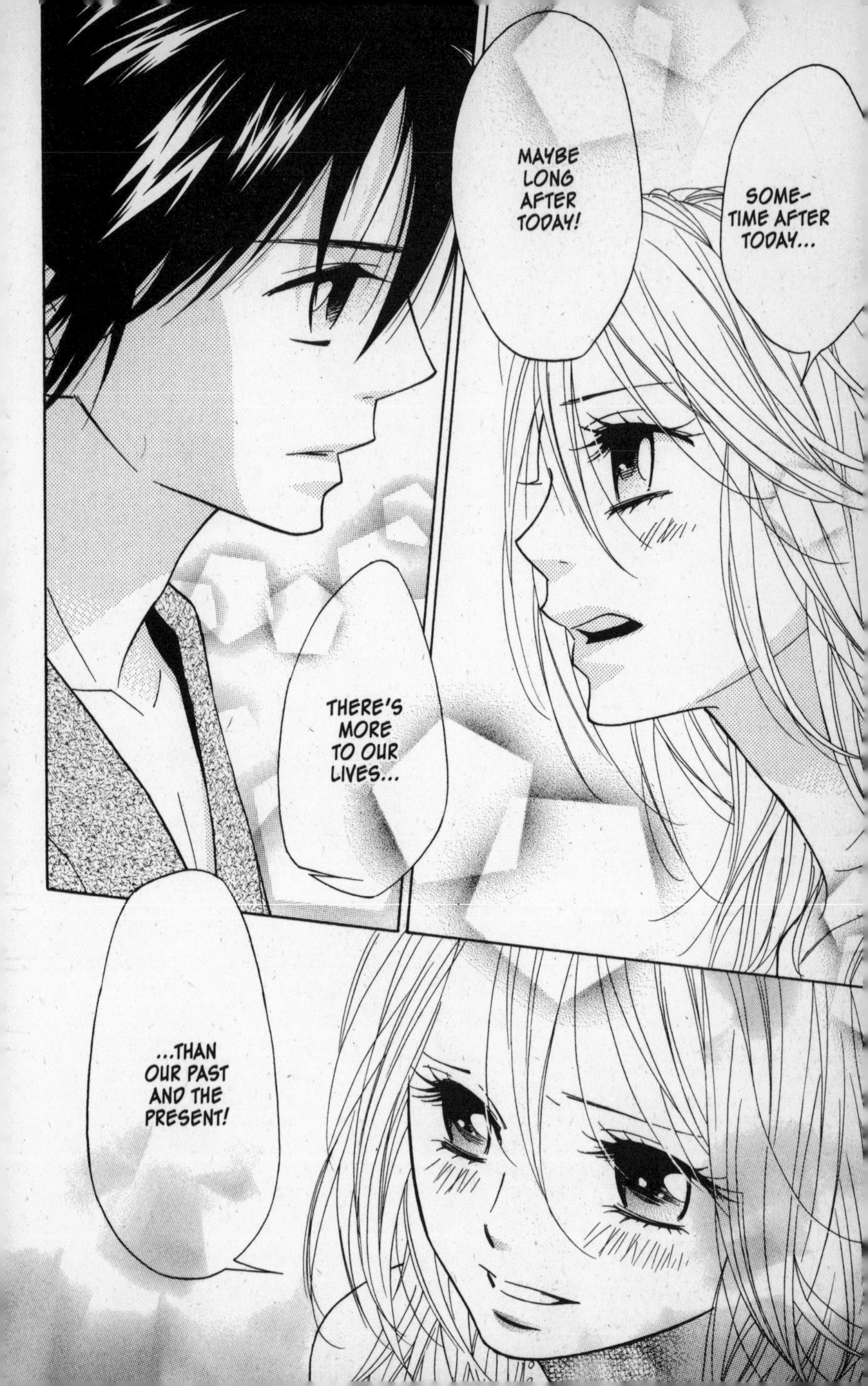
SOME-TIME AFTER TODAY...
MAYBE LONG AFTER TODAY!
THERE'S MORE TO OUR LIVES...
...THAN OUR PAST AND THE PRESENT!

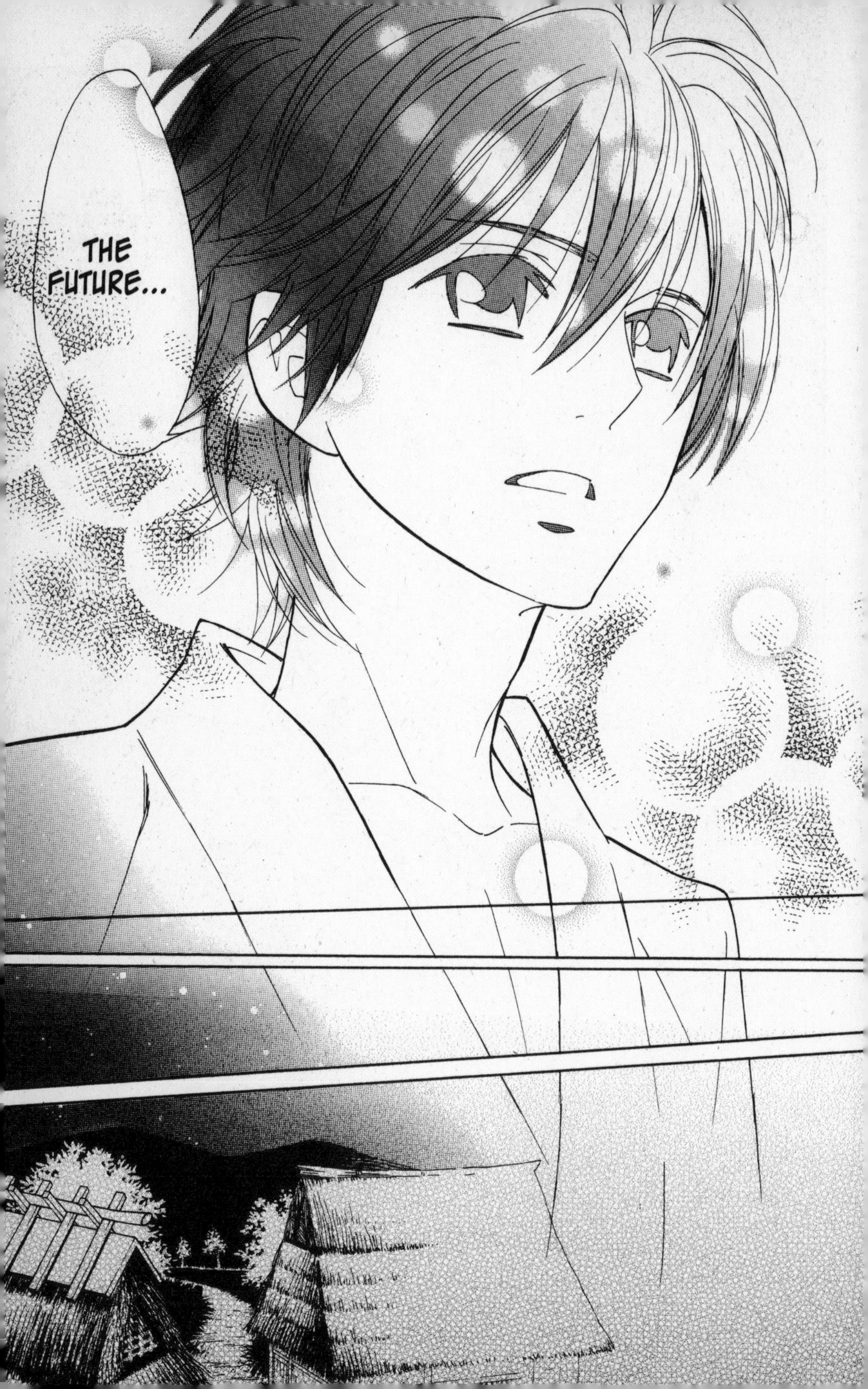
THE FUTURE...

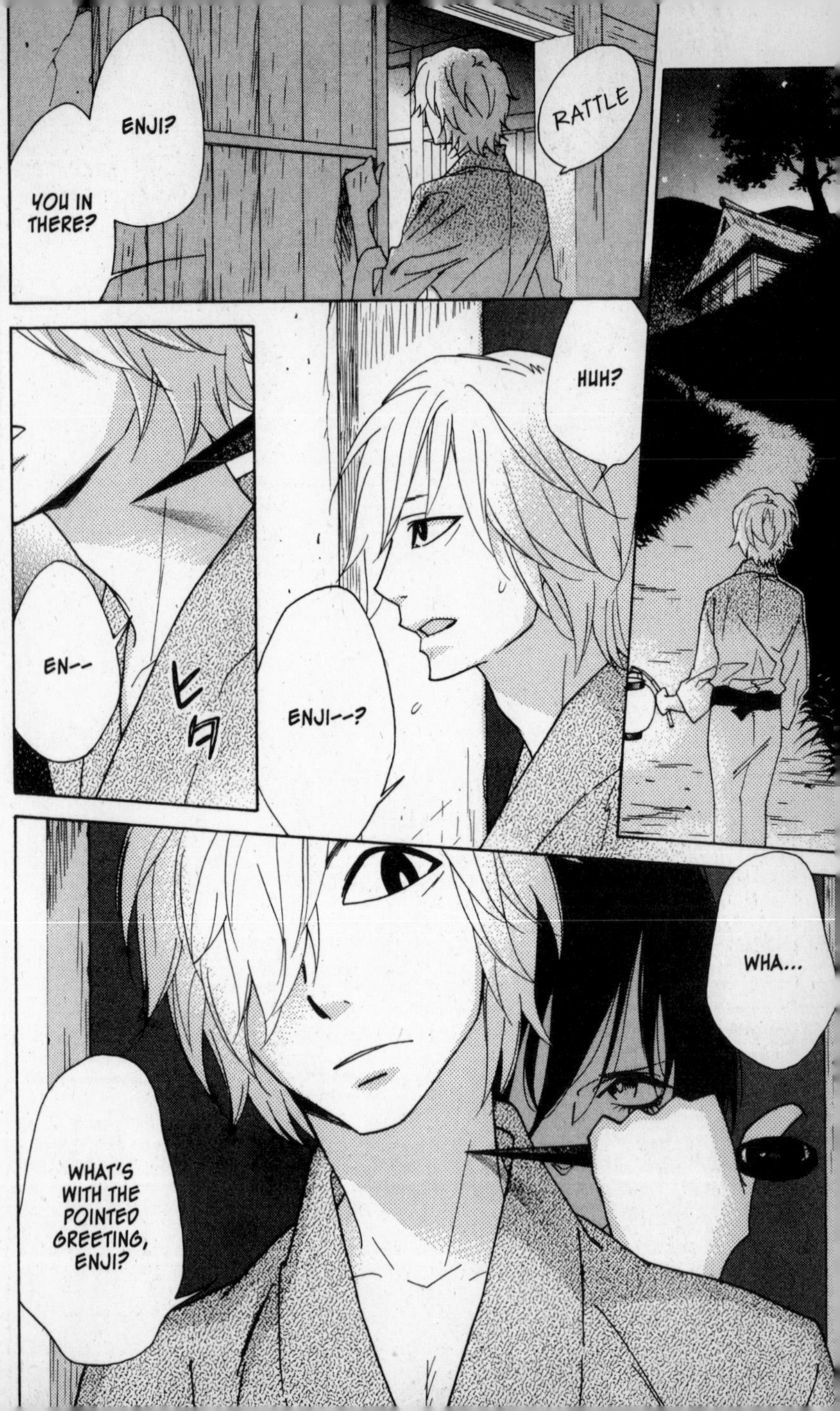
RATTLE
ENJI?
YOU IN THERE?
HUH?
ENJI--?
EN--
ヒタ
WHA...
WHAT'S WITH THE POINTED GREETING, ENJI?

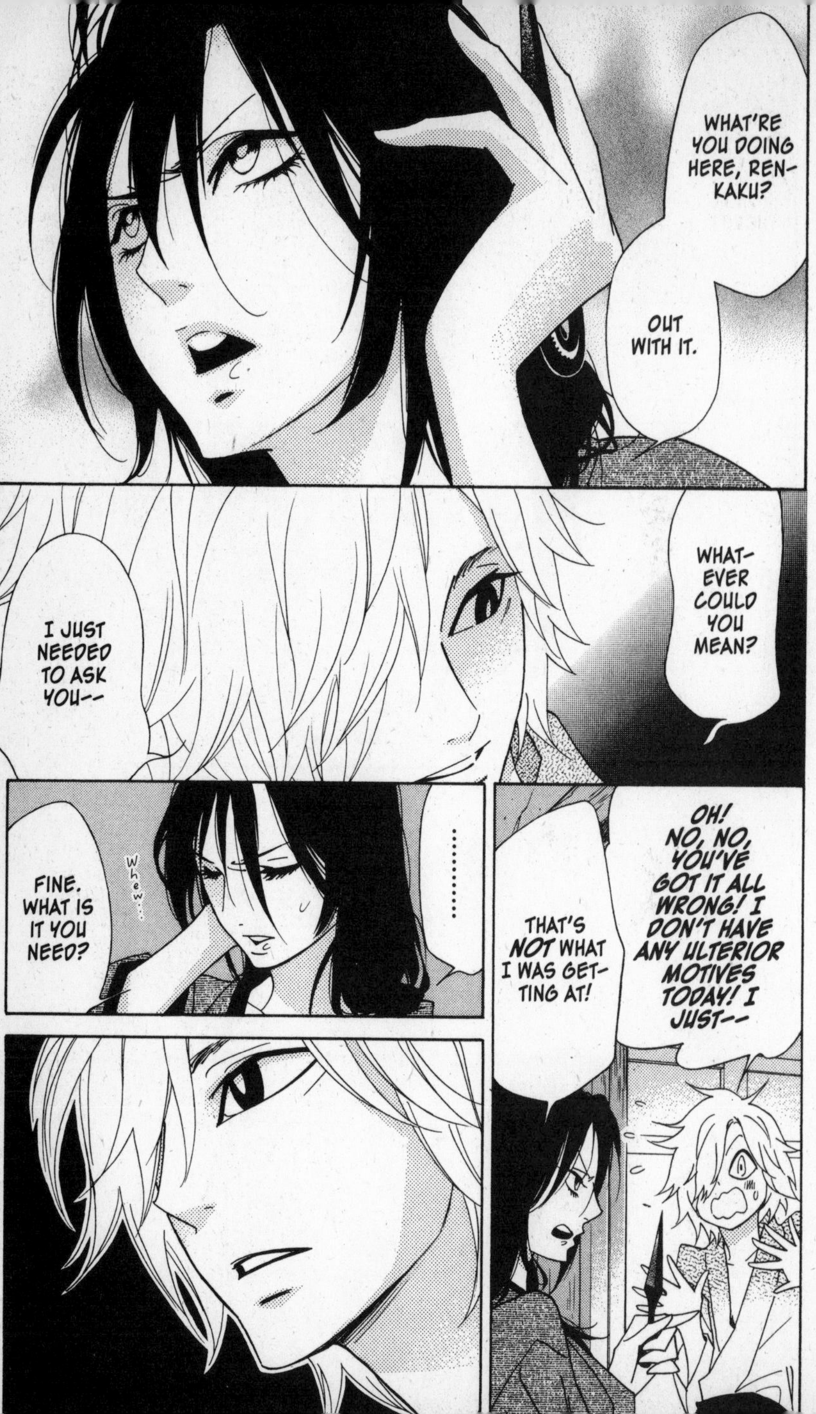
WHAT'RE YOU DOING HERE, REN-KAKU?
OUT WITH IT.
WHAT-EVER COULD YOU MEAN?
I JUST NEEDED TO ASK YOU--
....
Whew...
FINE. WHAT IS IT YOU NEED?
OH! NO, NO, YOU'VE GOT IT ALL WRONG! I DON'T HAVE ANY ULTERIOR MOTIVES TODAY! I JUST--
THAT'S NOT WHAT I WAS GET-TING AT!

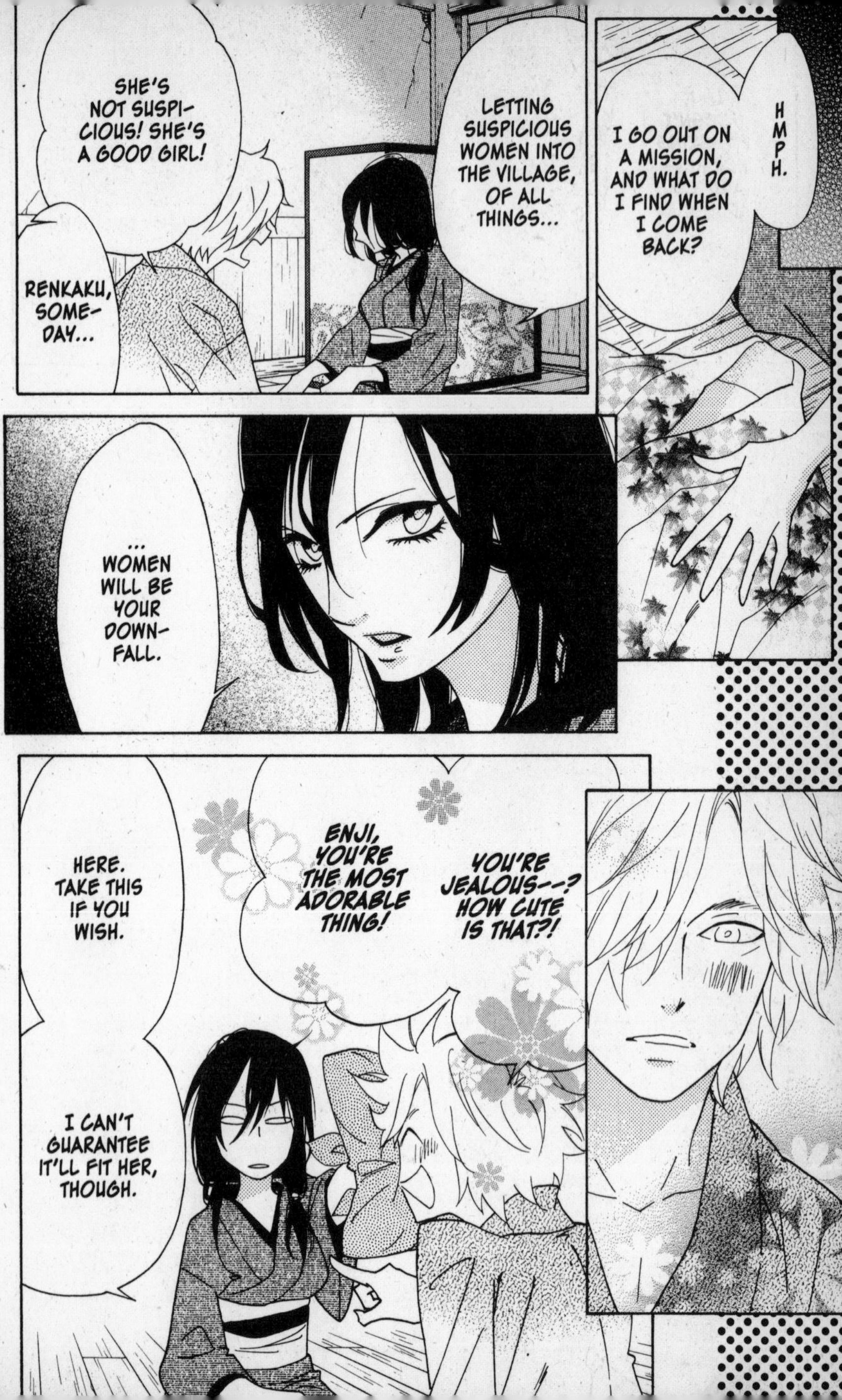
HMPH.
I GO OUT ON A MISSION, AND WHAT DO I FIND WHEN I COME BACK?
LETTING SUSPICIOUS WOMEN INTO THE VILLAGE, OF ALL THINGS...
SHE'S NOT SUSPICIOUS! SHE'S A GOOD GIRL!
RENKAKU, SOMEDAY...
...WOMEN WILL BE YOUR DOWNFALL.
YOU'RE JEALOUS--? HOW CUTE IS THAT?!
ENJI, YOU'RE THE MOST ADORABLE THING!
HERE. TAKE THIS IF YOU WISH.
I CAN'T GUARANTEE IT'LL FIT HER, THOUGH.

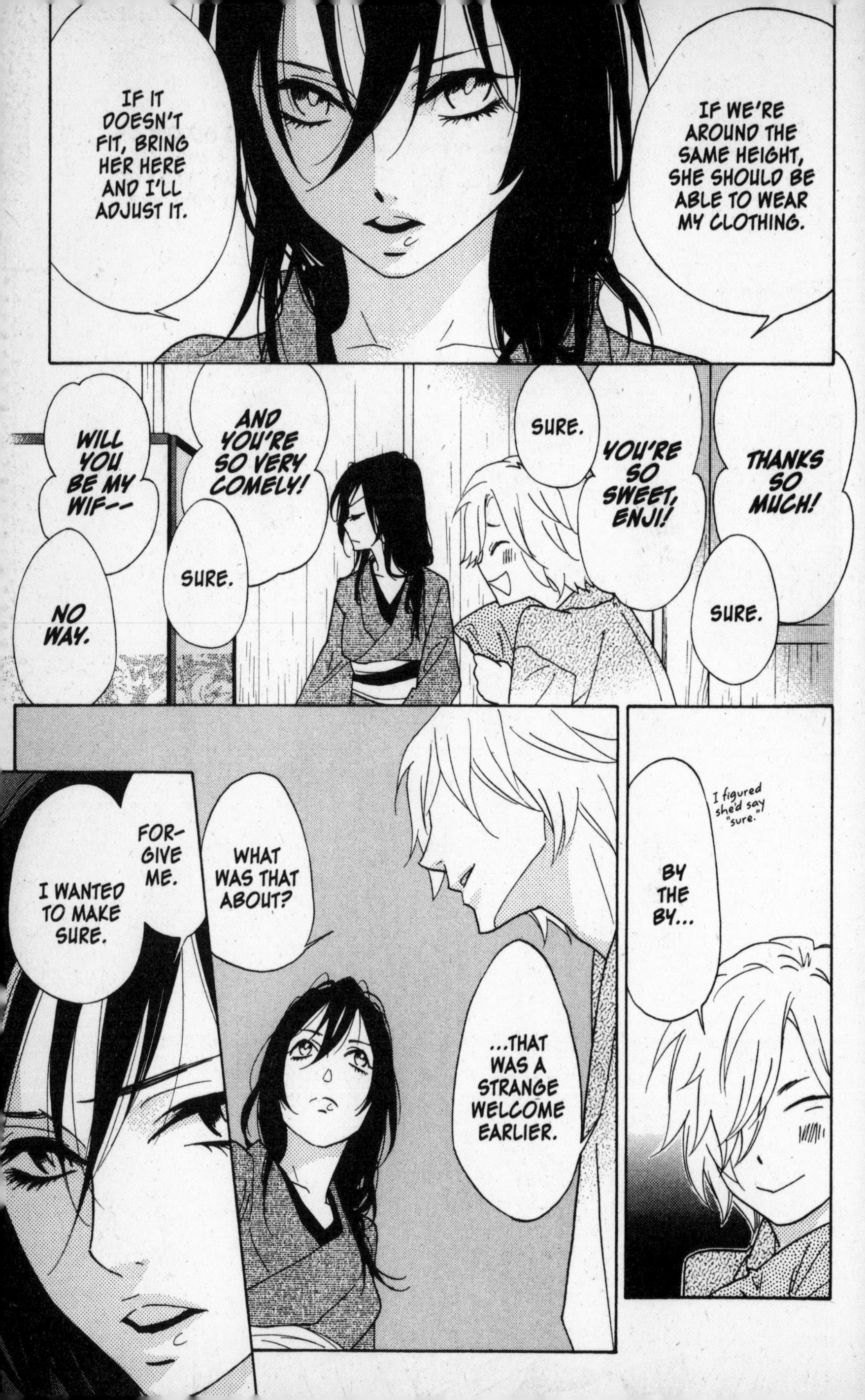
IF WE'RE AROUND THE SAME HEIGHT, SHE SHOULD BE ABLE TO WEAR MY CLOTHING.
IF IT DOESN'T FIT, BRING HER HERE AND I'LL ADJUST IT.
THANKS SO MUCH!
SURE.
YOU'RE SO SWEET, ENJI!
SURE.
AND YOU'RE SO VERY COMELY!
SURE.
WILL YOU BE MY WIF--
NO WAY.
I figured she'd say "sure."
BY THE BY...
...THAT WAS A STRANGE WELCOME EARLIER.
WHAT WAS THAT ABOUT?
FOR-GIVE ME.
I WANTED TO MAKE SURE.

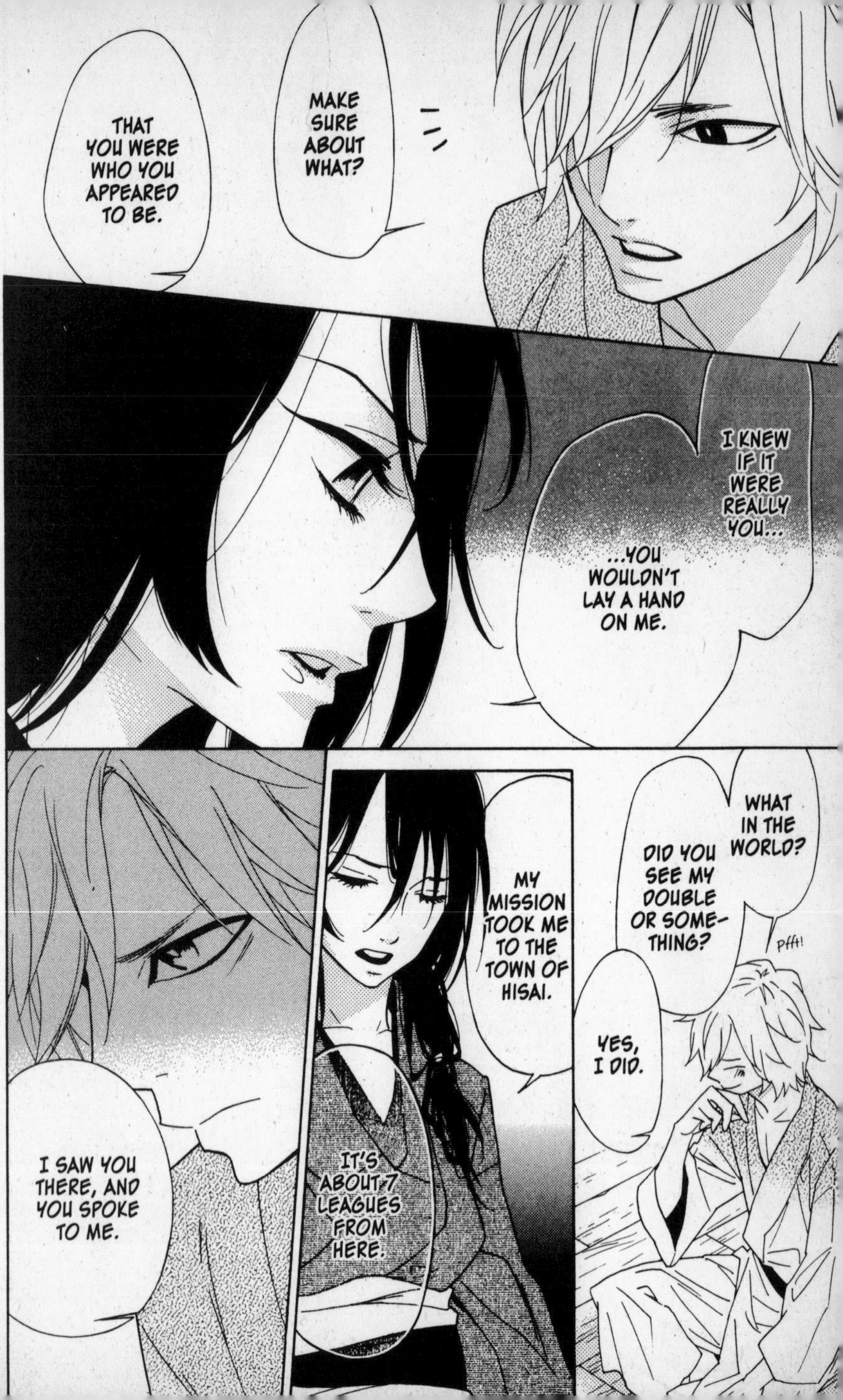
MAKE SURE ABOUT WHAT?
THAT YOU WERE WHO YOU APPEARED TO BE.
I KNEW IF IT WERE REALLY YOU...
...YOU WOULDN'T LAY A HAND ON ME.
WHAT IN THE WORLD?
DID YOU SEE MY DOUBLE OR SOME-THING?
Pfft!
YES, I DID.
MY MISSION TOOK ME TO THE TOWN OF HISAI.
IT'S ABOUT 7 LEAGUES FROM HERE.
I SAW YOU THERE, AND YOU SPOKE TO ME.

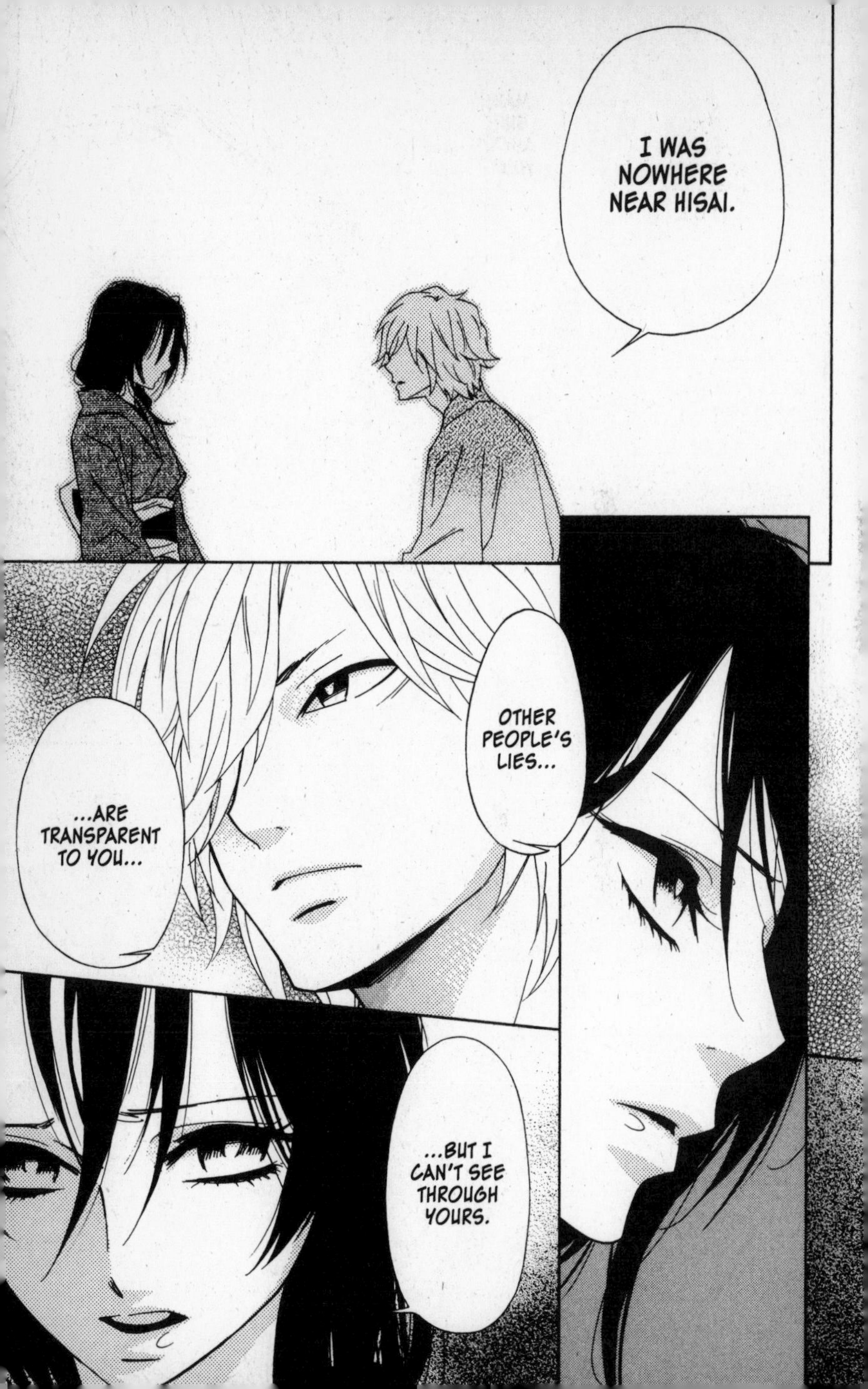
I WAS NOWHERE NEAR HISAI.
OTHER PEOPLE'S LIES...
...ARE TRANSPARENT TO YOU...
...BUT I CAN'T SEE THROUGH YOURS.

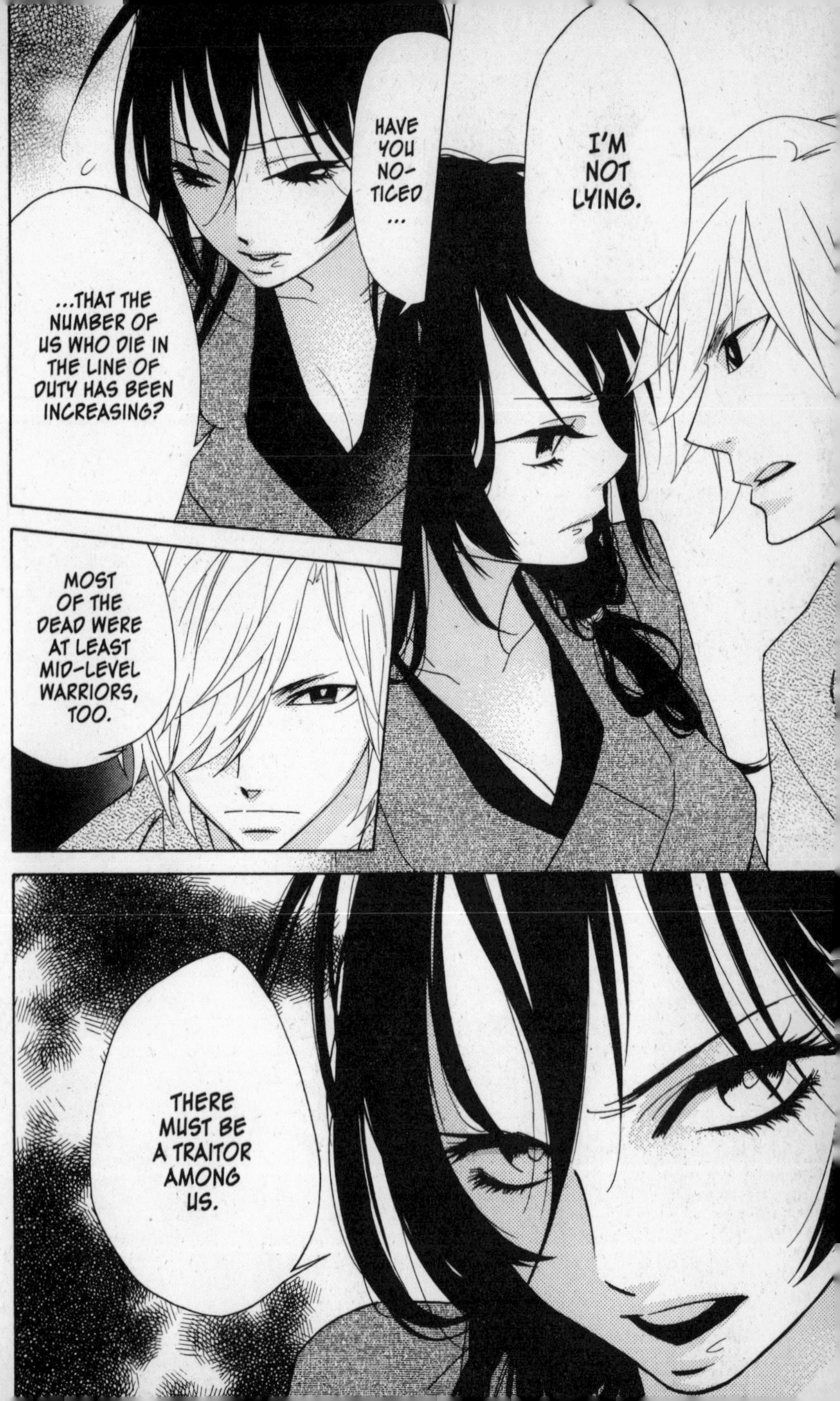
I'M NOT LYING.
HAVE YOU NO-TICED ...
...THAT THE NUMBER OF US WHO DIE IN THE LINE OF DUTY HAS BEEN INCREASING?
MOST OF THE DEAD WERE AT LEAST MID-LEVEL WARRIORS, TOO.
THERE MUST BE A TRAITOR AMONG US.

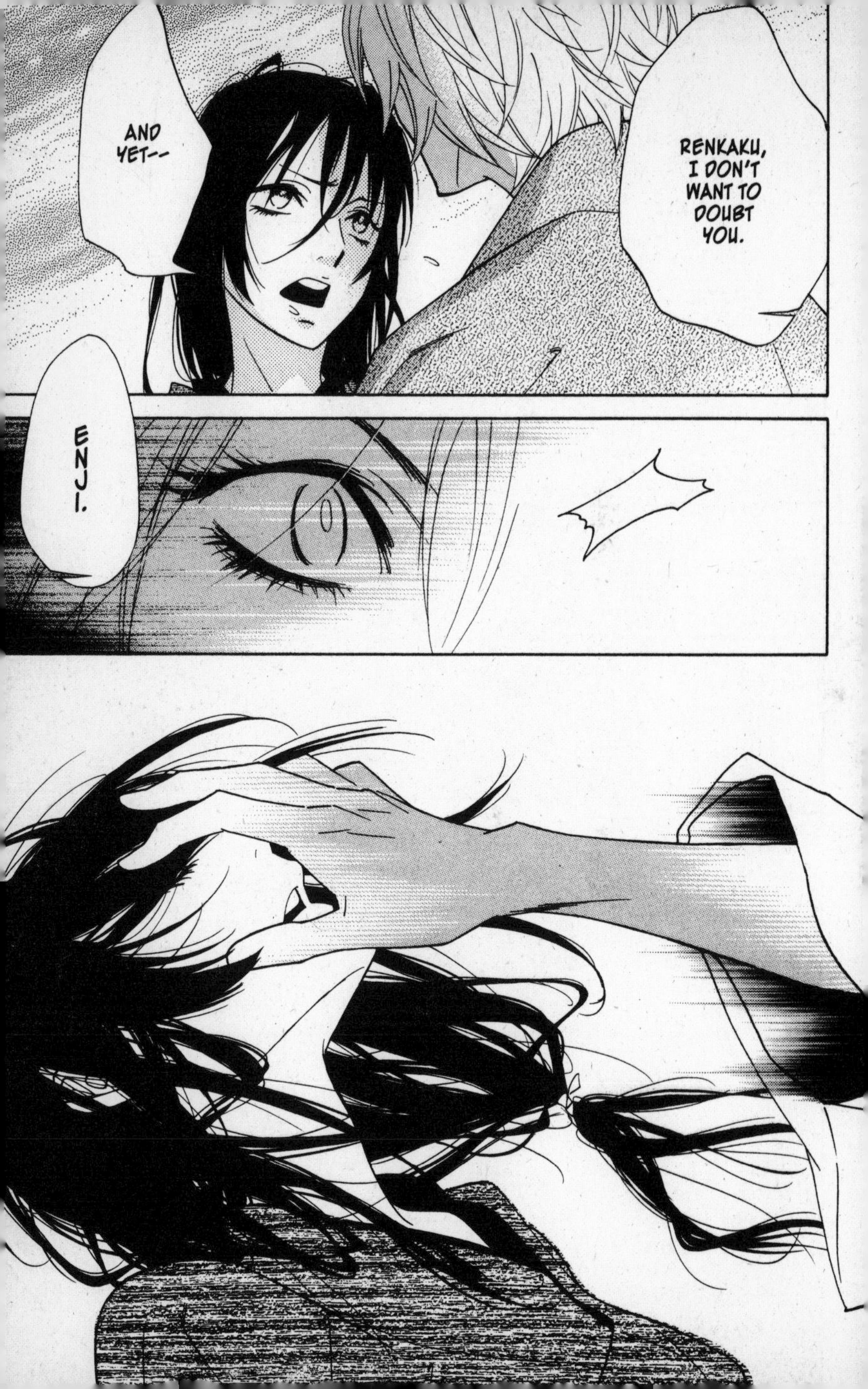
RENKAKU, I DON'T WANT TO DOUBT YOU.
AND YET--
ENJI.

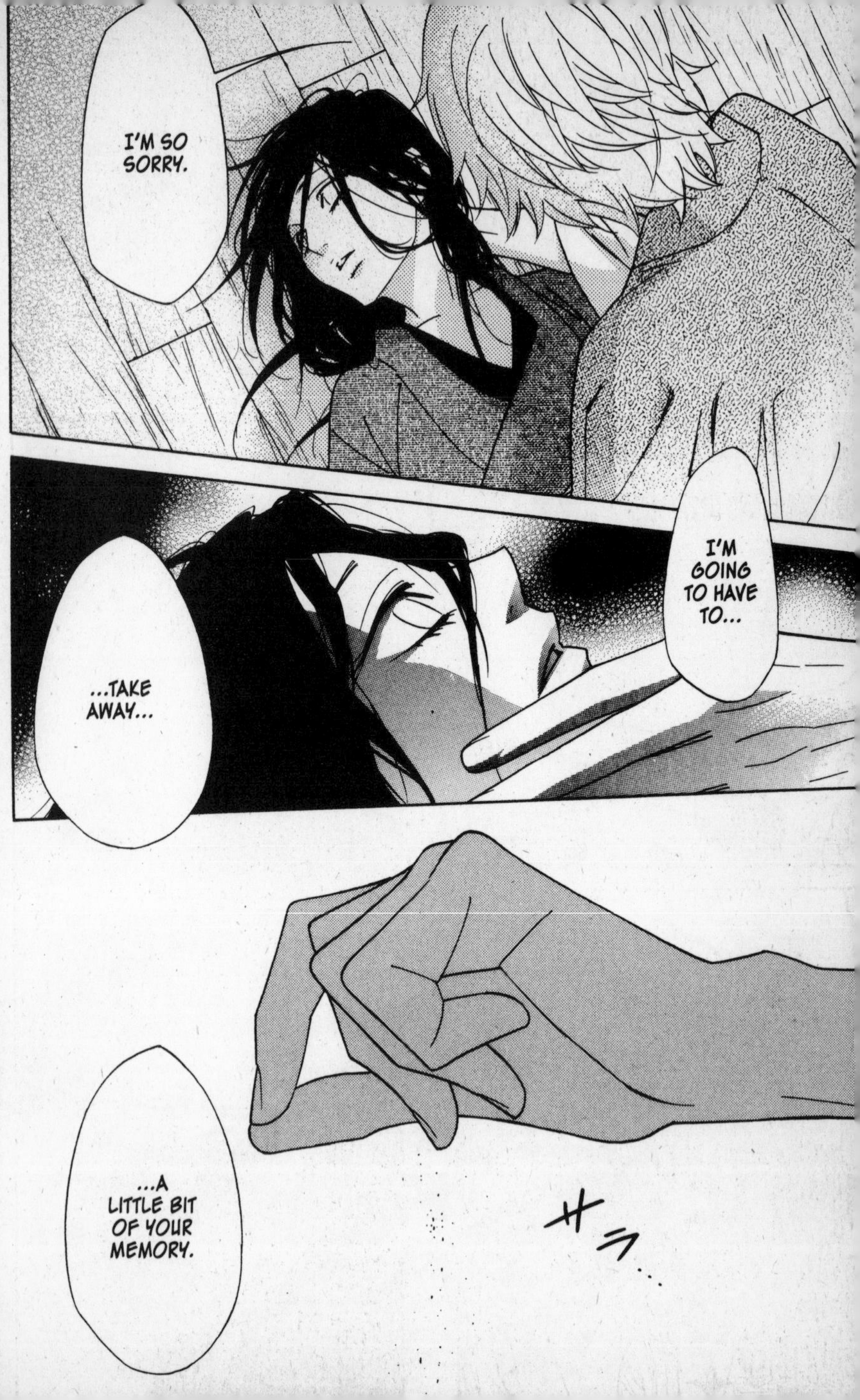
I'M SO SORRY.
I'M GOING TO HAVE TO...
...TAKE AWAY...
...A LITTLE BIT OF YOUR MEMORY.
サラ…

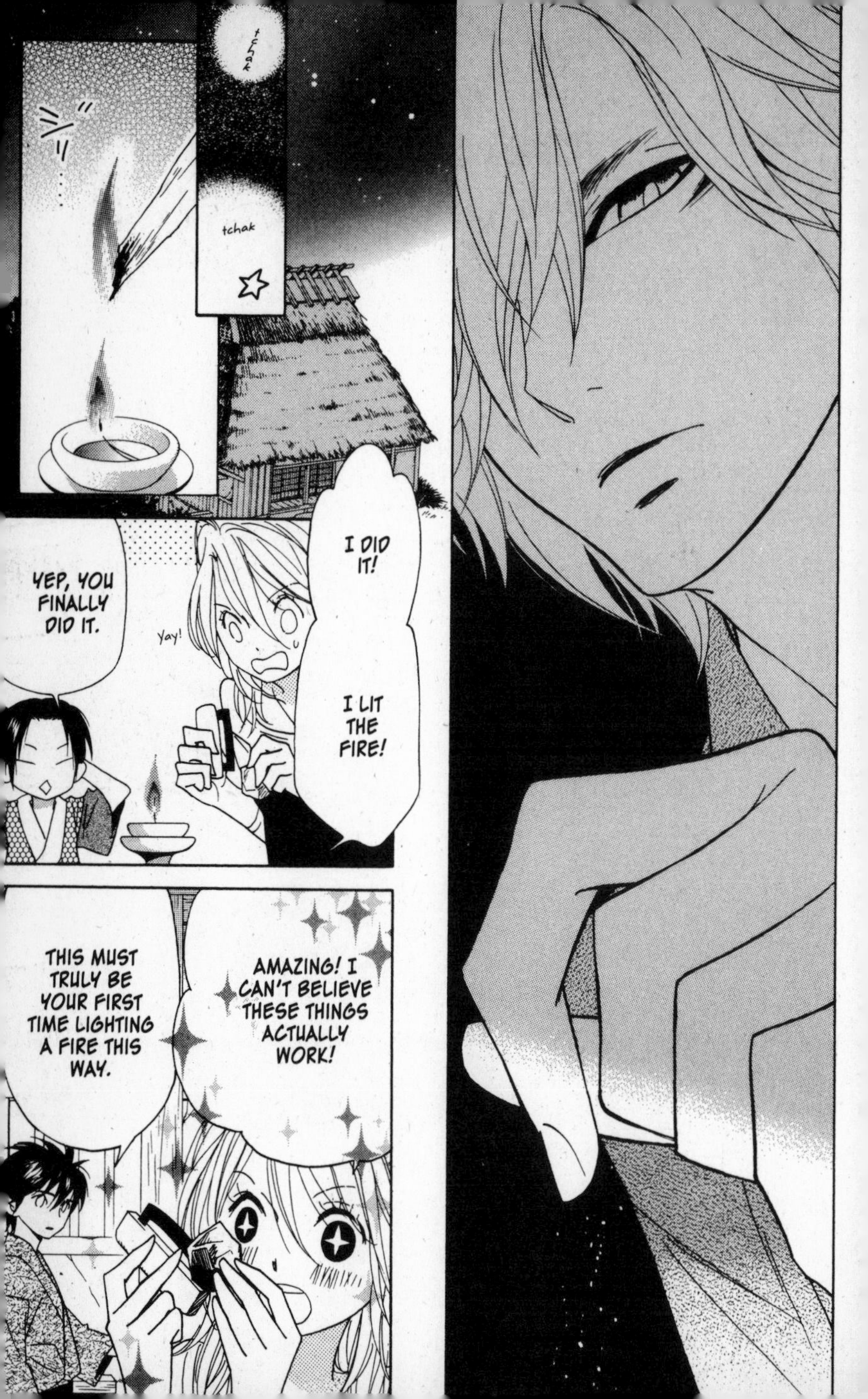

tchak
tchak
I DID IT!
I LIT THE FIRE!
Yay!
YEP, YOU FINALLY DID IT.
AMAZING! I CAN'T BELIEVE THESE THINGS ACTUALLY WORK!
THIS MUST TRULY BE YOUR FIRST TIME LIGHTING A FIRE THIS WAY.

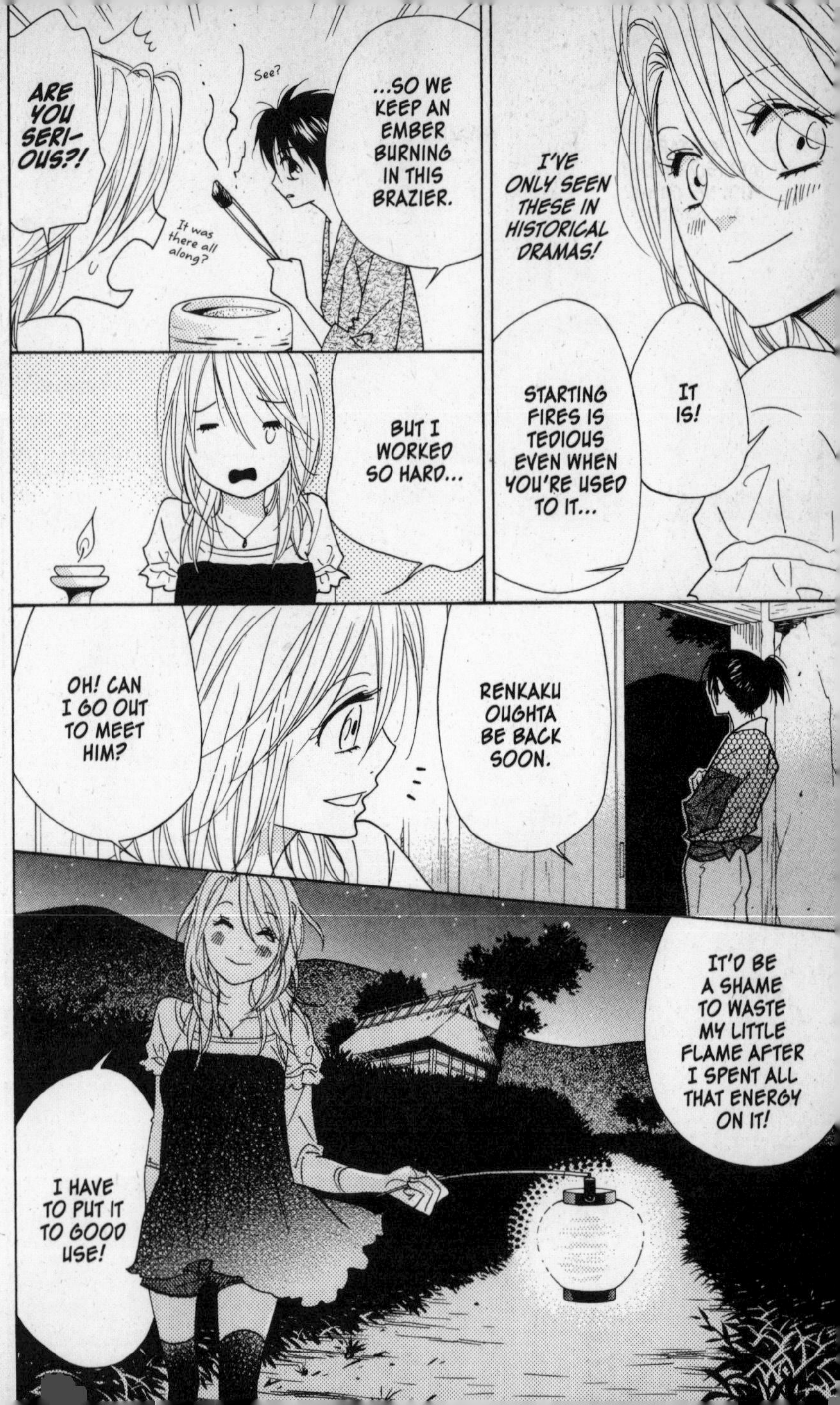

See?
...SO WE KEEP AN EMBER BURNING IN THIS BRAZIER.
ARE YOU SERI-OUS?!
It was there all along?
I'VE ONLY SEEN THESE IN HISTORICAL DRAMAS!
BUT I WORKED SO HARD...
IT IS!
STARTING FIRES IS TEDIOUS EVEN WHEN YOU'RE USED TO IT...
RENKAKU OUGHTA BE BACK SOON.
OH! CAN I GO OUT TO MEET HIM?
IT'D BE A SHAME TO WASTE MY LITTLE FLAME AFTER I SPENT ALL THAT ENERGY ON IT!
I HAVE TO PUT IT TO GOOD USE!

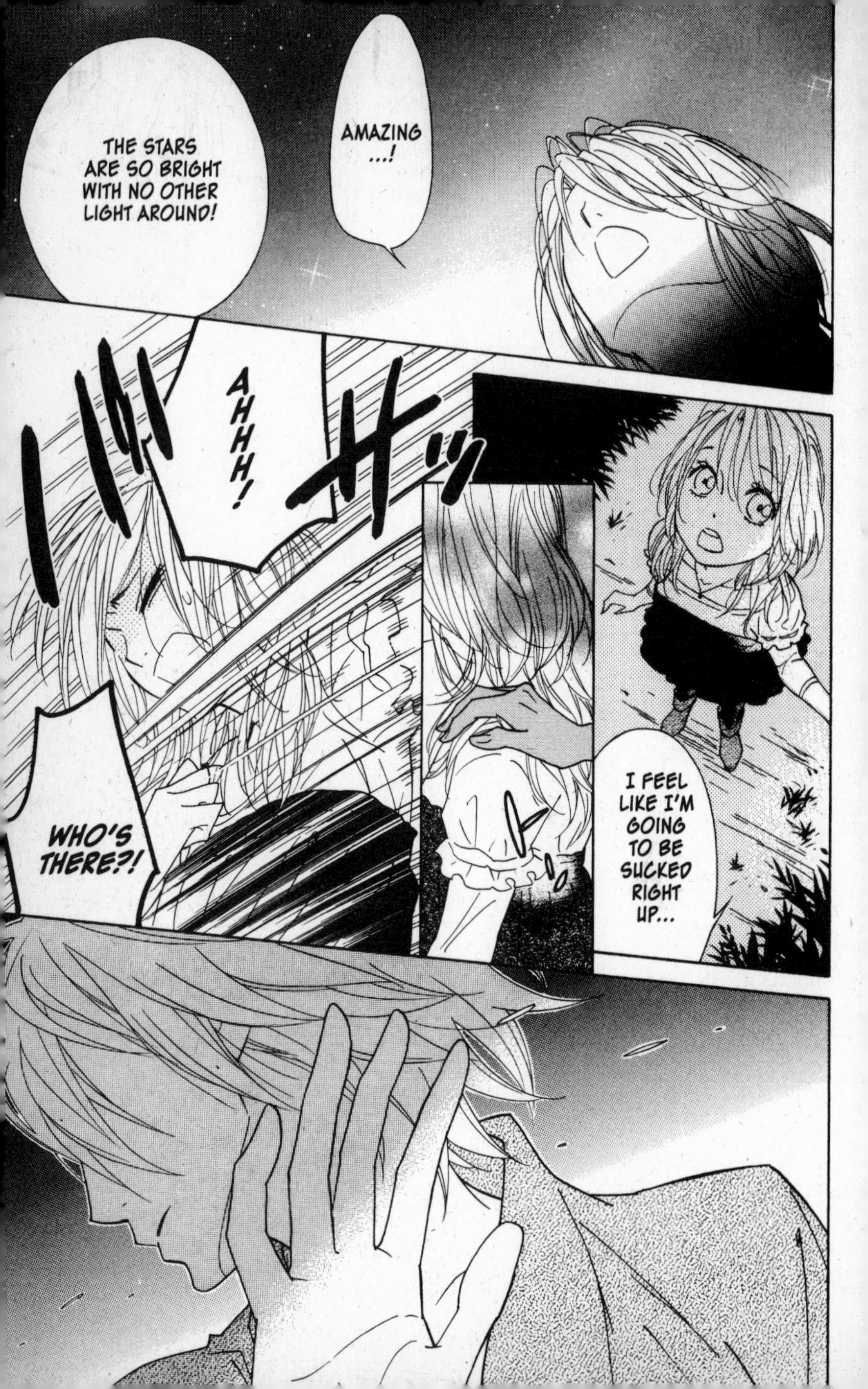
AMAZING ...!
THE STARS ARE SO BRIGHT WITH NO OTHER LIGHT AROUND!
I FEEL LIKE I'M GOING TO BE SUCKED RIGHT UP...
AHHHH!
WHO'S THERE?!

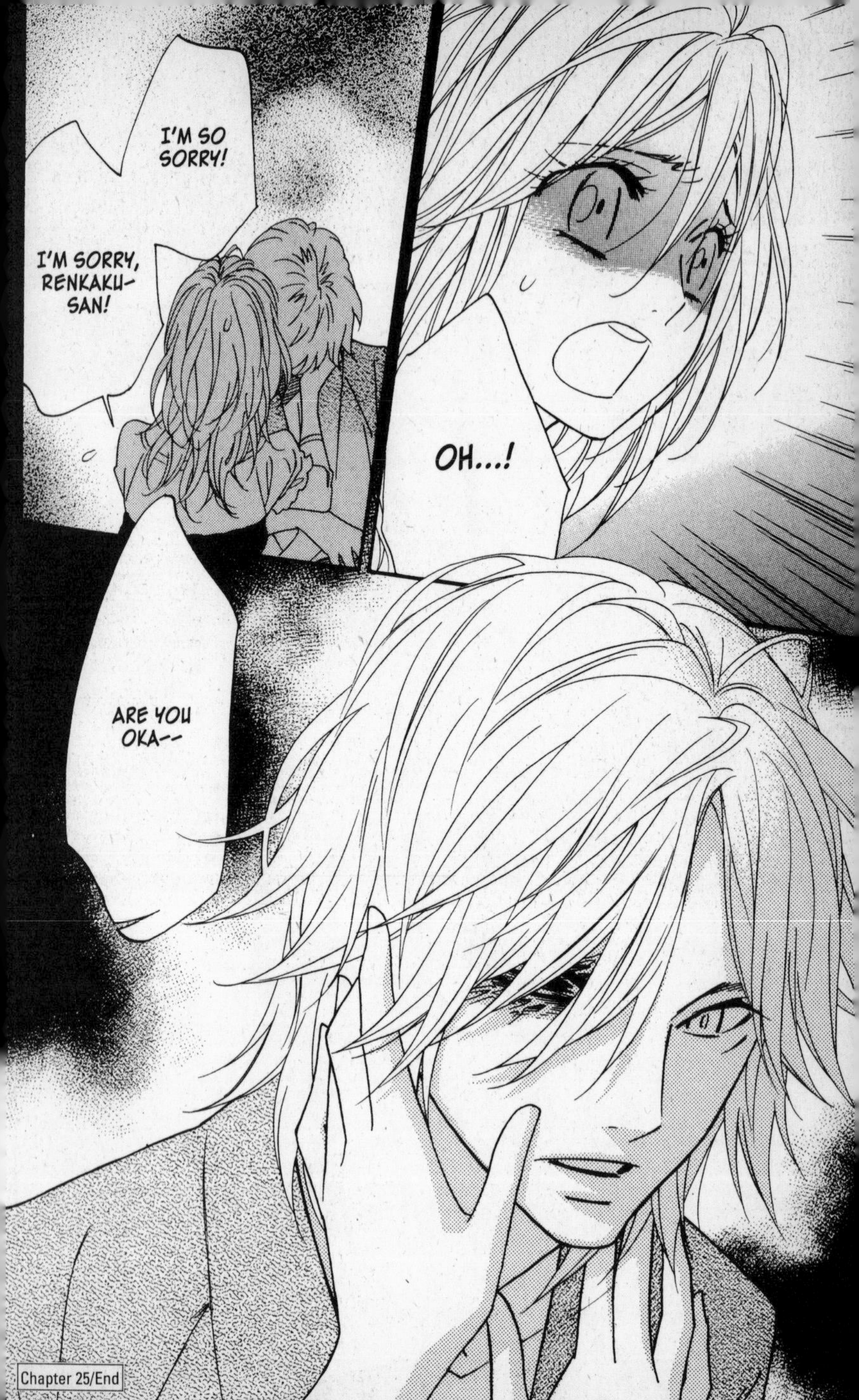
OH...!
I'M SO SORRY!
I'M SORRY, RENKAKU-SAN!
ARE YOU OKA--
Chapter 25/End

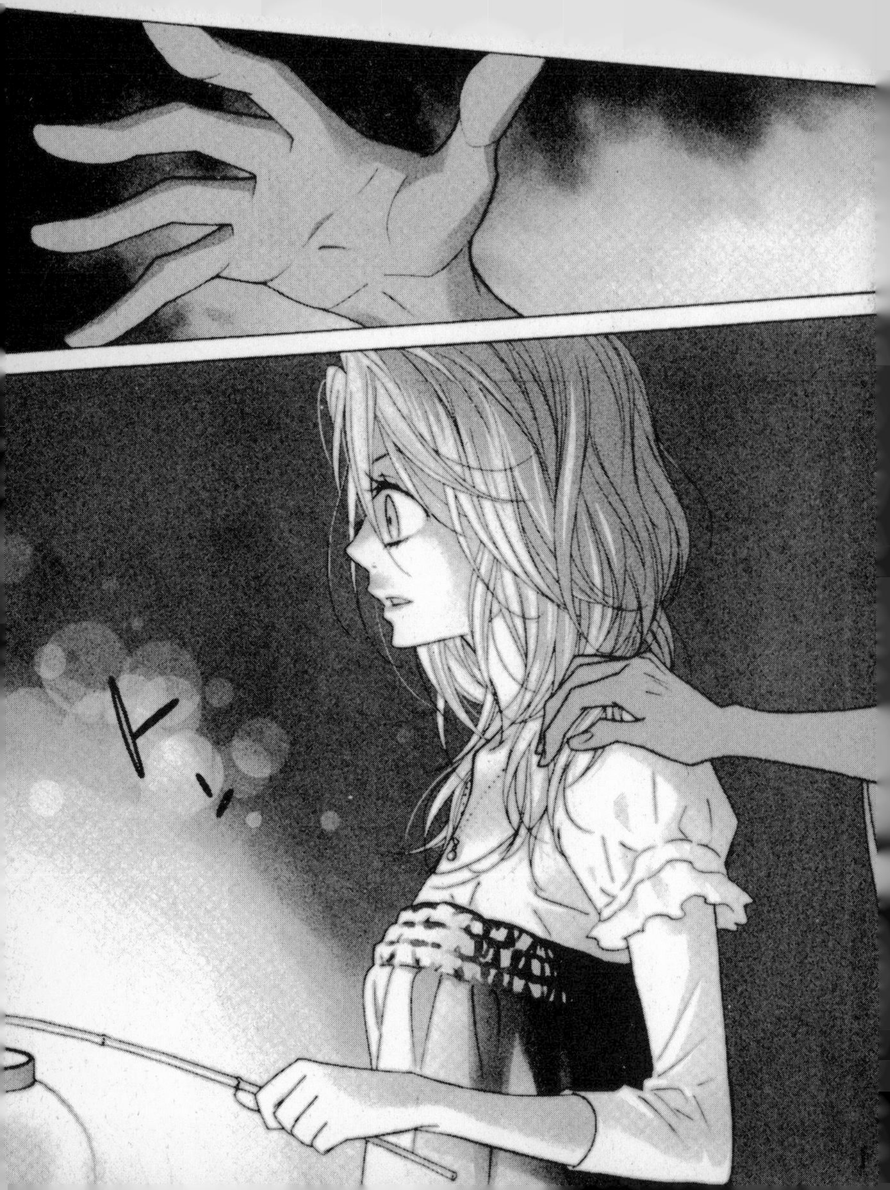

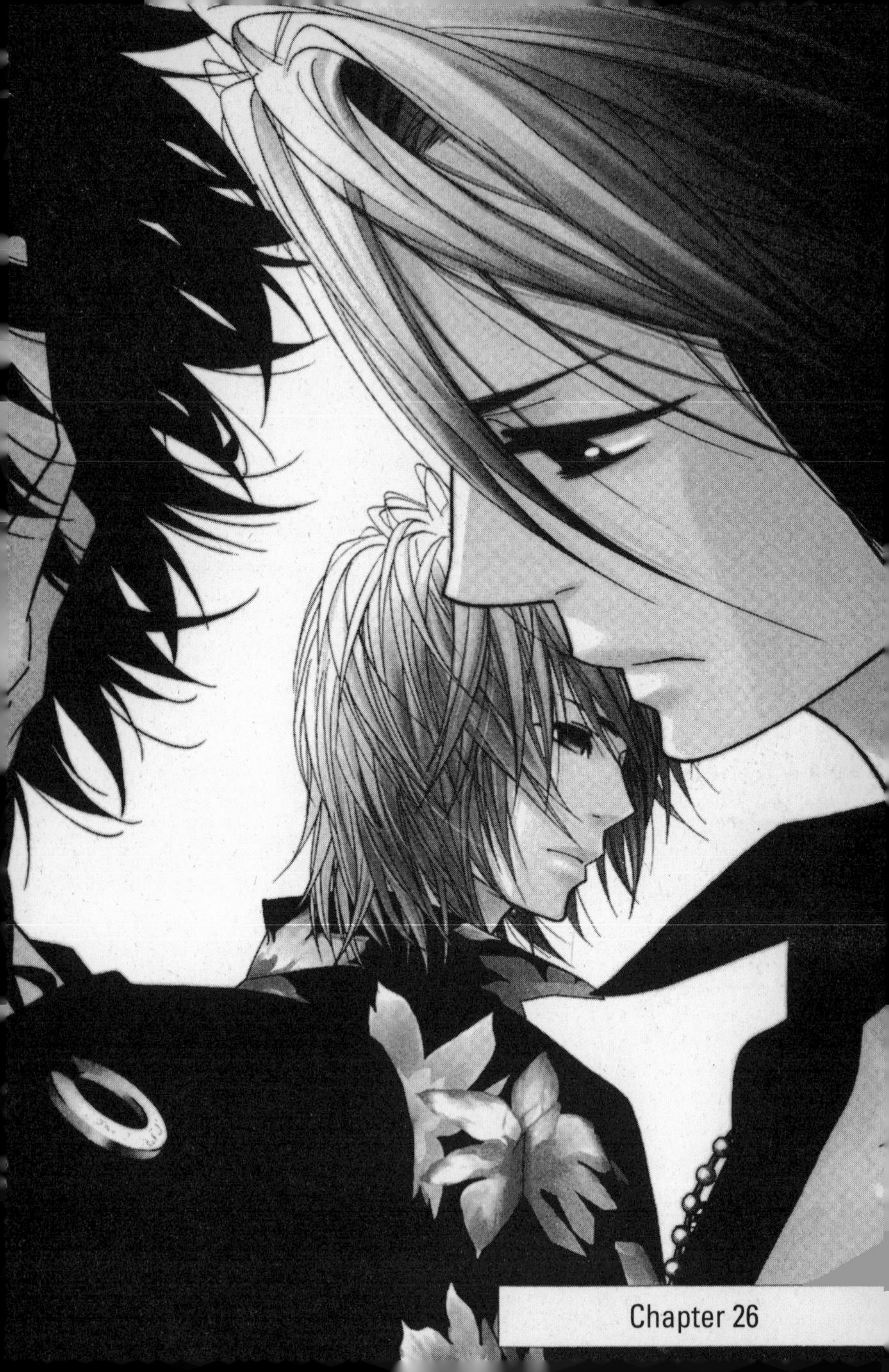
Chapter 26

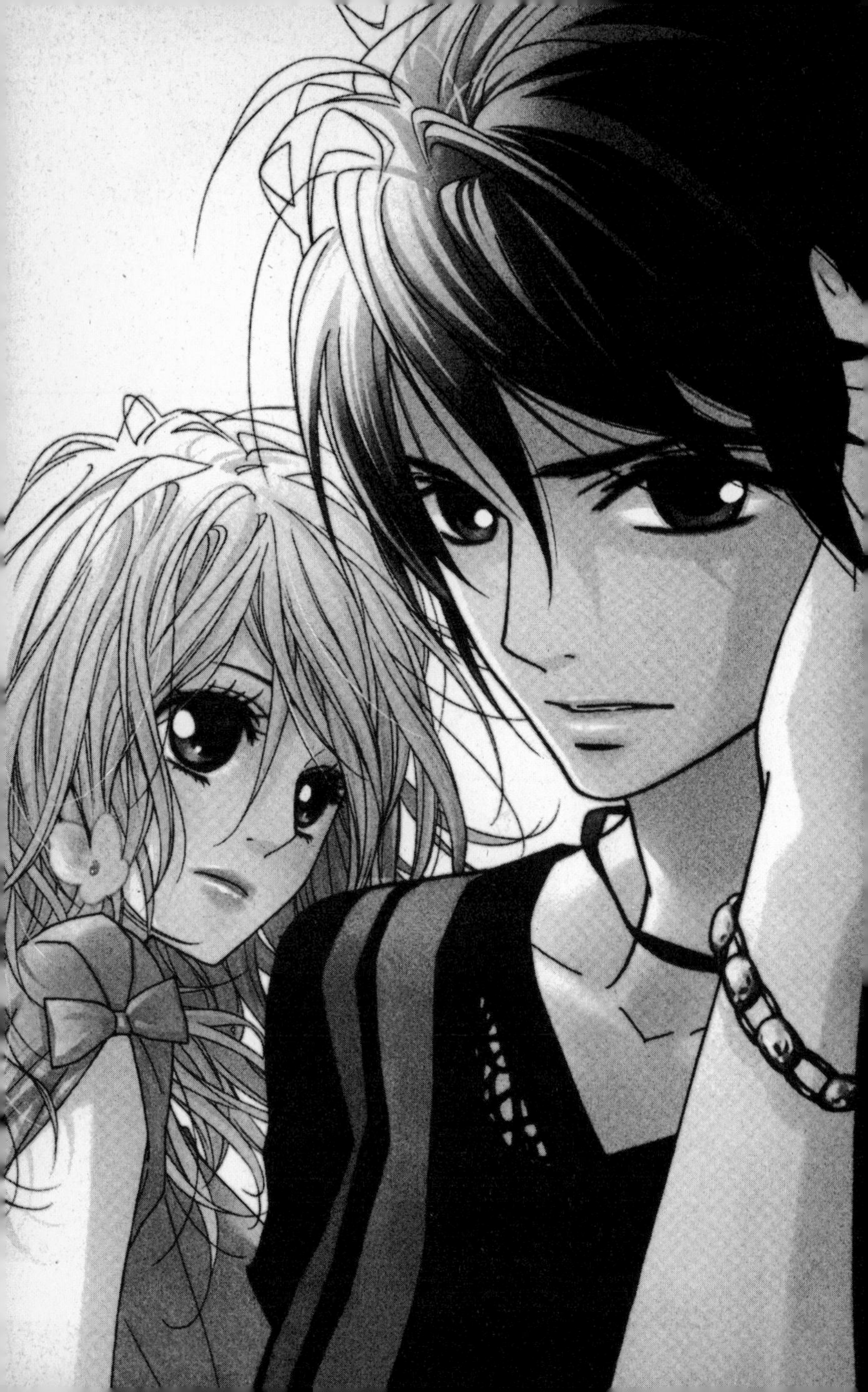

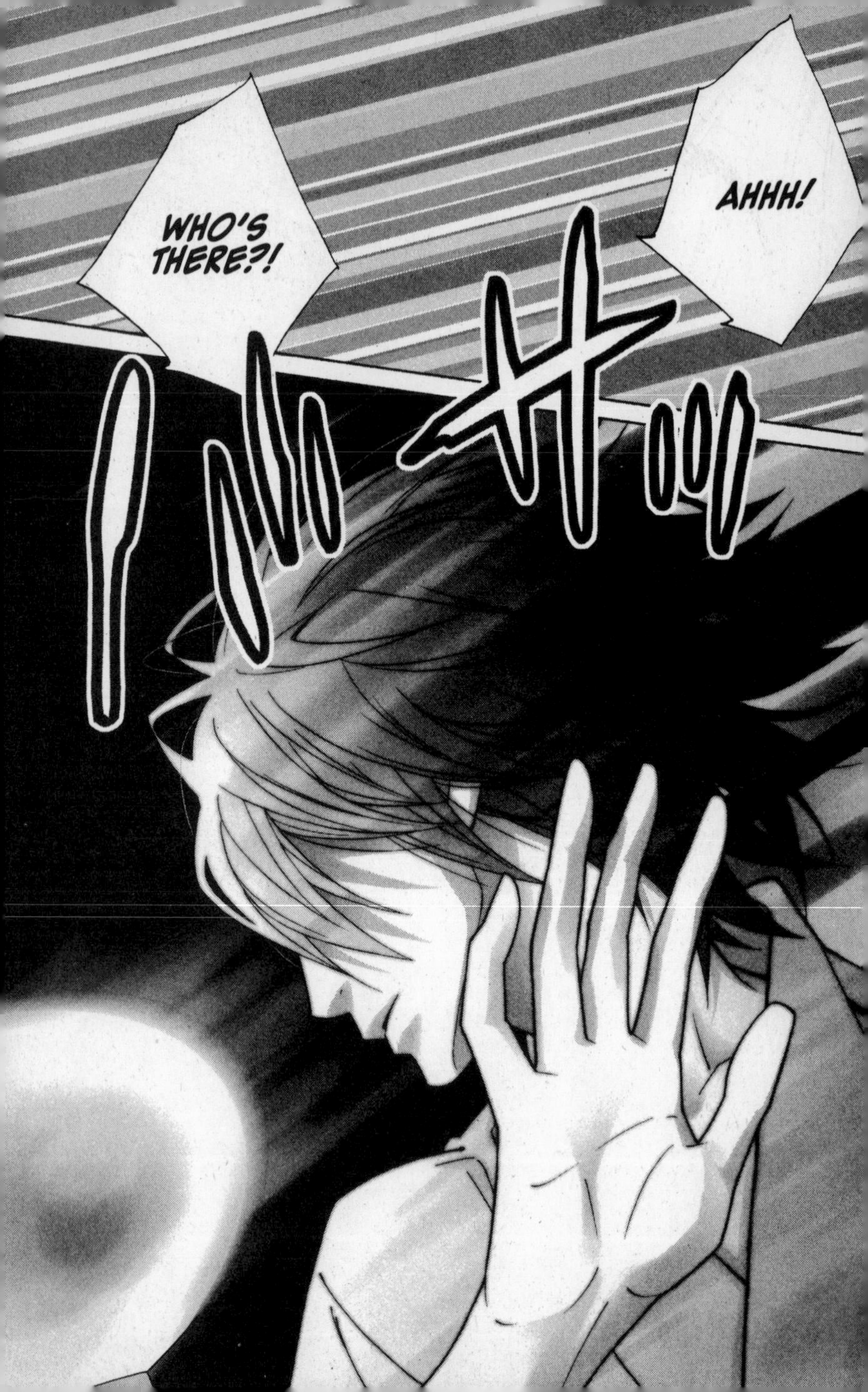
AHHH!
WHO'S THERE?!

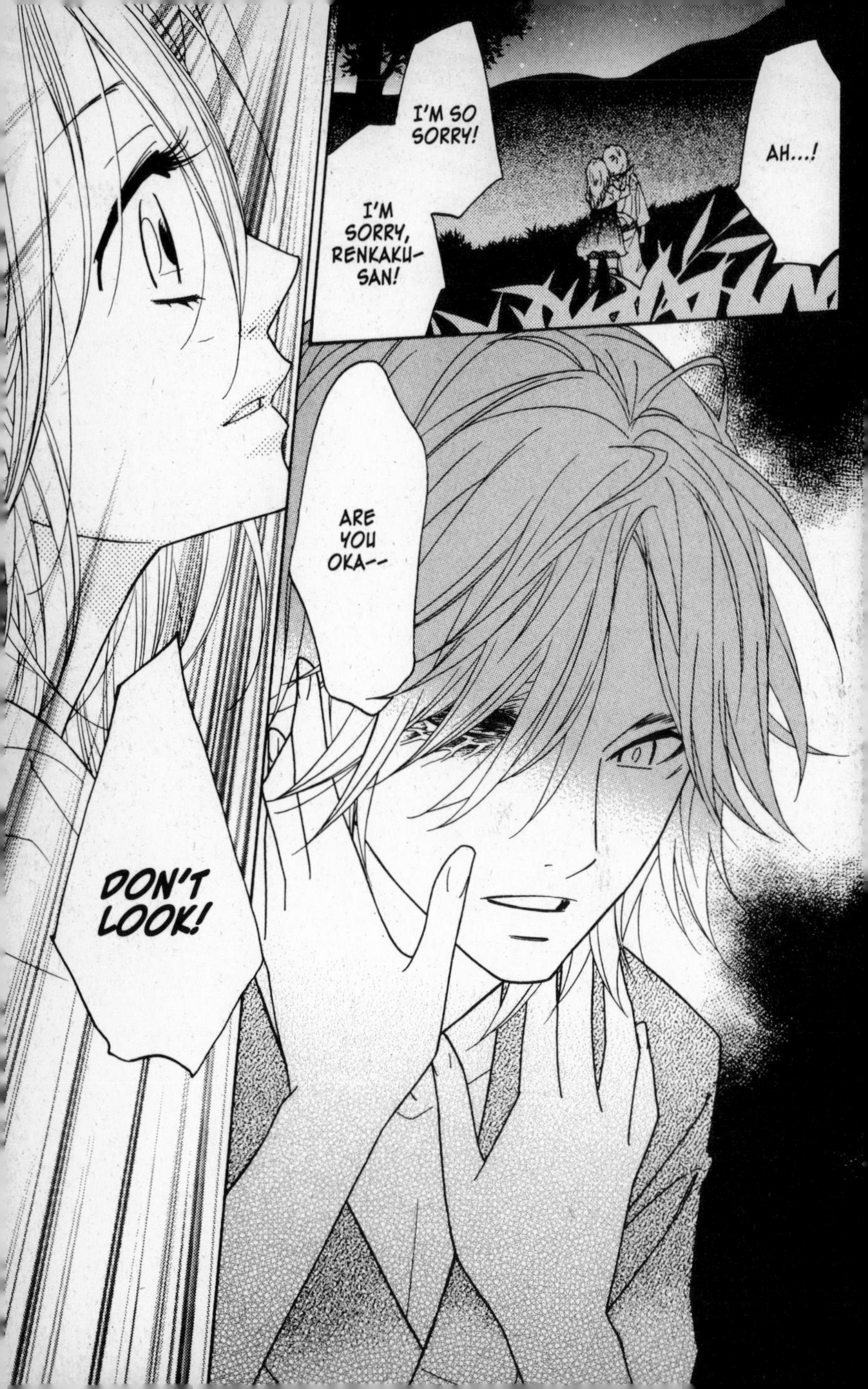
AH...!
I'M SO SORRY!
I'M SORRY, RENKAKU-SAN!
ARE YOU OKA--
DON'T LOOK!

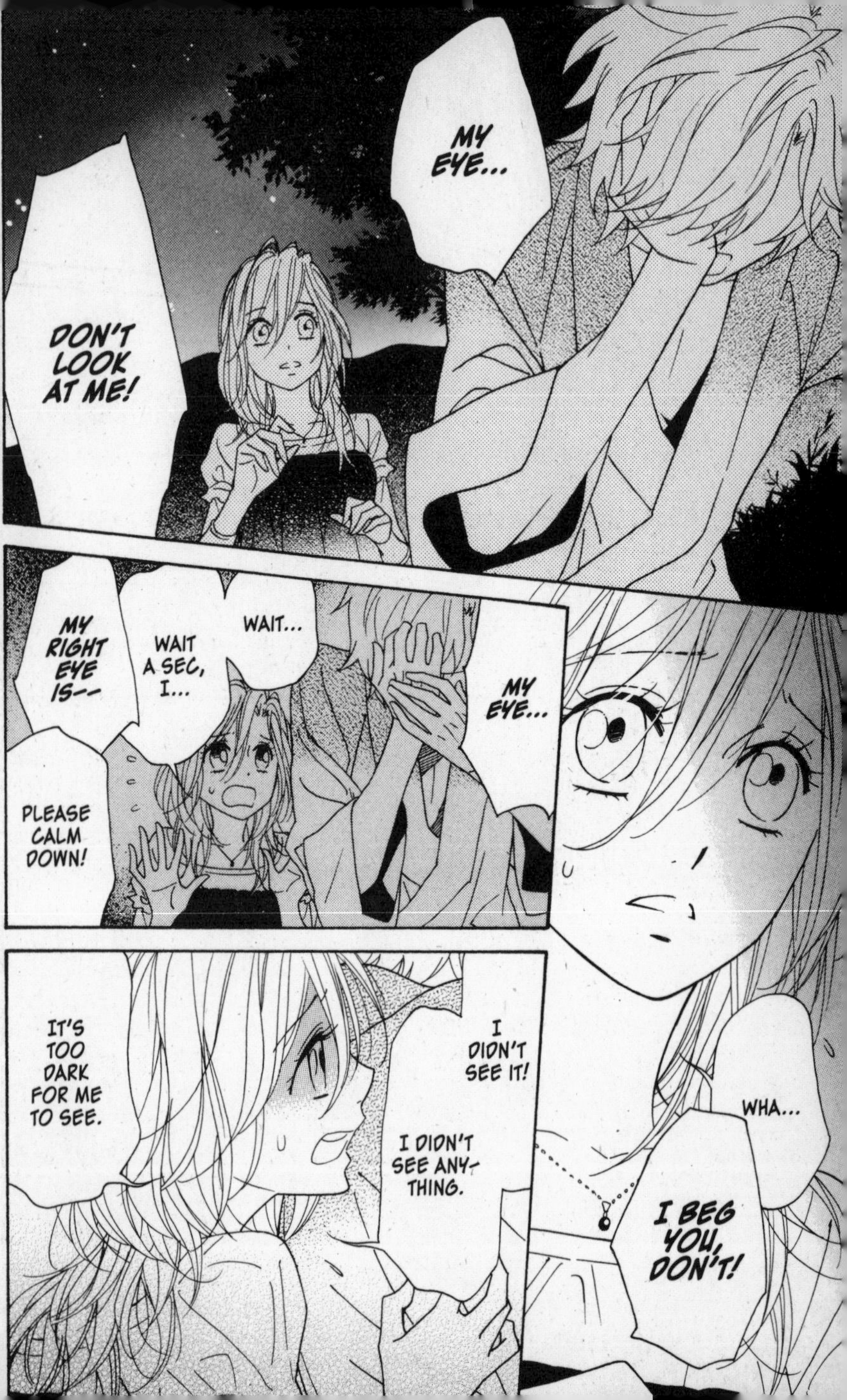
MY EYE...
DON'T LOOK AT ME!
MY EYE...
WAIT...
WAIT A SEC, I...
MY RIGHT EYE IS--
PLEASE CALM DOWN!
WHA...
I BEG YOU, DON'T!
I DIDN'T SEE IT!
I DIDN'T SEE ANY-THING.
IT'S TOO DARK FOR ME TO SEE.

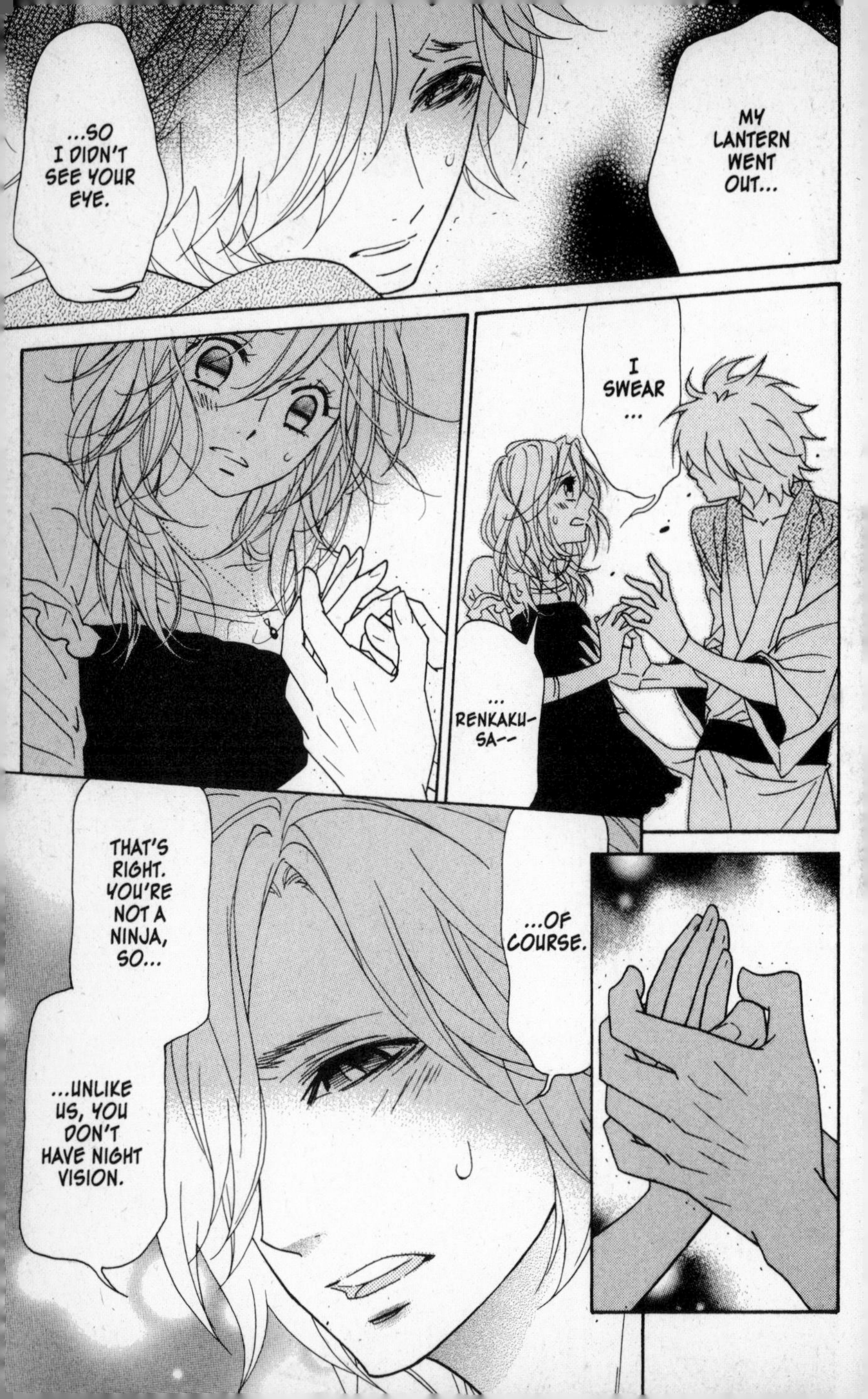
MY LANTERN WENT OUT...
...SO I DIDN'T SEE YOUR EYE.
I SWEAR ...
... RENKAKU-SA--
...OF COURSE.
THAT'S RIGHT. YOU'RE NOT A NINJA, SO...
...UNLIKE US, YOU DON'T HAVE NIGHT VISION.

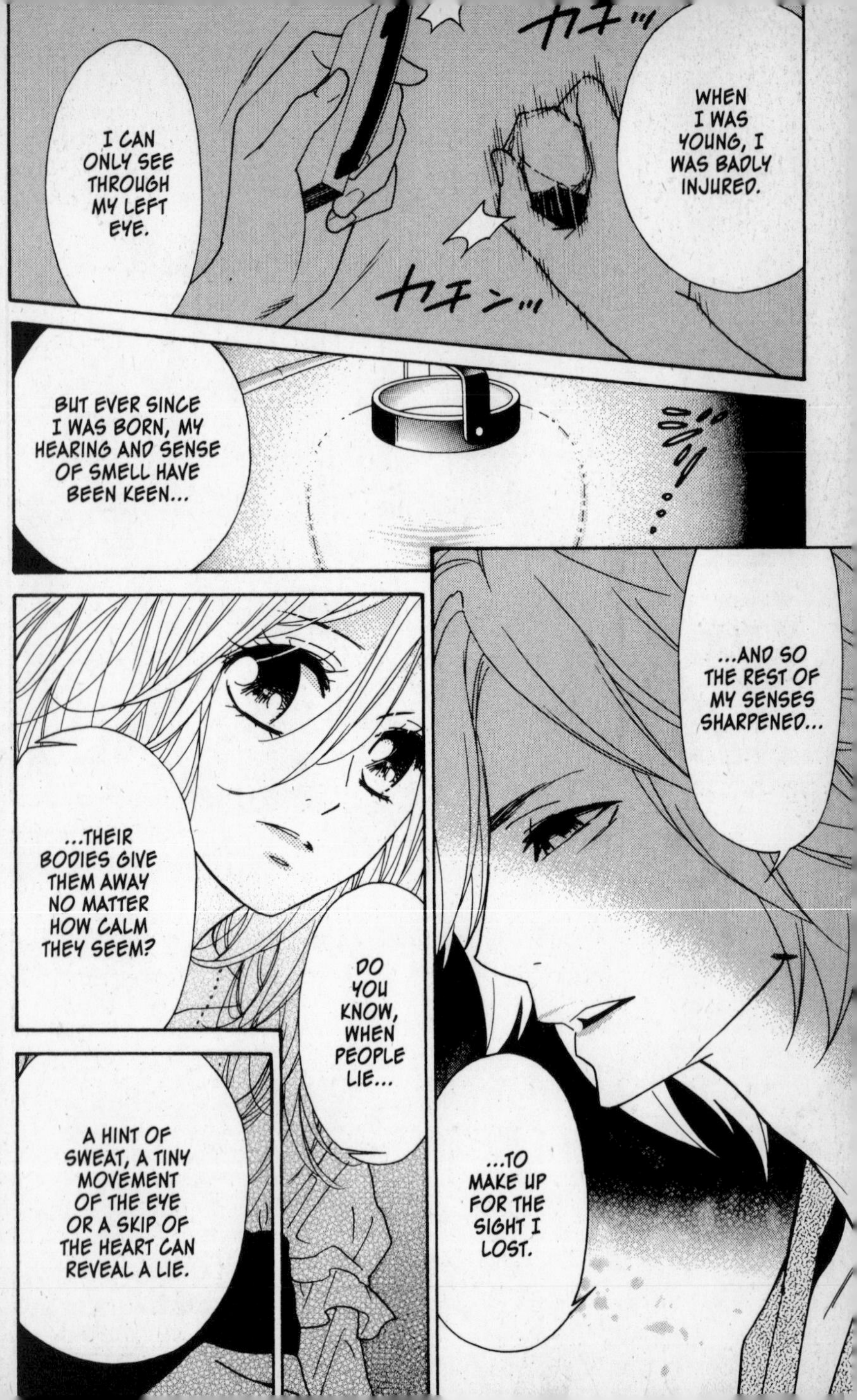

カチッ
WHEN I WAS YOUNG, I WAS BADLY INJURED.
I CAN ONLY SEE THROUGH MY LEFT EYE.
カチンッ
BUT EVER SINCE I WAS BORN, MY HEARING AND SENSE OF SMELL HAVE BEEN KEEN...
...AND SO THE REST OF MY SENSES SHARPENED...
...TO MAKE UP FOR THE SIGHT I LOST.
DO YOU KNOW, WHEN PEOPLE LIE...
...THEIR BODIES GIVE THEM AWAY NO MATTER HOW CALM THEY SEEM?
A HINT OF SWEAT, A TINY MOVEMENT OF THE EYE OR A SKIP OF THE HEART CAN REVEAL A LIE.

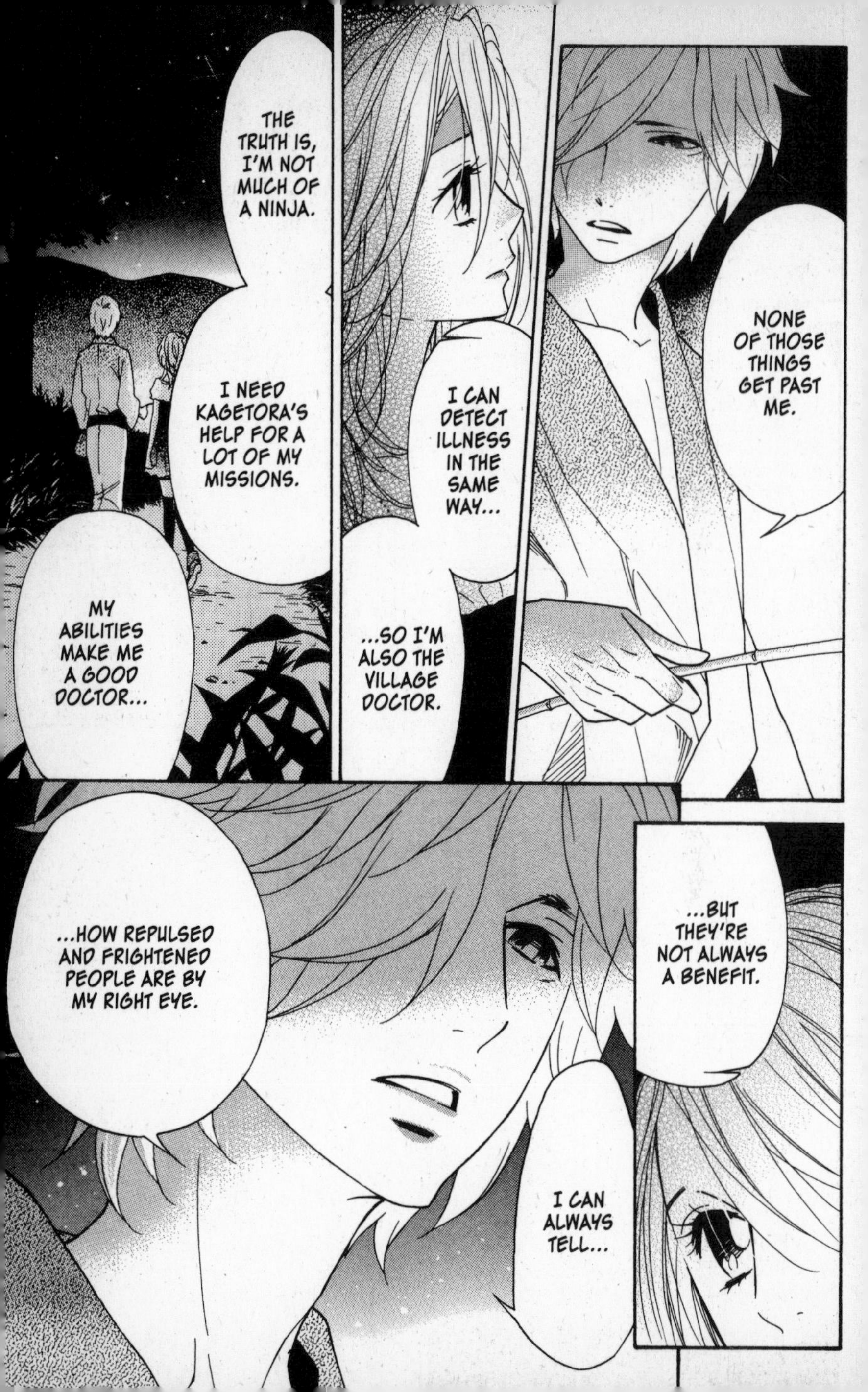
NONE OF THOSE THINGS GET PAST ME.
I CAN DETECT ILLNESS IN THE SAME WAY...
...SO I'M ALSO THE VILLAGE DOCTOR.
THE TRUTH IS, I'M NOT MUCH OF A NINJA.
I NEED KAGETORA'S HELP FOR A LOT OF MY MISSIONS.
MY ABILITIES MAKE ME A GOOD DOCTOR...
...BUT THEY'RE NOT ALWAYS A BENEFIT.
I CAN ALWAYS TELL...
...HOW REPULSED AND FRIGHTENED PEOPLE ARE BY MY RIGHT EYE.

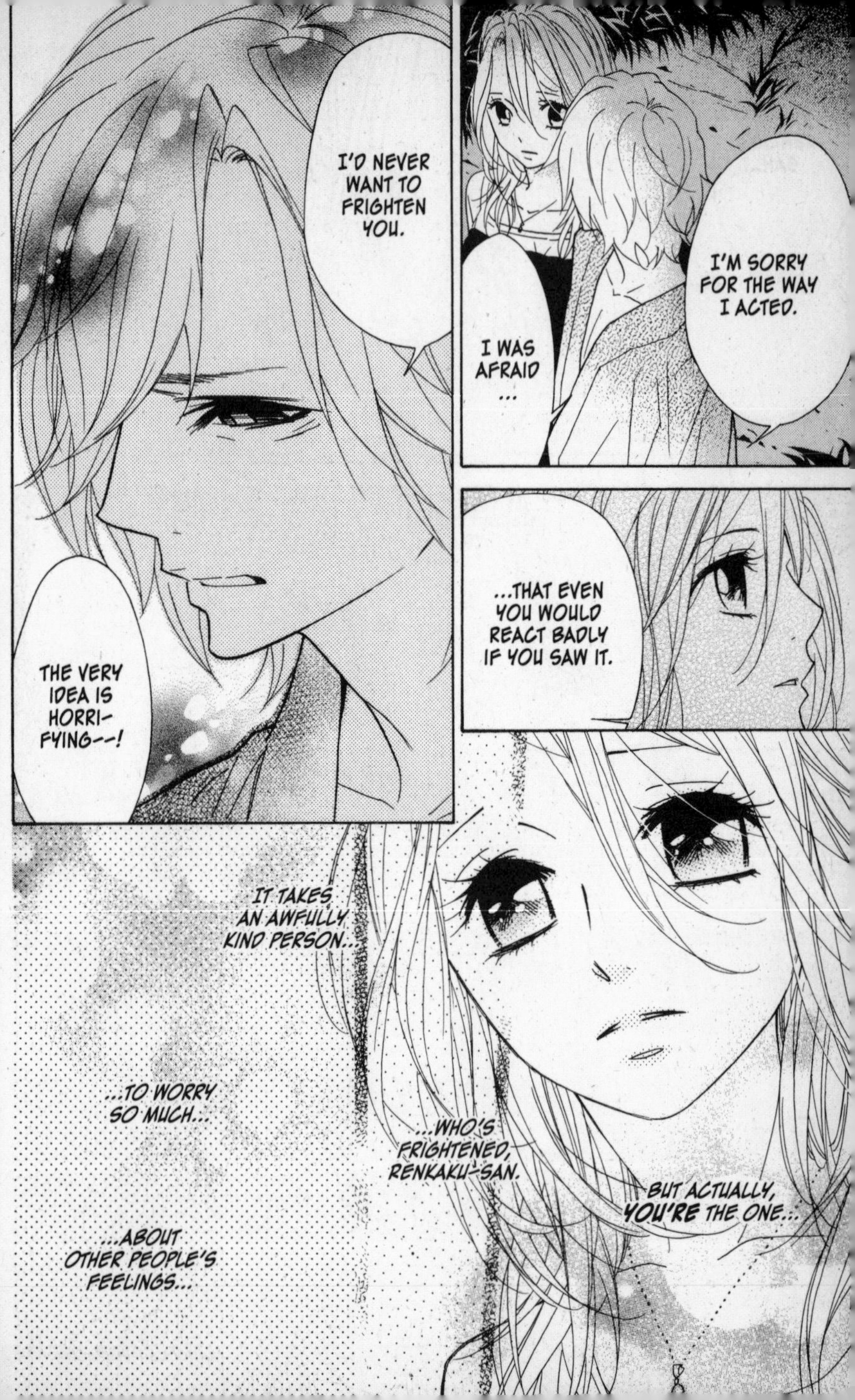

I'M SORRY FOR THE WAY I ACTED.
I WAS AFRAID ...
...THAT EVEN YOU WOULD REACT BADLY IF YOU SAW IT.
I'D NEVER WANT TO FRIGHTEN YOU.
THE VERY IDEA IS HORRI-FYING--!
IT TAKES AN AWFULLY KIND PERSON...
...TO WORRY SO MUCH...
...ABOUT OTHER PEOPLE'S FEELINGS...
BUT ACTUALLY, YOU'RE THE ONE...
...WHO'S FRIGHTENED, RENKAKU-SAN.

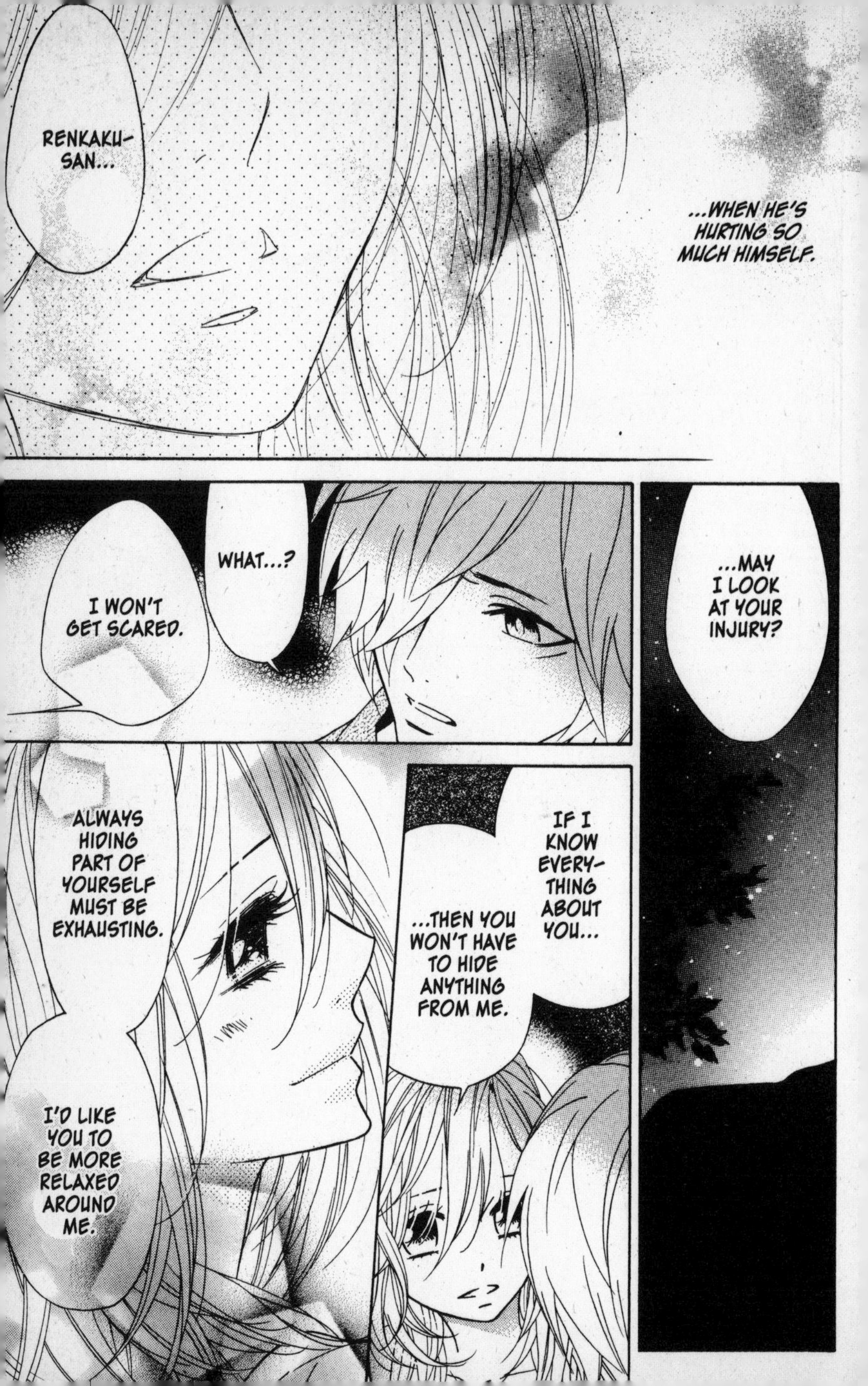
...WHEN HE'S HURTING SO MUCH HIMSELF.
RENKAKU-SAN...
...MAY I LOOK AT YOUR INJURY?
WHAT...?
I WON'T GET SCARED.
IF I KNOW EVERY-THING ABOUT YOU...
...THEN YOU WON'T HAVE TO HIDE ANYTHING FROM ME.
ALWAYS HIDING PART OF YOURSELF MUST BE EXHAUSTING.
I'D LIKE YOU TO BE MORE RELAXED AROUND ME.

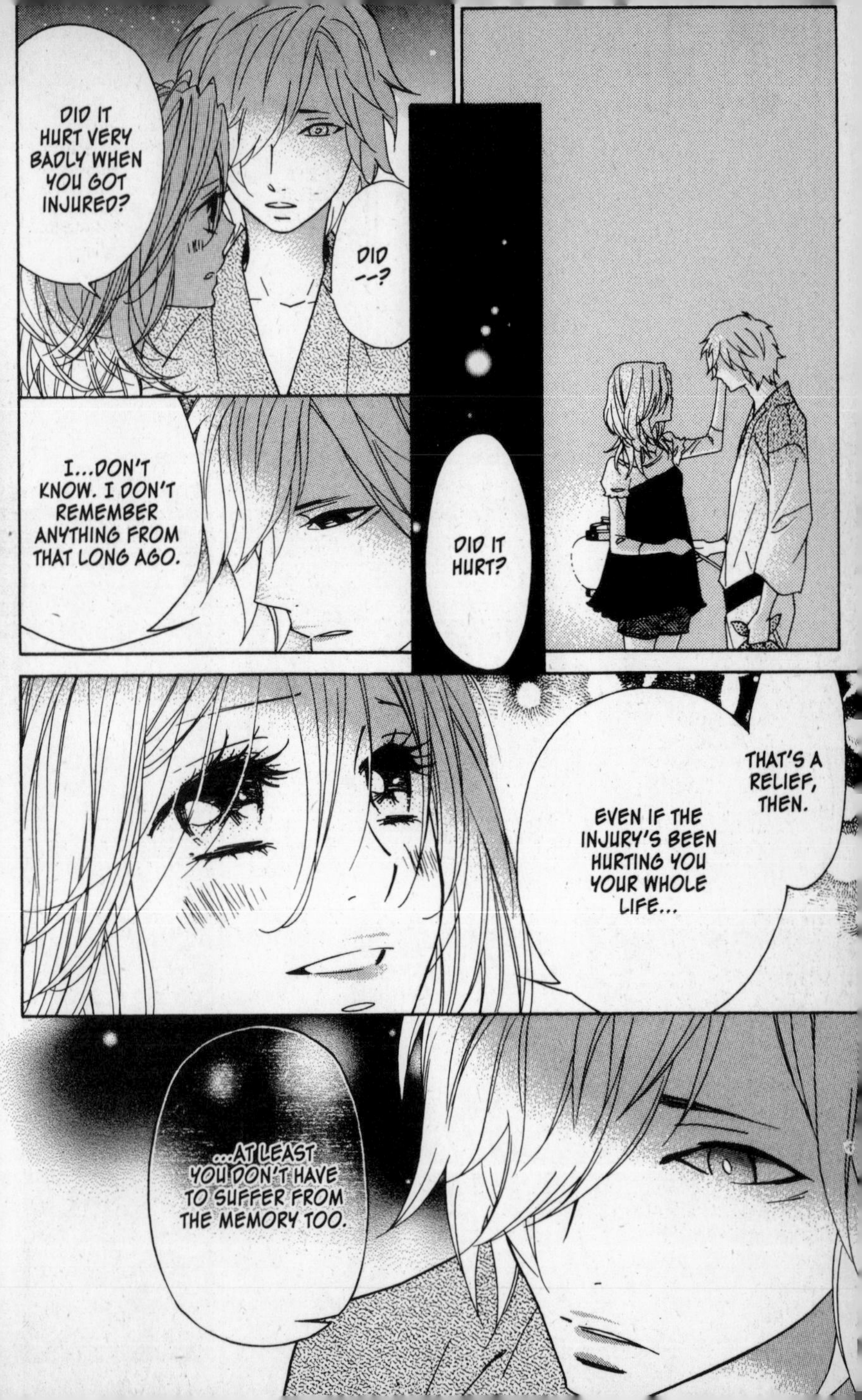
DID IT HURT VERY BADLY WHEN YOU GOT INJURED?
DID --?
I...DON'T KNOW. I DON'T REMEMBER ANYTHING FROM THAT LONG AGO.
DID IT HURT?
THAT'S A RELIEF, THEN.
EVEN IF THE INJURY'S BEEN HURTING YOU YOUR WHOLE LIFE...
...AT LEAST YOU DON'T HAVE TO SUFFER FROM THE MEMORY TOO.

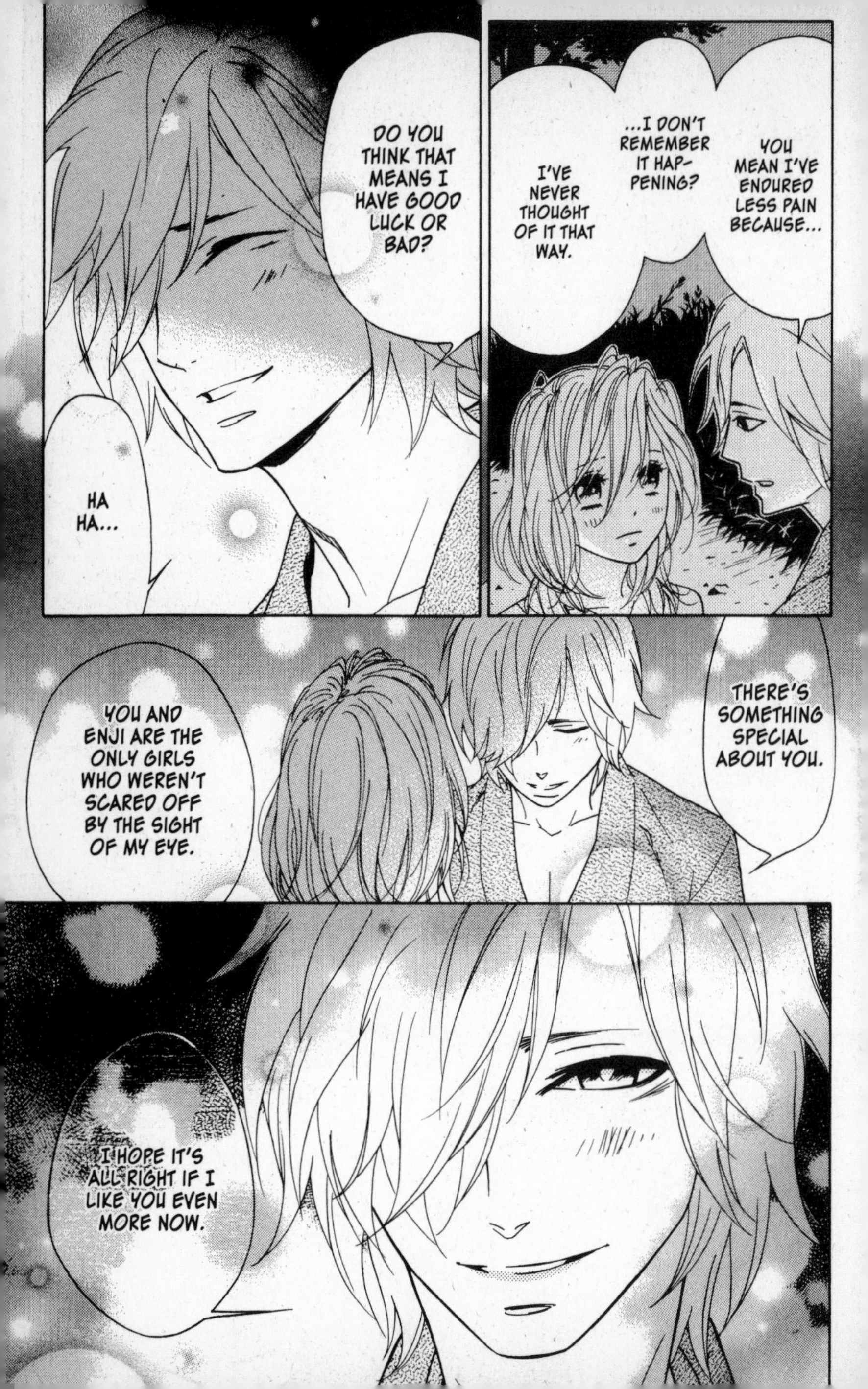
YOU MEAN I'VE ENDURED LESS PAIN BECAUSE...
...I DON'T REMEMBER IT HAP-PENING?
I'VE NEVER THOUGHT OF IT THAT WAY.
DO YOU THINK THAT MEANS I HAVE GOOD LUCK OR BAD?
HA HA...
THERE'S SOMETHING SPECIAL ABOUT YOU.
YOU AND ENJI ARE THE ONLY GIRLS WHO WEREN'T SCARED OFF BY THE SIGHT OF MY EYE.
I HOPE IT'S ALL RIGHT IF I LIKE YOU EVEN MORE NOW.

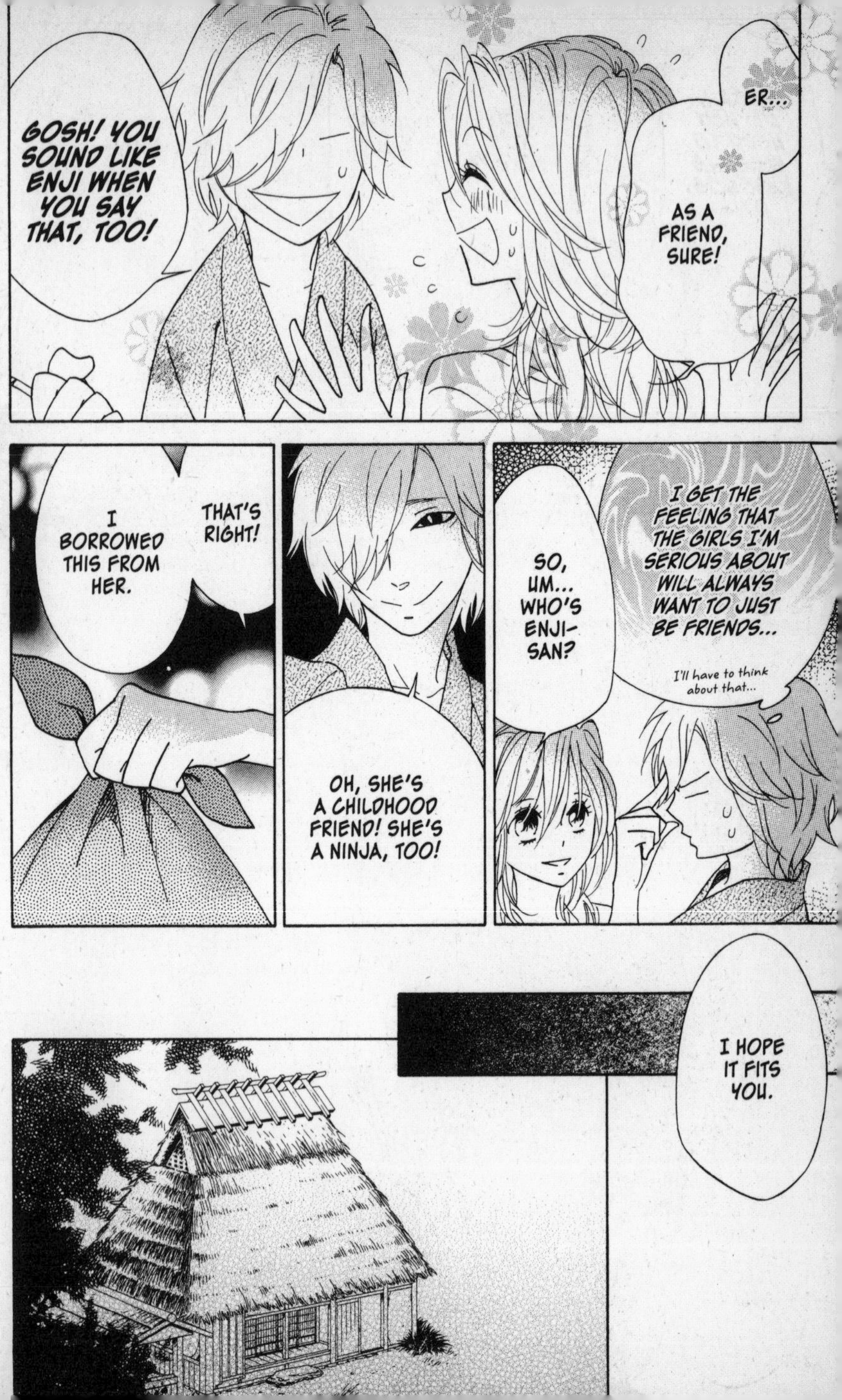
ER...
AS A FRIEND, SURE!
GOSH! YOU SOUND LIKE ENJI WHEN YOU SAY THAT, TOO!
I GET THE FEELING THAT THE GIRLS I'M SERIOUS ABOUT WILL ALWAYS WANT TO JUST BE FRIENDS...
I'll have to think about that...
SO, UM... WHO'S ENJI-SAN?
OH, SHE'S A CHILDHOOD FRIEND! SHE'S A NINJA, TOO!
THAT'S RIGHT!
I BORROWED THIS FROM HER.
I HOPE IT FITS YOU.

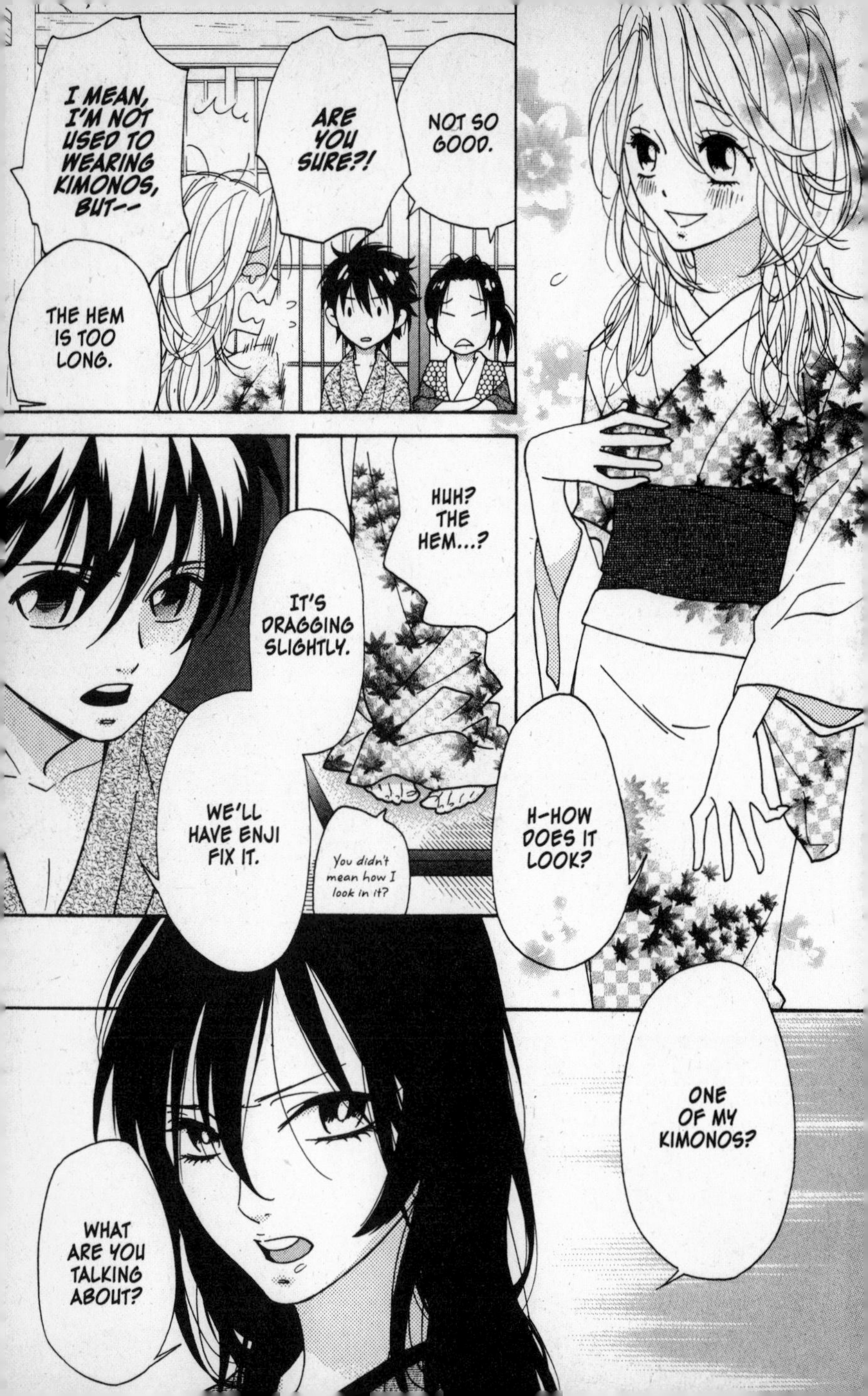
H-HOW DOES IT LOOK?
NOT SO GOOD.
ARE YOU SURE?!
I MEAN, I'M NOT USED TO WEARING KIMONOS, BUT--
THE HEM IS TOO LONG.
HUH? THE HEM...?
IT'S DRAGGING SLIGHTLY.
WE'LL HAVE ENJI FIX IT.
You didn't mean how I look in it?
ONE OF MY KIMONOS?
WHAT ARE YOU TALKING ABOUT?

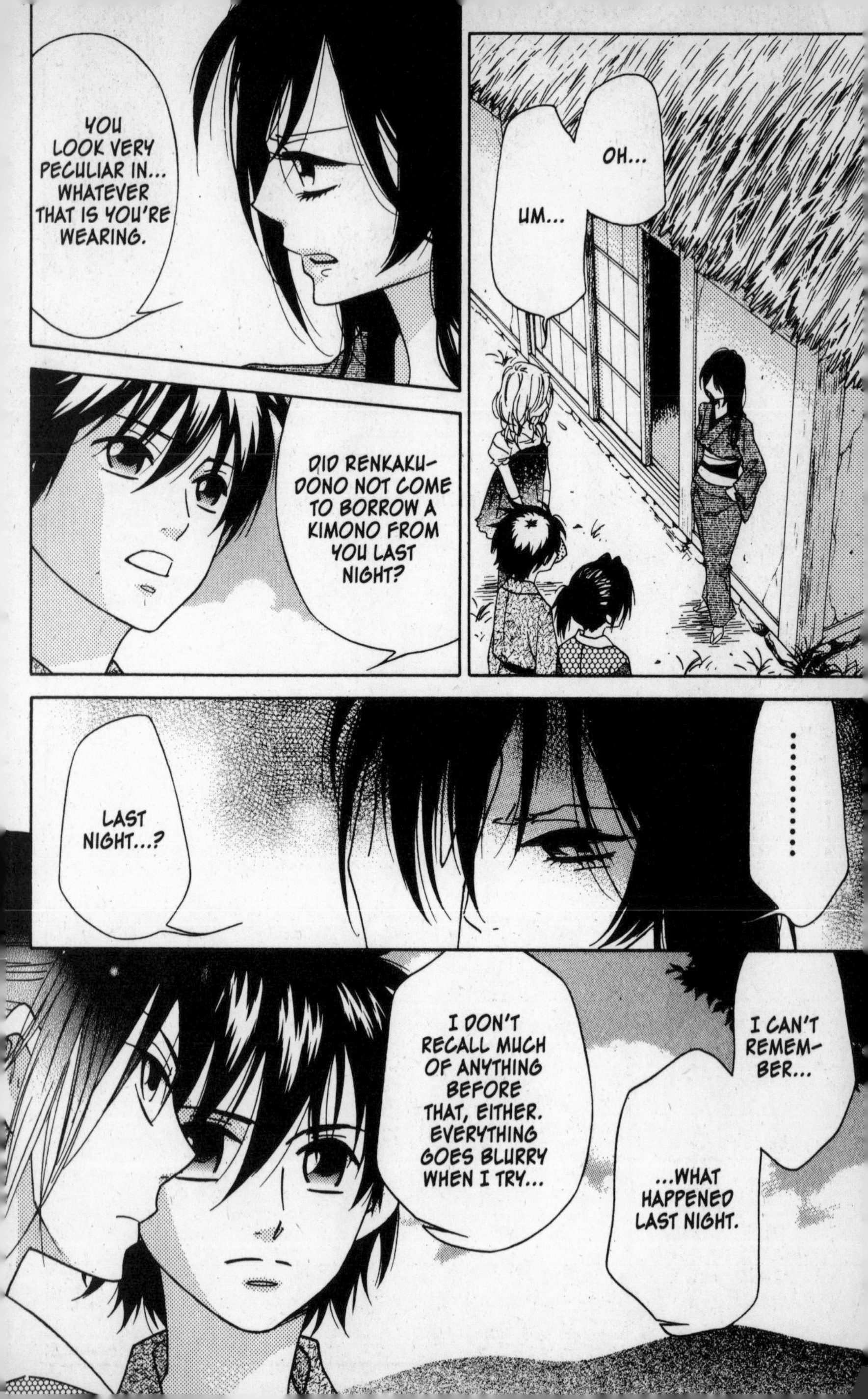
OH...
UM...
YOU LOOK VERY PECULIAR IN... WHATEVER THAT IS YOU'RE WEARING.
DID RENKAKU-DONO NOT COME TO BORROW A KIMONO FROM YOU LAST NIGHT?
......
LAST NIGHT...?
I CAN'T REMEMBER...
...WHAT HAPPENED LAST NIGHT.
I DON'T RECALL MUCH OF ANYTHING BEFORE THAT, EITHER. EVERYTHING GOES BLURRY WHEN I TRY...

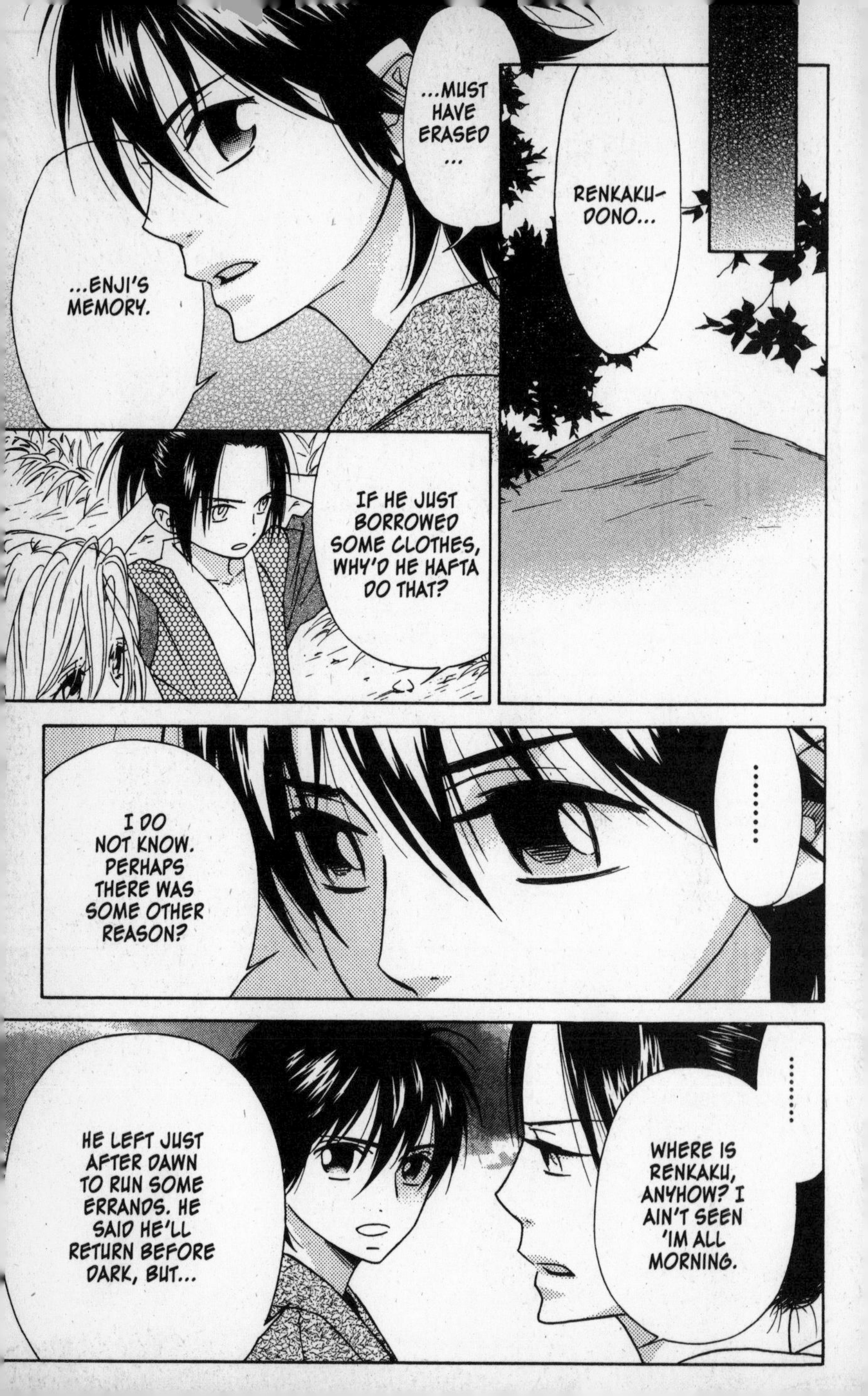
RENKAKU-DONO...
...MUST HAVE ERASED...
...ENJI'S MEMORY.
IF HE JUST BORROWED SOME CLOTHES, WHY'D HE HAFTA DO THAT?
......
I DO NOT KNOW. PERHAPS THERE WAS SOME OTHER REASON?
......
WHERE IS RENKAKU, ANYHOW? I AIN'T SEEN 'IM ALL MORNING.
HE LEFT JUST AFTER DAWN TO RUN SOME ERRANDS. HE SAID HE'LL RETURN BEFORE DARK, BUT...

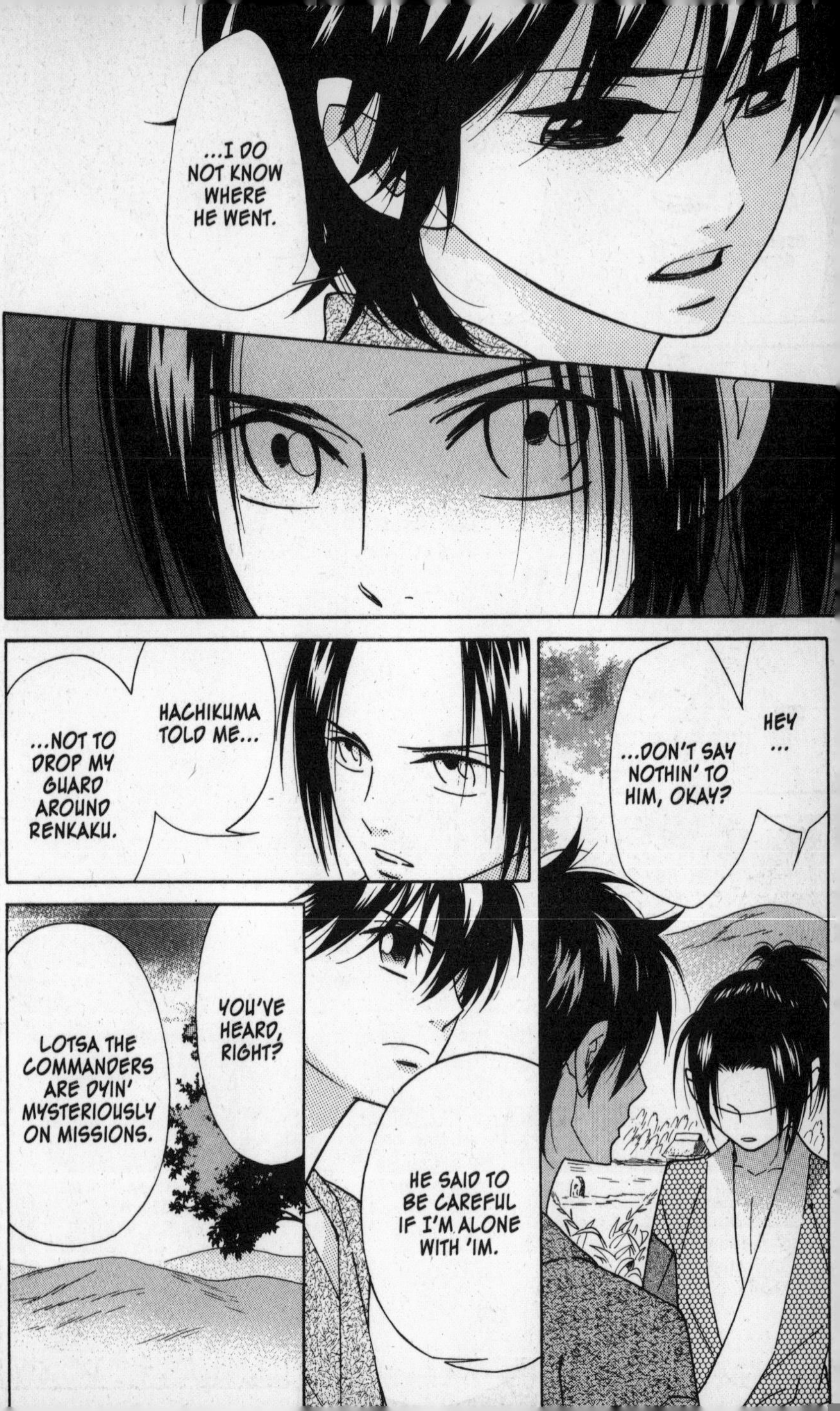
...I DO NOT KNOW WHERE HE WENT.
HEY ...
...DON'T SAY NOTHIN' TO HIM, OKAY?
HACHIKUMA TOLD ME...
...NOT TO DROP MY GUARD AROUND RENKAKU.
HE SAID TO BE CAREFUL IF I'M ALONE WITH 'IM.
YOU'VE HEARD, RIGHT?
LOTSA THE COMMANDERS ARE DYIN' MYSTERIOUSLY ON MISSIONS.

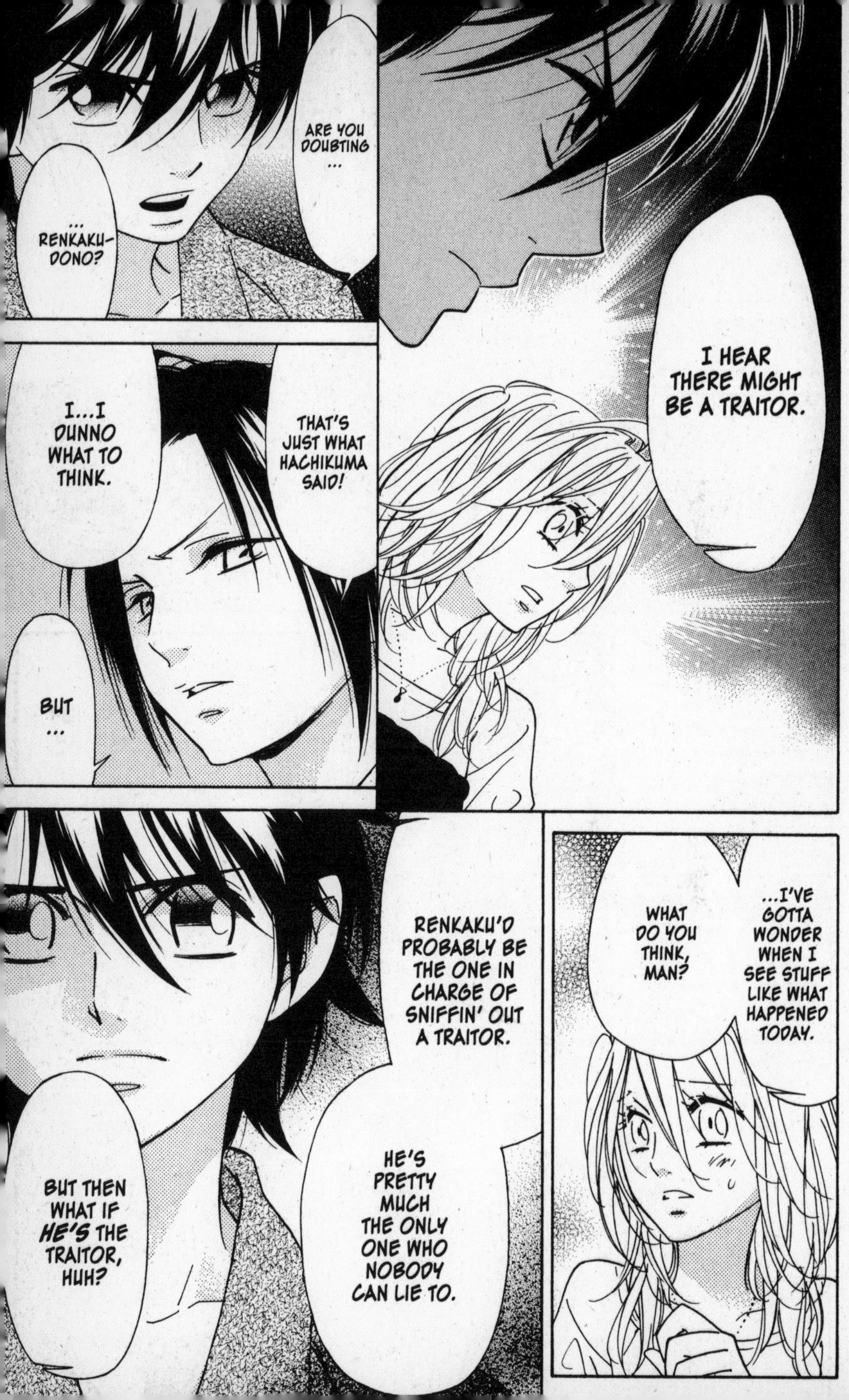
I HEAR THERE MIGHT BE A TRAITOR.
ARE YOU DOUBTING ...
... RENKAKU-DONO?
THAT'S JUST WHAT HACHIKUMA SAID!
I...I DUNNO WHAT TO THINK.
BUT ...
...I'VE GOTTA WONDER WHEN I SEE STUFF LIKE WHAT HAPPENED TODAY.
WHAT DO YOU THINK, MAN?
RENKAKU'D PROBABLY BE THE ONE IN CHARGE OF SNIFFIN' OUT A TRAITOR.
HE'S PRETTY MUCH THE ONLY ONE WHO NOBODY CAN LIE TO.
BUT THEN WHAT IF *HE'S* THE TRAITOR, HUH?

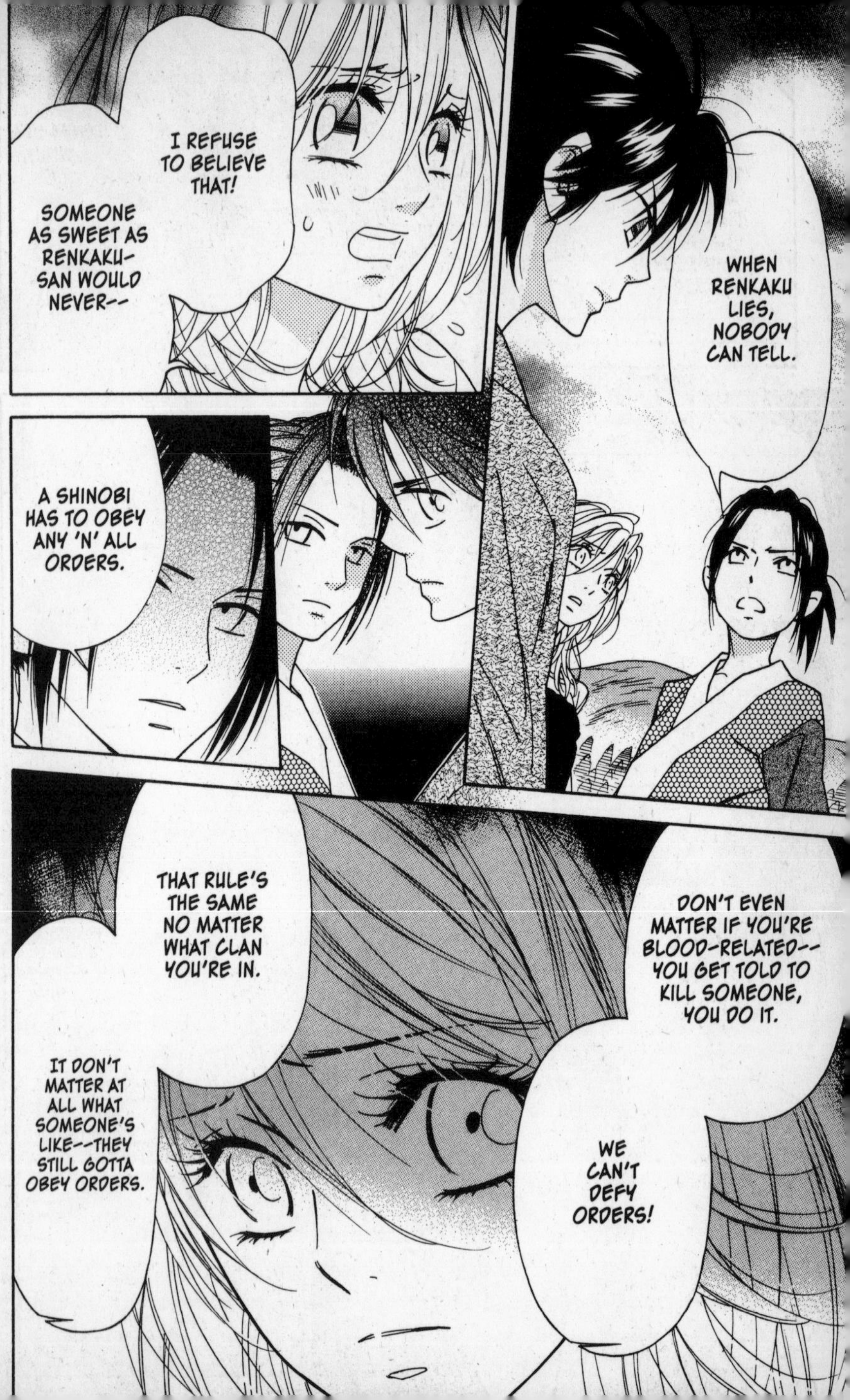
WHEN RENKAKU LIES, NOBODY CAN TELL.
I REFUSE TO BELIEVE THAT!
SOMEONE AS SWEET AS RENKAKU-SAN WOULD NEVER--
A SHINOBI HAS TO OBEY ANY 'N' ALL ORDERS.
DON'T EVEN MATTER IF YOU'RE BLOOD-RELATED--YOU GET TOLD TO KILL SOMEONE, YOU DO IT.
THAT RULE'S THE SAME NO MATTER WHAT CLAN YOU'RE IN.
IT DON'T MATTER AT ALL WHAT SOMEONE'S LIKE--THEY STILL GOTTA OBEY ORDERS.
WE CAN'T DEFY ORDERS!

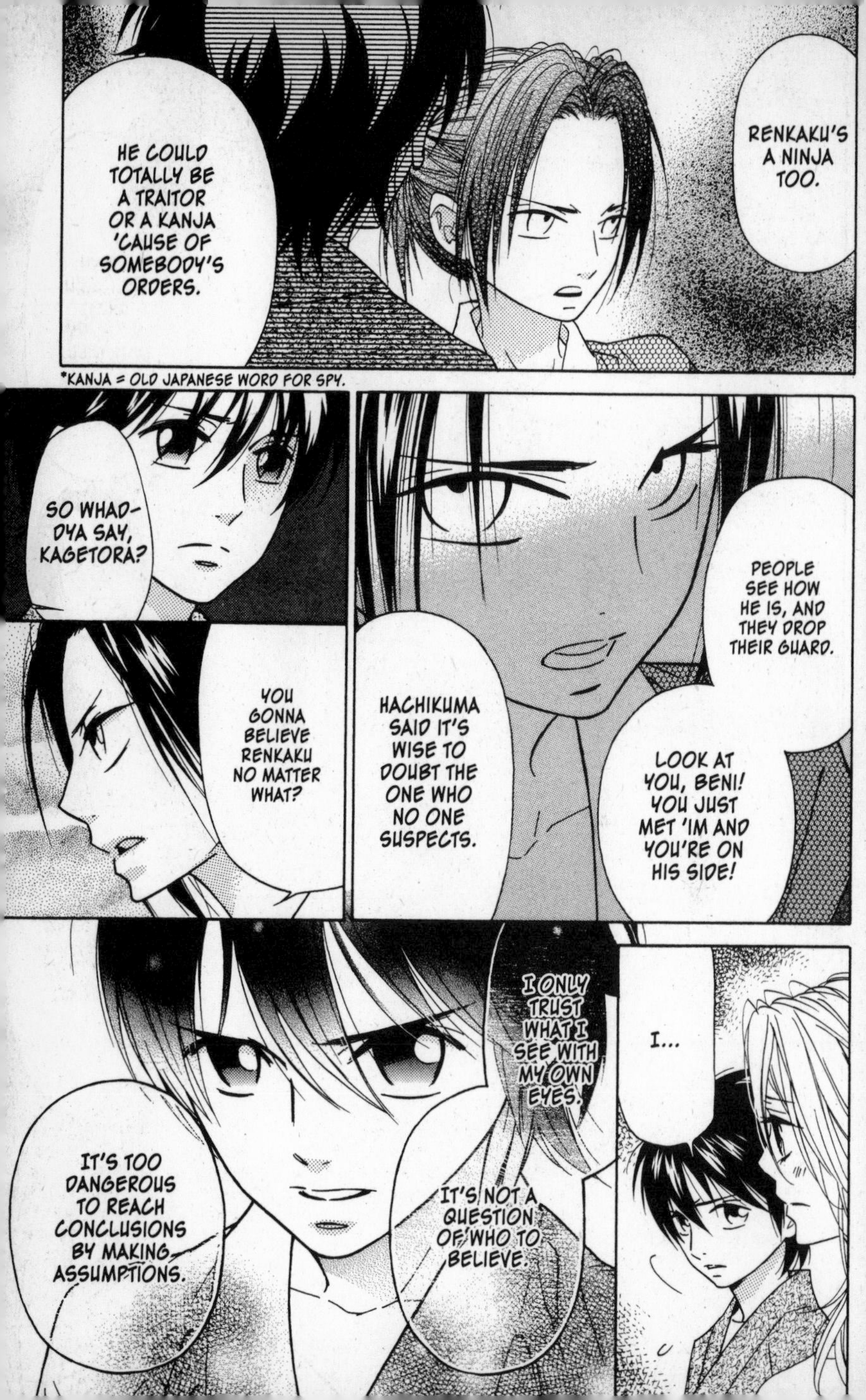
RENKAKU'S A NINJA TOO.
HE COULD TOTALLY BE A TRAITOR OR A KANJA 'CAUSE OF SOMEBODY'S ORDERS.
PEOPLE SEE HOW HE IS, AND THEY DROP THEIR GUARD.
LOOK AT YOU, BENI! YOU JUST MET 'IM AND YOU'RE ON HIS SIDE!
HACHIKUMA SAID IT'S WISE TO DOUBT THE ONE WHO NO ONE SUSPECTS.
SO WHAD-DYA SAY, KAGETORA?
YOU GONNA BELIEVE RENKAKU NO MATTER WHAT?
I...
I ONLY TRUST WHAT I SEE WITH MY OWN EYES.
IT'S NOT A QUESTION OF WHO TO BELIEVE.
IT'S TOO DANGEROUS TO REACH CONCLUSIONS BY MAKING ASSUMPTIONS.

*KANJA = OLD JAPANESE WORD FOR SPY.

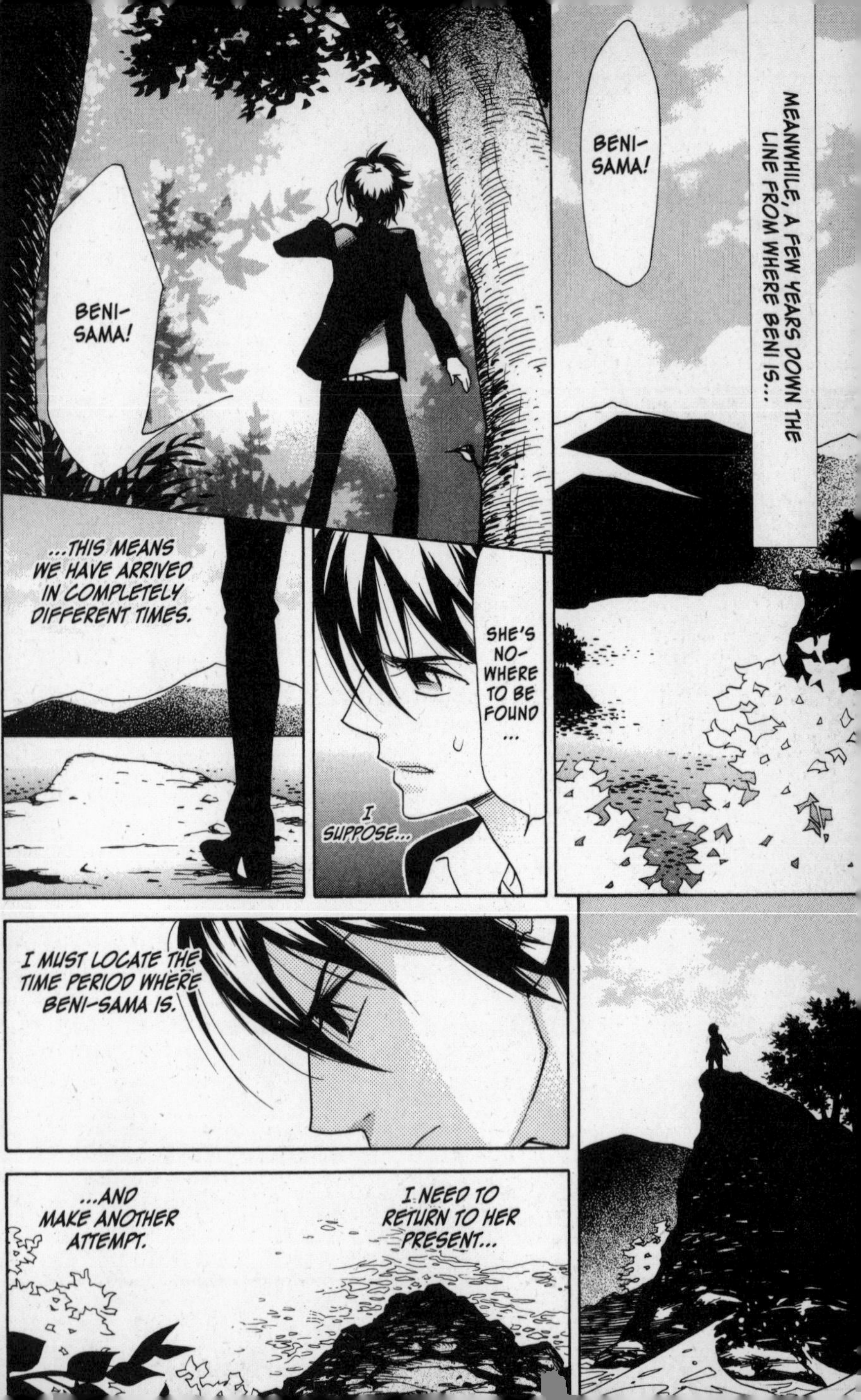
MEANWHILE, A FEW YEARS DOWN THE LINE FROM WHERE BENI IS...
BENI-SAMA!
BENI-SAMA!
SHE'S NO-WHERE TO BE FOUND ...
I SUPPOSE...
...THIS MEANS WE HAVE ARRIVED IN COMPLETELY DIFFERENT TIMES.
I MUST LOCATE THE TIME PERIOD WHERE BENI-SAMA IS.
I NEED TO RETURN TO HER PRESENT...
...AND MAKE ANOTHER ATTEMPT.

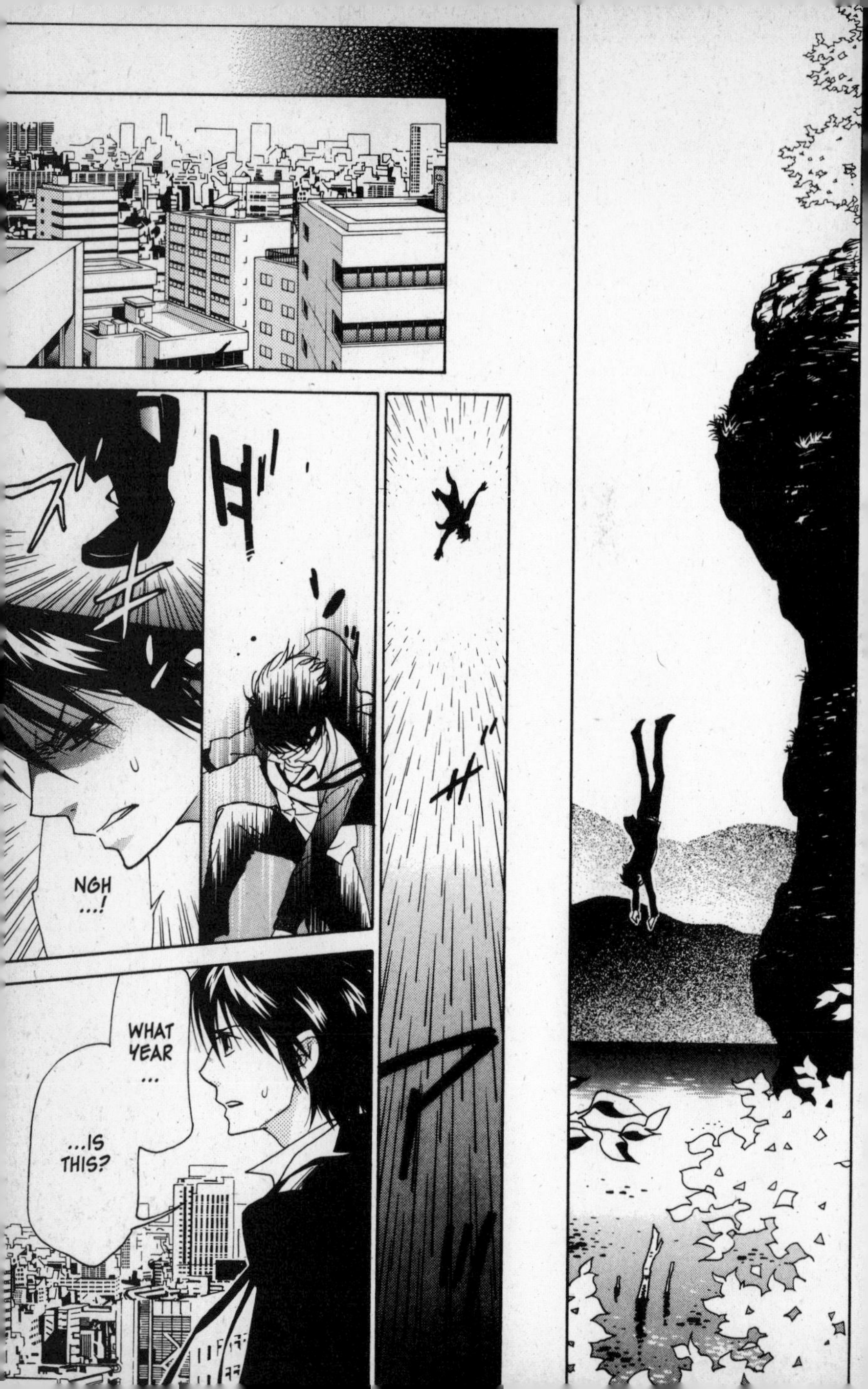
NGH ...!
WHAT YEAR ...
...IS THIS?

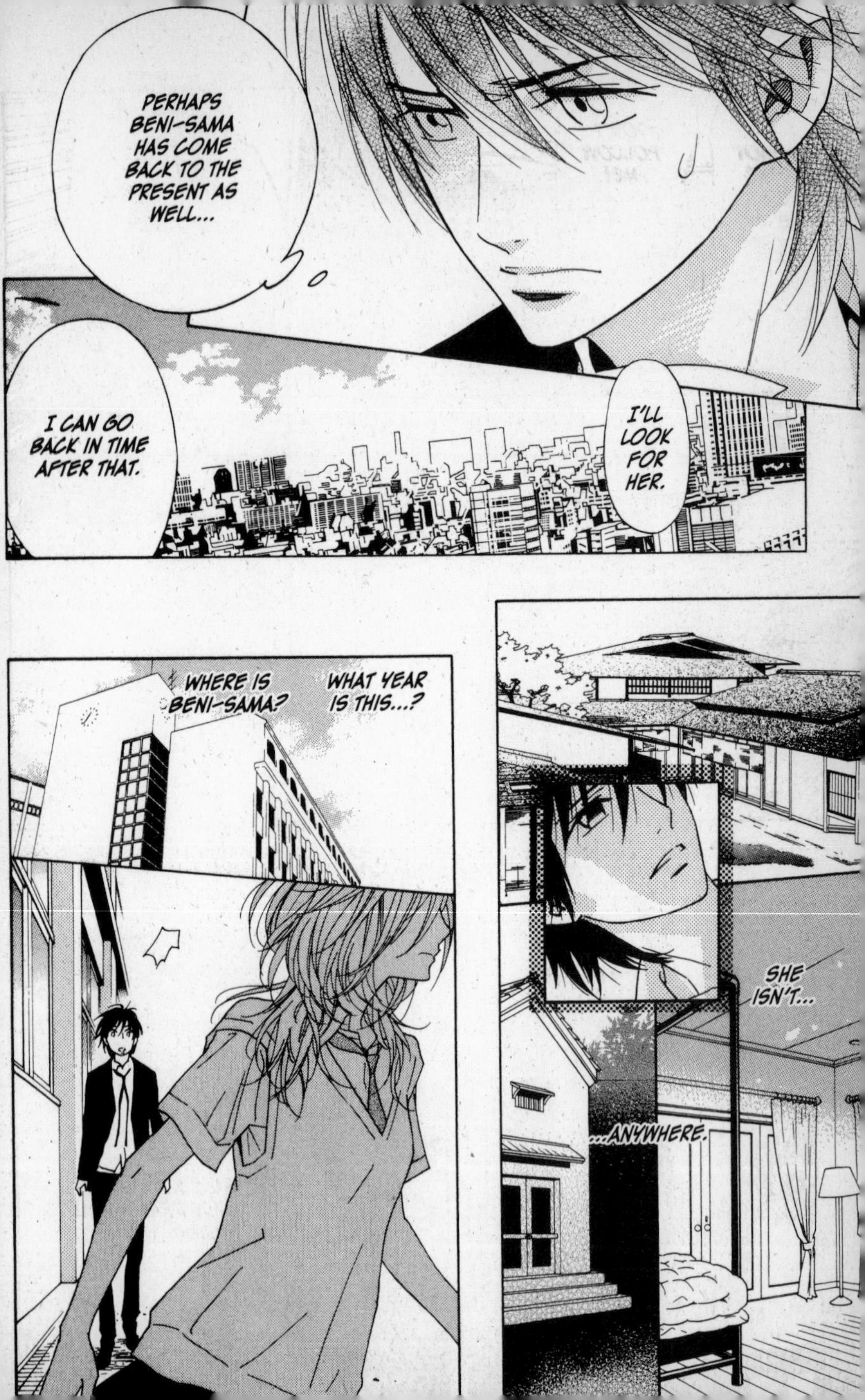
PERHAPS BENI-SAMA HAS COME BACK TO THE PRESENT AS WELL...
I'LL LOOK FOR HER.
I CAN GO BACK IN TIME AFTER THAT.
WHAT YEAR IS THIS...?
WHERE IS BENI-SAMA?
SHE ISN'T...
...ANYWHERE.

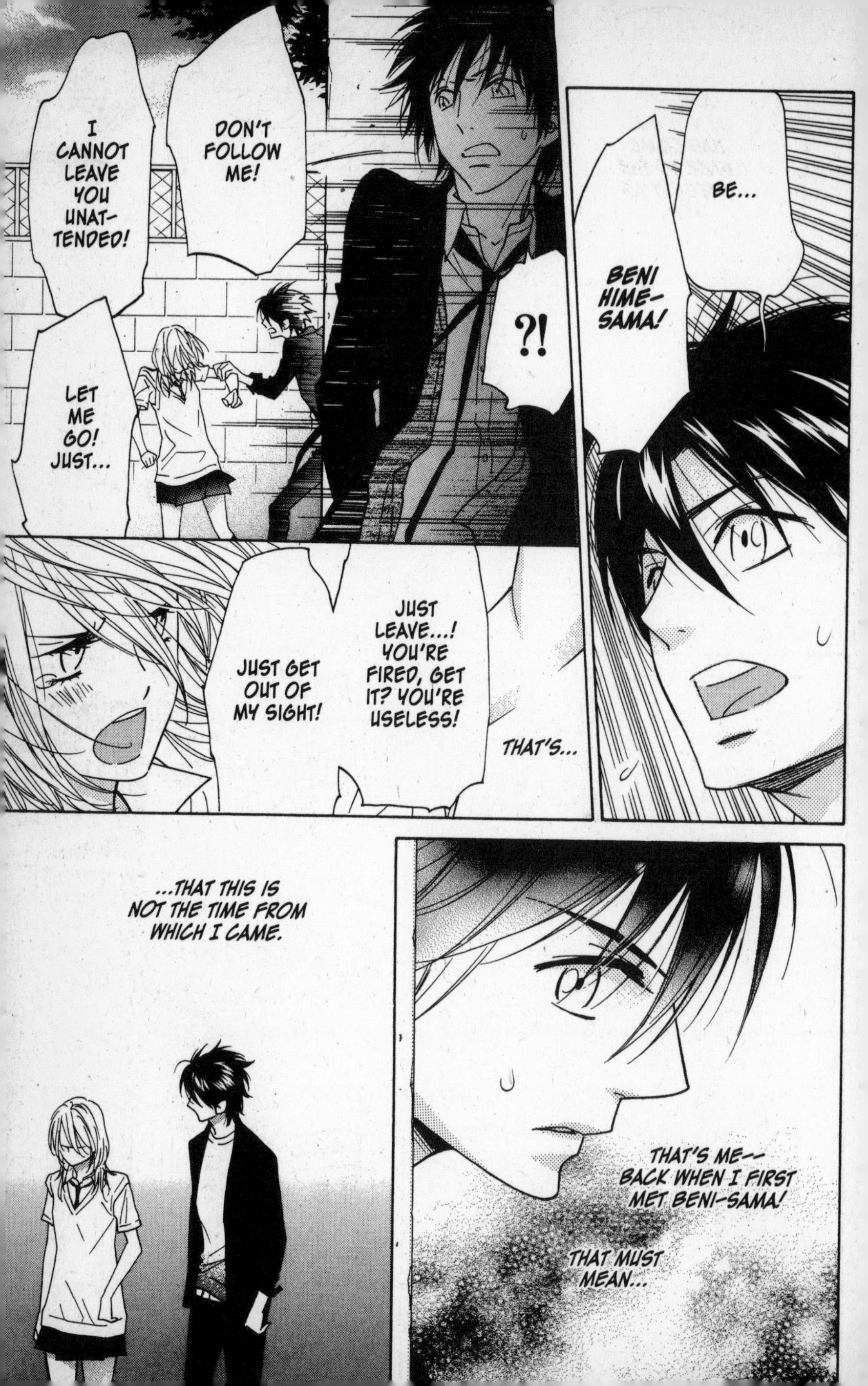
BE...
BENI HIME-SAMA!
?!
DON'T FOLLOW ME!
I CANNOT LEAVE YOU UNAT-TENDED!
LET ME GO! JUST...
JUST LEAVE...! YOU'RE FIRED, GET IT? YOU'RE USELESS!
JUST GET OUT OF MY SIGHT!
THAT'S...
THAT'S ME-- BACK WHEN I FIRST MET BENI-SAMA!
THAT MUST MEAN...
...THAT THIS IS NOT THE TIME FROM WHICH I CAME.

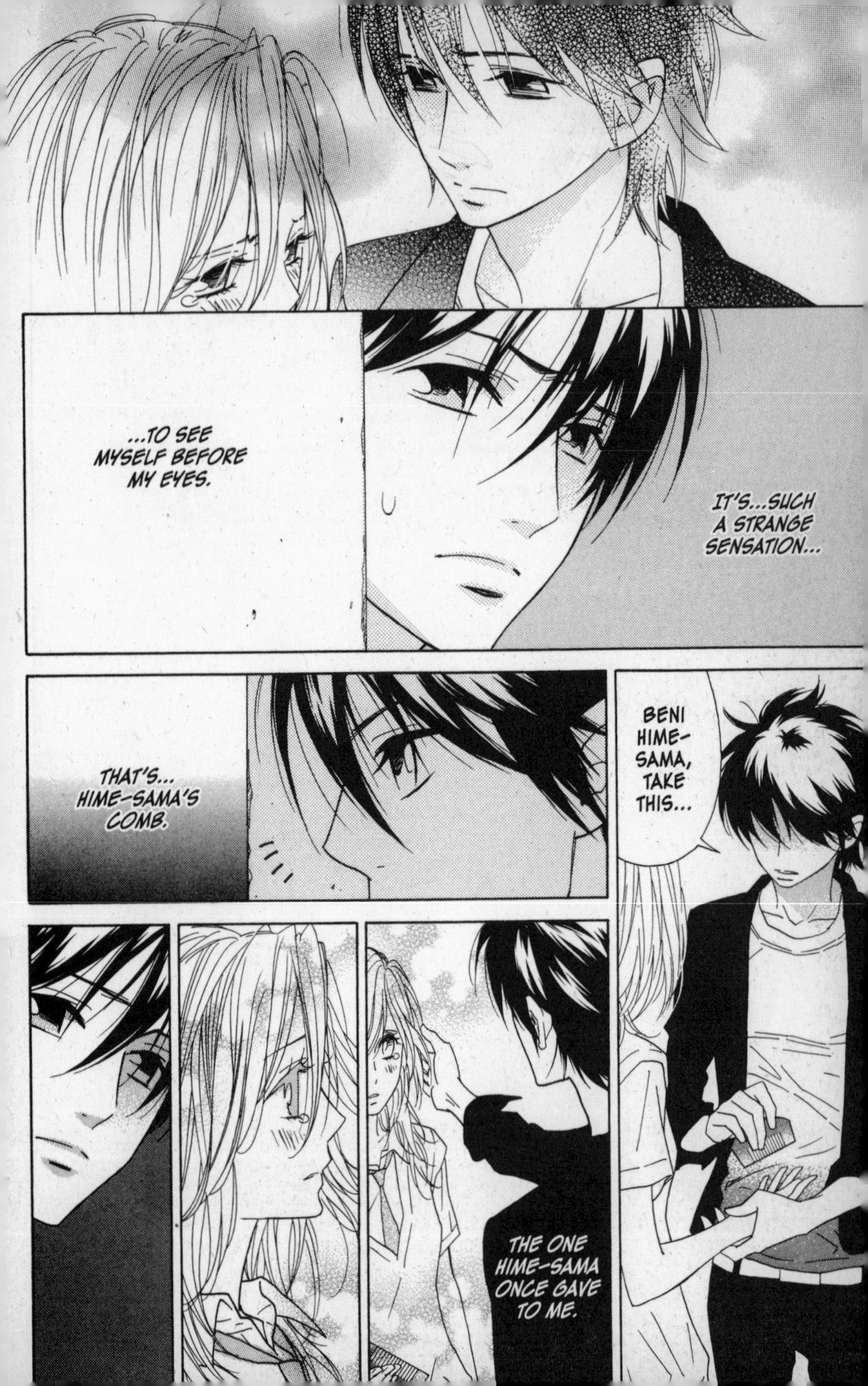
IT'S...SUCH A STRANGE SENSATION...
...TO SEE MYSELF BEFORE MY EYES.
BENI HIME-SAMA, TAKE THIS...
THAT'S... HIME-SAMA'S COMB.
THE ONE HIME-SAMA ONCE GAVE TO ME.

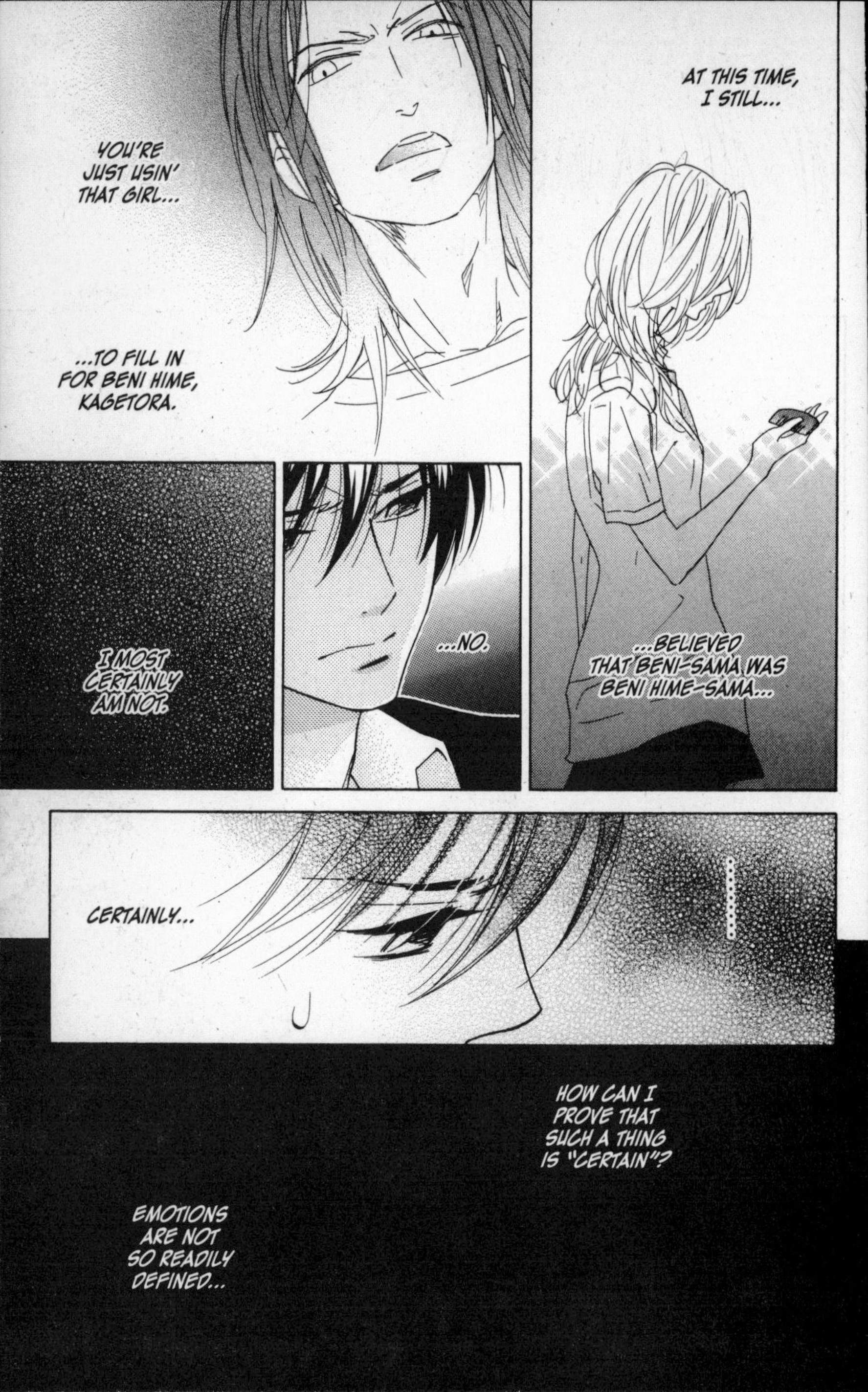
AT THIS TIME, I STILL...
...BELIEVED THAT BENI-SAMA WAS BENI HIME-SAMA...
YOU'RE JUST USIN' THAT GIRL...
...TO FILL IN FOR BENI HIME, KAGETORA.
...NO.
I MOST CERTAINLY AM NOT.
....
CERTAINLY...
HOW CAN I PROVE THAT SUCH A THING IS "CERTAIN"?
EMOTIONS ARE NOT SO READILY DEFINED...

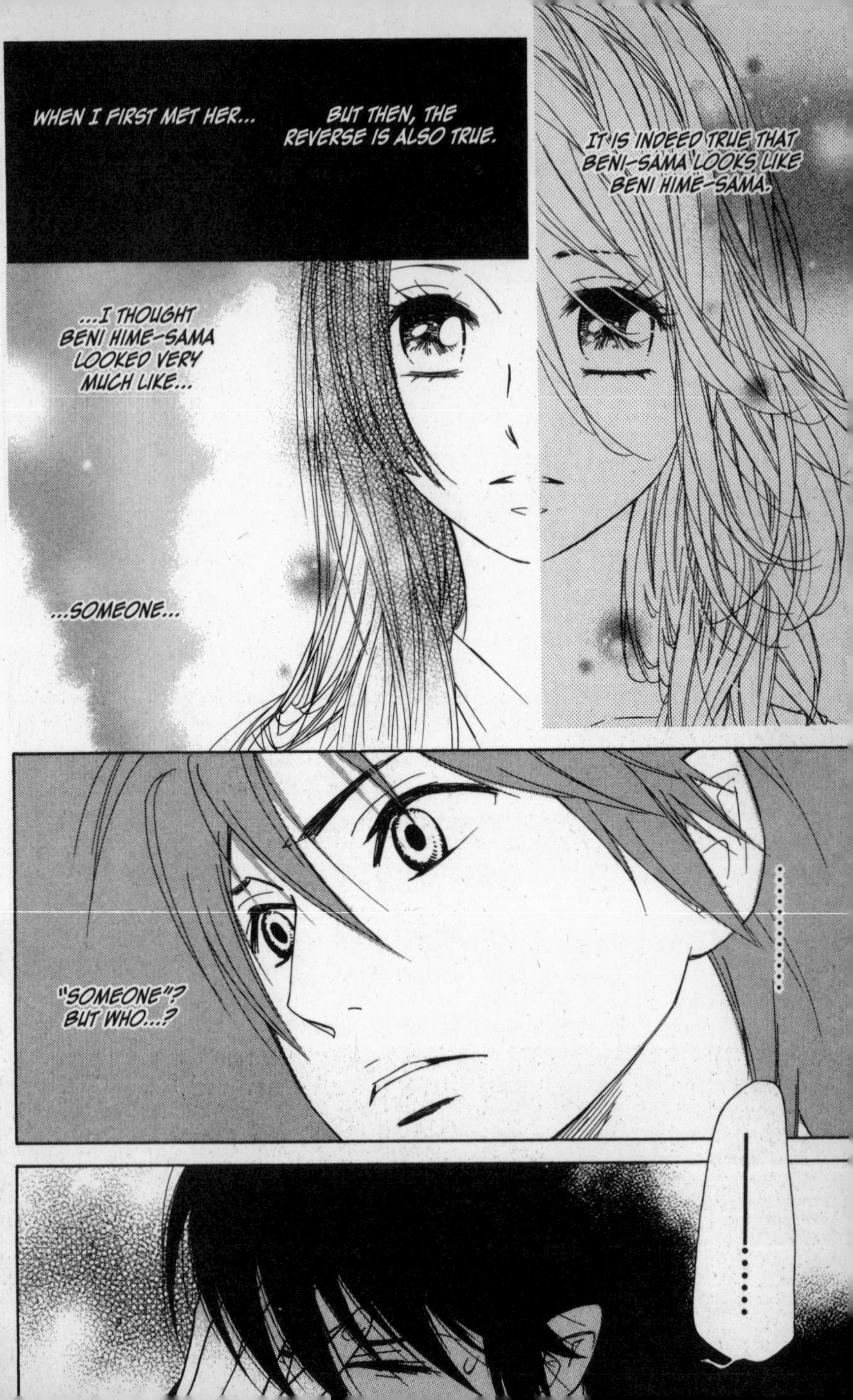
IT IS INDEED TRUE THAT BENI-SAMA LOOKS LIKE BENI HIME-SAMA.
BUT THEN, THE REVERSE IS ALSO TRUE.
WHEN I FIRST MET HER...
...I THOUGHT BENI HIME-SAMA LOOKED VERY MUCH LIKE...
...SOMEONE...
....
"SOMEONE"? BUT WHO...?
—......

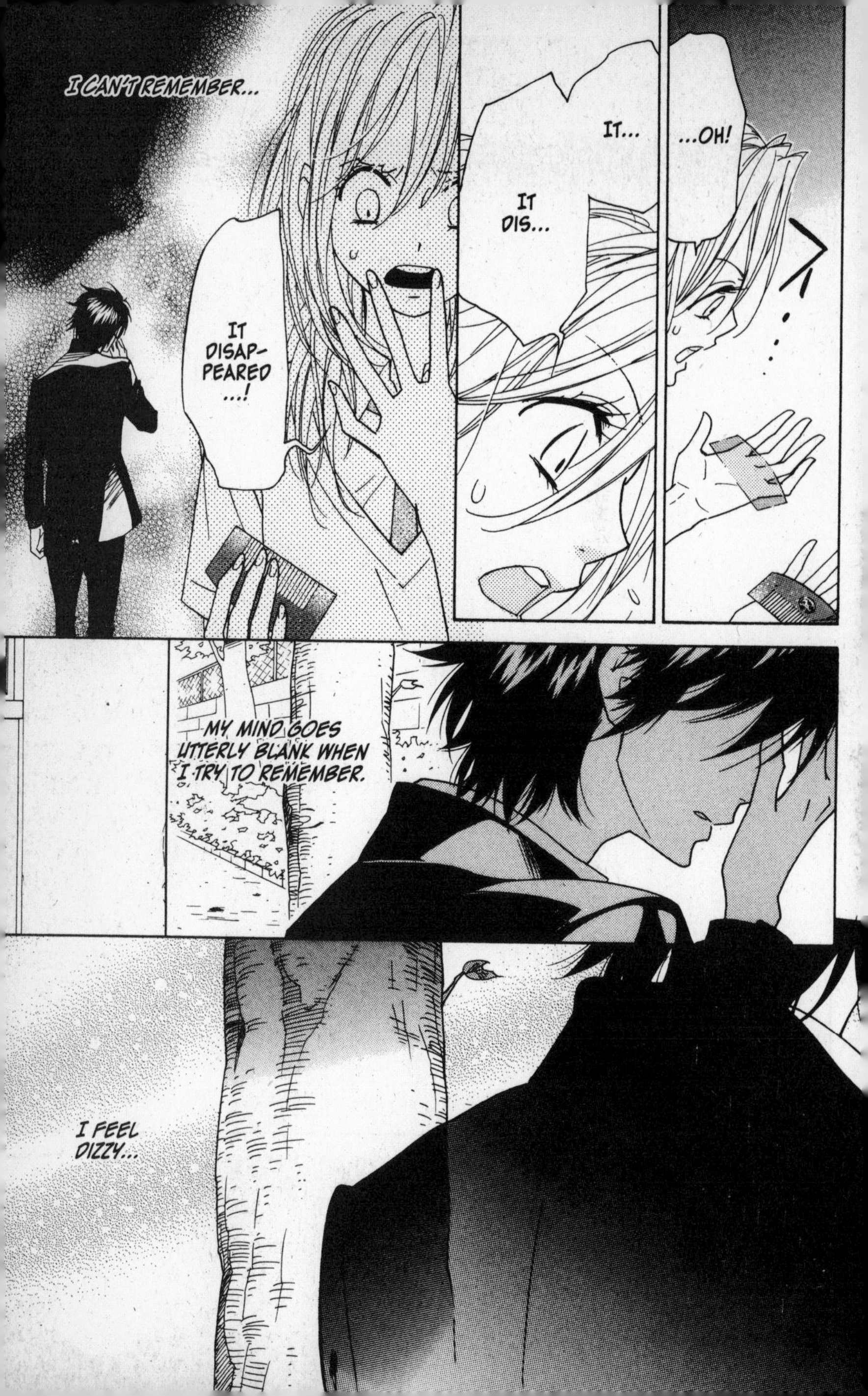
...OH!
IT...
IT DIS...
IT DISAP-PEARED ....!
I CAN'T REMEMBER...
MY MIND GOES UTTERLY BLANK WHEN I TRY TO REMEMBER.
I FEEL DIZZY...

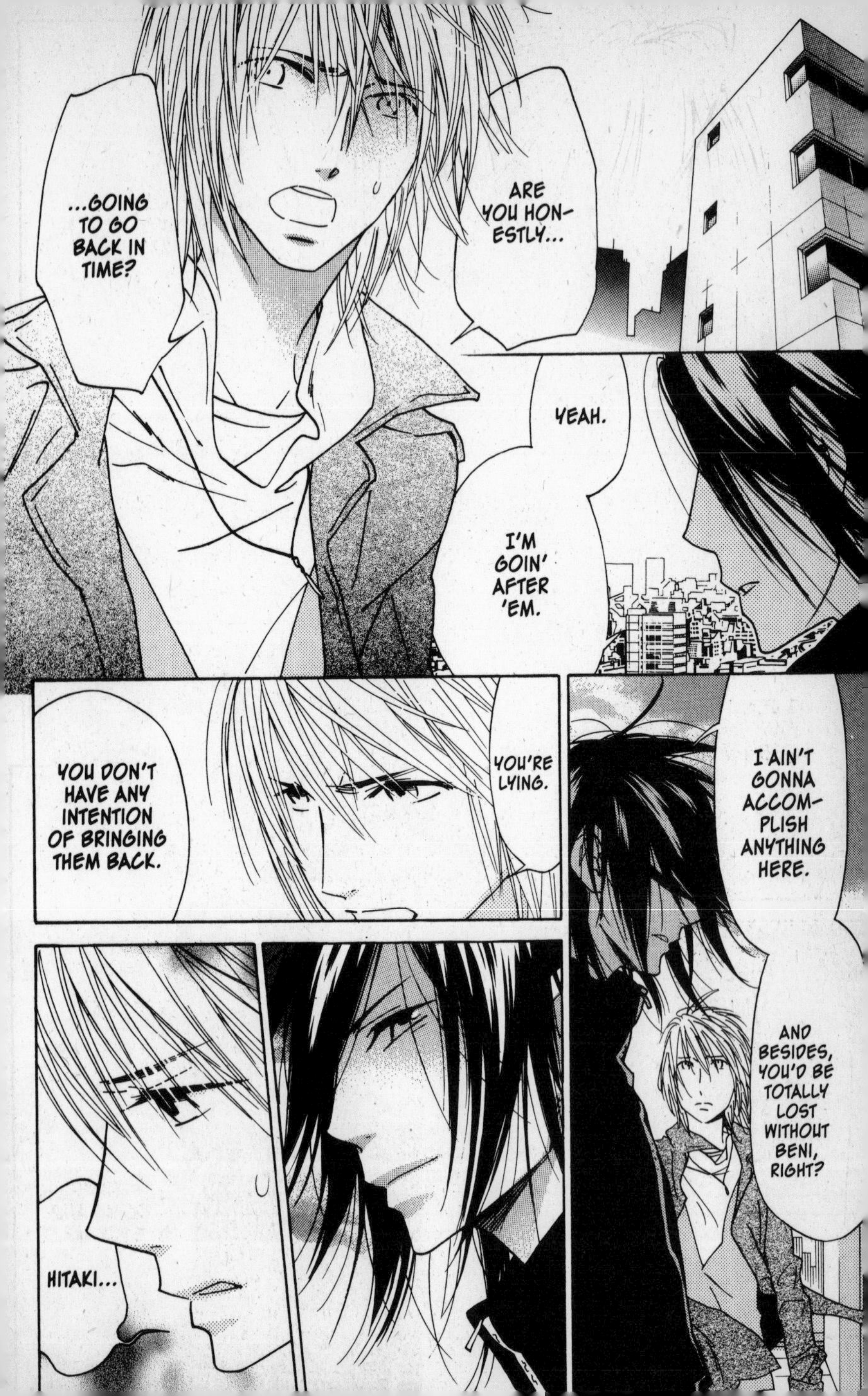
ARE YOU HON-ESTLY...
...GOING TO GO BACK IN TIME?
YEAH.
I'M GOIN' AFTER 'EM.
I AIN'T GONNA ACCOM-PLISH ANYTHING HERE.
YOU'RE LYING.
YOU DON'T HAVE ANY INTENTION OF BRINGING THEM BACK.
AND BESIDES, YOU'D BE TOTALLY LOST WITHOUT BENI, RIGHT?
HITAKI...

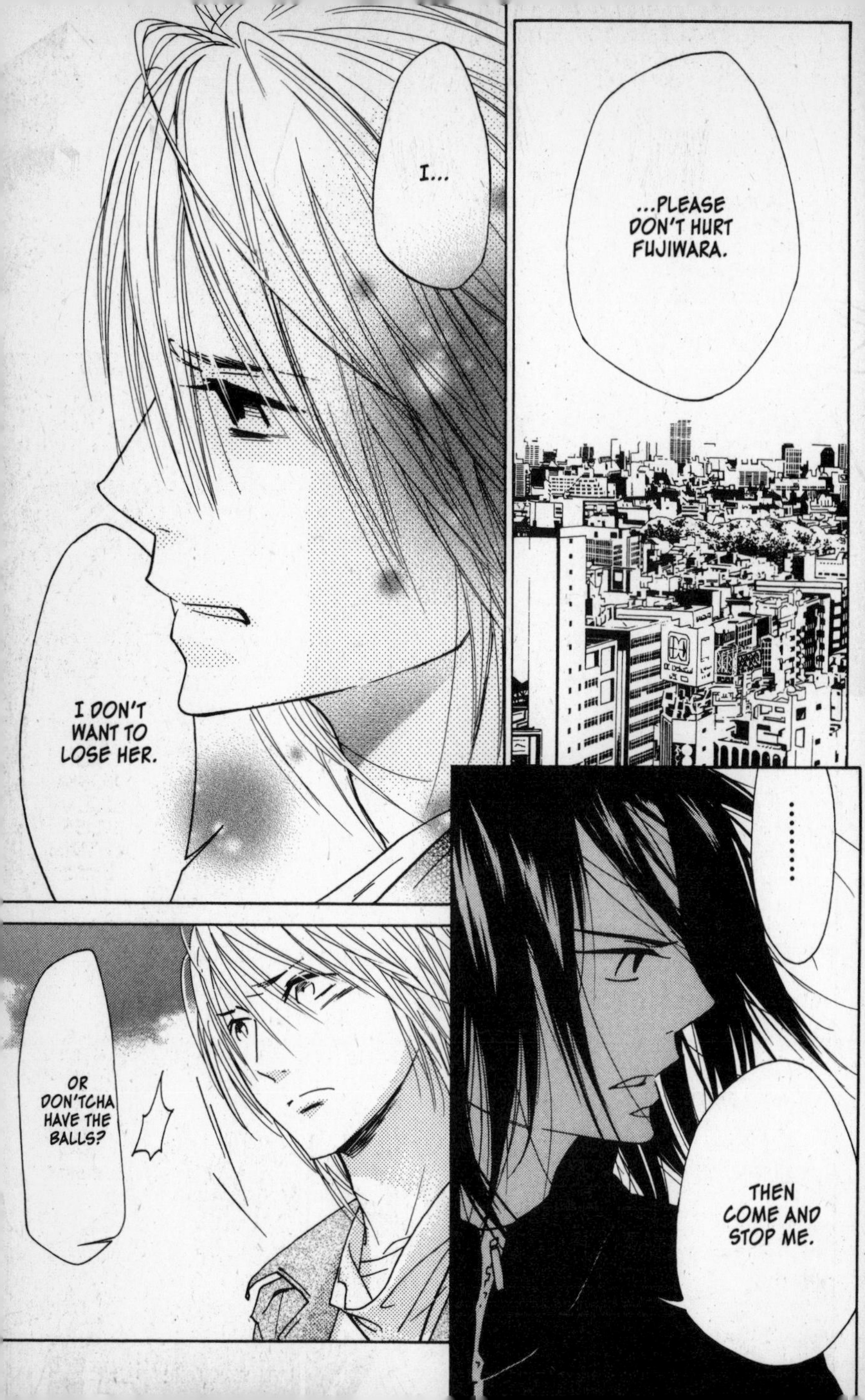
...PLEASE DON'T HURT FUJIWARA.
I...
I DON'T WANT TO LOSE HER.
....
THEN COME AND STOP ME.
OR DON'TCHA HAVE THE BALLS?

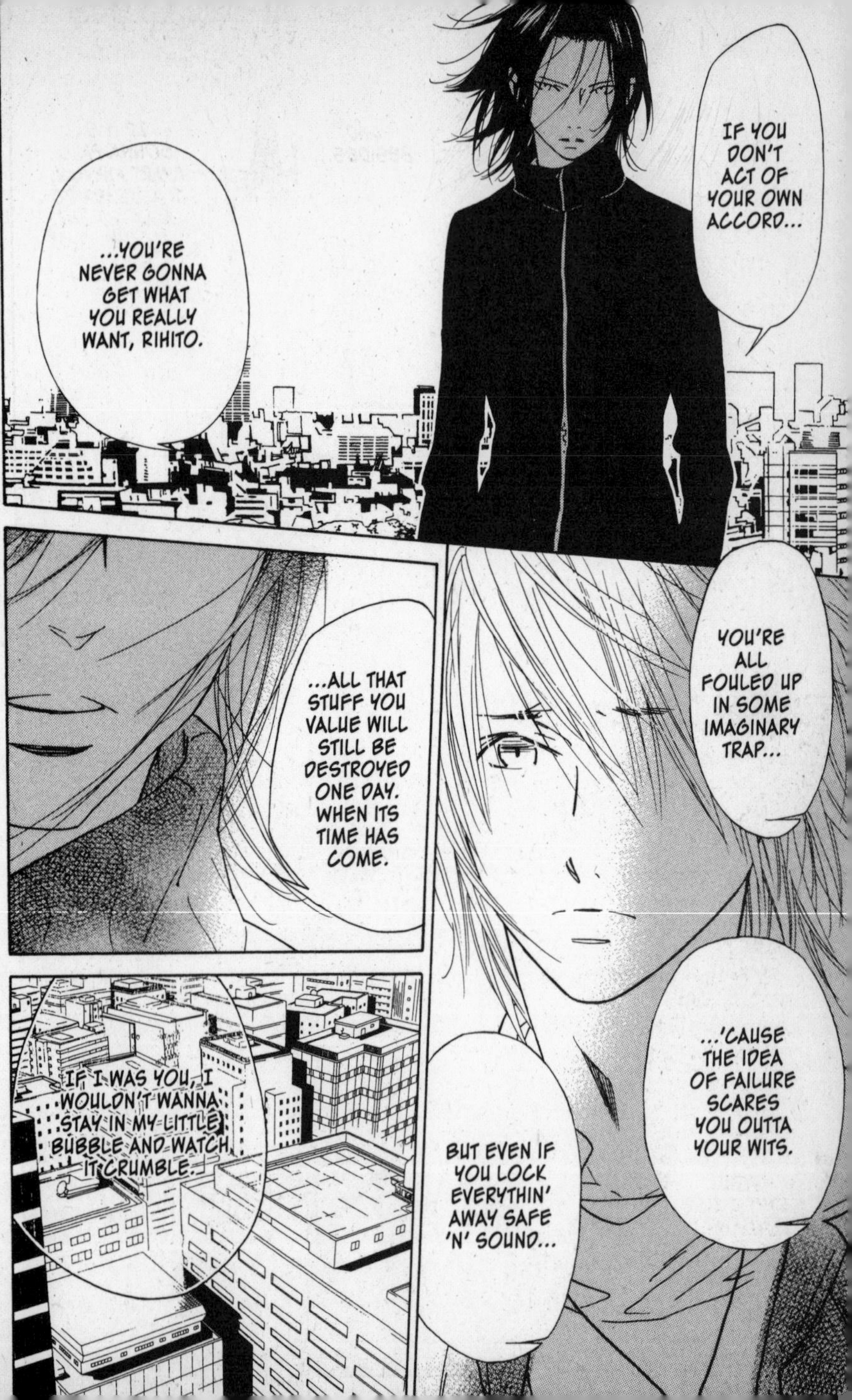
IF YOU DON'T ACT OF YOUR OWN ACCORD...
...YOU'RE NEVER GONNA GET WHAT YOU REALLY WANT, RIHITO.
YOU'RE ALL FOULED UP IN SOME IMAGINARY TRAP...
...'CAUSE THE IDEA OF FAILURE SCARES YOU OUTTA YOUR WITS.
BUT EVEN IF YOU LOCK EVERYTHIN' AWAY SAFE 'N' SOUND...
...ALL THAT STUFF YOU VALUE WILL STILL BE DESTROYED ONE DAY. WHEN ITS TIME HAS COME.
IF I WAS YOU, I WOULDN'T WANNA STAY IN MY LITTLE BUBBLE AND WATCH IT CRUMBLE.

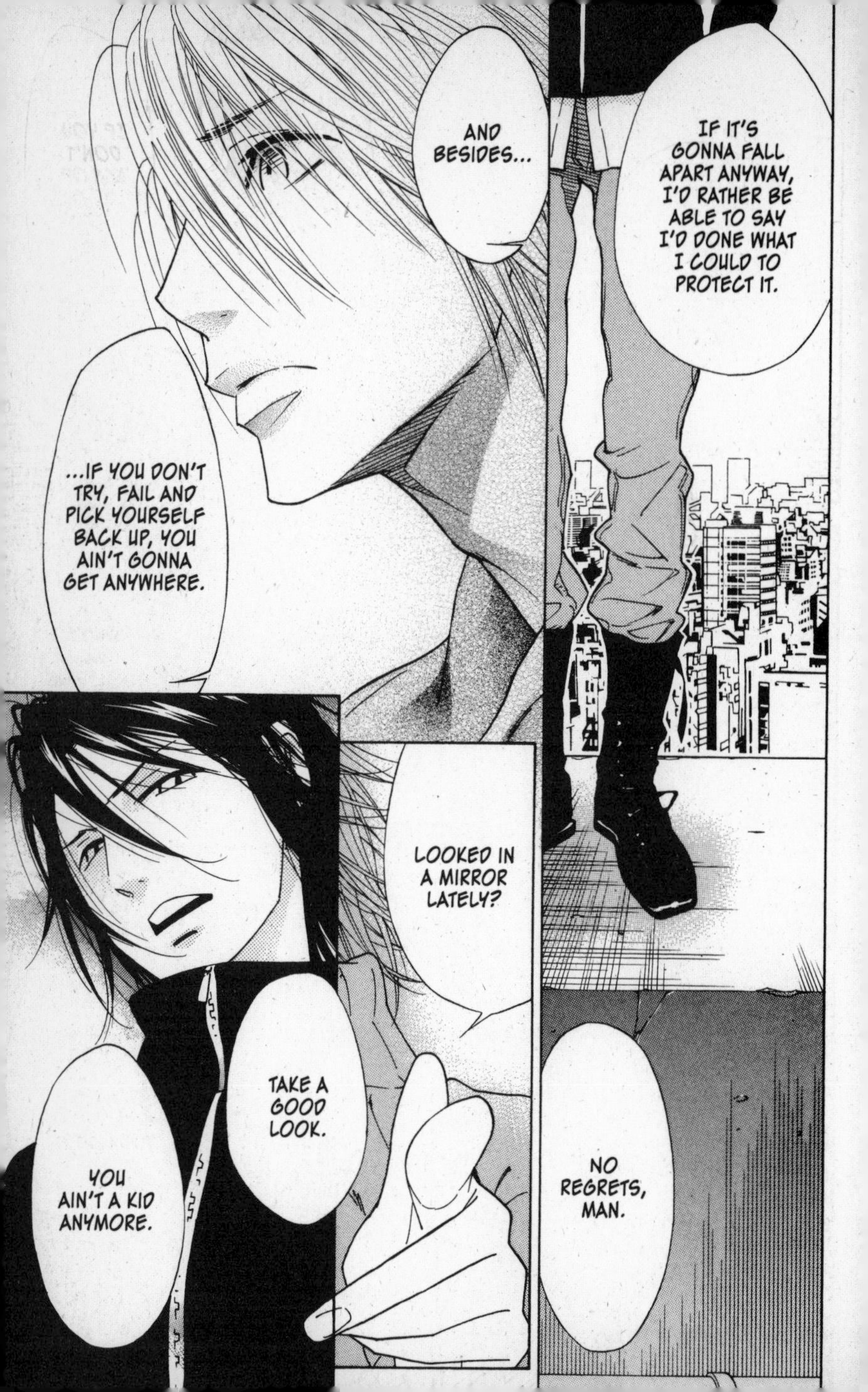
IF IT'S GONNA FALL APART ANYWAY, I'D RATHER BE ABLE TO SAY I'D DONE WHAT I COULD TO PROTECT IT.
AND BESIDES...
...IF YOU DON'T TRY, FAIL AND PICK YOURSELF BACK UP, YOU AIN'T GONNA GET ANYWHERE.
LOOKED IN A MIRROR LATELY?
TAKE A GOOD LOOK.
YOU AIN'T A KID ANYMORE.
NO REGRETS, MAN.

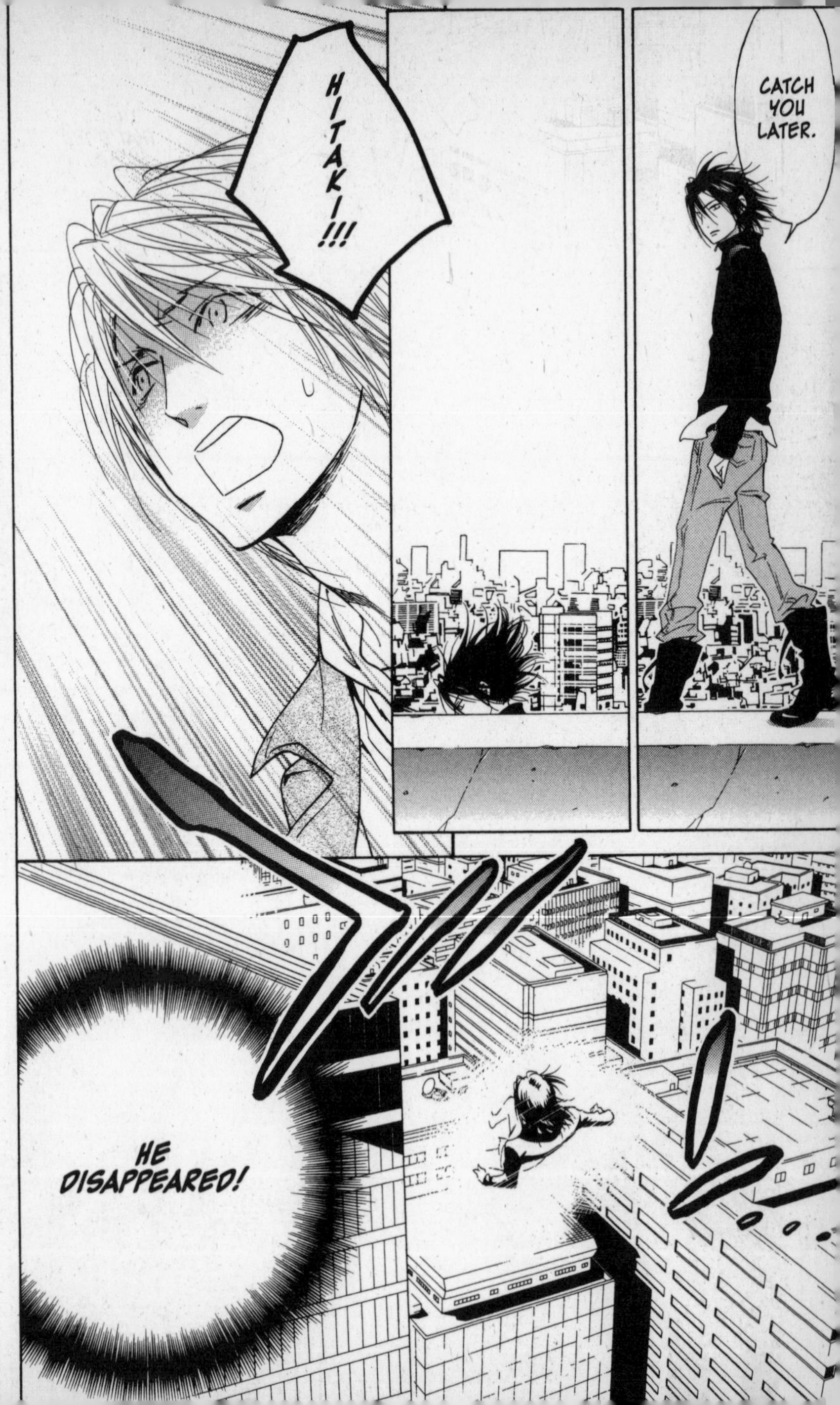
CATCH YOU LATER.
HITAKI!!!
HE DISAPPEARED!

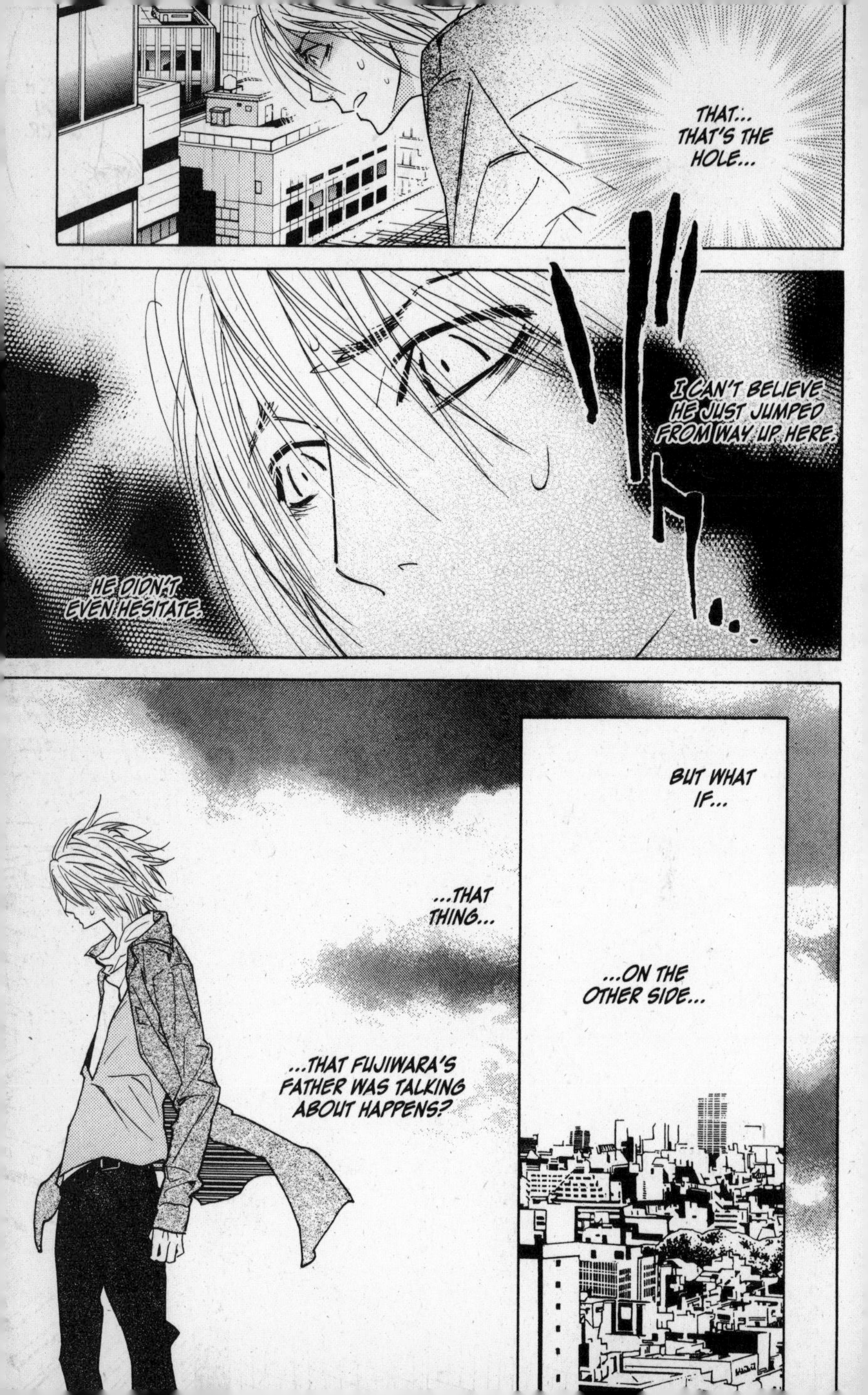
THAT... THAT'S THE HOLE...
I CAN'T BELIEVE HE JUST JUMPED FROM WAY UP HERE.
HE DIDN'T EVEN HESITATE.
BUT WHAT IF...
...THAT THING...
...ON THE OTHER SIDE...
...THAT FUJIWARA'S FATHER WAS TALKING ABOUT HAPPENS?

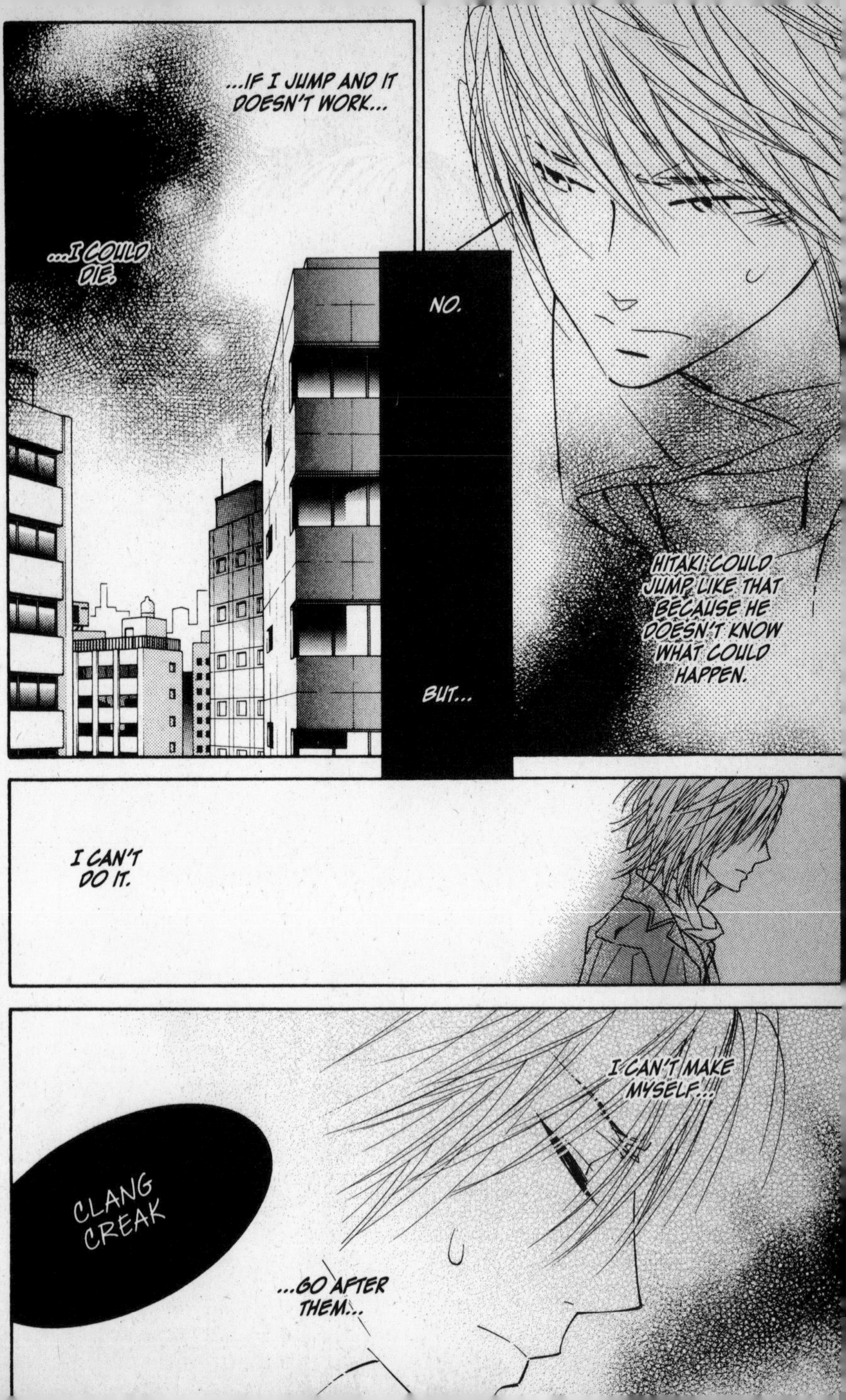

...IF I JUMP AND IT DOESN'T WORK...
...I COULD DIE.
NO.
HITAKI COULD JUMP LIKE THAT BECAUSE HE DOESN'T KNOW WHAT COULD HAPPEN.
BUT...
I CAN'T DO IT.
I CAN'T MAKE MYSELF...
...GO AFTER THEM...
CLANG CREAK

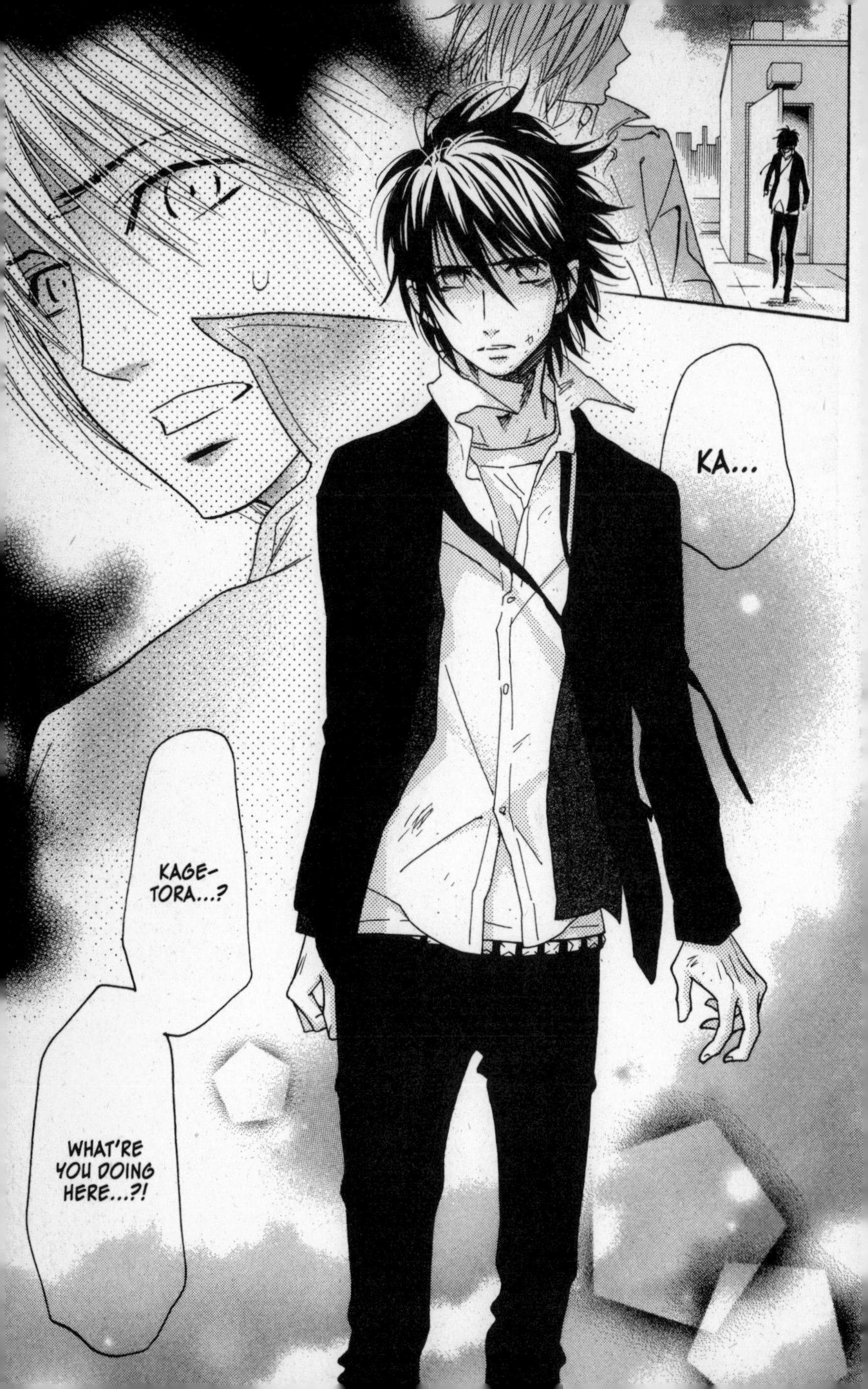
KA...
KAGE-TORA...?
WHAT'RE YOU DOING HERE...?!

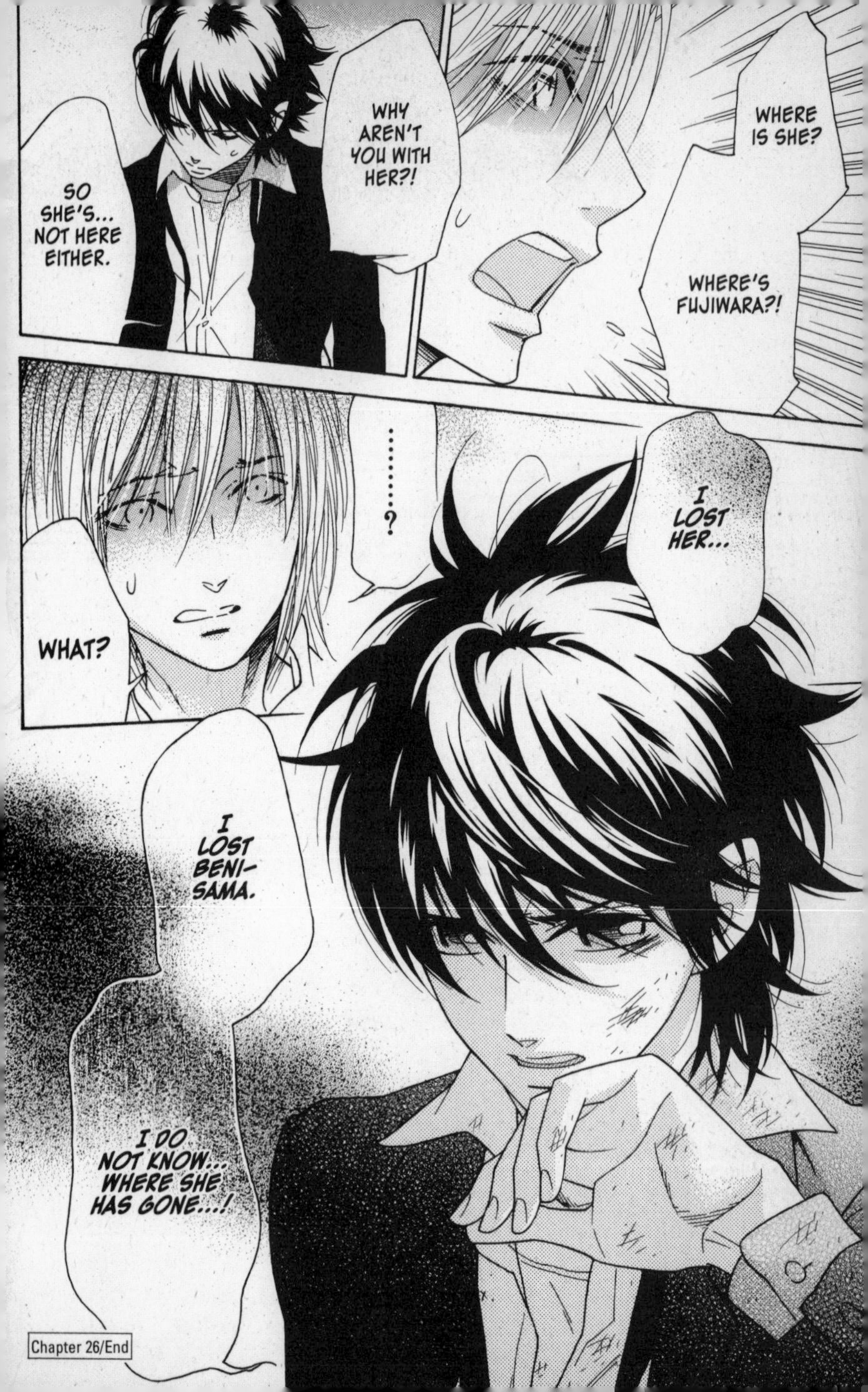
WHERE IS SHE?
WHERE'S FUJIWARA?!
WHY AREN'T YOU WITH HER?!
SO SHE'S... NOT HERE EITHER.
I LOST HER...
.......?
WHAT?
I LOST BENI-SAMA.
I DO NOT KNOW... WHERE SHE HAS GONE...!
Chapter 26/End

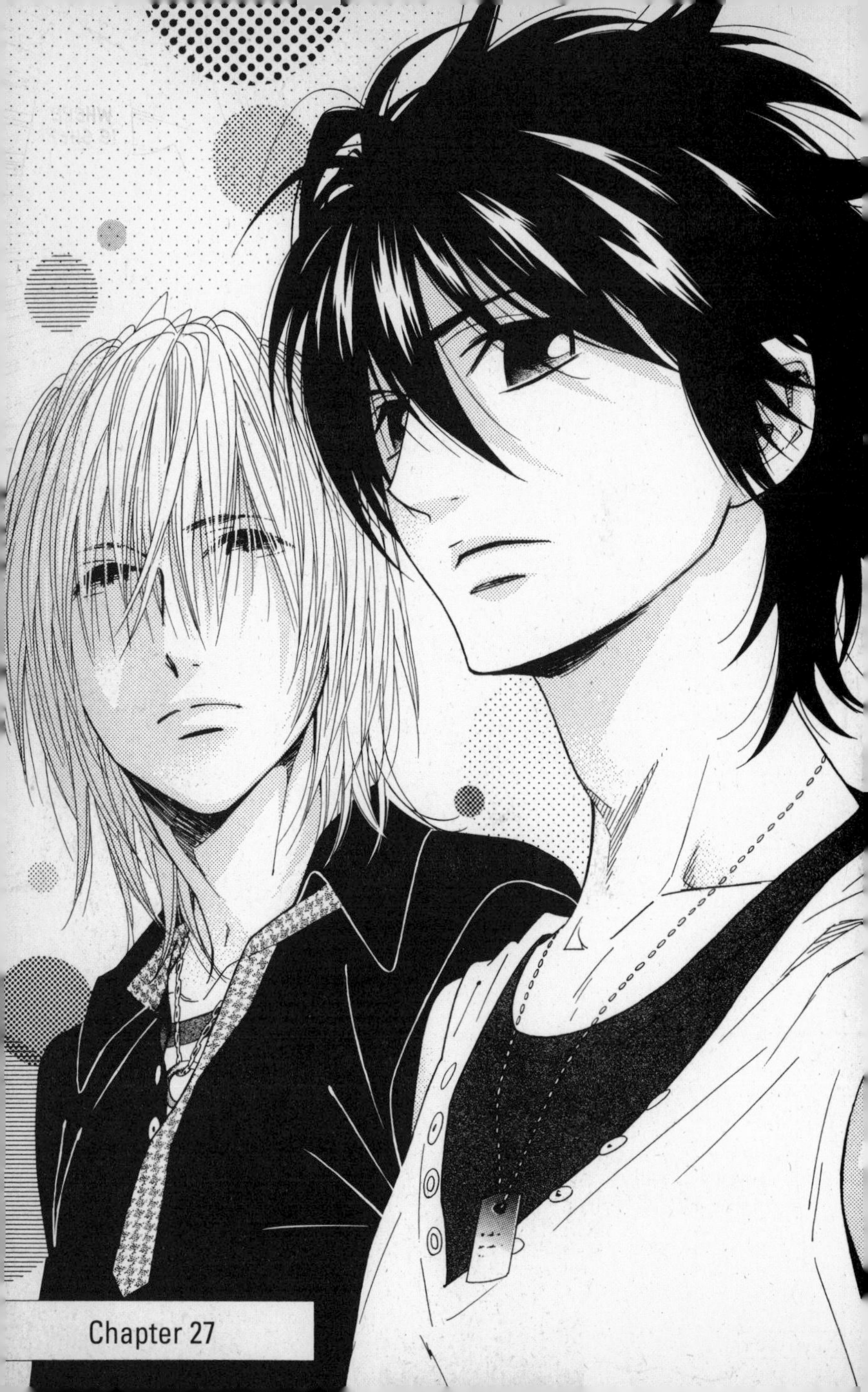

Chapter 27

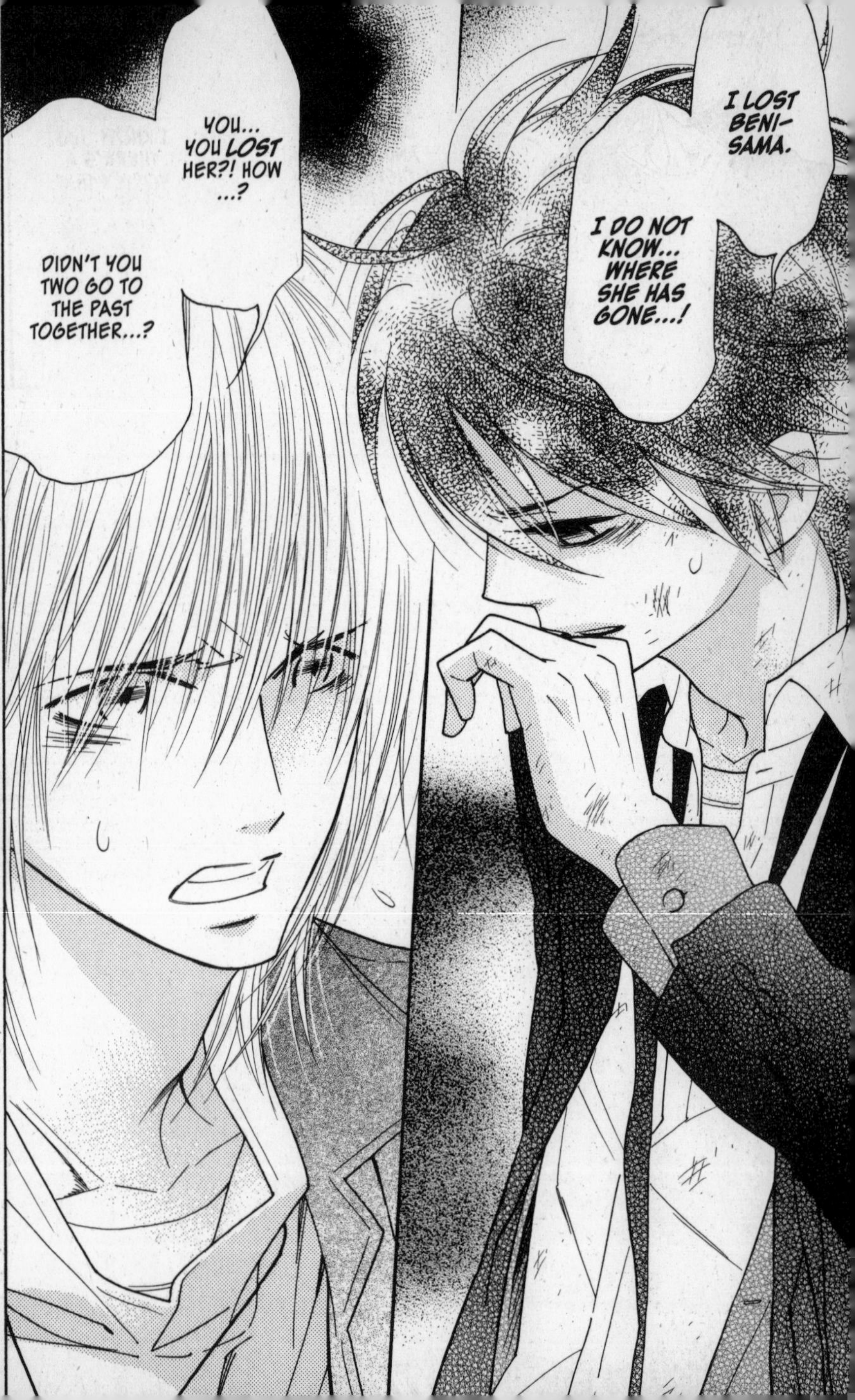
I LOST BENI-SAMA.
I DO NOT KNOW... WHERE SHE HAS GONE...!
YOU... YOU LOST HER?! HOW ...?
DIDN'T YOU TWO GO TO THE PAST TOGETHER...?

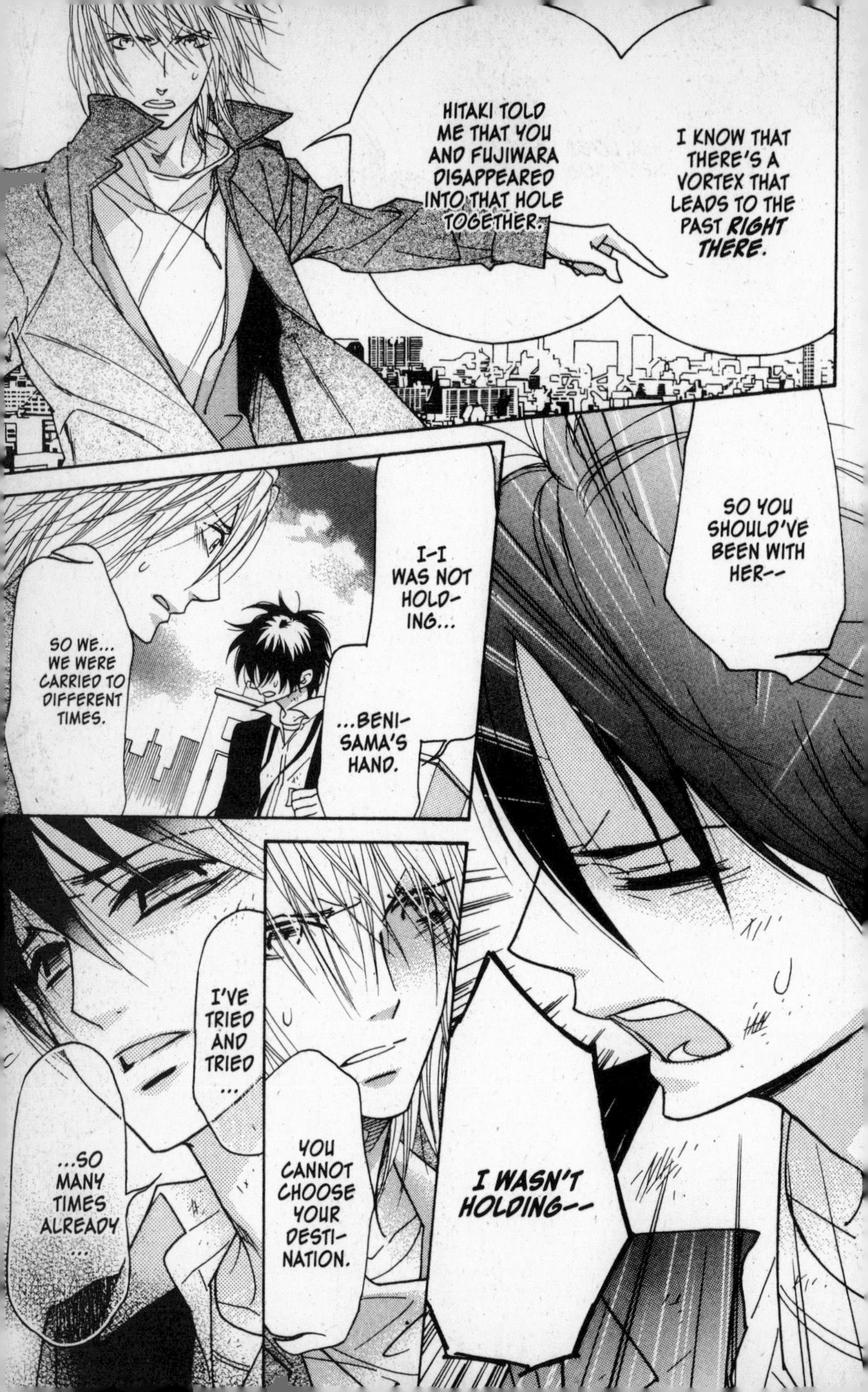
I KNOW THAT THERE'S A VORTEX THAT LEADS TO THE PAST *RIGHT THERE*.
HITAKI TOLD ME THAT YOU AND FUJIWARA DISAPPEARED INTO THAT HOLE TOGETHER.
SO YOU SHOULD'VE BEEN WITH HER--
I-I WAS NOT HOLDING...
...BENI-SAMA'S HAND.
SO WE... WE WERE CARRIED TO DIFFERENT TIMES.
I WASN'T HOLDING--
YOU CANNOT CHOOSE YOUR DESTINATION.
I'VE TRIED AND TRIED...
...SO MANY TIMES ALREADY...

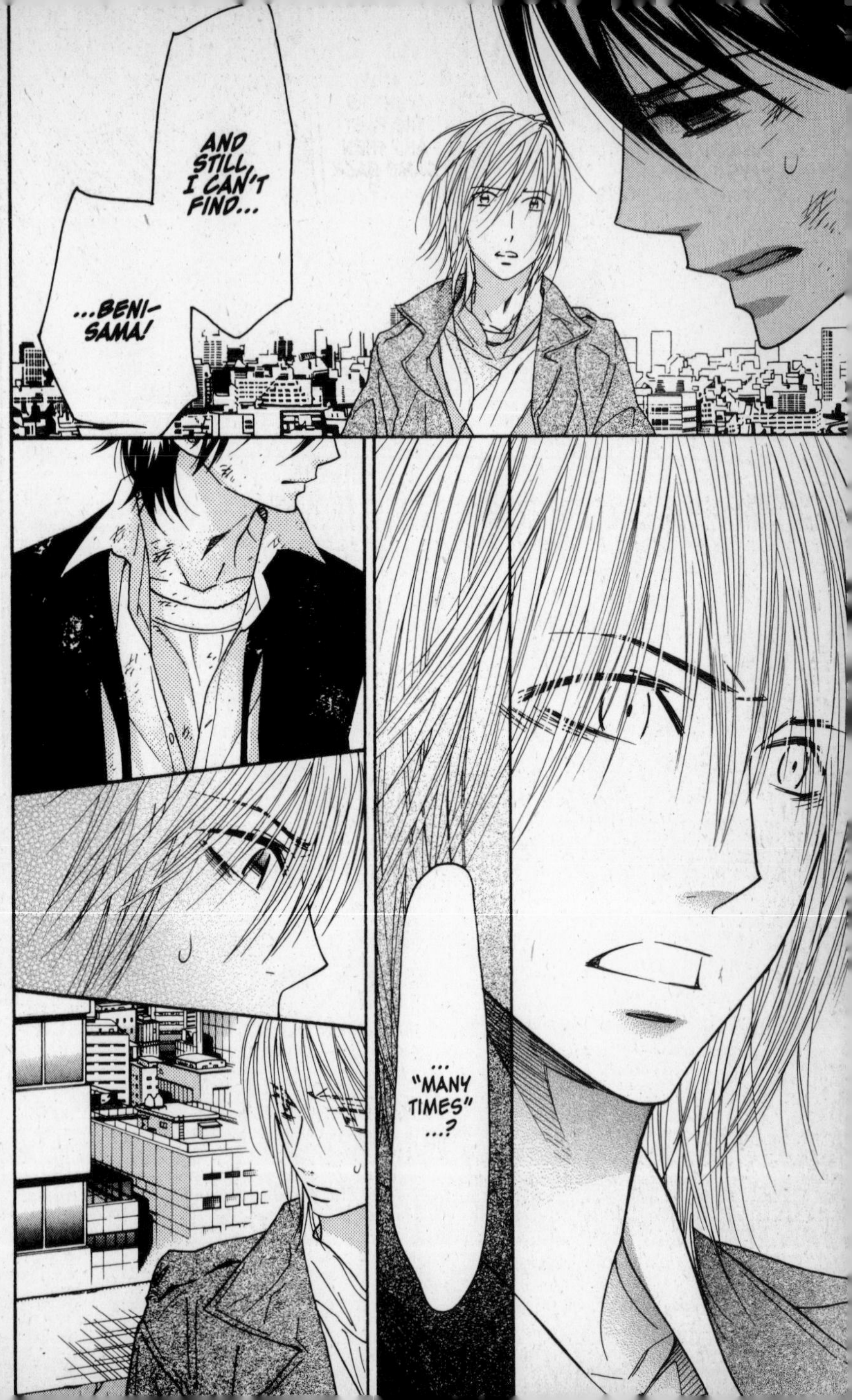
AND STILL, I CAN'T FIND...
...BENI-SAMA!
..."MANY TIMES"...?

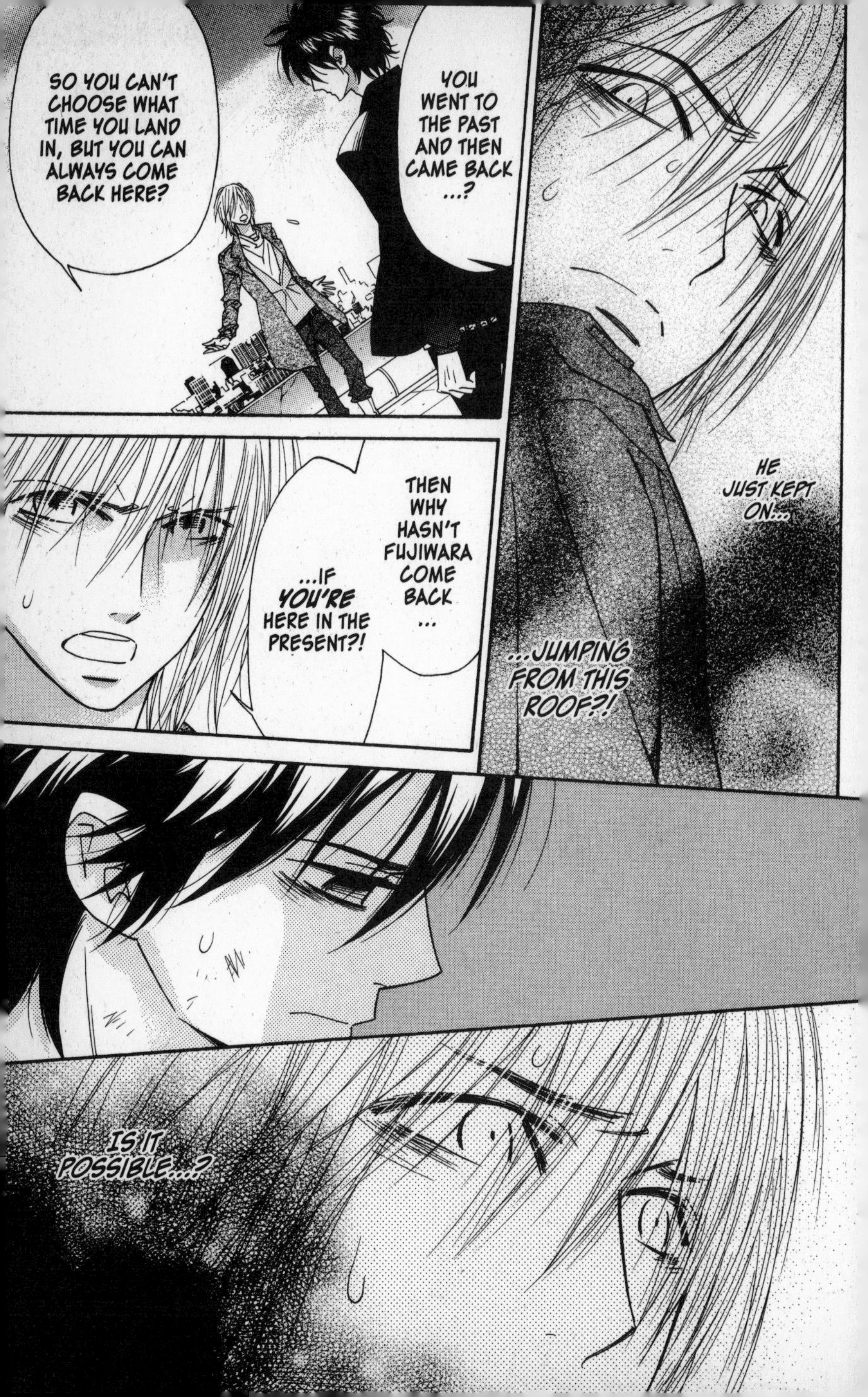
YOU WENT TO THE PAST AND THEN CAME BACK ...?
SO YOU CAN'T CHOOSE WHAT TIME YOU LAND IN, BUT YOU CAN ALWAYS COME BACK HERE?
THEN WHY HASN'T FUJIWARA COME BACK ...
...IF *YOU'RE* HERE IN THE PRESENT?!
HE JUST KEPT ON...
...JUMPING FROM THIS ROOF?!
IS IT POSSIBLE...?

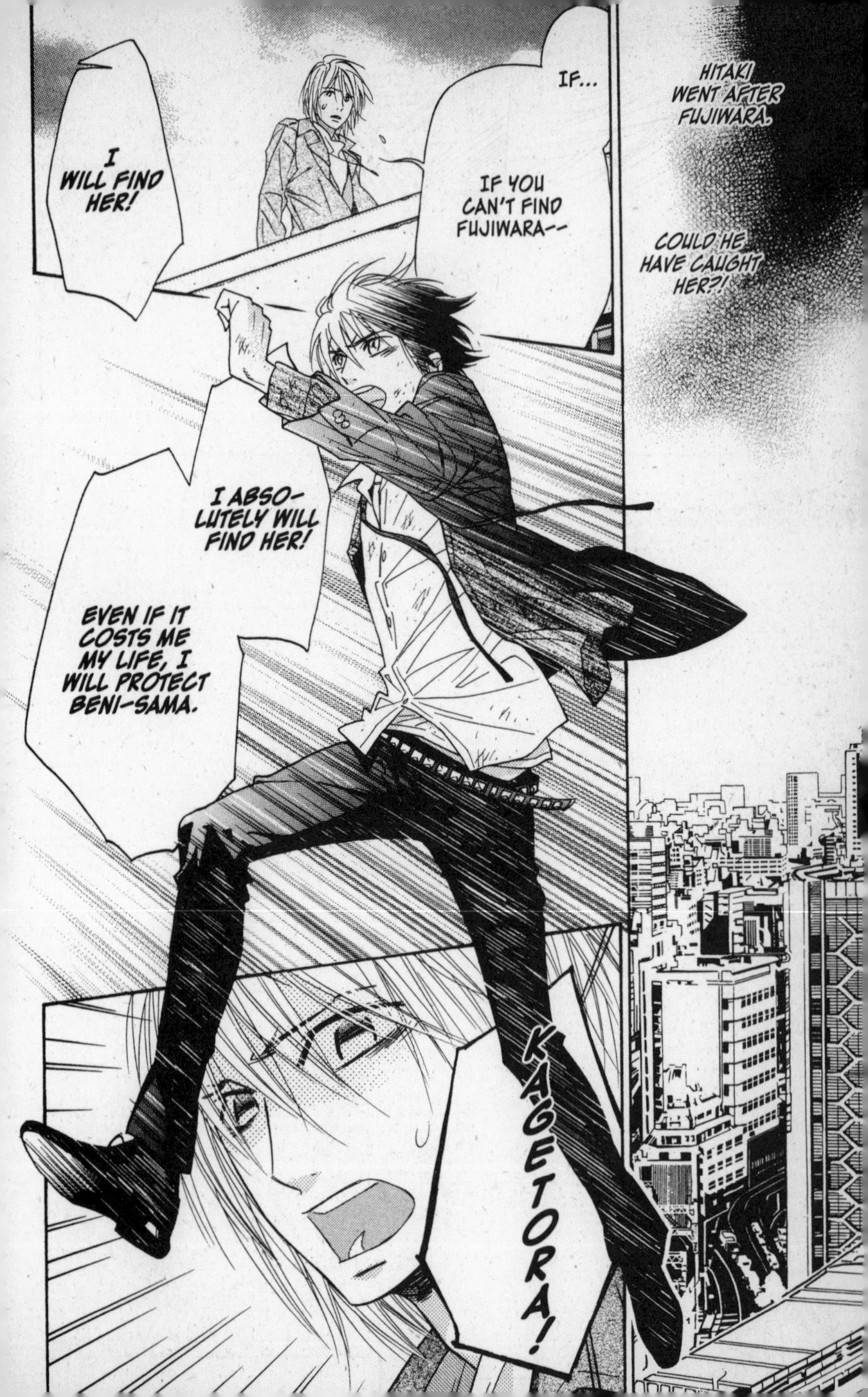
HITAKI WENT AFTER FUJIWARA.
COULD HE HAVE CAUGHT HER?!
IF...
IF YOU CAN'T FIND FUJIWARA--
I WILL FIND HER!
I ABSOLUTELY WILL FIND HER!
EVEN IF IT COSTS ME MY LIFE, I WILL PROTECT BENI-SAMA.
KAGETORA!

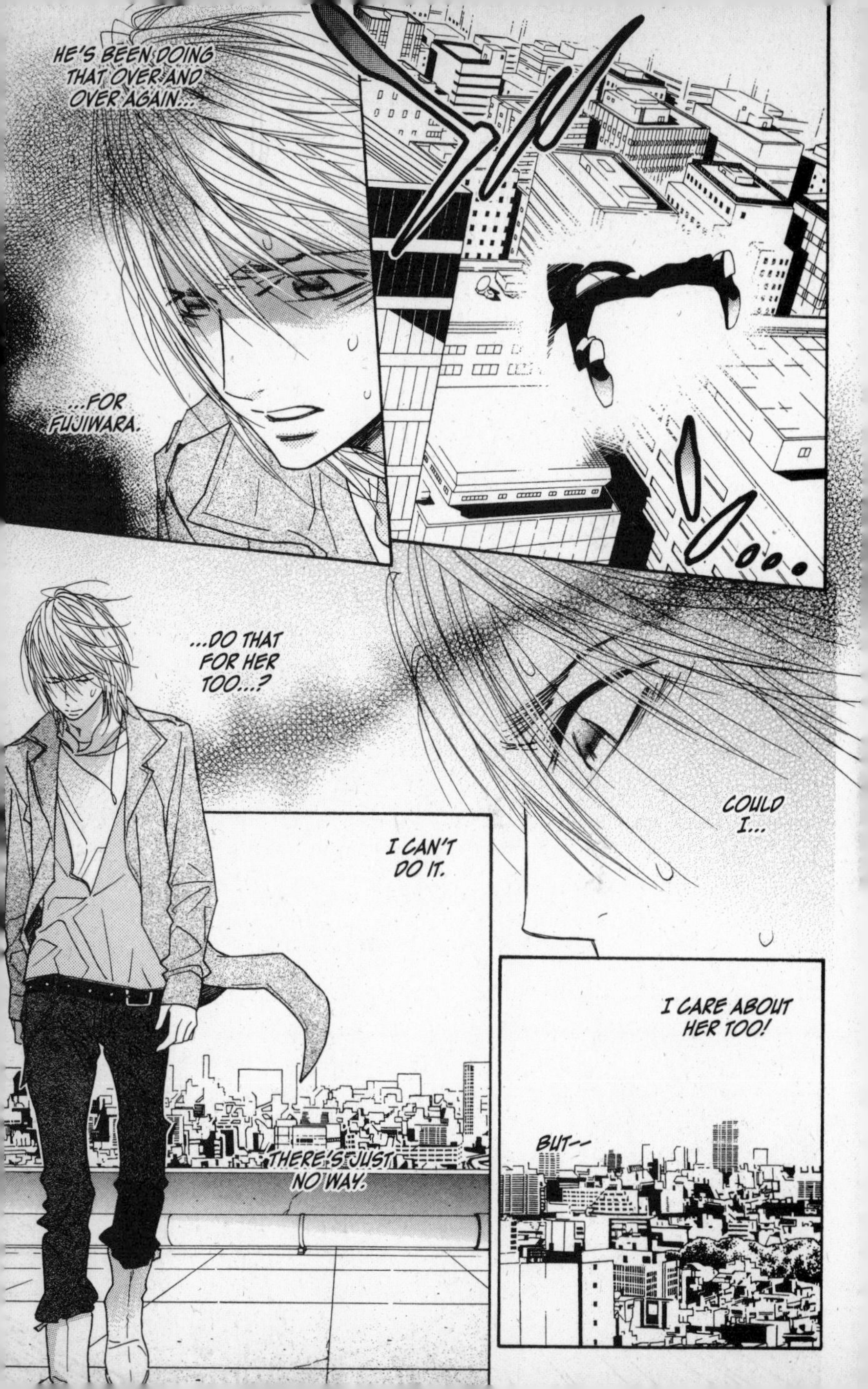
HE'S BEEN DOING THAT OVER AND OVER AGAIN...
...FOR FUJIWARA.
COULD I...
...DO THAT FOR HER TOO...?
I CARE ABOUT HER TOO!
BUT--
I CAN'T DO IT.
THERE'S JUST NO WAY.

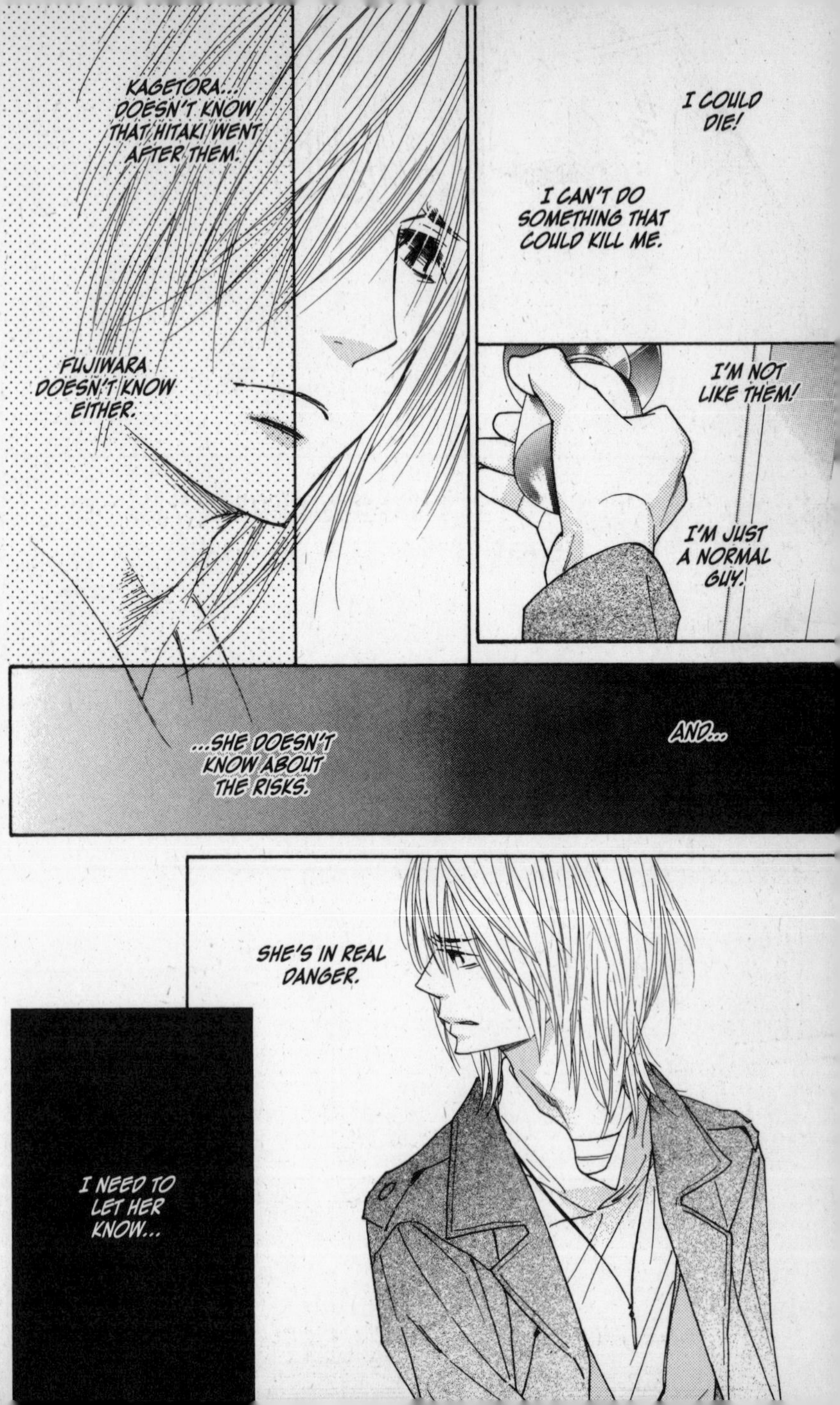

I COULD DIE!
I CAN'T DO SOMETHING THAT COULD KILL ME.
I'M NOT LIKE THEM!
I'M JUST A NORMAL GUY.
KAGETORA... DOESN'T KNOW THAT HITAKI WENT AFTER THEM.
FUJIWARA DOESN'T KNOW EITHER.
AND...
...SHE DOESN'T KNOW ABOUT THE RISKS.
SHE'S IN REAL DANGER.
I NEED TO LET HER KNOW...

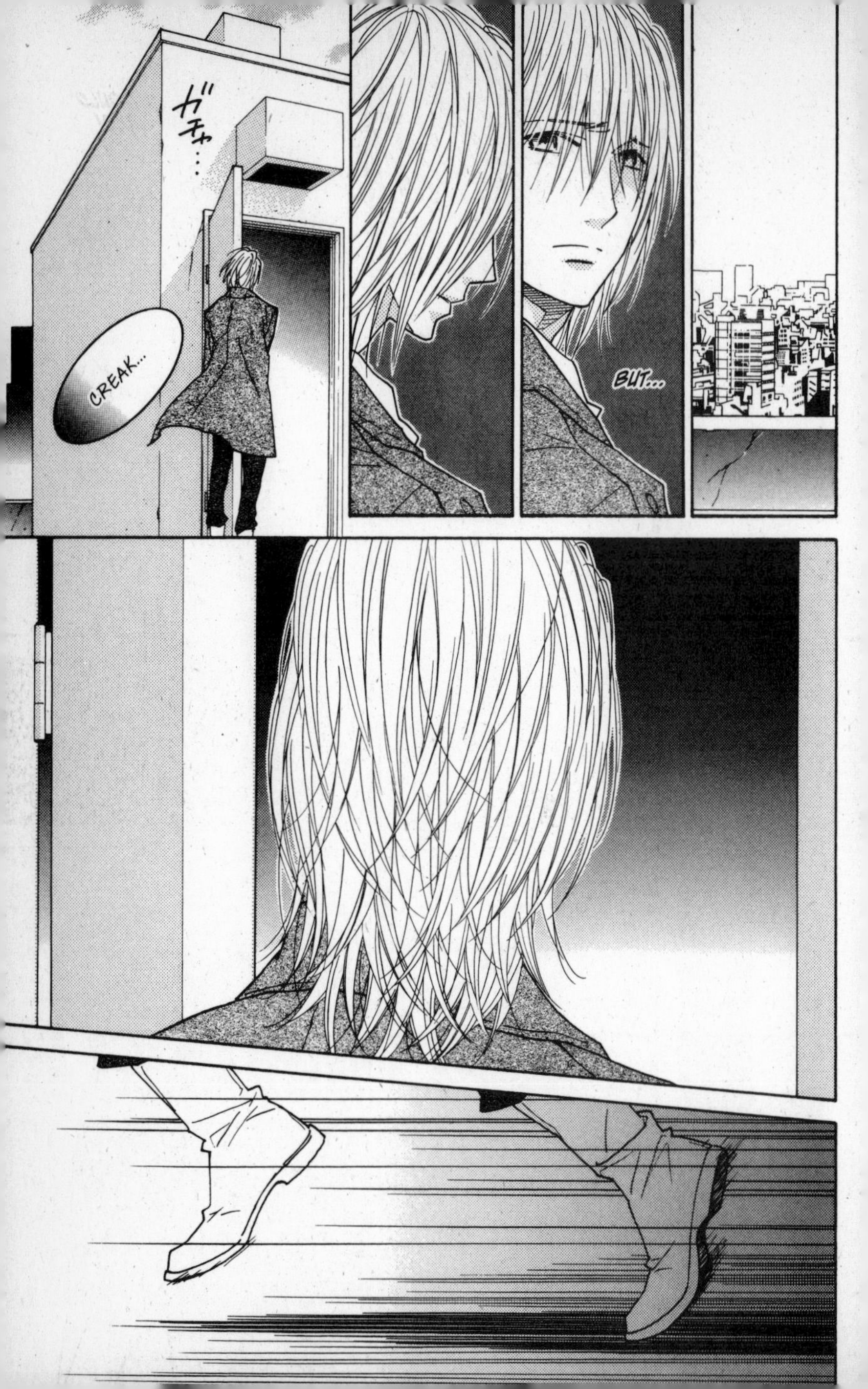
ガチャ…
CREAK...
BUT...

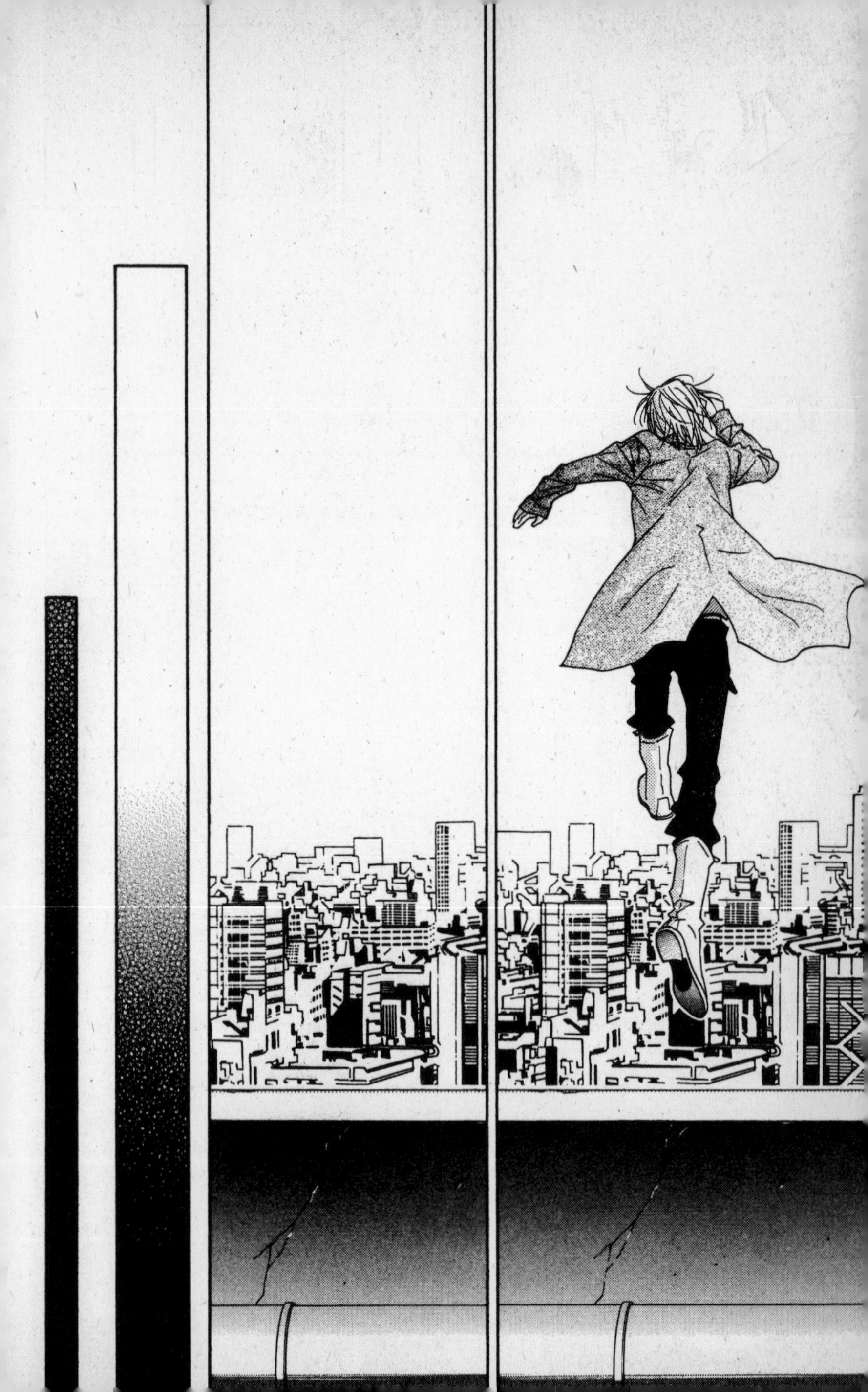

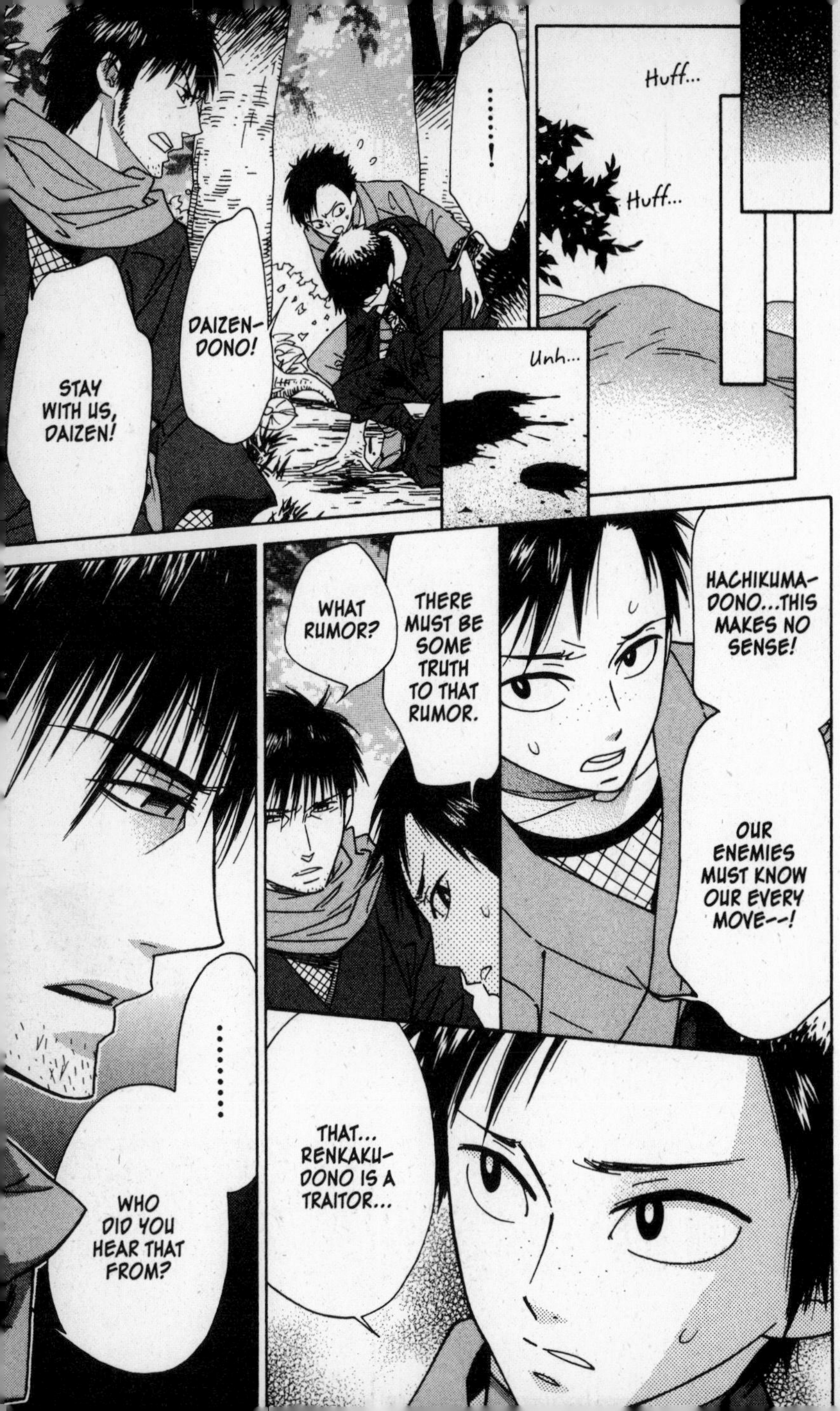
Huff...
Huff...
Unh...
......!
DAIZEN-DONO!
STAY WITH US, DAIZEN!
HACHIKUMA-DONO...THIS MAKES NO SENSE!
OUR ENEMIES MUST KNOW OUR EVERY MOVE--!
THERE MUST BE SOME TRUTH TO THAT RUMOR.
WHAT RUMOR?
THAT... RENKAKU-DONO IS A TRAITOR...
......
WHO DID YOU HEAR THAT FROM?

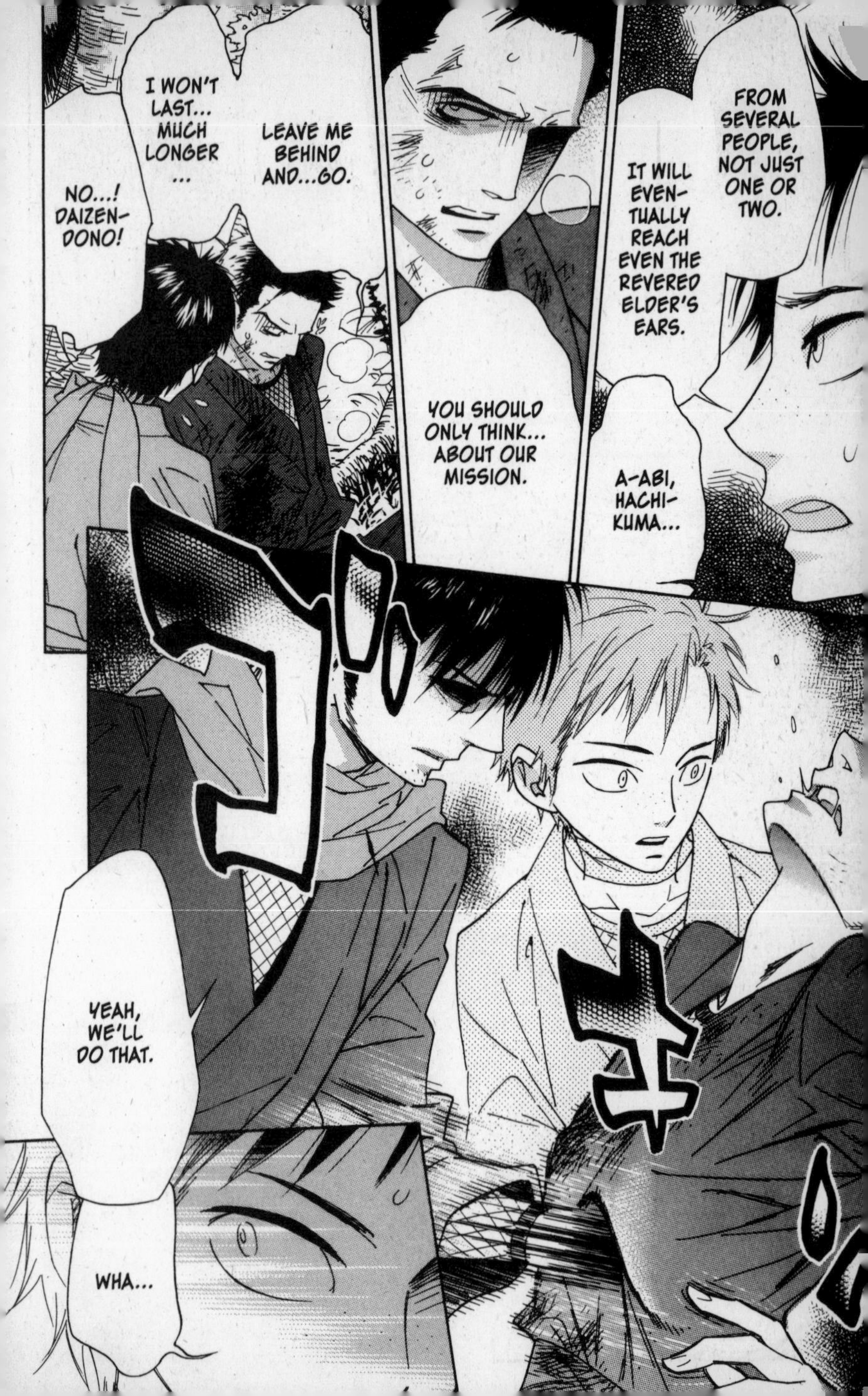
FROM SEVERAL PEOPLE, NOT JUST ONE OR TWO.
IT WILL EVENTUALLY REACH EVEN THE REVERED ELDER'S EARS.
A-ABI, HACHIKUMA...
YOU SHOULD ONLY THINK... ABOUT OUR MISSION.
LEAVE ME BEHIND AND...GO.
I WON'T LAST... MUCH LONGER...
NO...! DAIZEN-DONO!
YEAH, WE'LL DO THAT.
WHA...

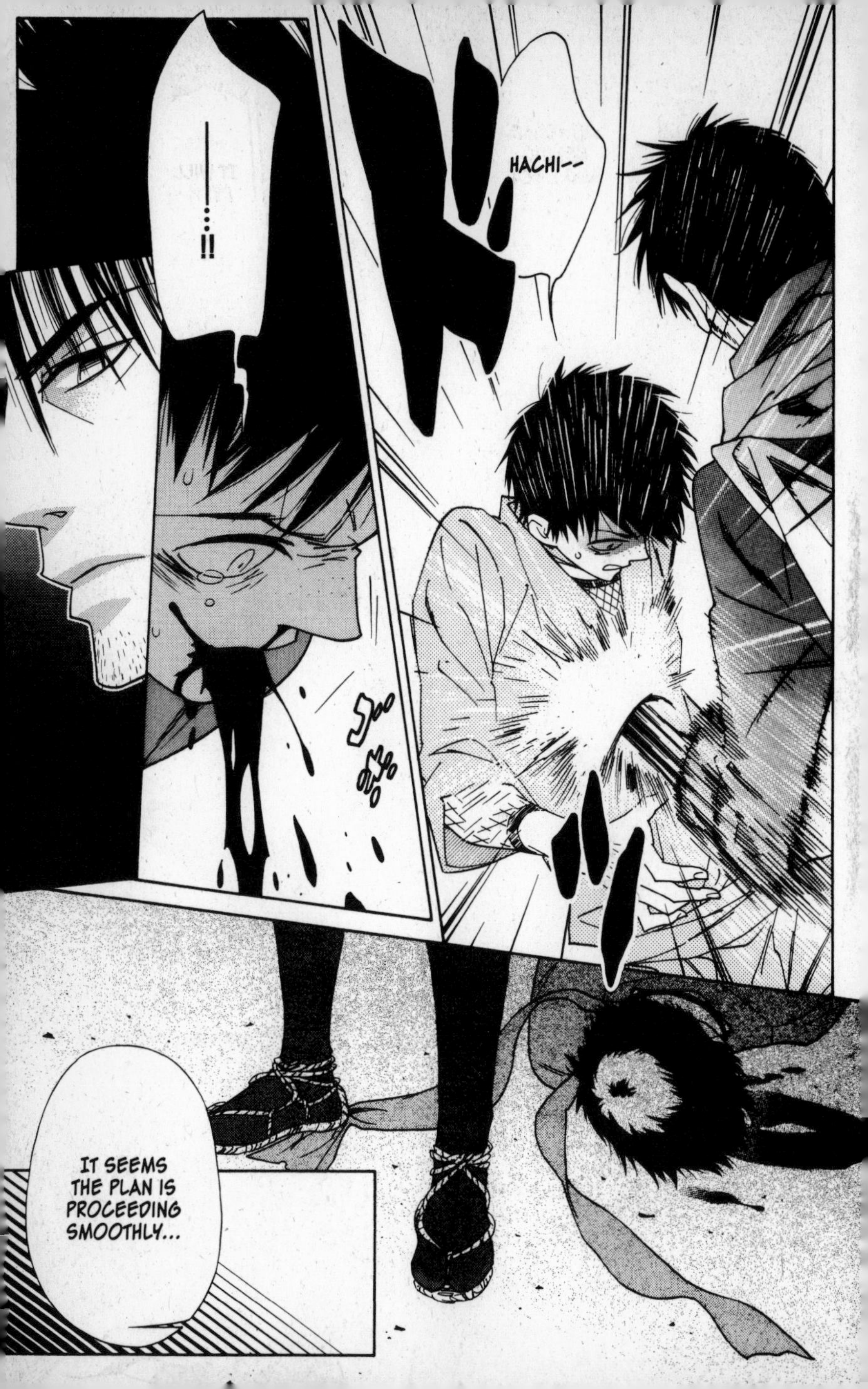

HACHI--
......!!
IT SEEMS THE PLAN IS PROCEEDING SMOOTHLY...

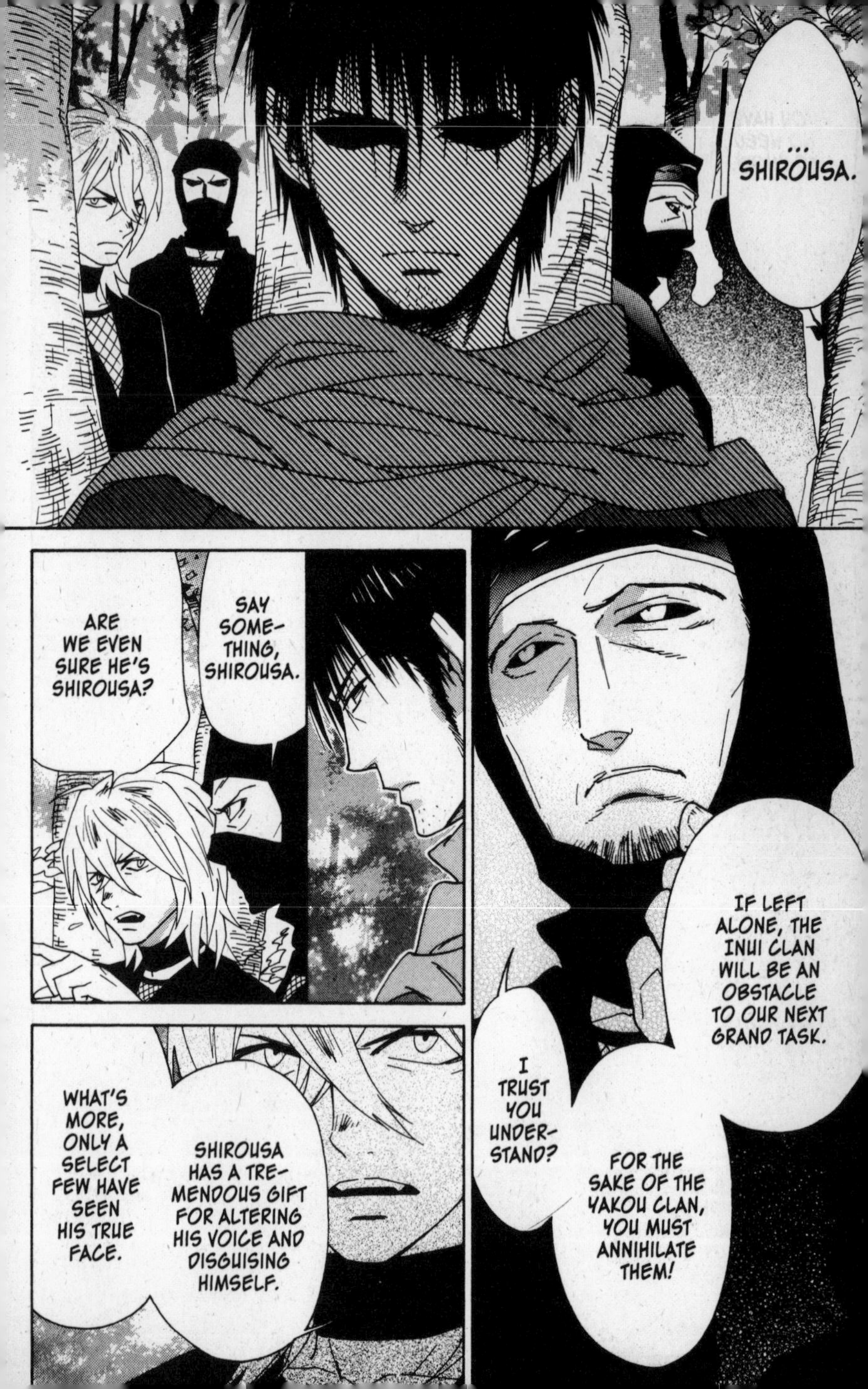
...SHIROUSA.
IF LEFT ALONE, THE INUI CLAN WILL BE AN OBSTACLE TO OUR NEXT GRAND TASK.
FOR THE SAKE OF THE YAKOU CLAN, YOU MUST ANNIHILATE THEM!
I TRUST YOU UNDER-STAND?
SAY SOME-THING, SHIROUSA.
ARE WE EVEN SURE HE'S SHIROUSA?
SHIROUSA HAS A TRE-MENDOUS GIFT FOR ALTERING HIS VOICE AND DISGUISING HIMSELF.
WHAT'S MORE, ONLY A SELECT FEW HAVE SEEN HIS TRUE FACE.

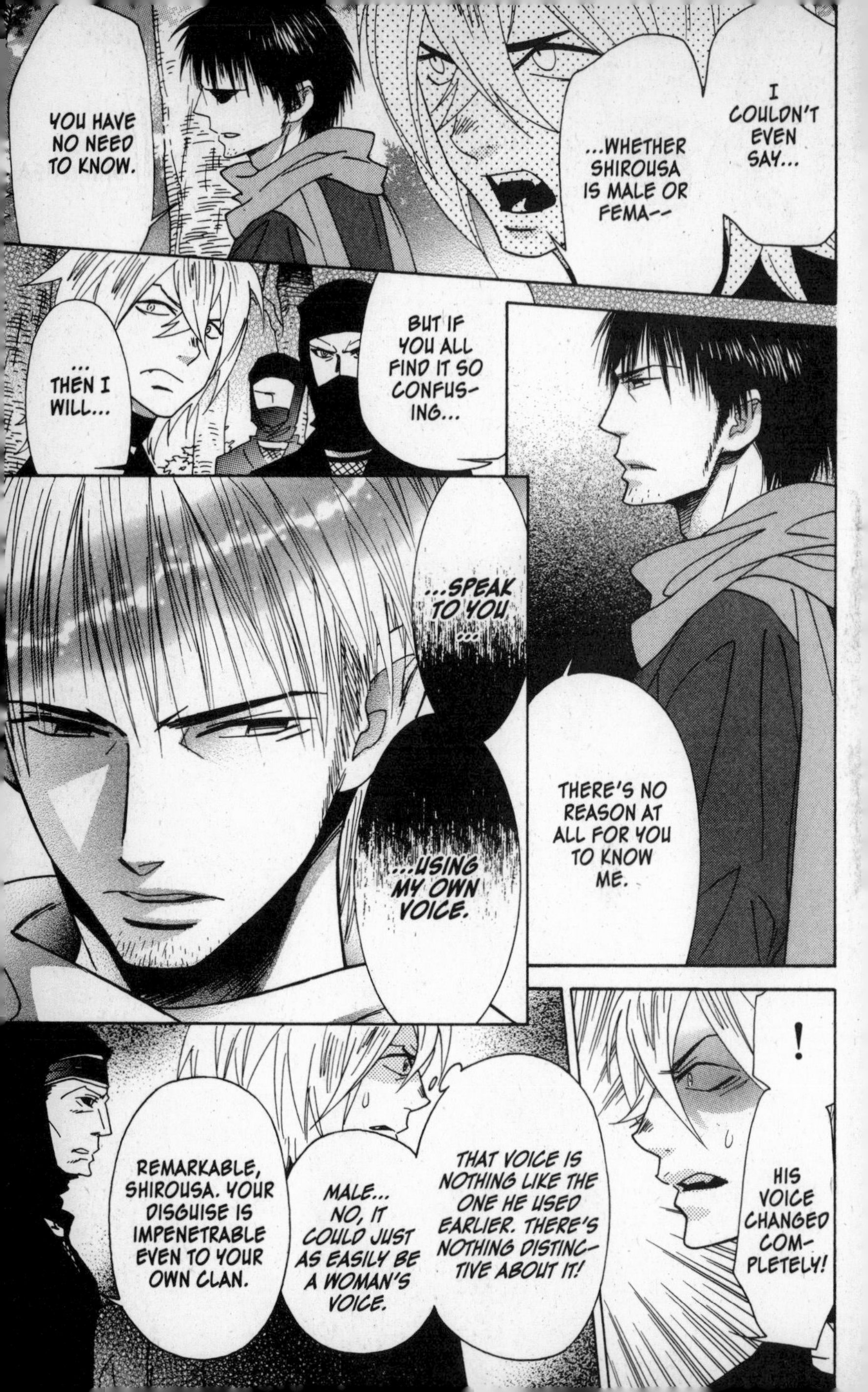

I COULDN'T EVEN SAY...
...WHETHER SHIROUSA IS MALE OR FEMA--
YOU HAVE NO NEED TO KNOW.
BUT IF YOU ALL FIND IT SO CONFUSING...
... THEN I WILL...
...SPEAK TO YOU ...
...USING MY OWN VOICE.
THERE'S NO REASON AT ALL FOR YOU TO KNOW ME.
!
HIS VOICE CHANGED COMPLETELY!
THAT VOICE IS NOTHING LIKE THE ONE HE USED EARLIER. THERE'S NOTHING DISTINCTIVE ABOUT IT!
MALE... NO, IT COULD JUST AS EASILY BE A WOMAN'S VOICE.
REMARKABLE, SHIROUSA. YOUR DISGUISE IS IMPENETRABLE EVEN TO YOUR OWN CLAN.

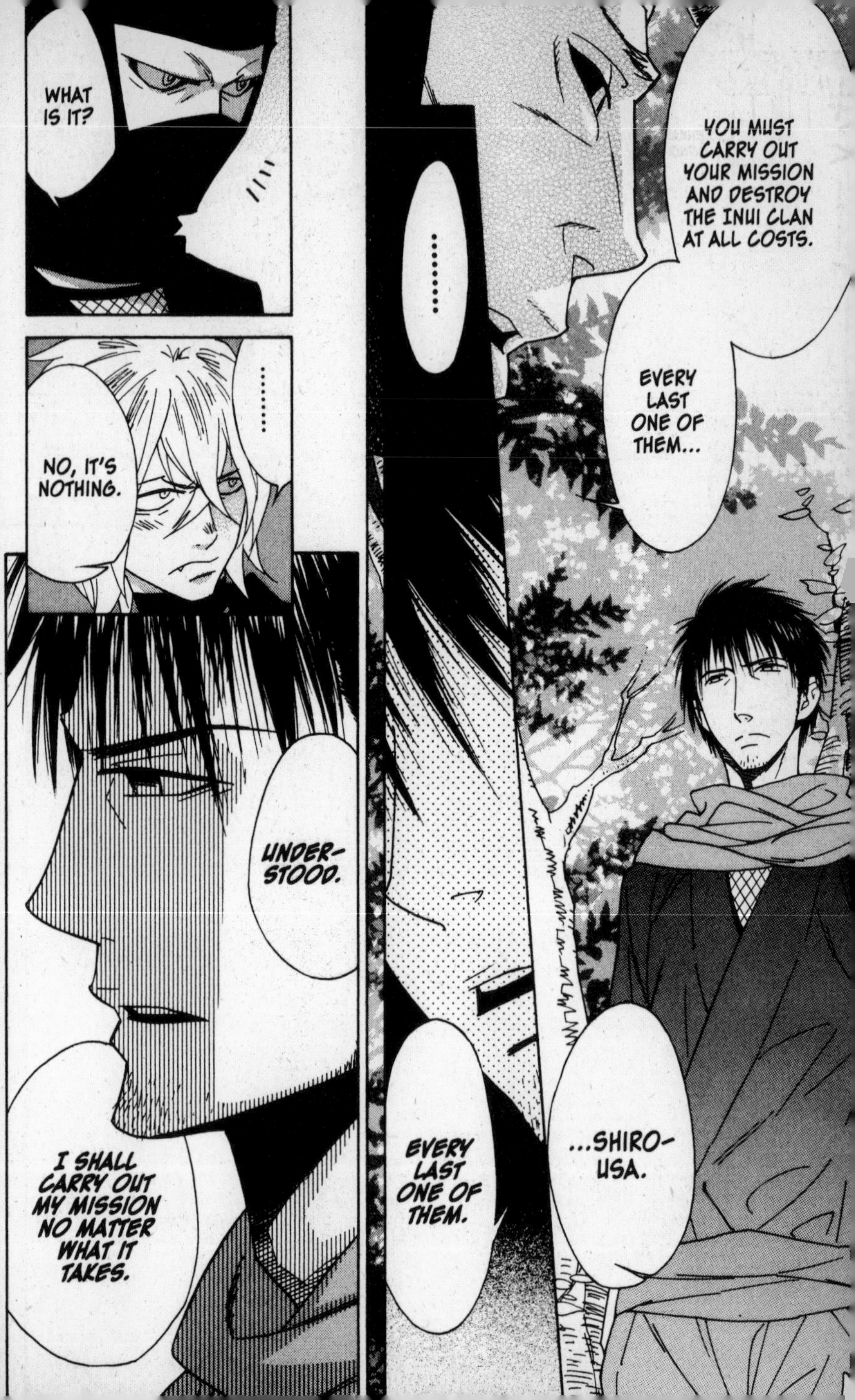
YOU MUST CARRY OUT YOUR MISSION AND DESTROY THE INUI CLAN AT ALL COSTS.
EVERY LAST ONE OF THEM...
....
WHAT IS IT?
....
NO, IT'S NOTHING.
...SHIRO-USA.
EVERY LAST ONE OF THEM.
UNDER-STOOD.
I SHALL CARRY OUT MY MISSION NO MATTER WHAT IT TAKES.

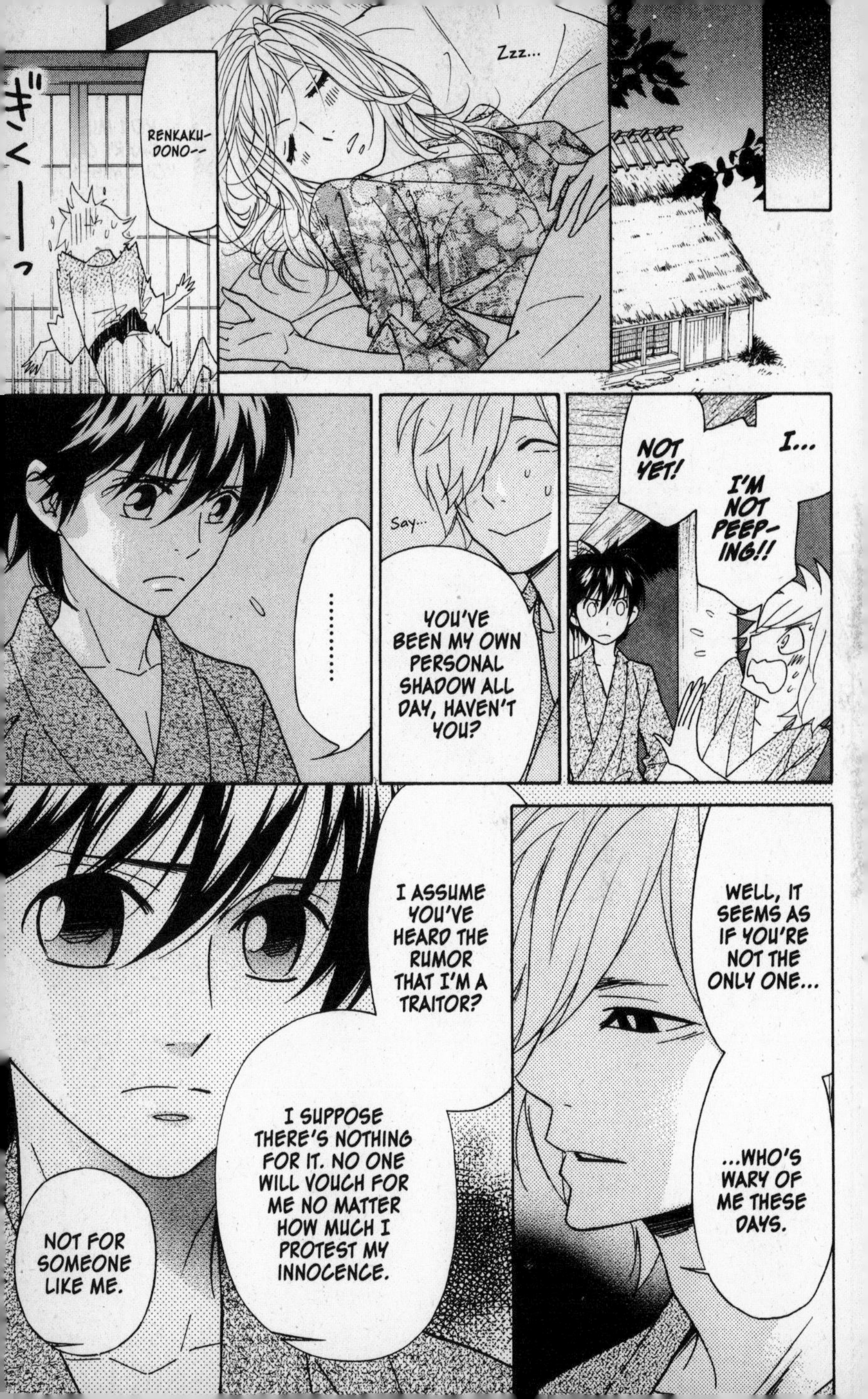

Zzz...
RENKAKU-DONO--
ギくーっ
I...
I'M NOT PEEPING!!
NOT YET!
Say...
YOU'VE BEEN MY OWN PERSONAL SHADOW ALL DAY, HAVEN'T YOU?
......
WELL, IT SEEMS AS IF YOU'RE NOT THE ONLY ONE...
...WHO'S WARY OF ME THESE DAYS.
I ASSUME YOU'VE HEARD THE RUMOR THAT I'M A TRAITOR?
I SUPPOSE THERE'S NOTHING FOR IT. NO ONE WILL VOUCH FOR ME NO MATTER HOW MUCH I PROTEST MY INNOCENCE.
NOT FOR SOMEONE LIKE ME.

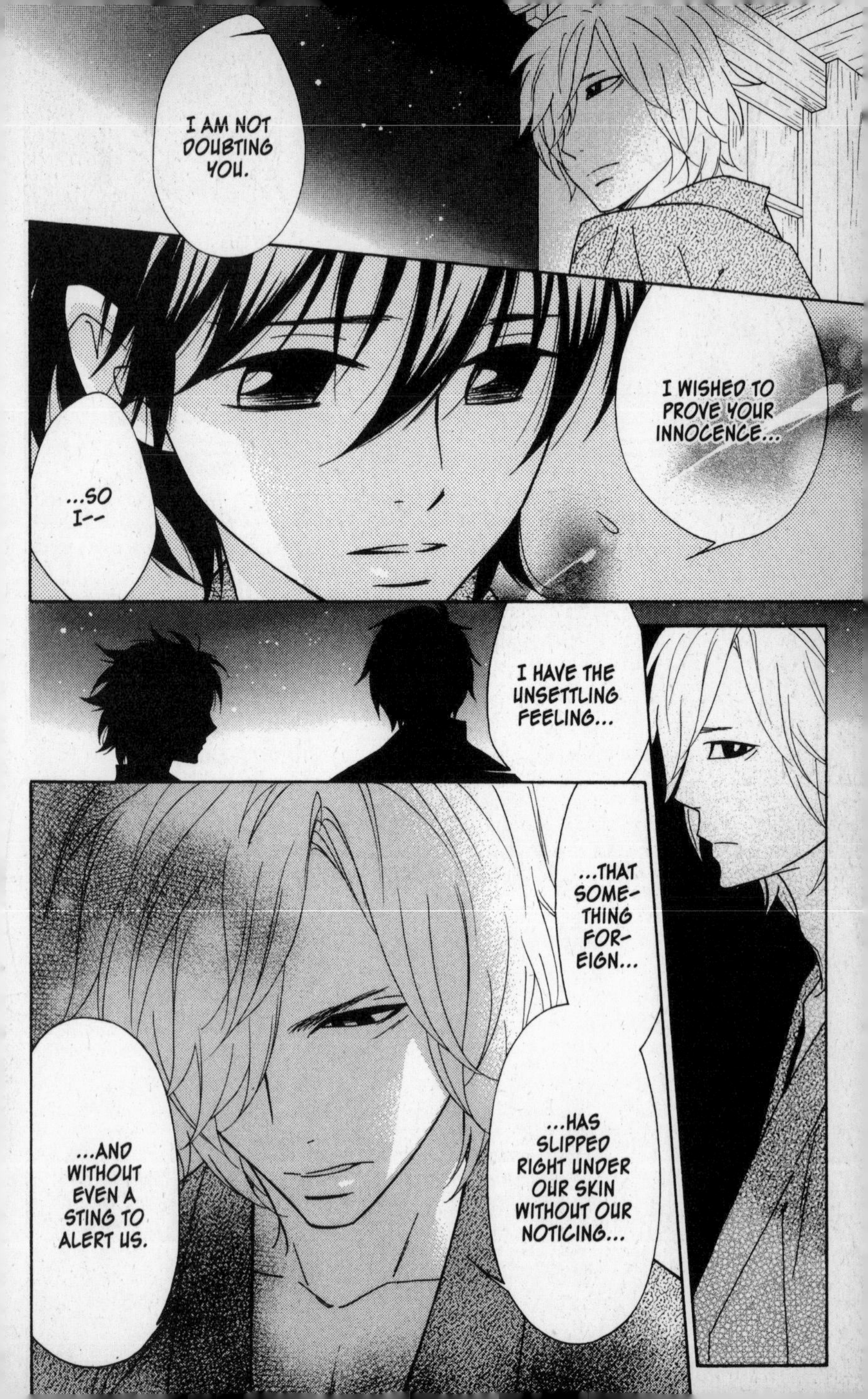
I AM NOT DOUBTING YOU.
I WISHED TO PROVE YOUR INNOCENCE...
...SO I--
I HAVE THE UNSETTLING FEELING...
...THAT SOME-THING FOR-EIGN...
...HAS SLIPPED RIGHT UNDER OUR SKIN WITHOUT OUR NOTICING...
...AND WITHOUT EVEN A STING TO ALERT US.

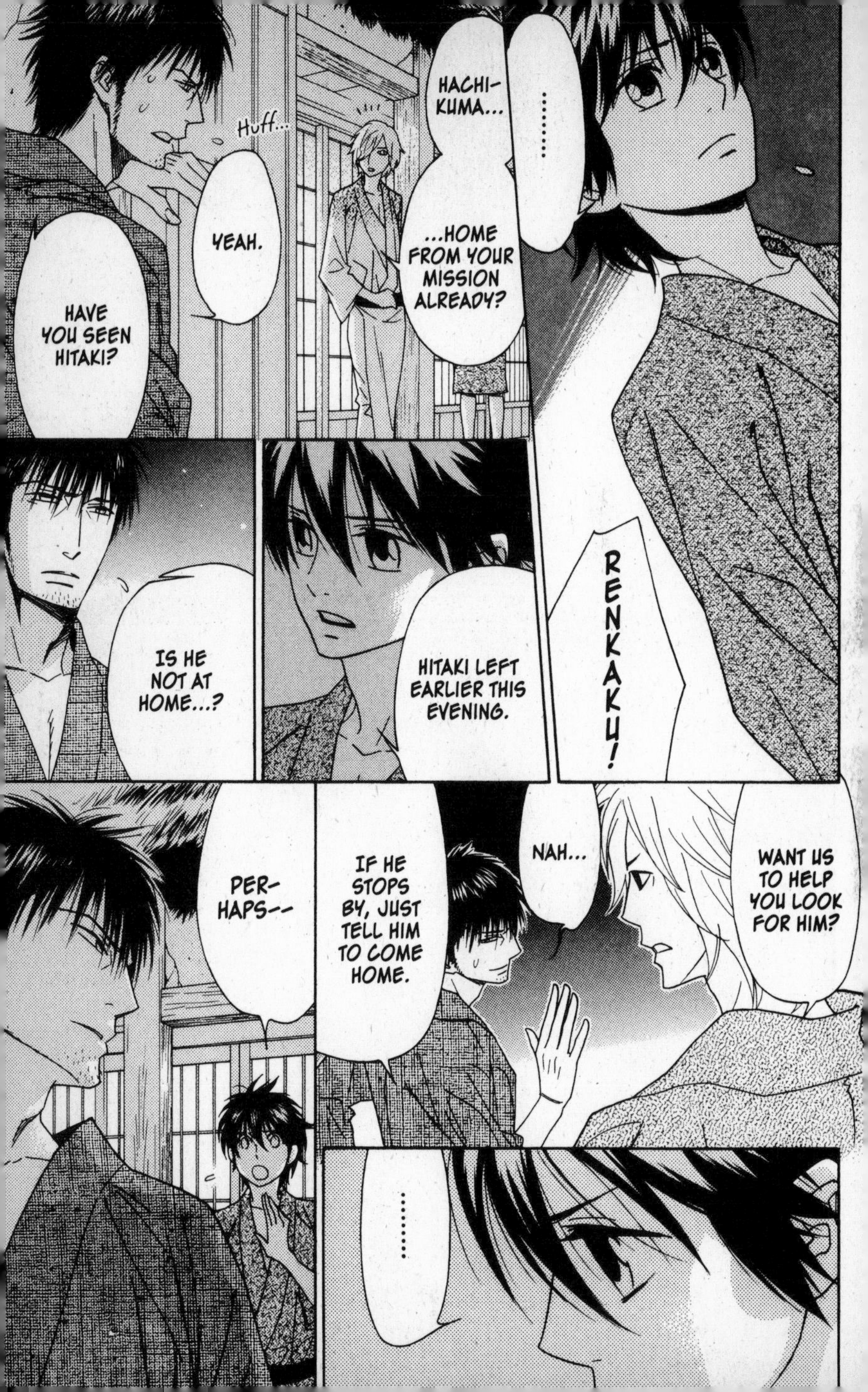

......
HACHI-KUMA...
...HOME FROM YOUR MISSION ALREADY?
Huff...
YEAH.
HAVE YOU SEEN HITAKI?
RENKAKU!
HITAKI LEFT EARLIER THIS EVENING.
IS HE NOT AT HOME...?
WANT US TO HELP YOU LOOK FOR HIM?
NAH...
IF HE STOPS BY, JUST TELL HIM TO COME HOME.
PER-HAPS--
......

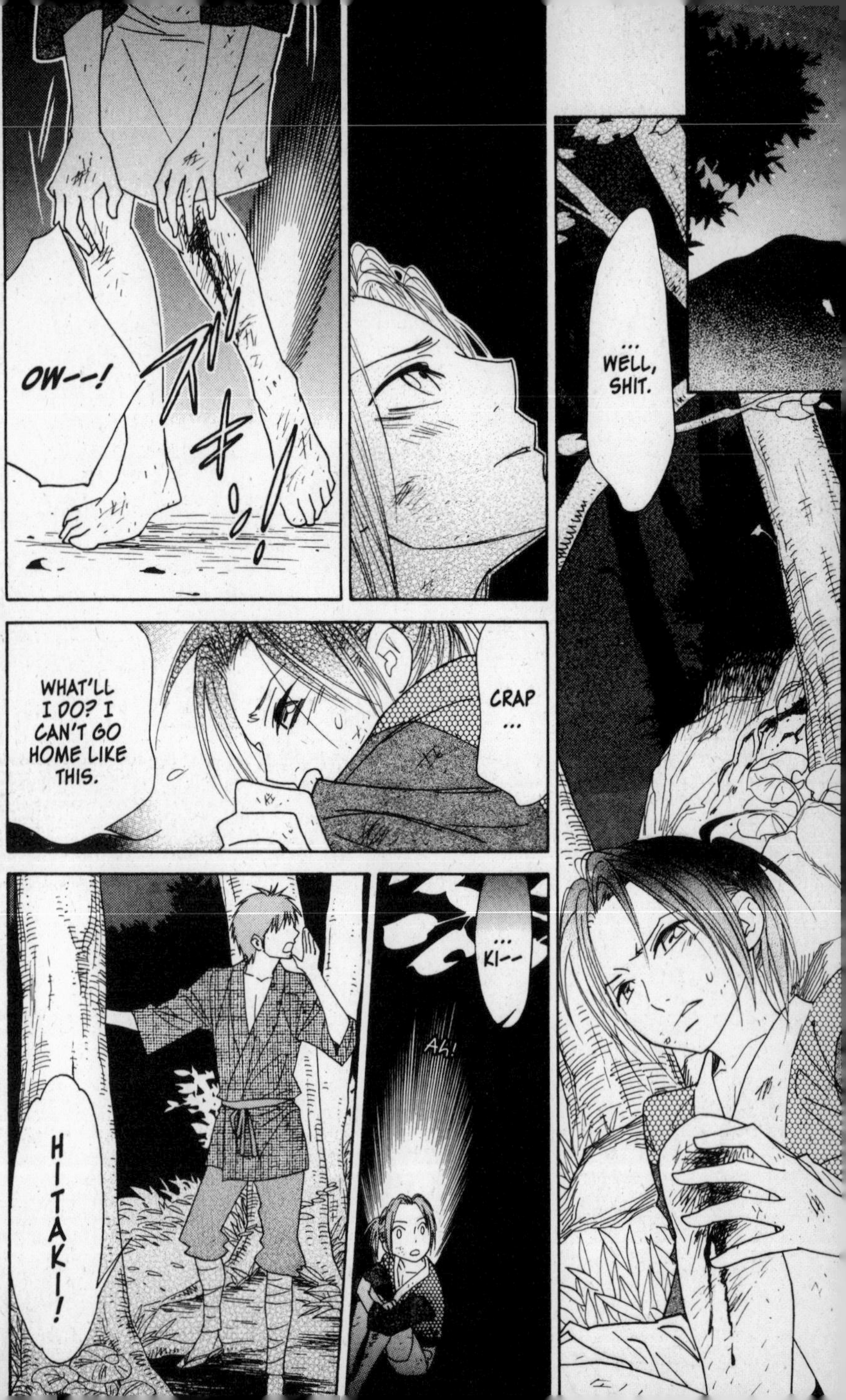
OW--!
... WELL, SHIT.
CRAP ...
WHAT'LL I DO? I CAN'T GO HOME LIKE THIS.
... KI--
AH!
HITAKI!

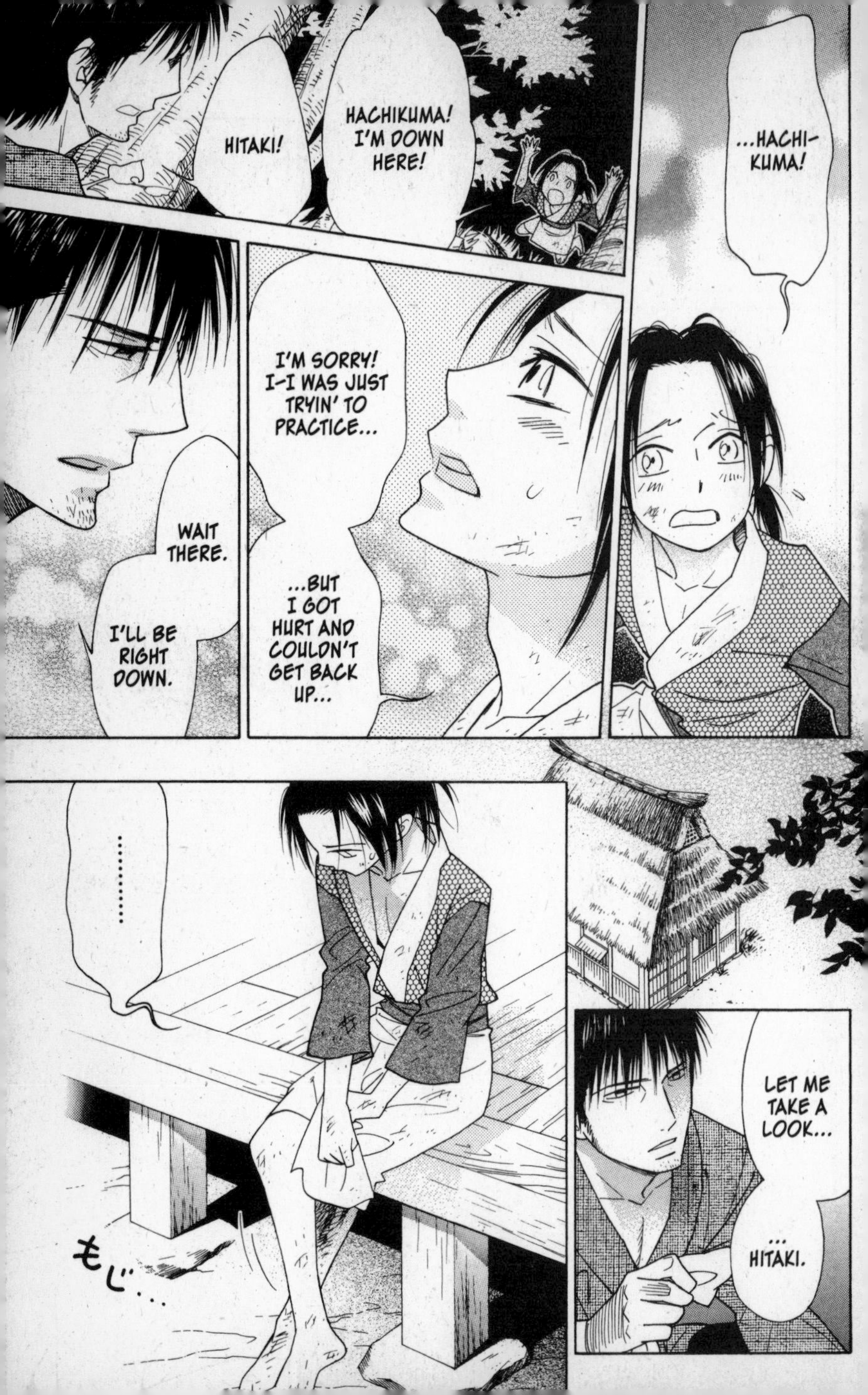
...HACHI-KUMA!
HACHIKUMA! I'M DOWN HERE!
HITAKI!
I'M SORRY! I-I WAS JUST TRYIN' TO PRACTICE...
...BUT I GOT HURT AND COULDN'T GET BACK UP...
WAIT THERE.
I'LL BE RIGHT DOWN.
LET ME TAKE A LOOK...
...HITAKI.
....
もじ...

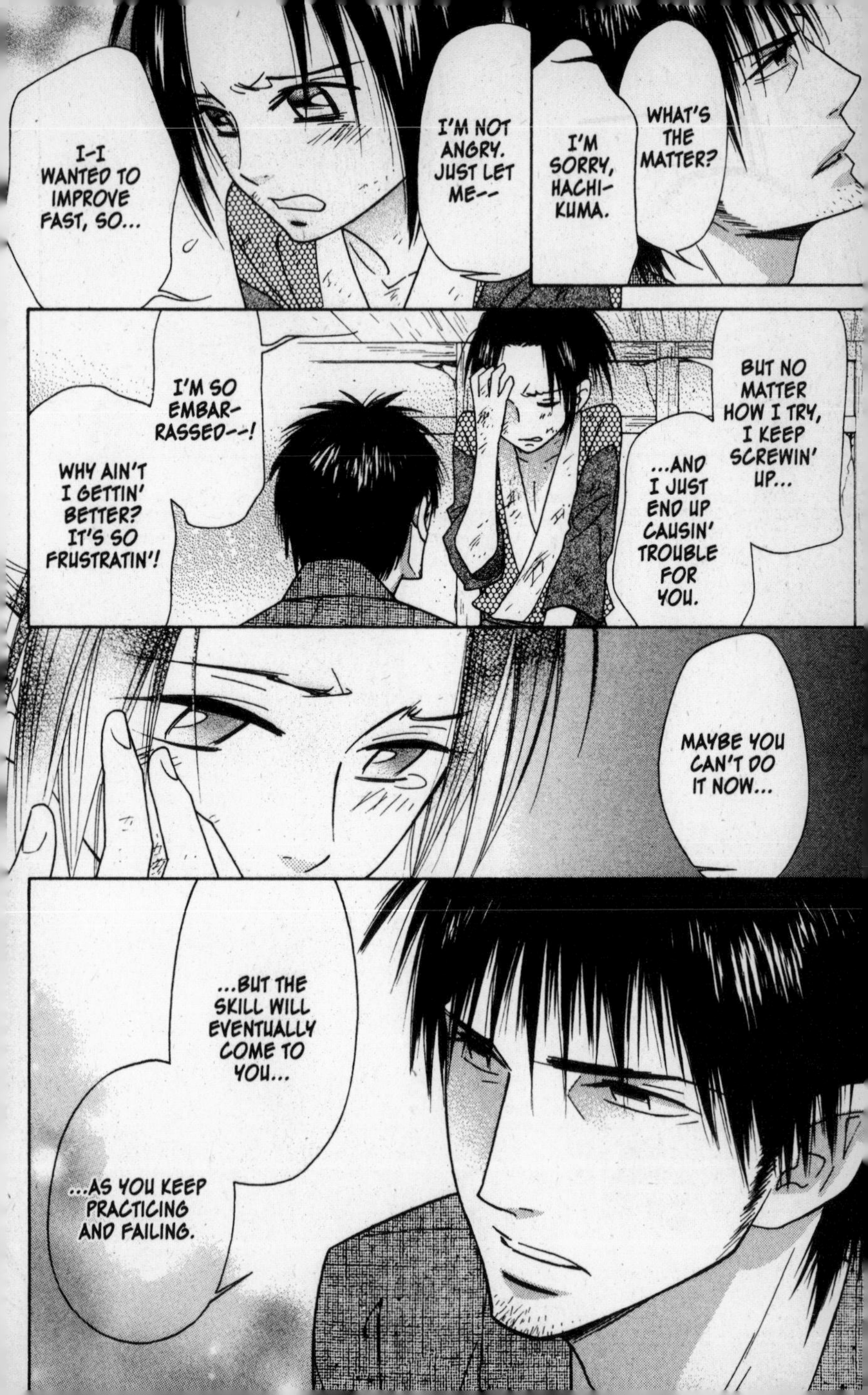
WHAT'S THE MATTER?
I'M SORRY, HACHI-KUMA.
I'M NOT ANGRY. JUST LET ME--
I-I WANTED TO IMPROVE FAST, SO...
BUT NO MATTER HOW I TRY, I KEEP SCREWIN' UP...
...AND I JUST END UP CAUSIN' TROUBLE FOR YOU.
I'M SO EMBAR-RASSED--!
WHY AIN'T I GETTIN' BETTER? IT'S SO FRUSTRATIN'!
MAYBE YOU CAN'T DO IT NOW...
...BUT THE SKILL WILL EVENTUALLY COME TO YOU...
...AS YOU KEEP PRACTICING AND FAILING.

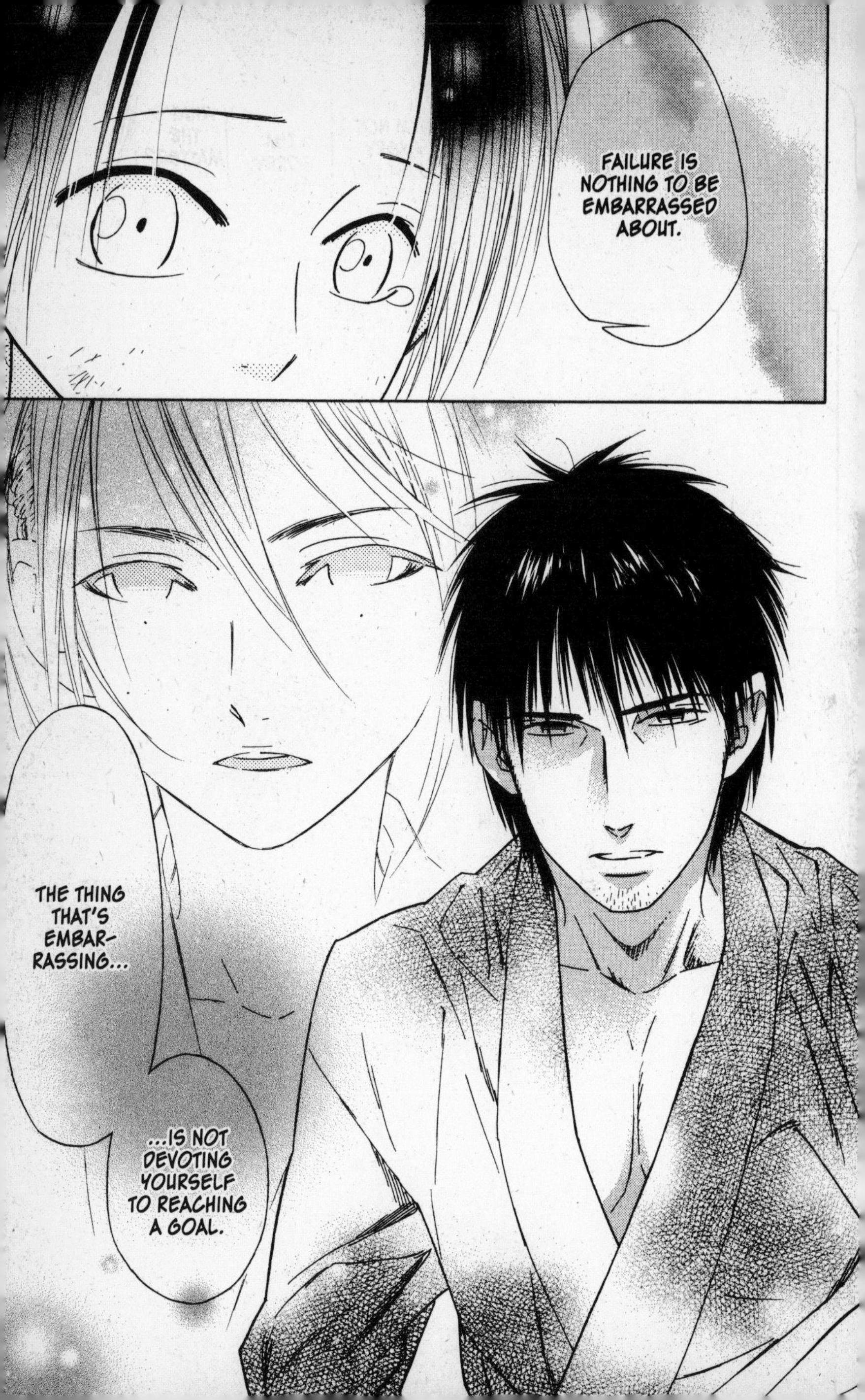
FAILURE IS NOTHING TO BE EMBARRASSED ABOUT.
THE THING THAT'S EMBAR-RASSING...
...IS NOT DEVOTING YOURSELF TO REACHING A GOAL.

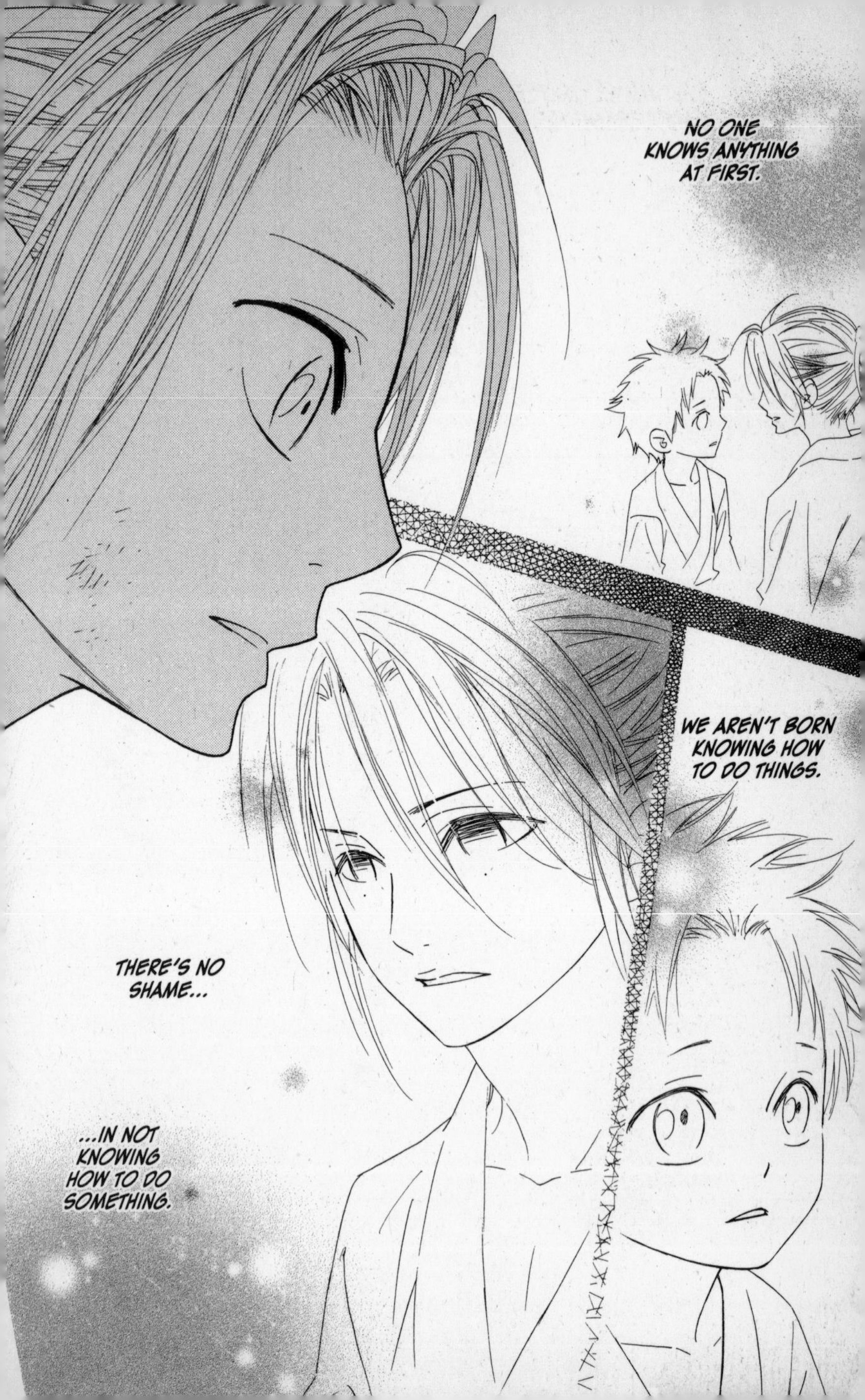
NO ONE KNOWS ANYTHING AT FIRST.
WE AREN'T BORN KNOWING HOW TO DO THINGS.
THERE'S NO SHAME...
...IN NOT KNOWING HOW TO DO SOMETHING.

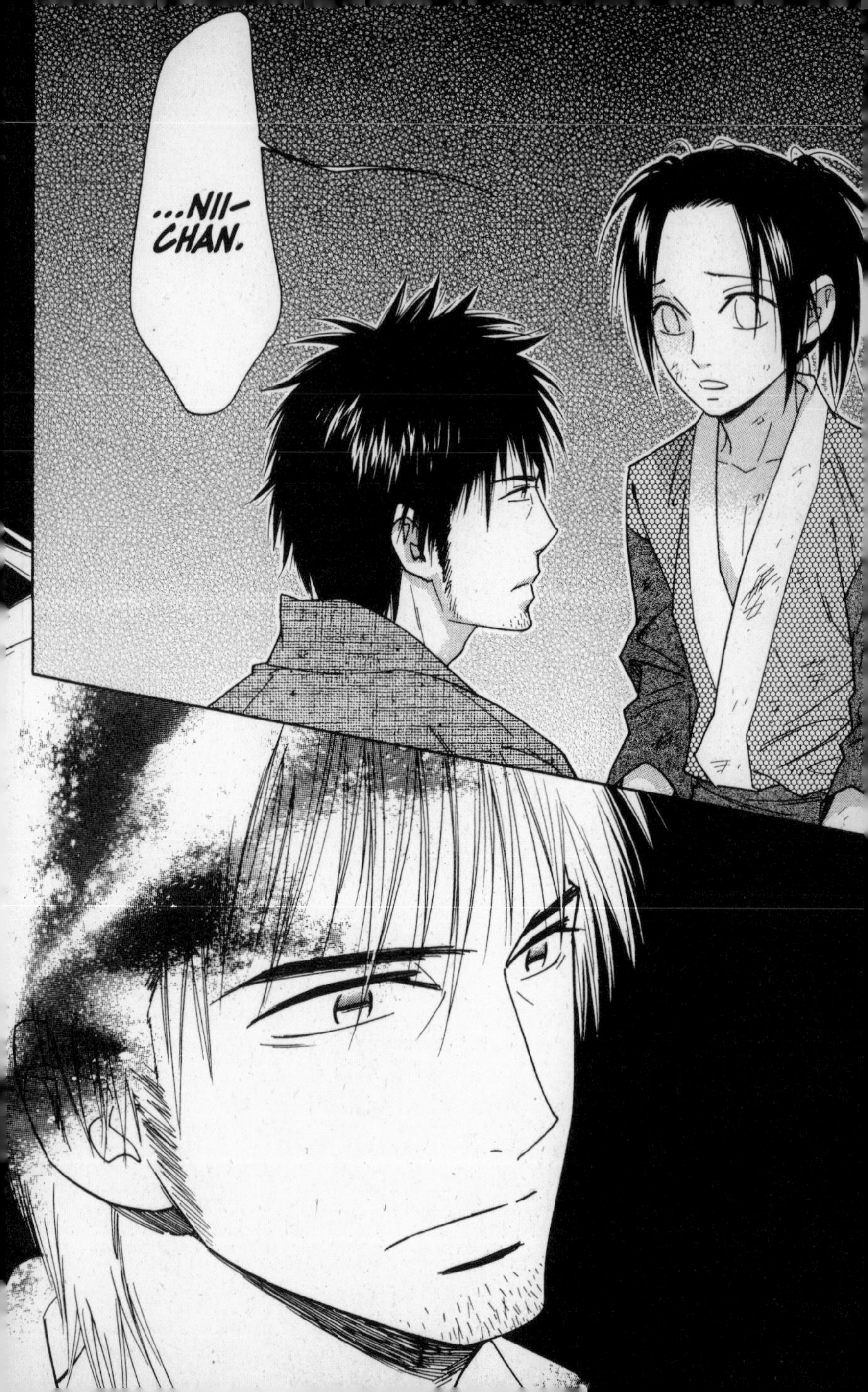
...NII-
CHAN.

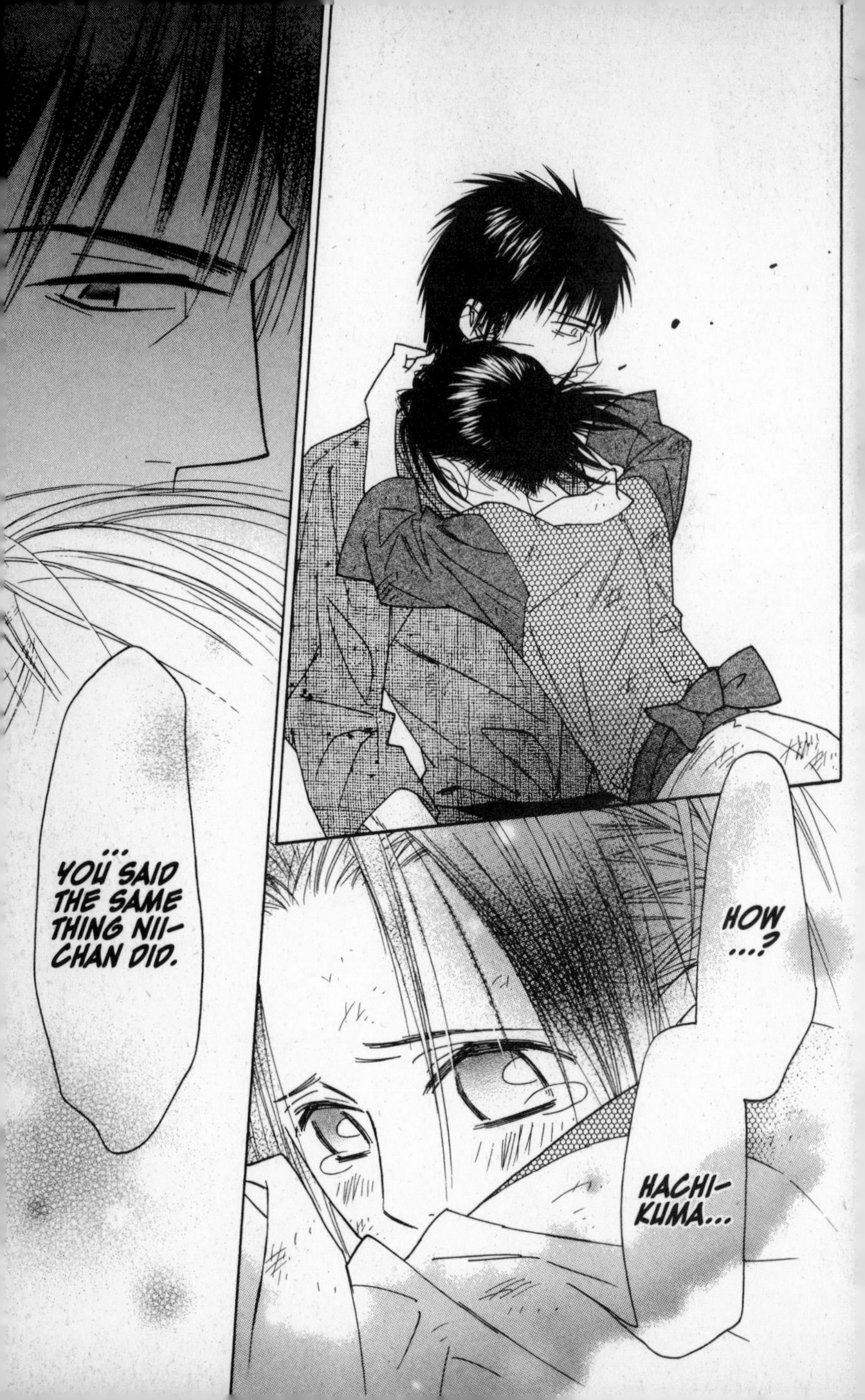
HOW ...?
HACHI-KUMA...
... YOU SAID THE SAME THING NII-CHAN DID.

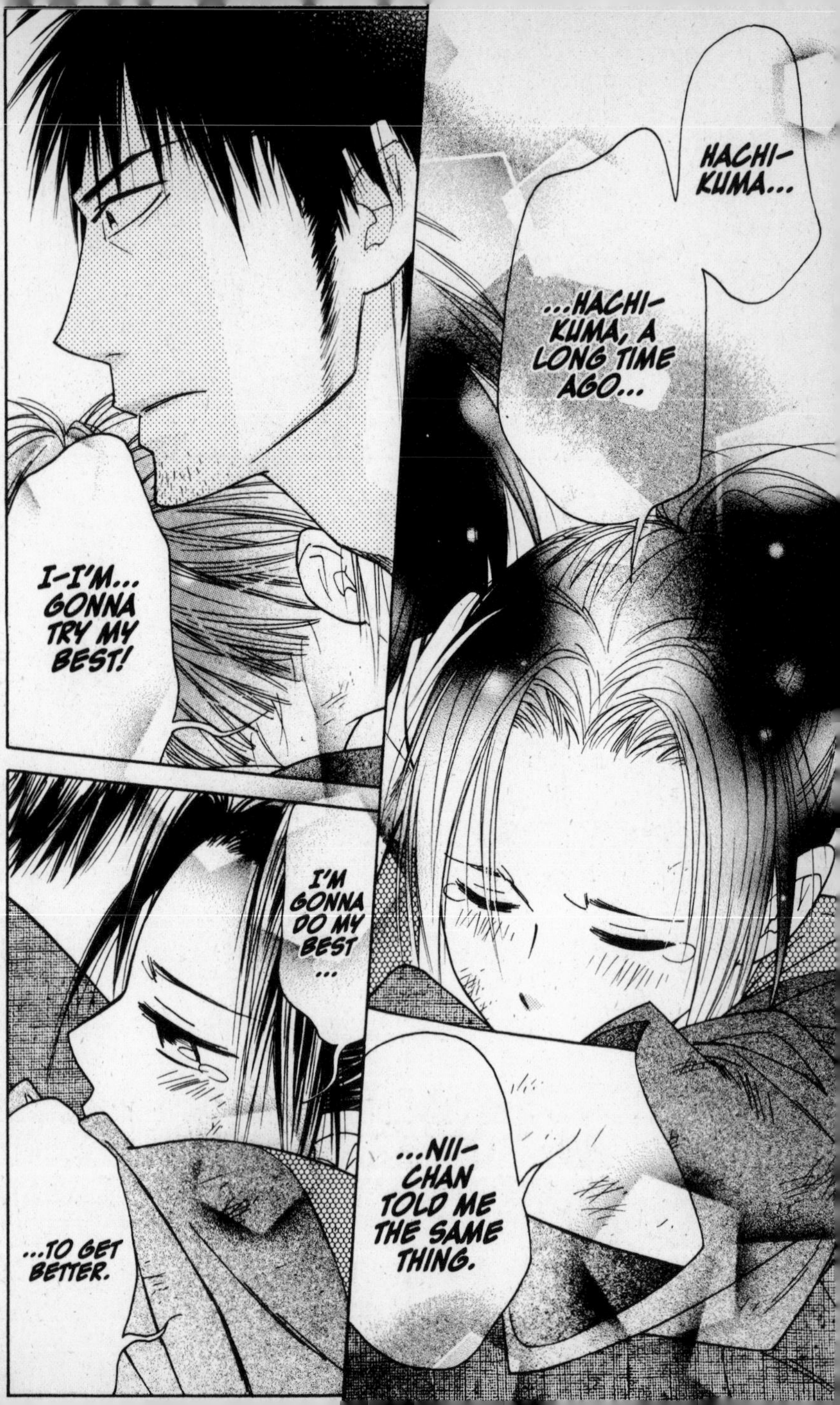
HACHI-KUMA...
...HACHI-KUMA, A LONG TIME AGO...
...NII-CHAN TOLD ME THE SAME THING.
I-I'M... GONNA TRY MY BEST!
I'M GONNA DO MY BEST ...
...TO GET BETTER.

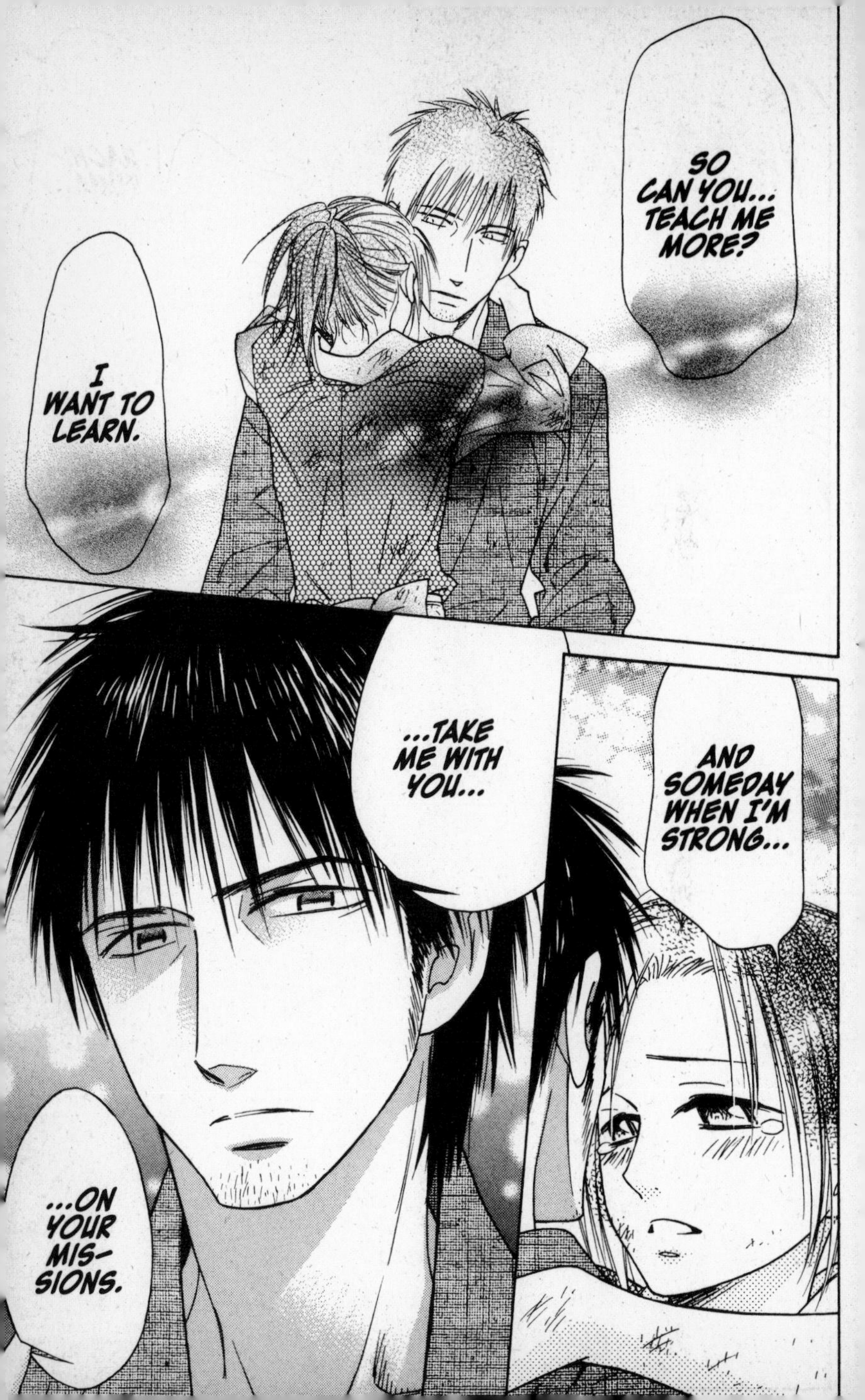
SO CAN YOU... TEACH ME MORE?
I WANT TO LEARN.
AND SOMEDAY WHEN I'M STRONG...
...TAKE ME WITH YOU...
...ON YOUR MIS-SIONS.

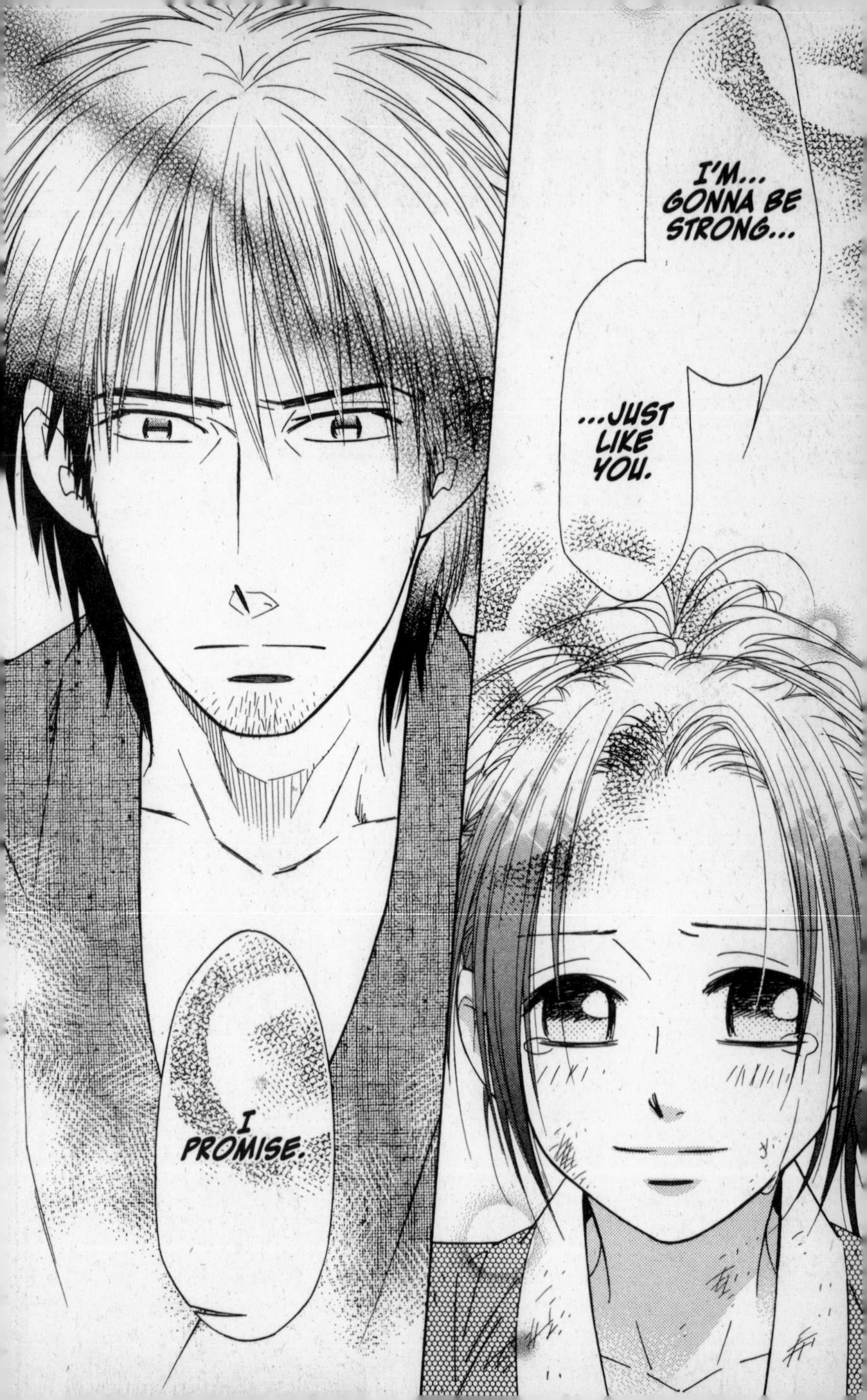
I'M... GONNA BE STRONG...
...JUST LIKE YOU.
I PROMISE.

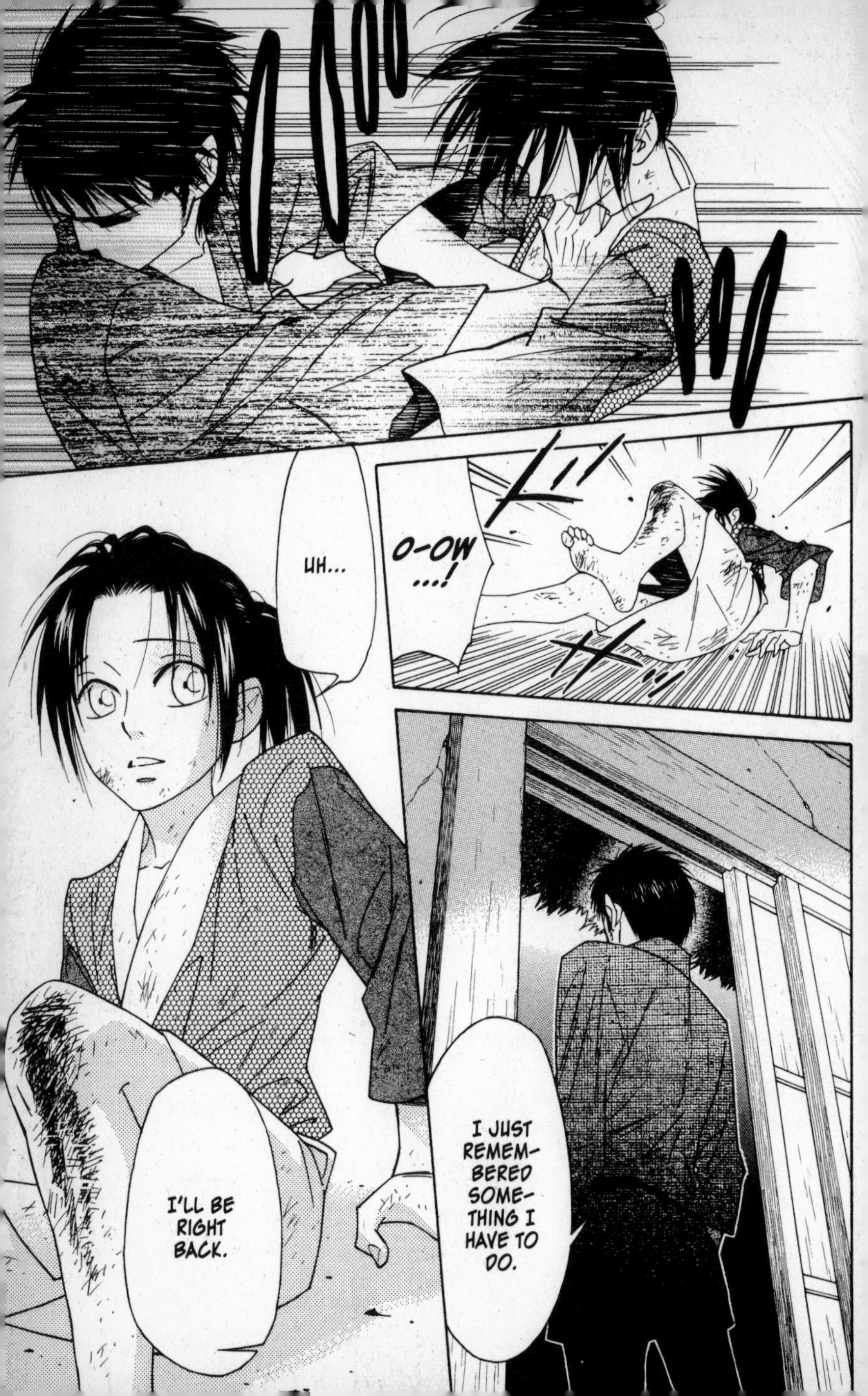
O-OW ...!
UH...
I JUST REMEMBERED SOMETHING I HAVE TO DO.
I'LL BE RIGHT BACK.

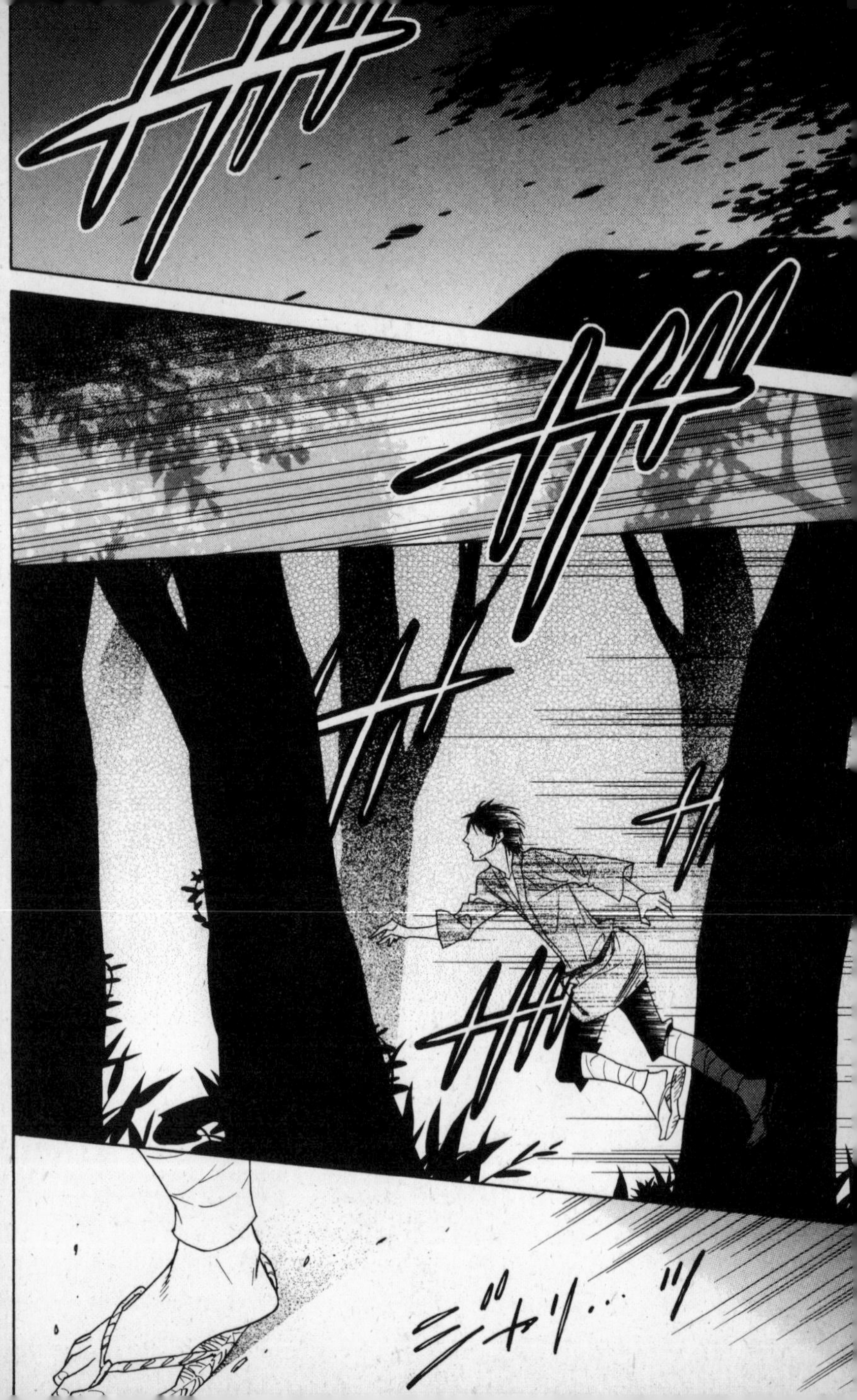
ジャリ…ッ

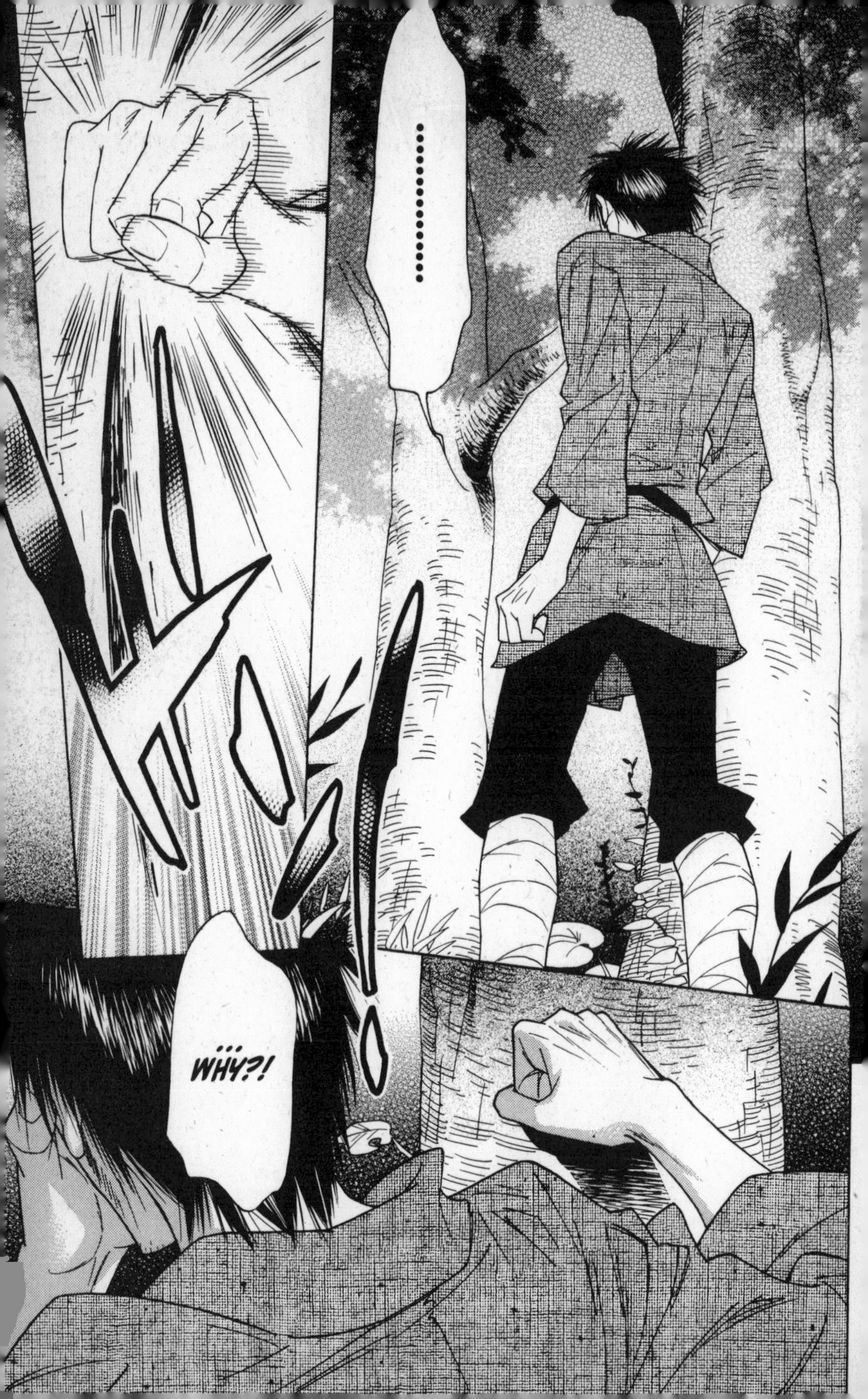
......
WHY?!

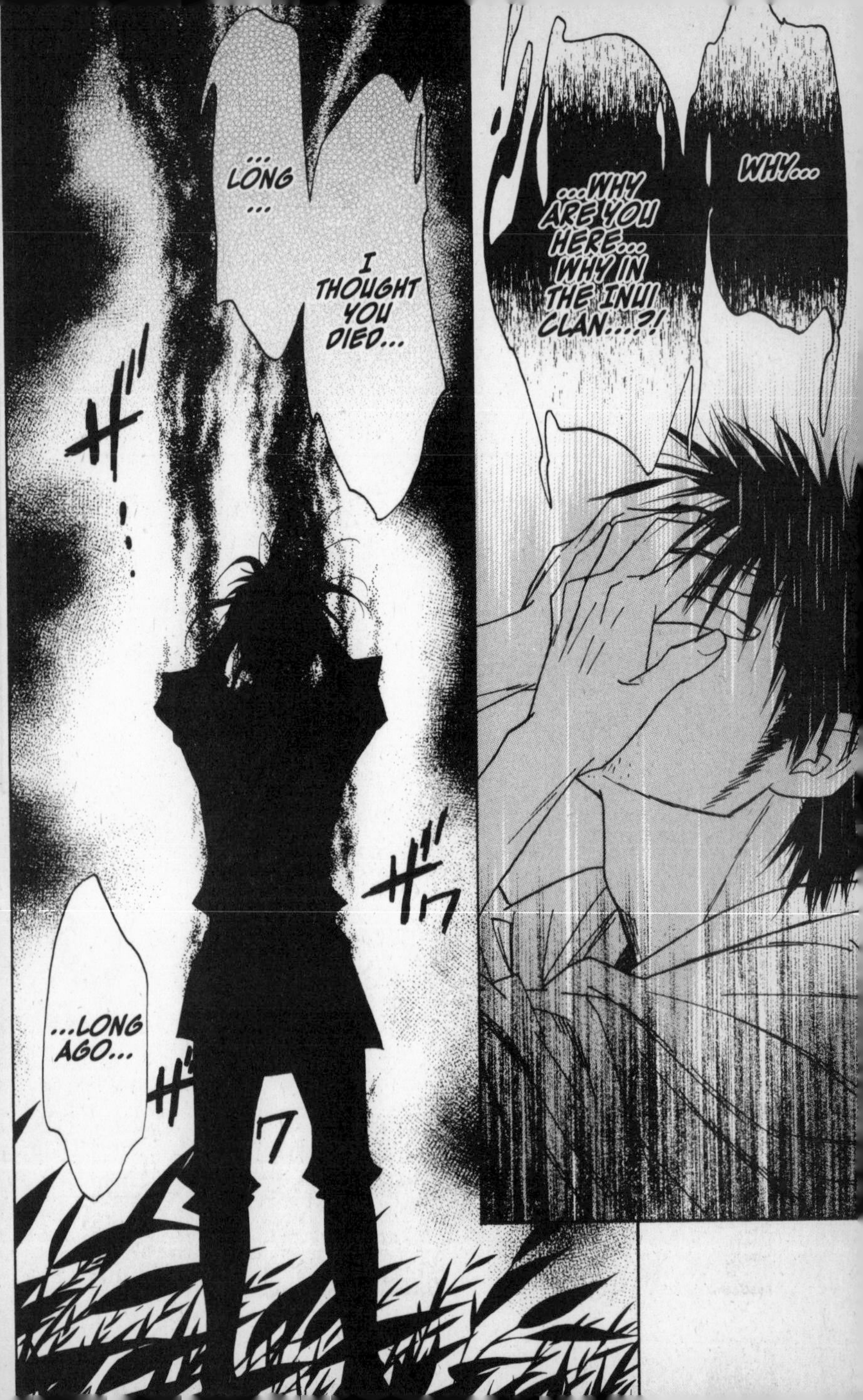
WHY...
...WHY ARE YOU HERE... WHY IN THE INUI CLAN...?!
...LONG...
I THOUGHT YOU DIED...
...LONG AGO...

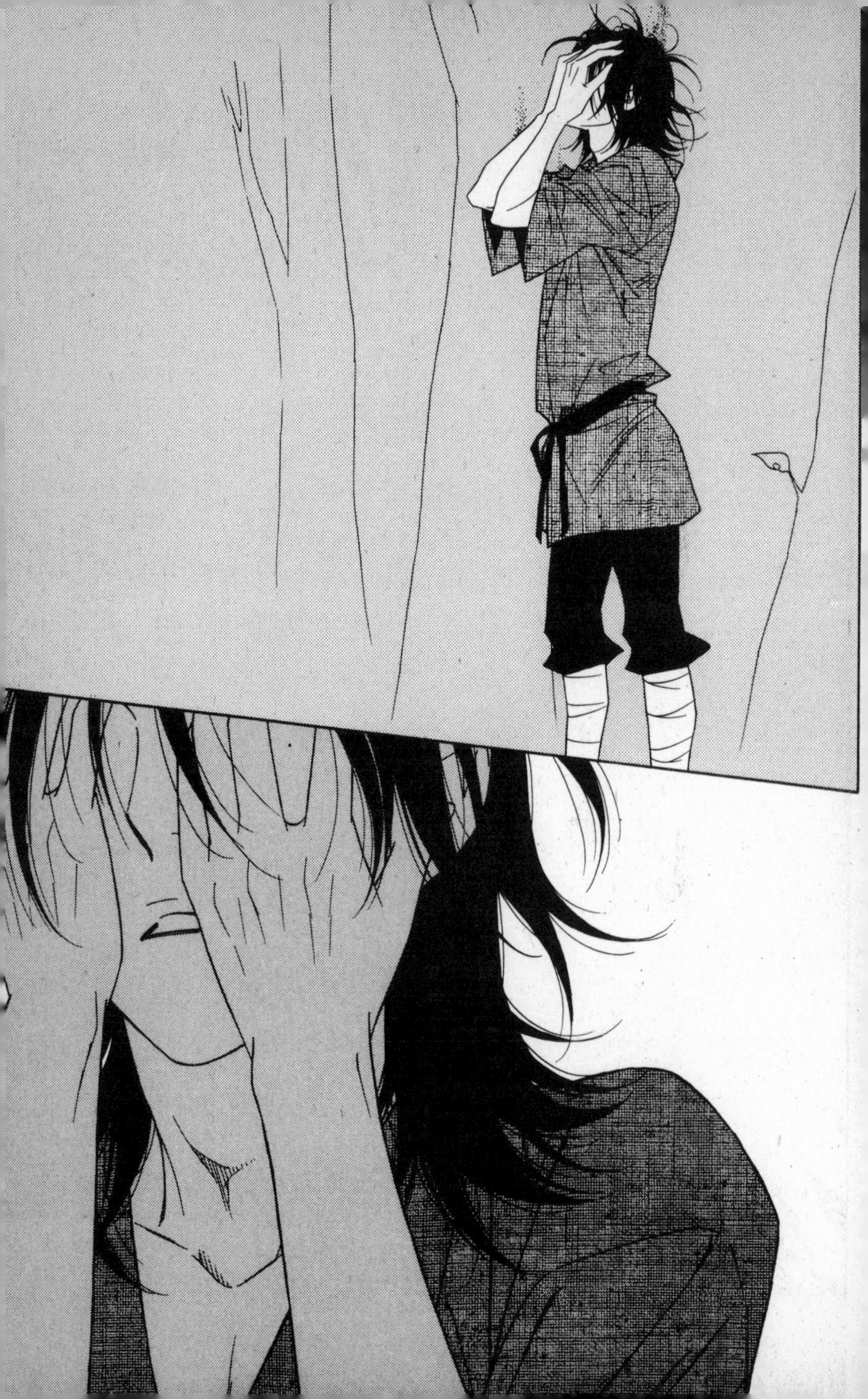

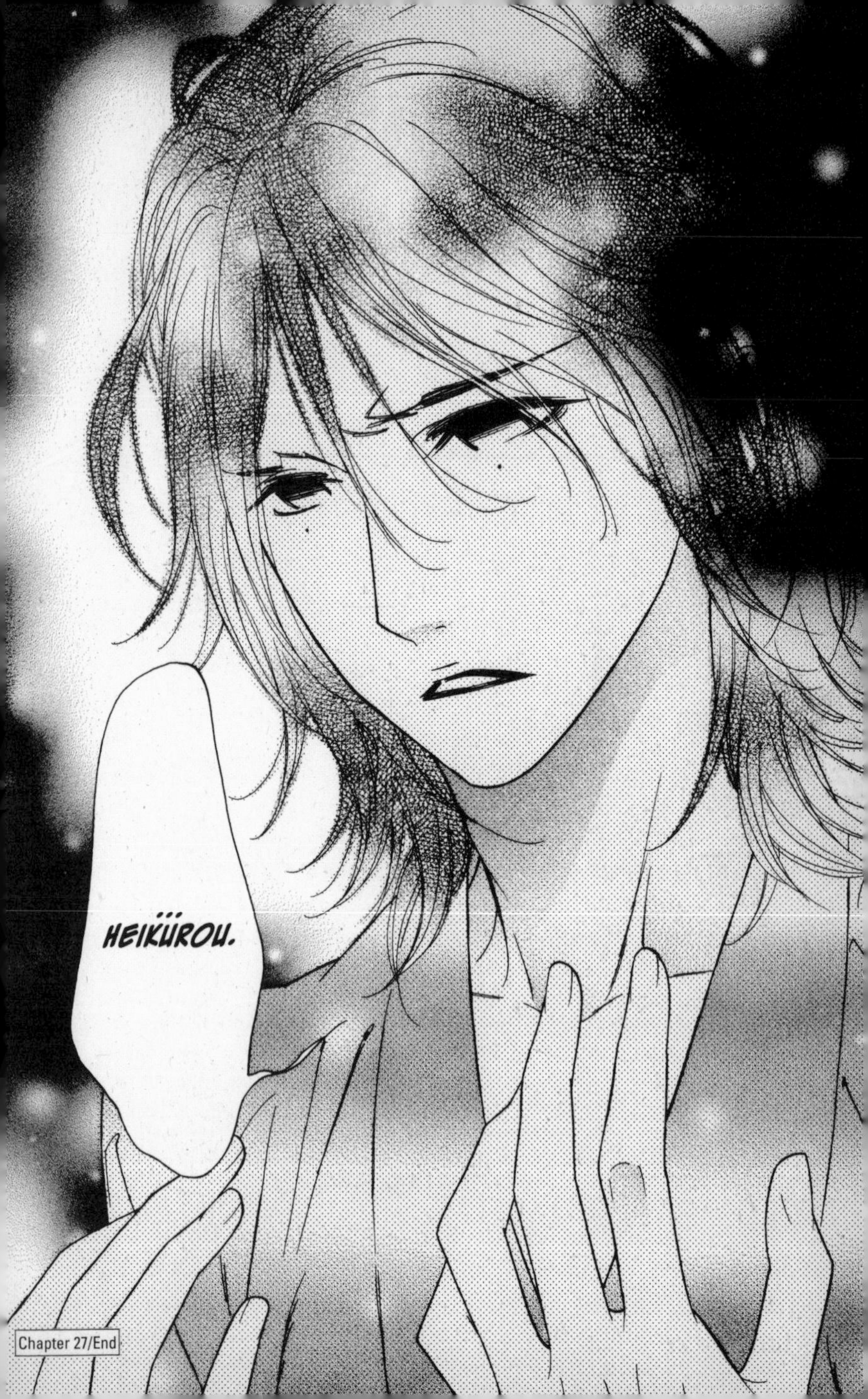
...HEIKŪROU.
Chapter 27/End

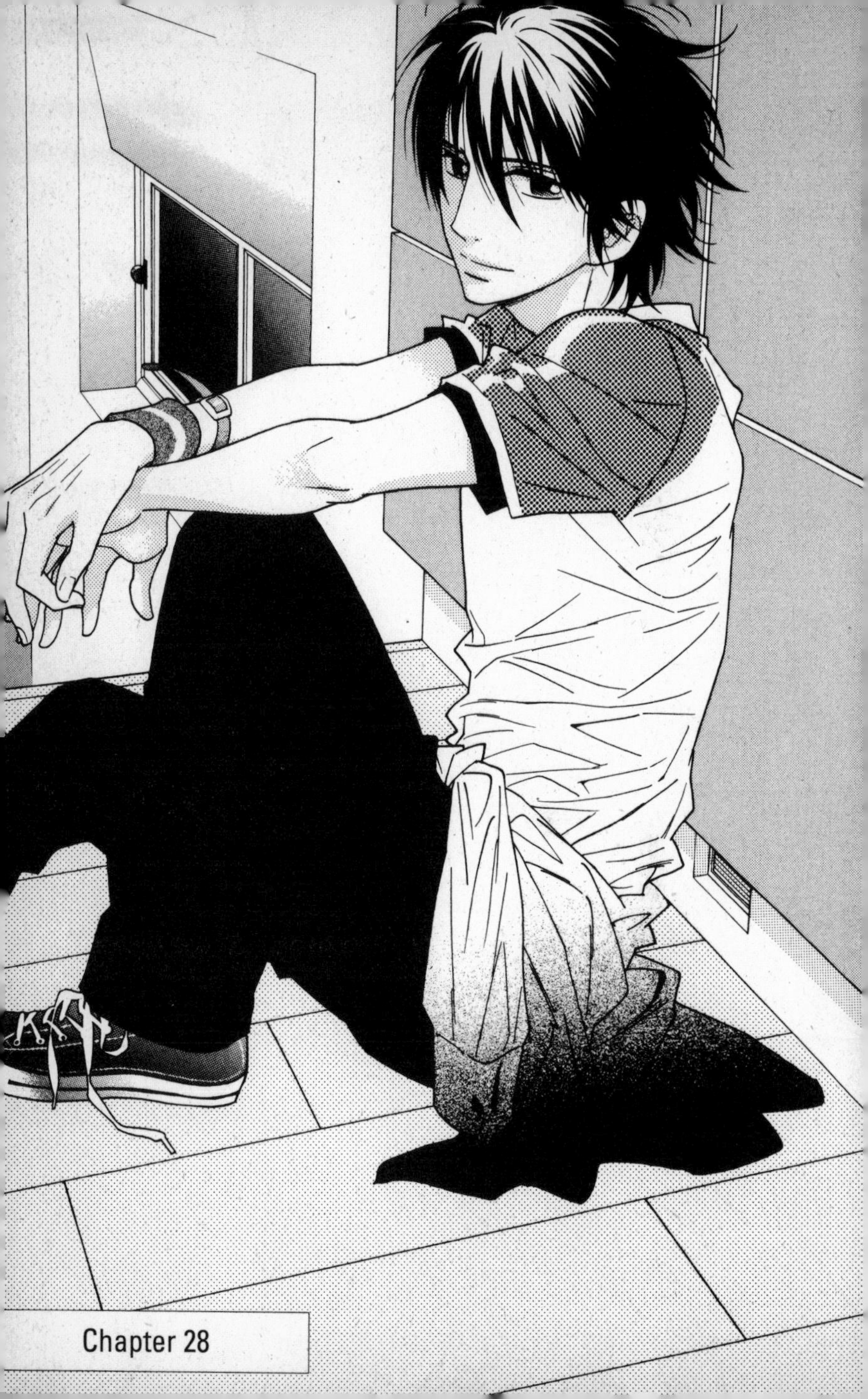

Chapter 28

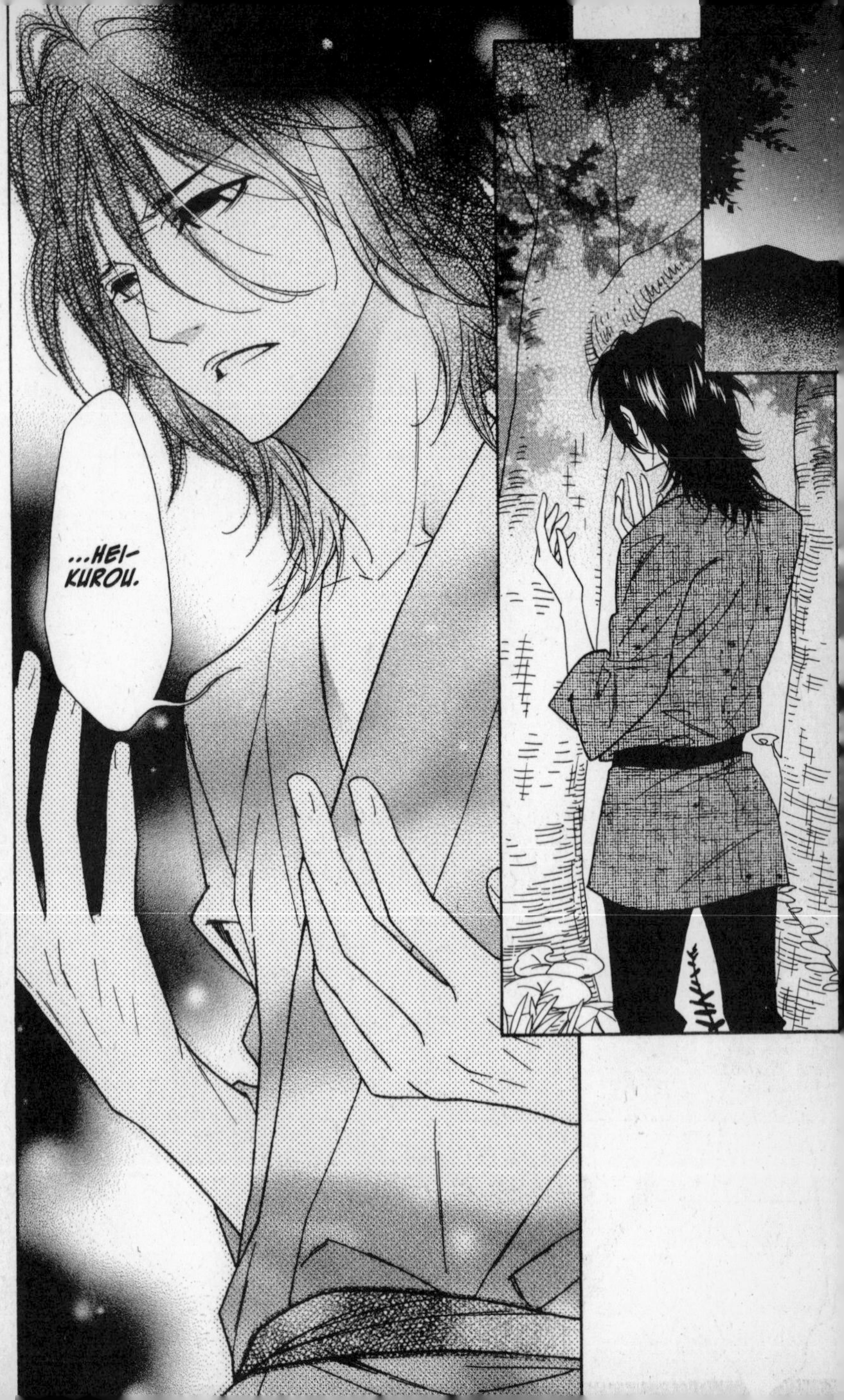
...HEI-KUROU.

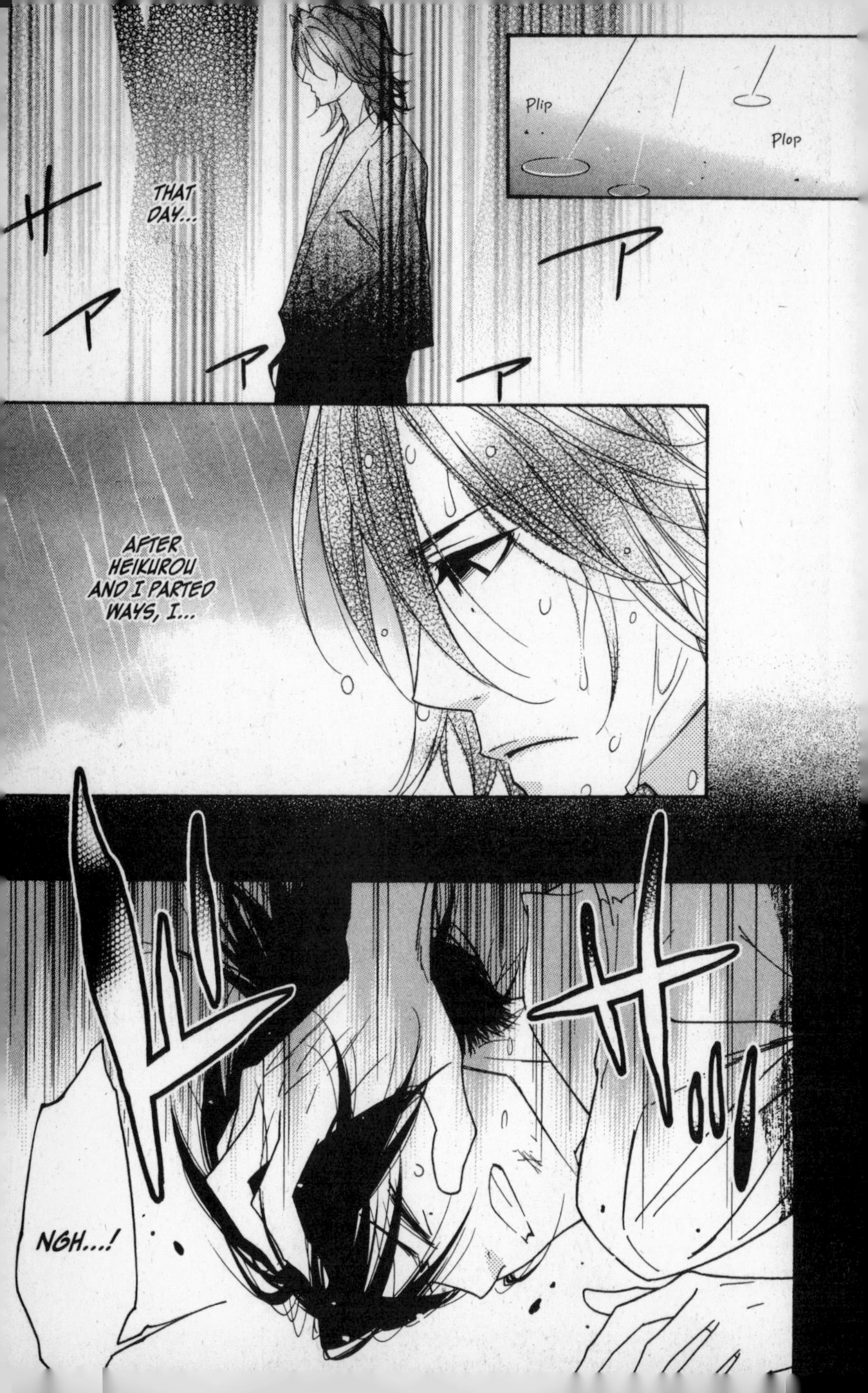
Plop
Plip
THAT DAY...
AFTER HEIKUROU AND I PARTED WAYS, I...
NGH...!

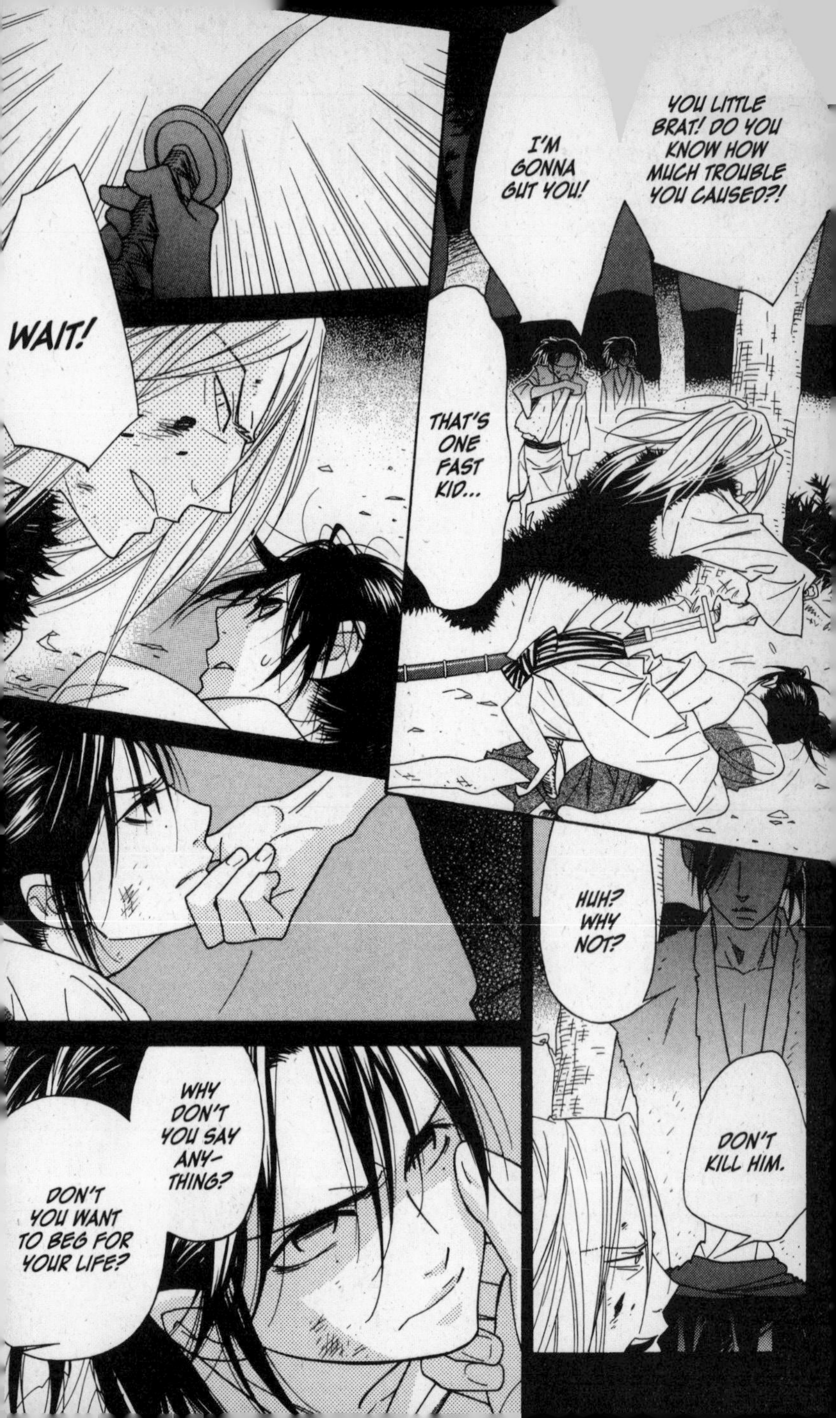
YOU LITTLE BRAT! DO YOU KNOW HOW MUCH TROUBLE YOU CAUSED?!
I'M GONNA GUT YOU!
THAT'S ONE FAST KID...
WAIT!
HUH? WHY NOT?
DON'T KILL HIM.
WHY DON'T YOU SAY ANY-THING?
DON'T YOU WANT TO BEG FOR YOUR LIFE?

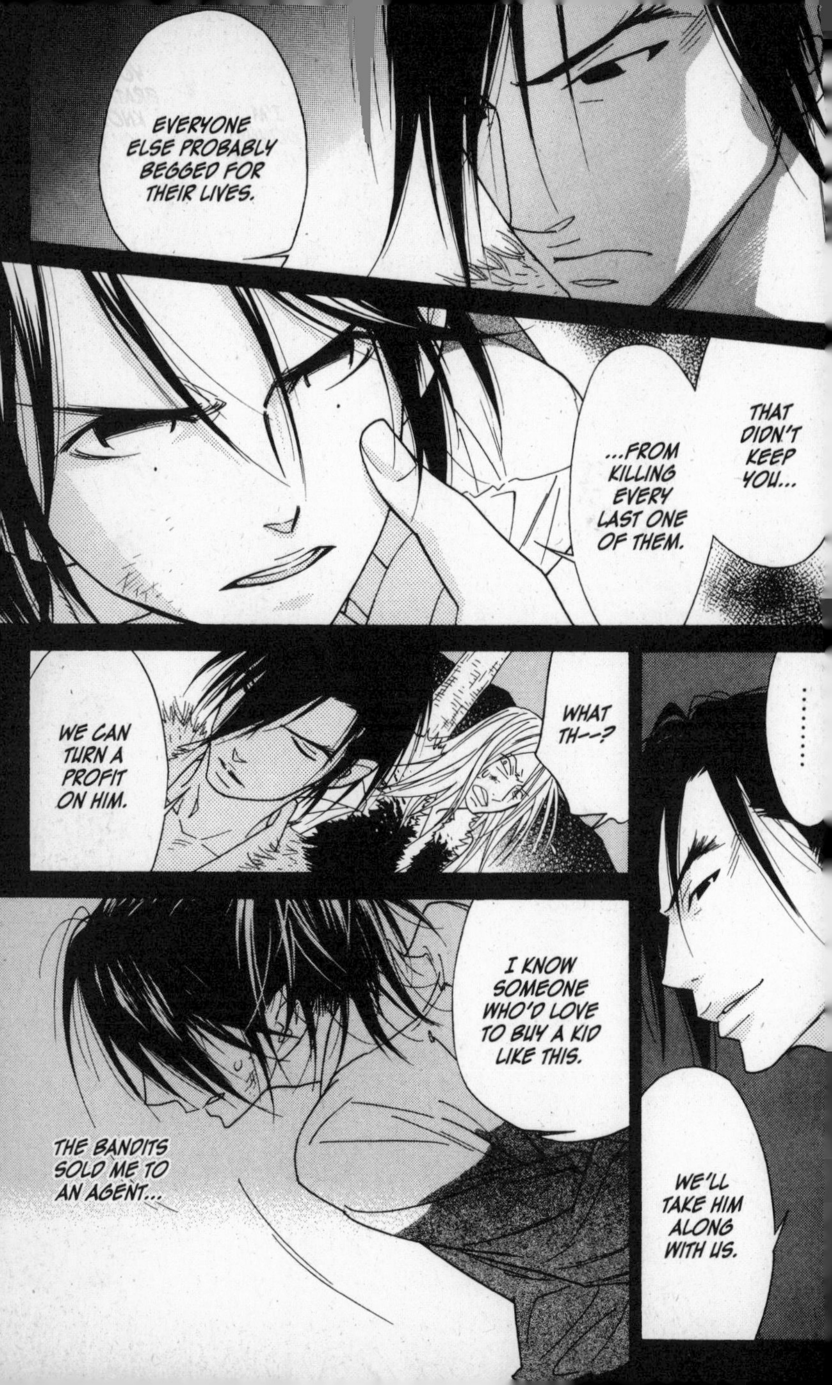
EVERYONE ELSE PROBABLY BEGGED FOR THEIR LIVES.
THAT DIDN'T KEEP YOU...
...FROM KILLING EVERY LAST ONE OF THEM.
......
WHAT TH--?
WE CAN TURN A PROFIT ON HIM.
I KNOW SOMEONE WHO'D LOVE TO BUY A KID LIKE THIS.
WE'LL TAKE HIM ALONG WITH US.
THE BANDITS SOLD ME TO AN AGENT...

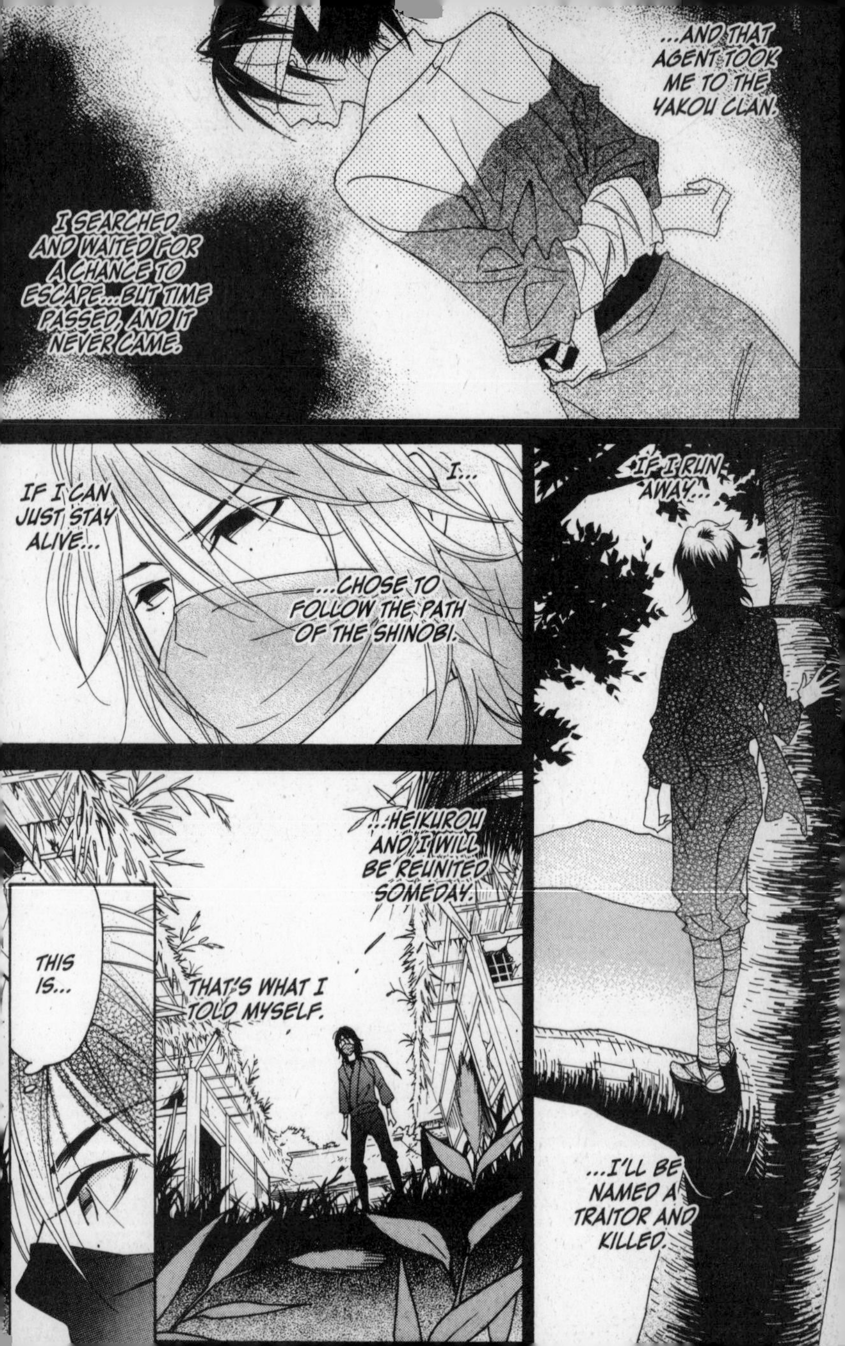
...AND THAT AGENT TOOK ME TO THE YAKOU CLAN.
I SEARCHED AND WAITED FOR A CHANCE TO ESCAPE...BUT TIME PASSED, AND IT NEVER CAME.
IF I RUN AWAY...
...I'LL BE NAMED A TRAITOR AND KILLED.
I...
...CHOSE TO FOLLOW THE PATH OF THE SHINOBI.
IF I CAN JUST STAY ALIVE...
...HEIKUROU AND I WILL BE REUNITED SOMEDAY.
THAT'S WHAT I TOLD MYSELF.
THIS IS...

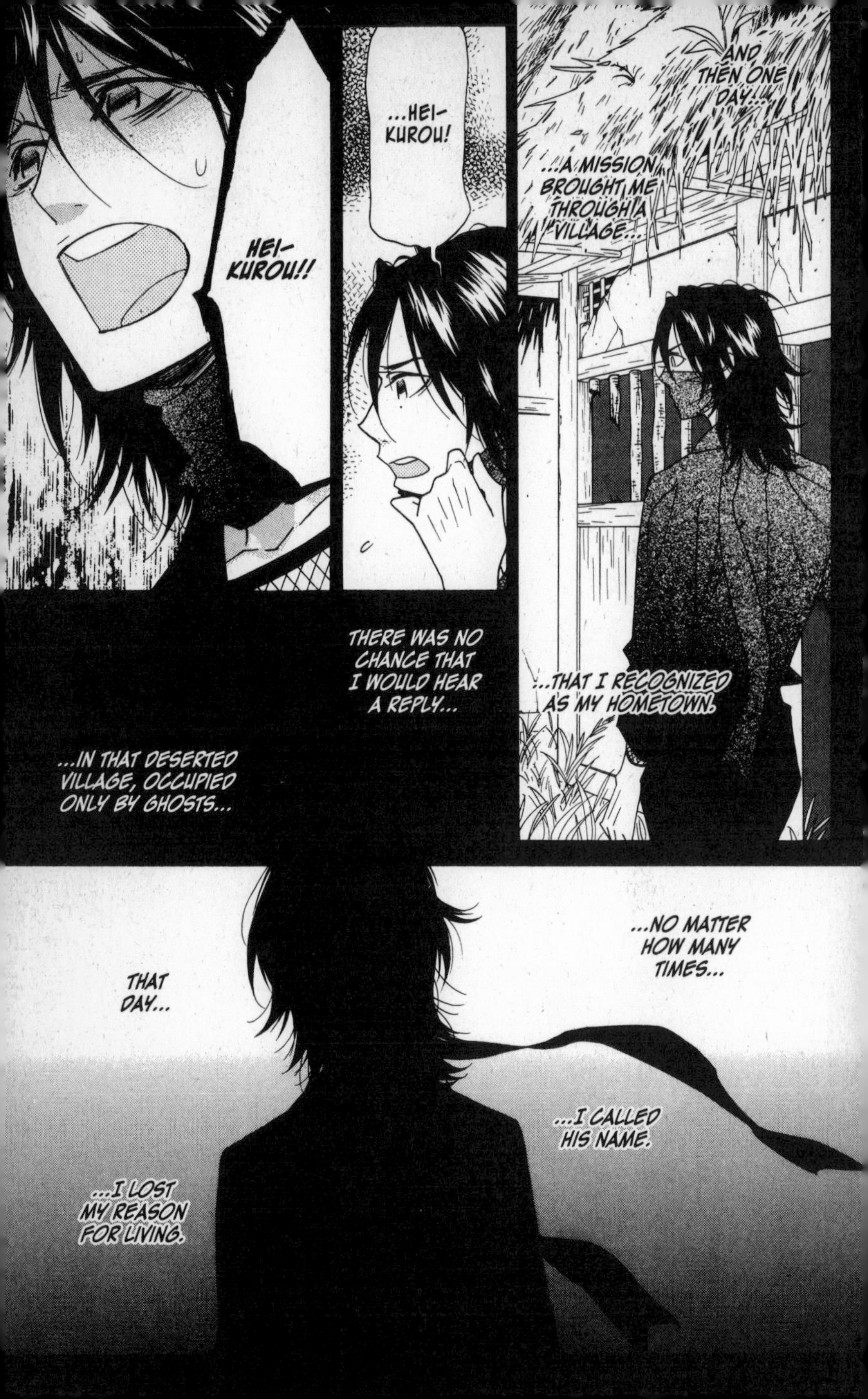
AND THEN ONE DAY...
...A MISSION BROUGHT ME THROUGH A VILLAGE...
...THAT I RECOGNIZED AS MY HOMETOWN.
...HEI-KUROU!
THERE WAS NO CHANCE THAT I WOULD HEAR A REPLY...
HEI-KUROU!!
...IN THAT DESERTED VILLAGE, OCCUPIED ONLY BY GHOSTS...
...NO MATTER HOW MANY TIMES...
...I CALLED HIS NAME.
THAT DAY...
...I LOST MY REASON FOR LIVING.

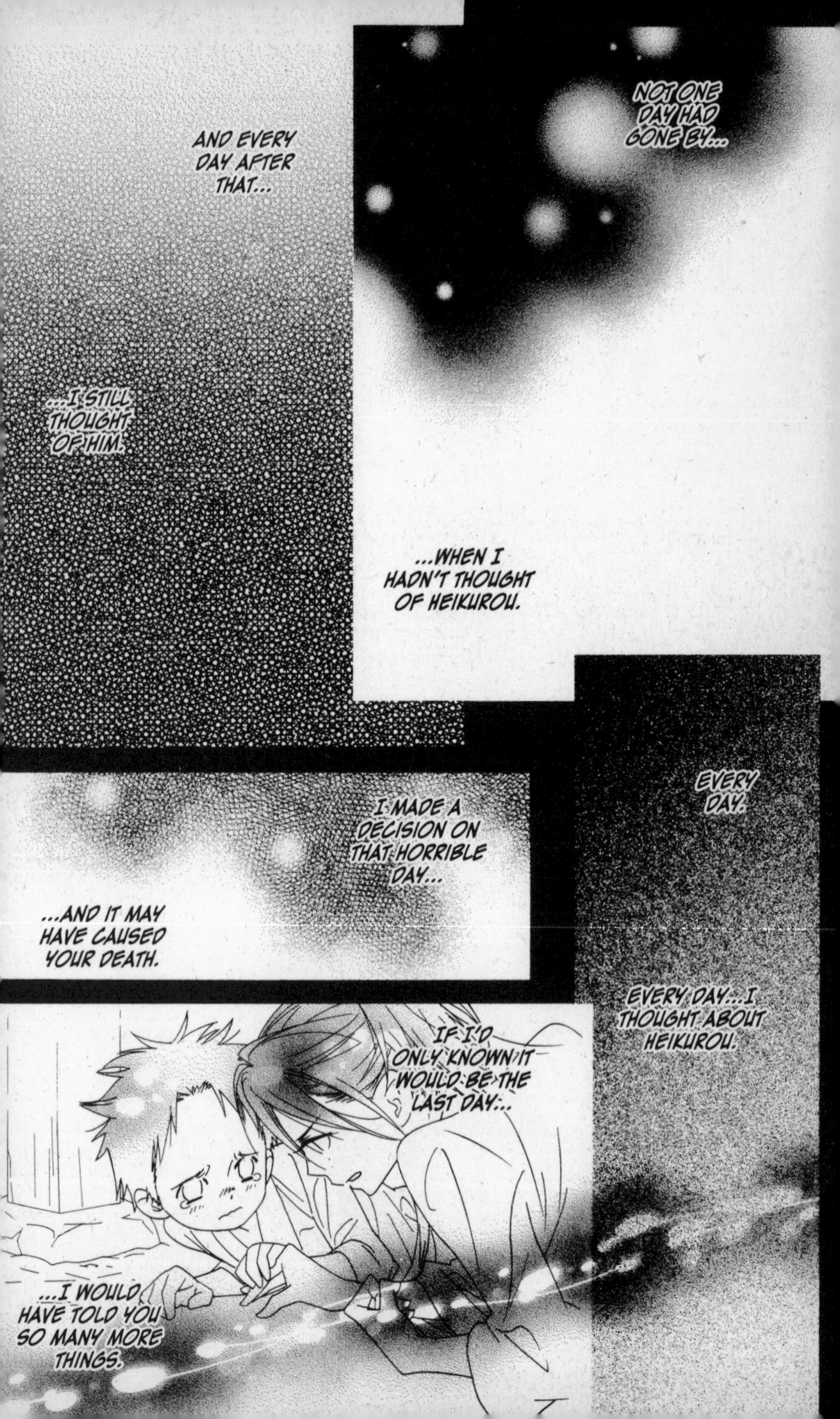
NOT ONE DAY HAD GONE BY...
...WHEN I HADN'T THOUGHT OF HEIKUROU.
AND EVERY DAY AFTER THAT...
...I STILL THOUGHT OF HIM.
EVERY DAY.
EVERY DAY...I THOUGHT ABOUT HEIKUROU.
I MADE A DECISION ON THAT HORRIBLE DAY...
...AND IT MAY HAVE CAUSED YOUR DEATH.
IF I'D ONLY KNOWN IT WOULD BE THE LAST DAY...
...I WOULD HAVE TOLD YOU SO MANY MORE THINGS.

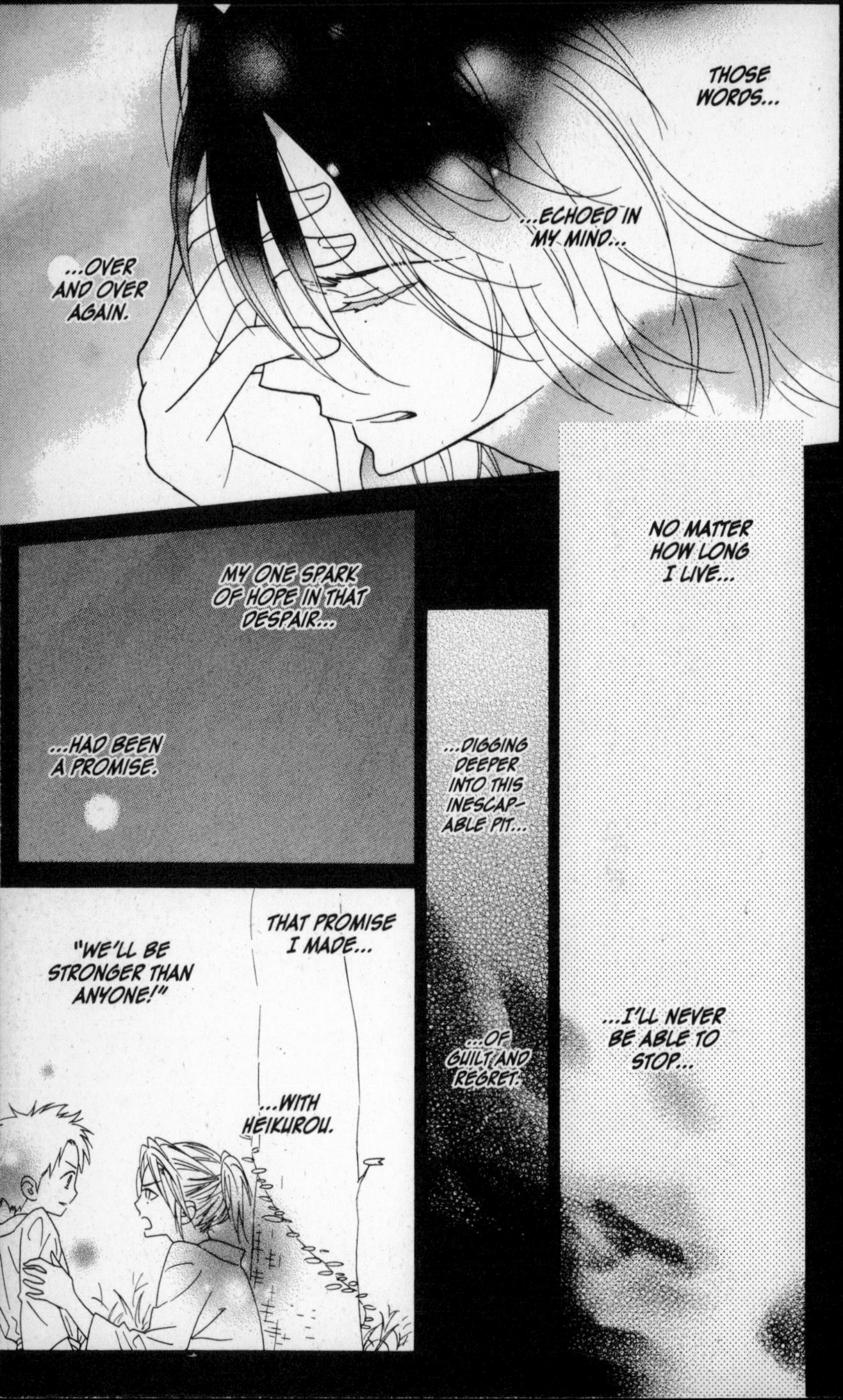
THOSE WORDS...
...ECHOED IN MY MIND...
...OVER AND OVER AGAIN.
NO MATTER HOW LONG I LIVE...
...I'LL NEVER BE ABLE TO STOP...
...DIGGING DEEPER INTO THIS INESCAPABLE PIT...
...OF GUILT AND REGRET.
MY ONE SPARK OF HOPE IN THAT DESPAIR...
...HAD BEEN A PROMISE.
THAT PROMISE I MADE...
...WITH HEIKUROU.
"WE'LL BE STRONGER THAN ANYONE!"

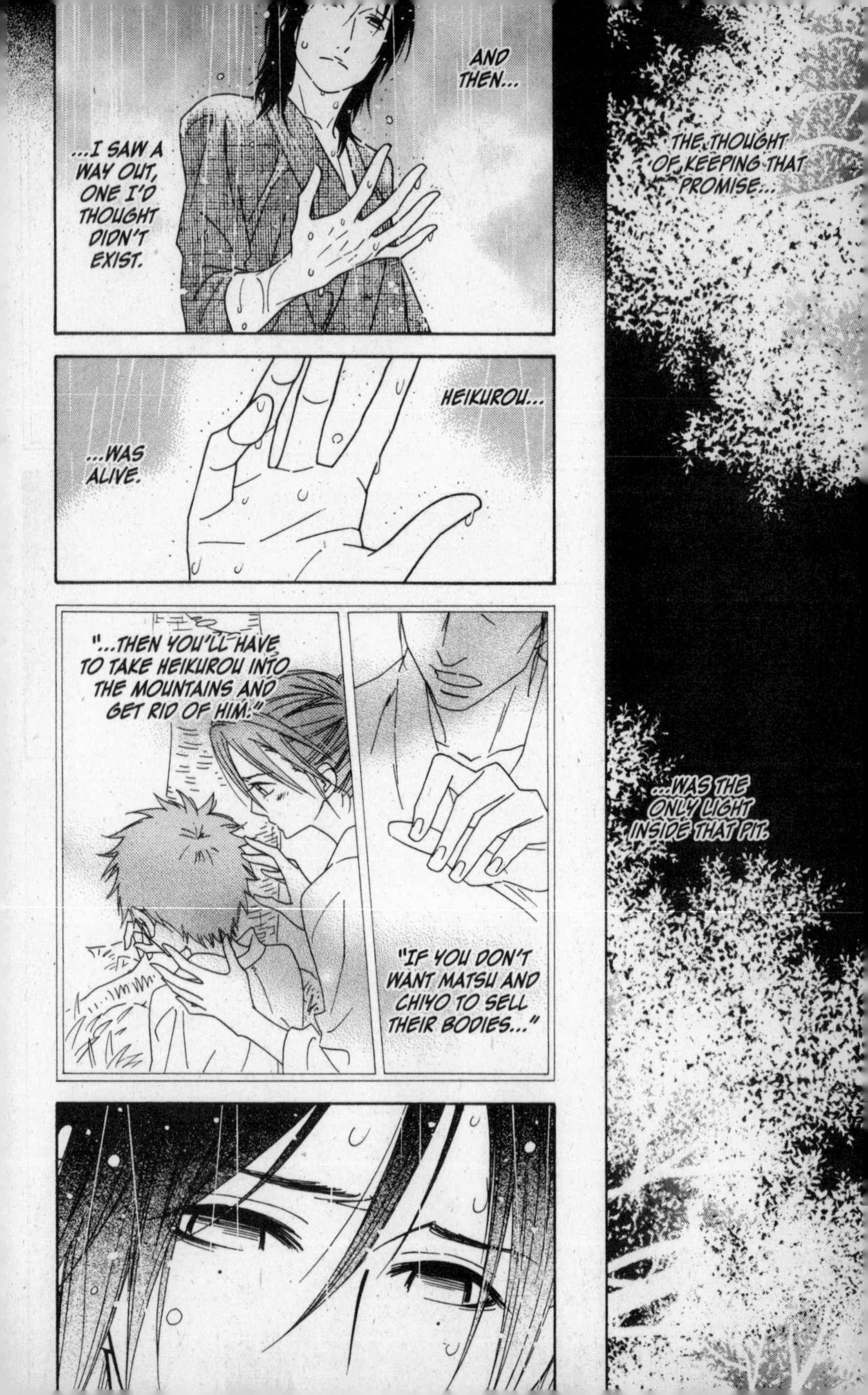
THE THOUGHT OF KEEPING THAT PROMISE...
...WAS THE ONLY LIGHT INSIDE THAT PIT.
AND THEN...
...I SAW A WAY OUT, ONE I'D THOUGHT DIDN'T EXIST.
HEIKUROU...
...WAS ALIVE.
"IF YOU DON'T WANT MATSU AND CHIYO TO SELL THEIR BODIES..."
"...THEN YOU'LL HAVE TO TAKE HEIKUROU INTO THE MOUNTAINS AND GET RID OF HIM."

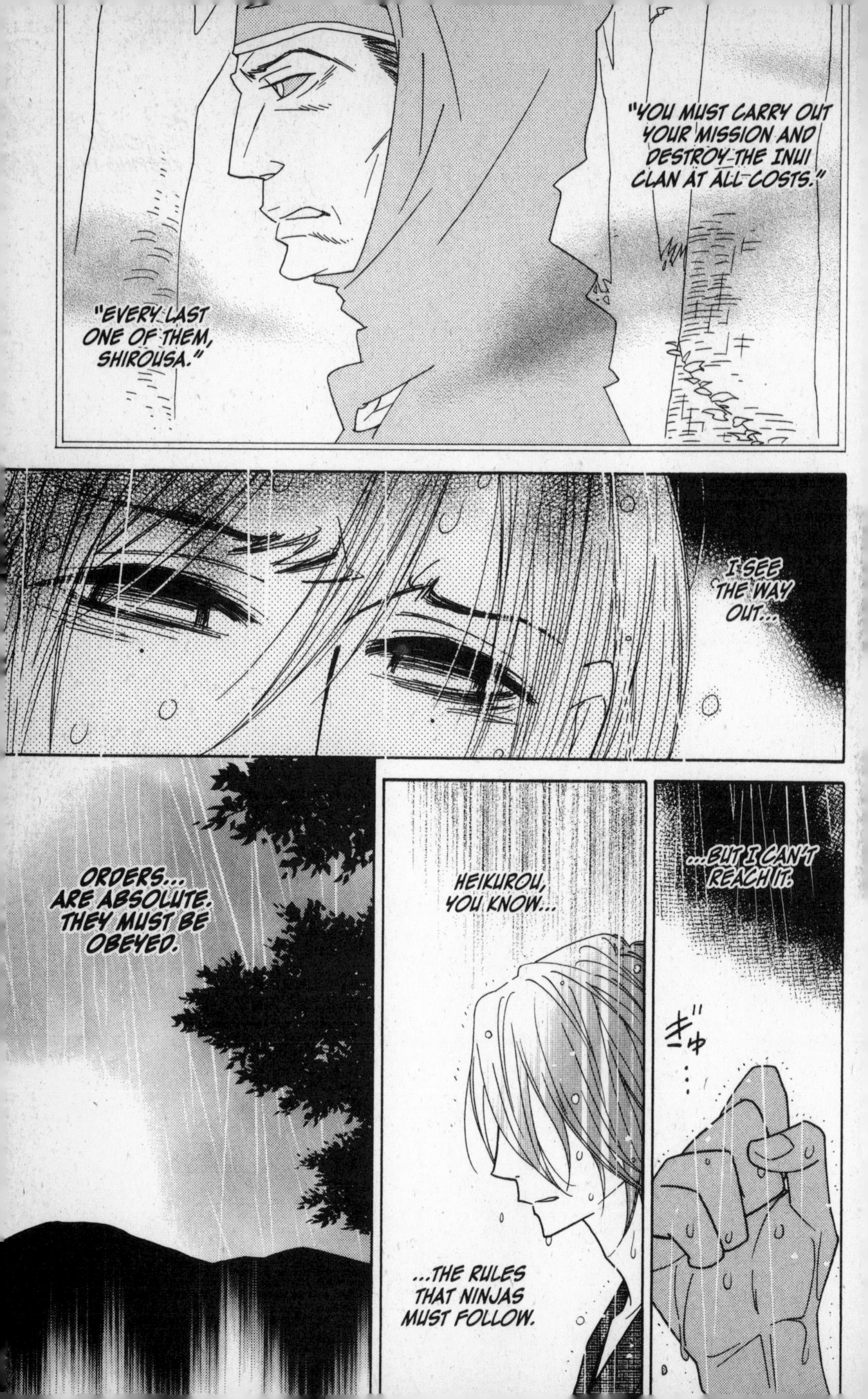
"YOU MUST CARRY OUT YOUR MISSION AND DESTROY THE INUI CLAN AT ALL COSTS."
"EVERY LAST ONE OF THEM, SHIROUSA."
I SEE THE WAY OUT...
...BUT I CAN'T REACH IT.
ぎゅ
HEIKUROU, YOU KNOW...
...THE RULES THAT NINJAS MUST FOLLOW.
ORDERS... ARE ABSOLUTE. THEY MUST BE OBEYED.

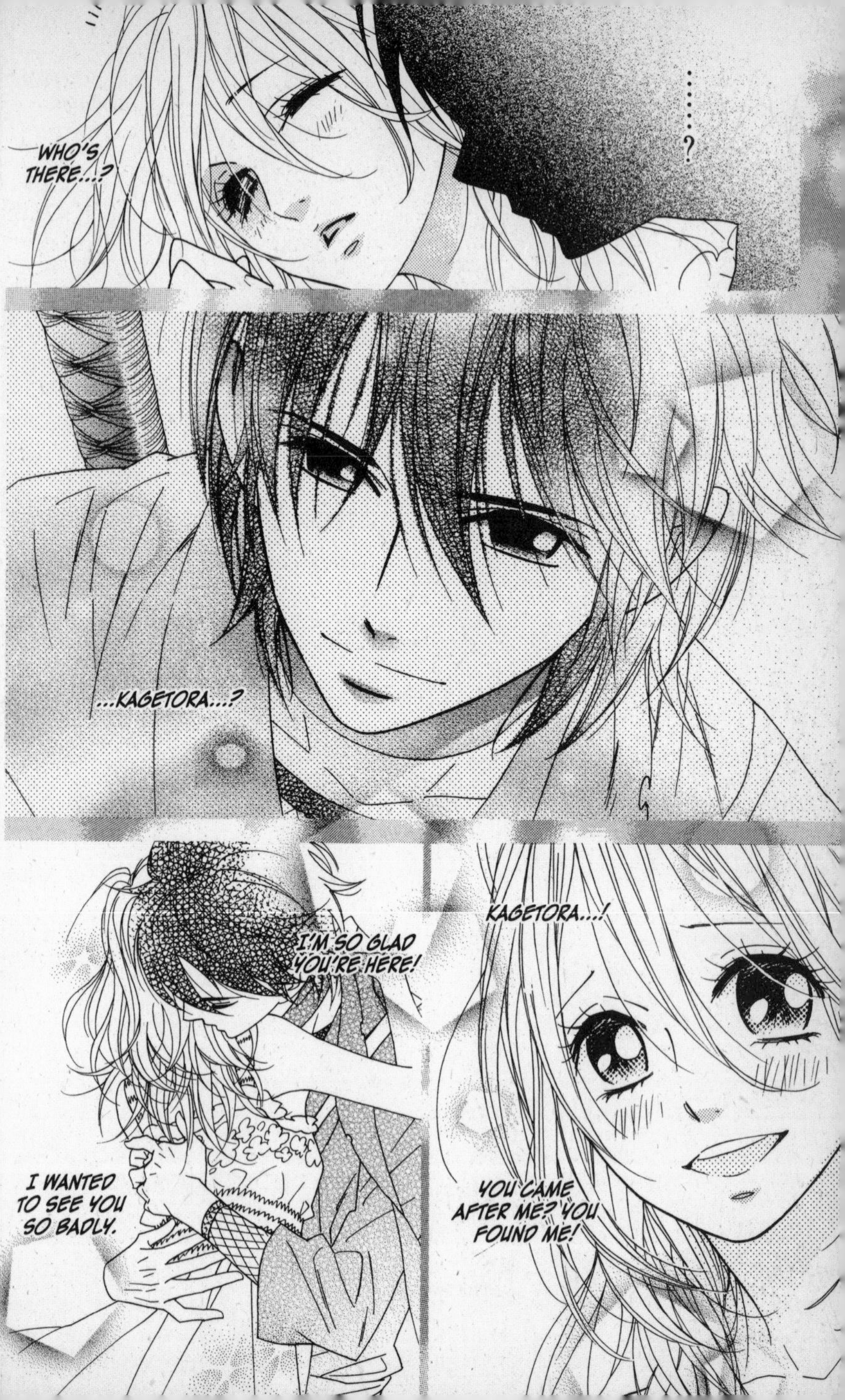
......?
WHO'S THERE...?
...KAGETORA...?
KAGETORA...!
YOU CAME AFTER ME? YOU FOUND ME!
I'M SO GLAD YOU'RE HERE!
I WANTED TO SEE YOU SO BADLY.

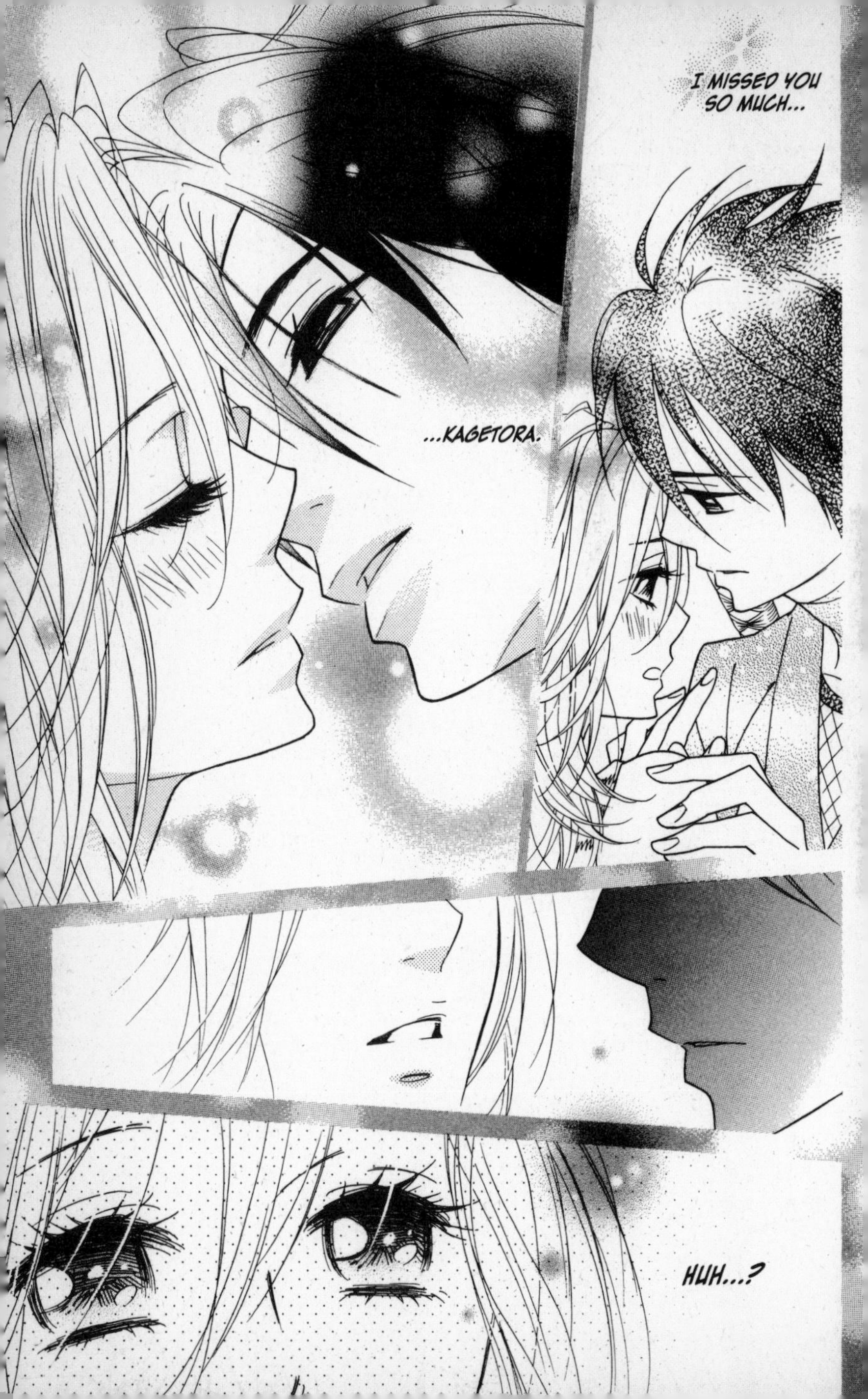
I MISSED YOU SO MUCH...
...KAGETORA.
HUH...?

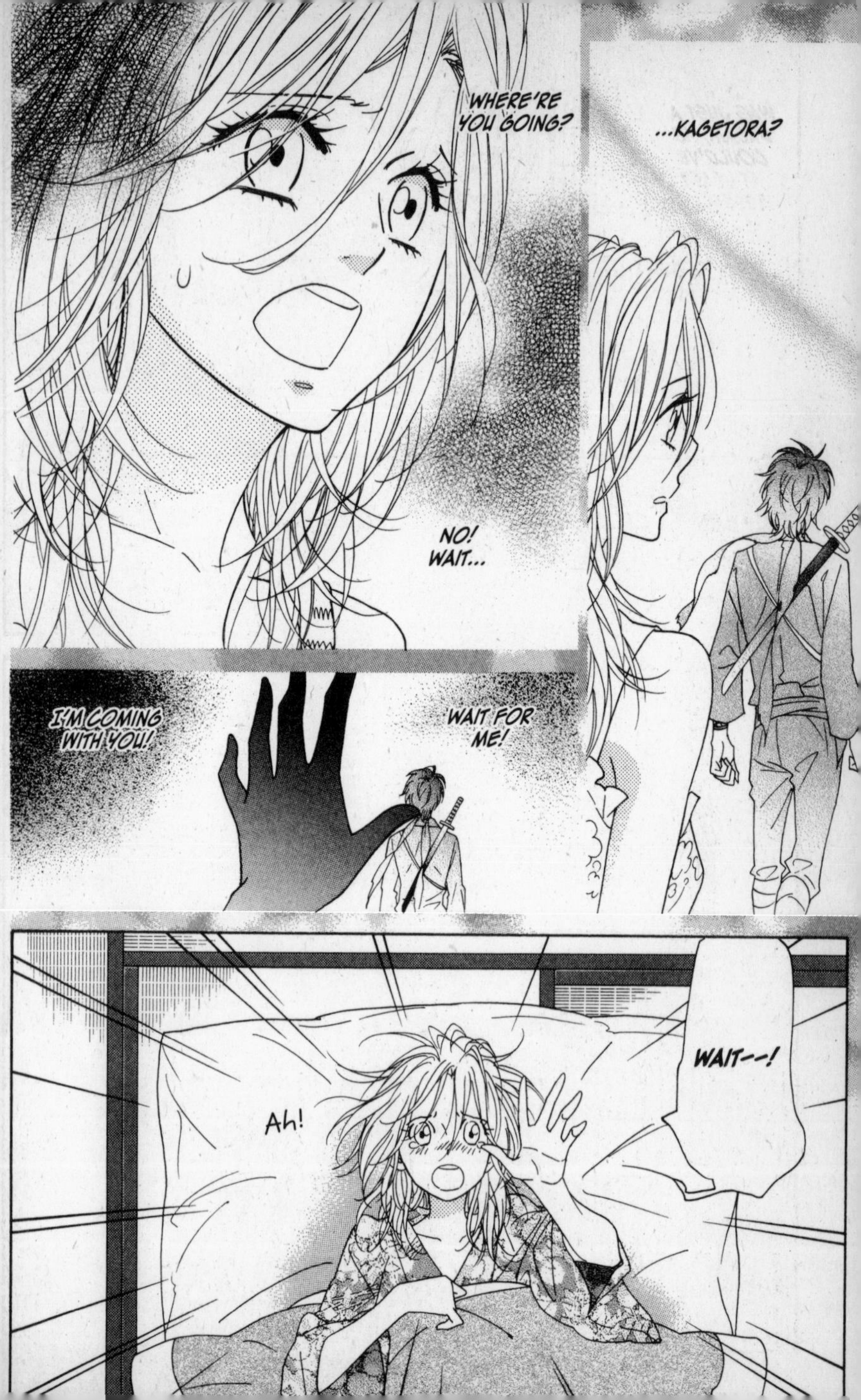
...KAGETORA?
WHERE'RE YOU GOING?
NO! WAIT...
WAIT FOR ME!
I'M COMING WITH YOU!
WAIT--!
Ah!

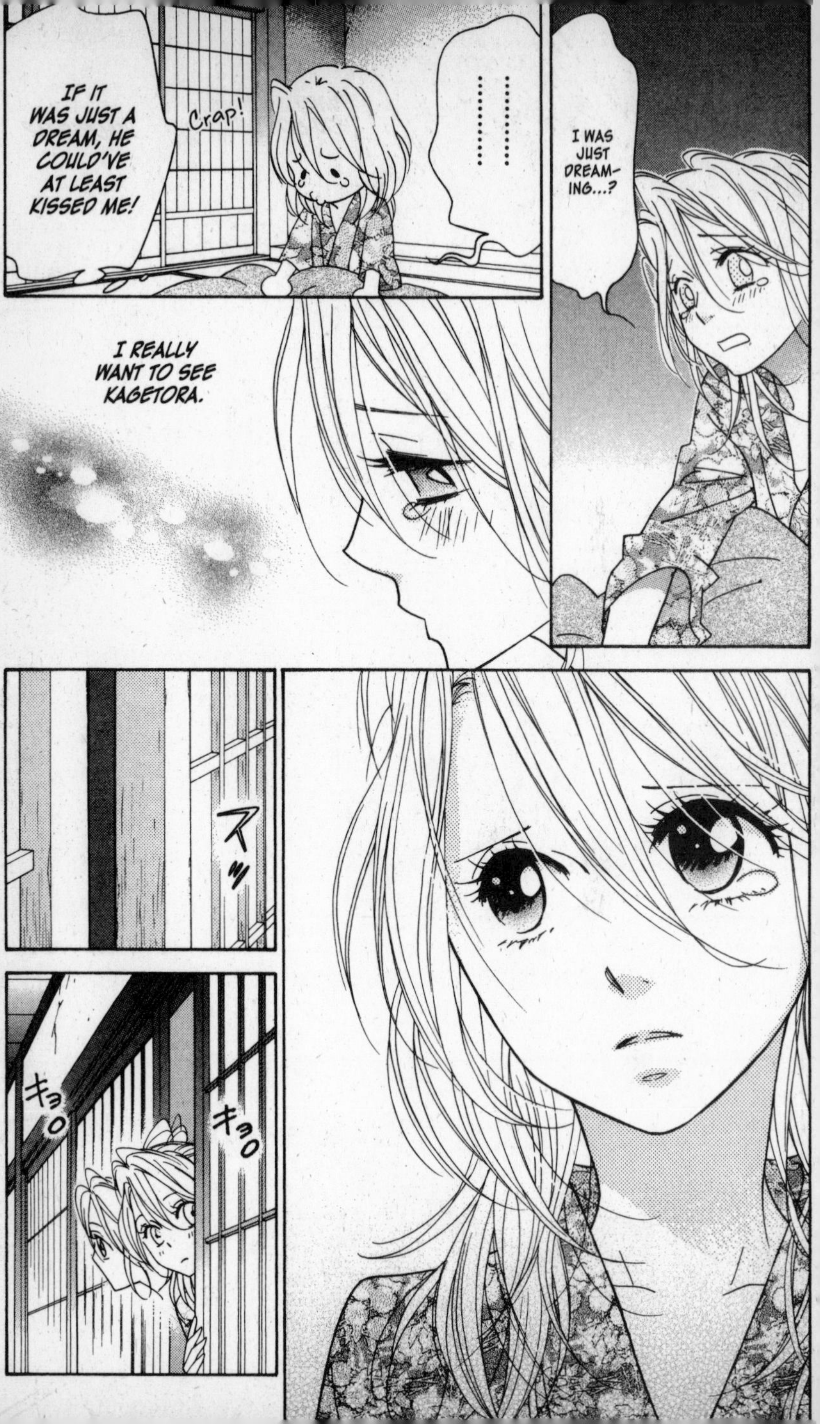
I WAS JUST DREAMING...?
......
Crap!
IF IT WAS JUST A DREAM, HE COULD'VE AT LEAST KISSED ME!
I REALLY WANT TO SEE KAGETORA.
スッ
キョロ
キョロ

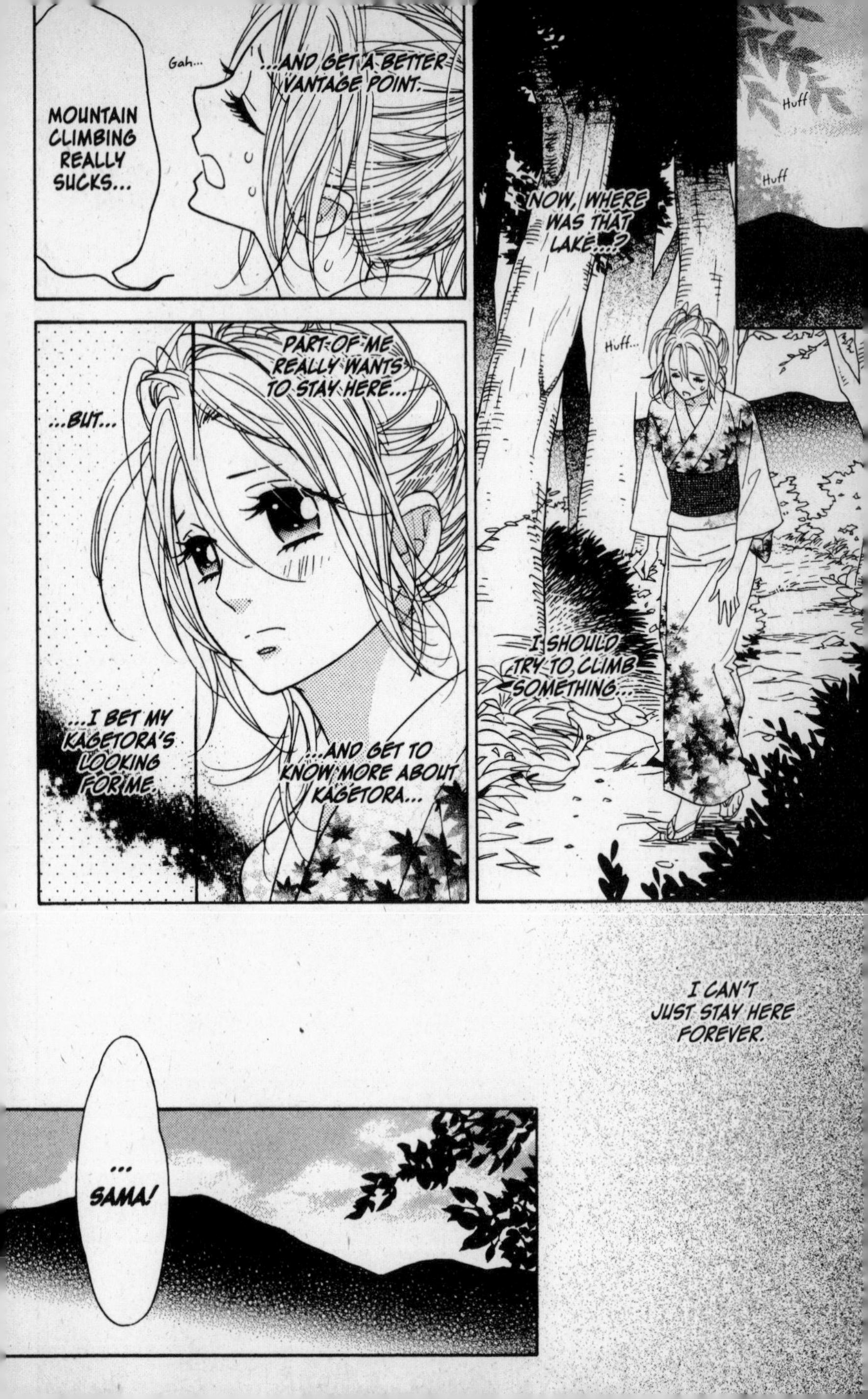
Huff
Huff
NOW, WHERE WAS THAT LAKE...?
Huff...
I SHOULD TRY TO CLIMB SOMETHING...
...AND GET A BETTER VANTAGE POINT.
Gah...
MOUNTAIN CLIMBING REALLY SUCKS...
PART OF ME REALLY WANTS TO STAY HERE...
...AND GET TO KNOW MORE ABOUT KAGETORA...
...BUT...
...I BET MY KAGETORA'S LOOKING FOR ME.
I CAN'T JUST STAY HERE FOREVER.
... SAMA!

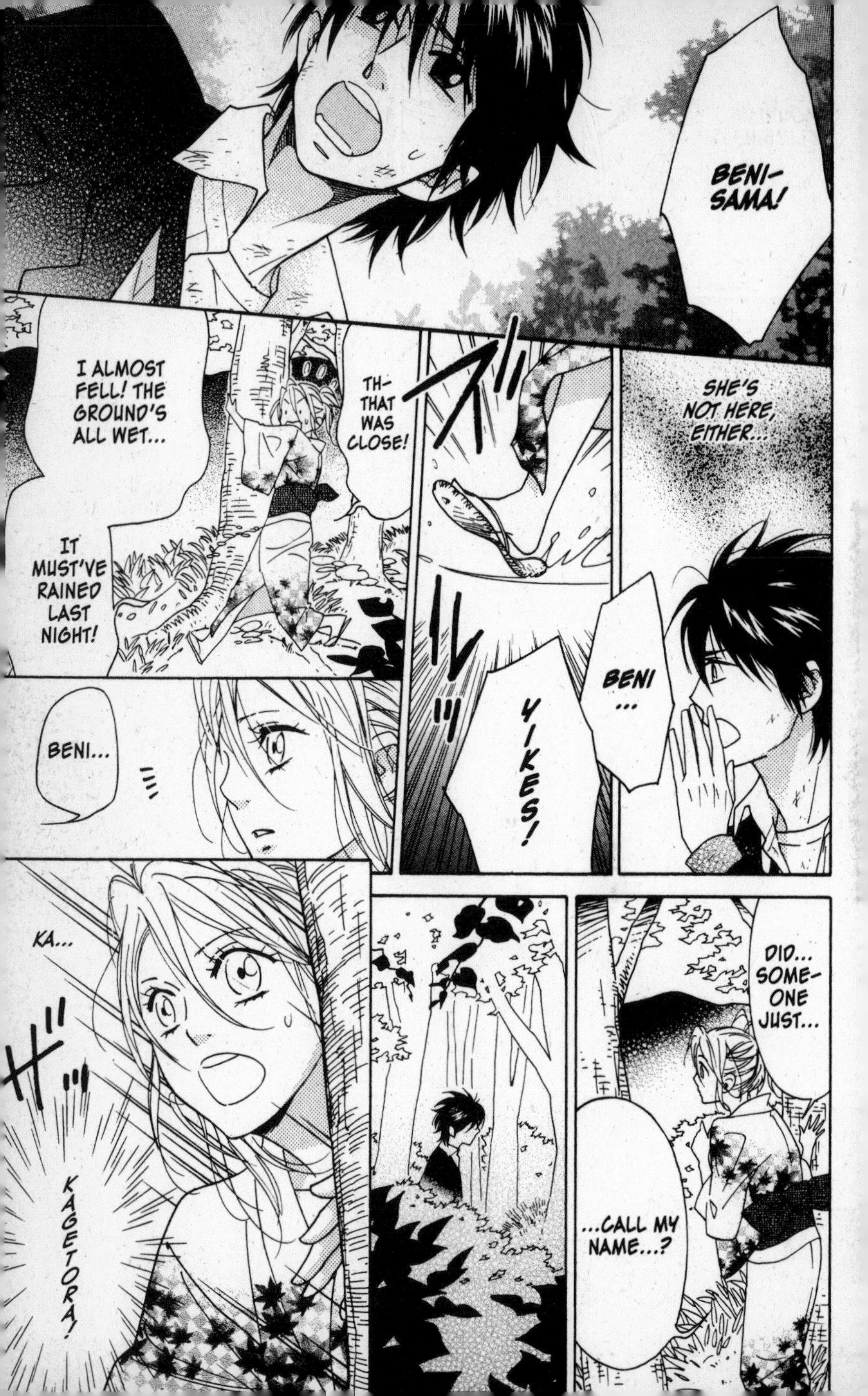
BENI-SAMA!
SHE'S NOT HERE, EITHER...
BENI...
TH-THAT WAS CLOSE!
YIKES!
I ALMOST FELL! THE GROUND'S ALL WET...
IT MUST'VE RAINED LAST NIGHT!
BENI...
DID... SOMEONE JUST...
...CALL MY NAME...?
KA...
KAGETORA!

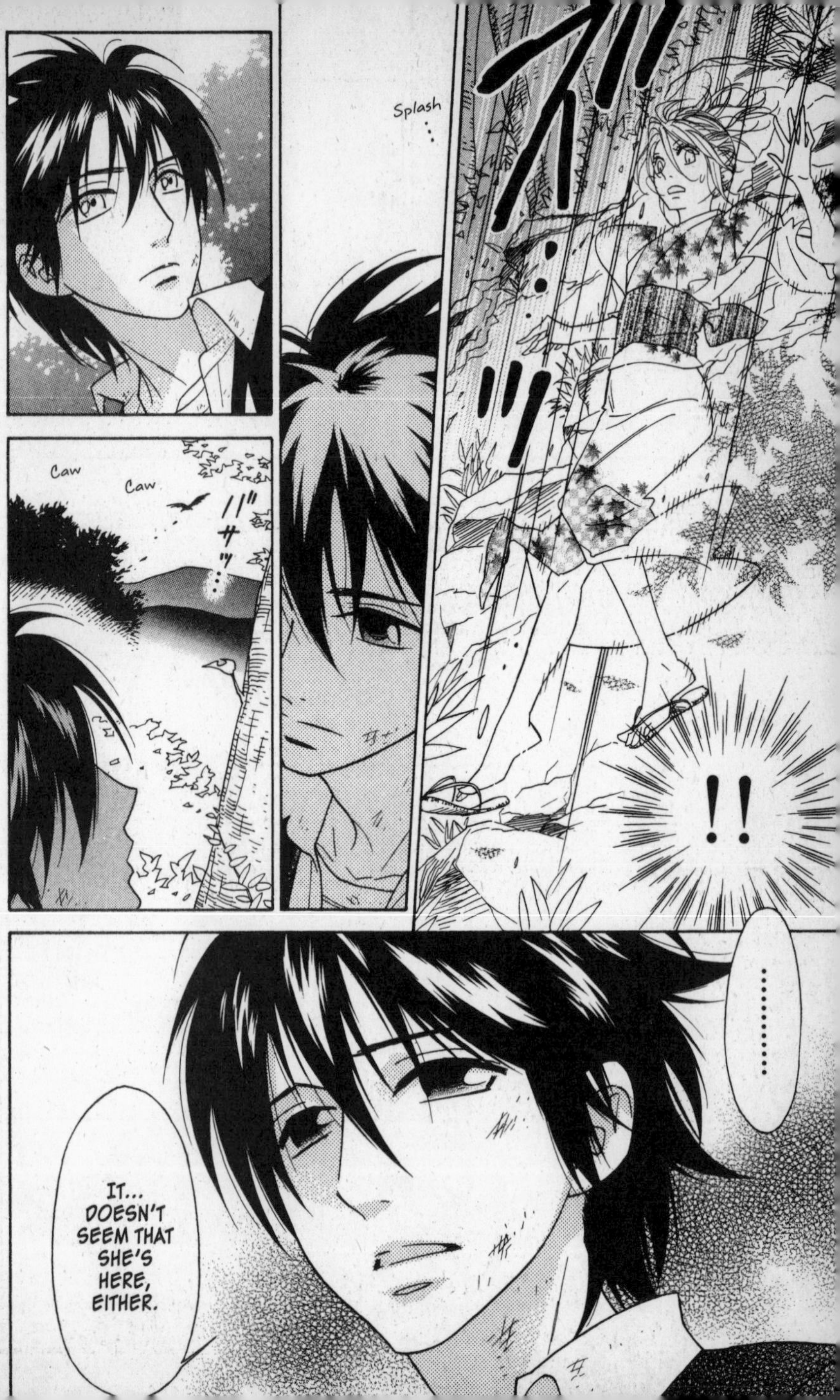

!!
Splash...
Caw
Caw
バサッ…
......
IT... DOESN'T SEEM THAT SHE'S HERE, EITHER.

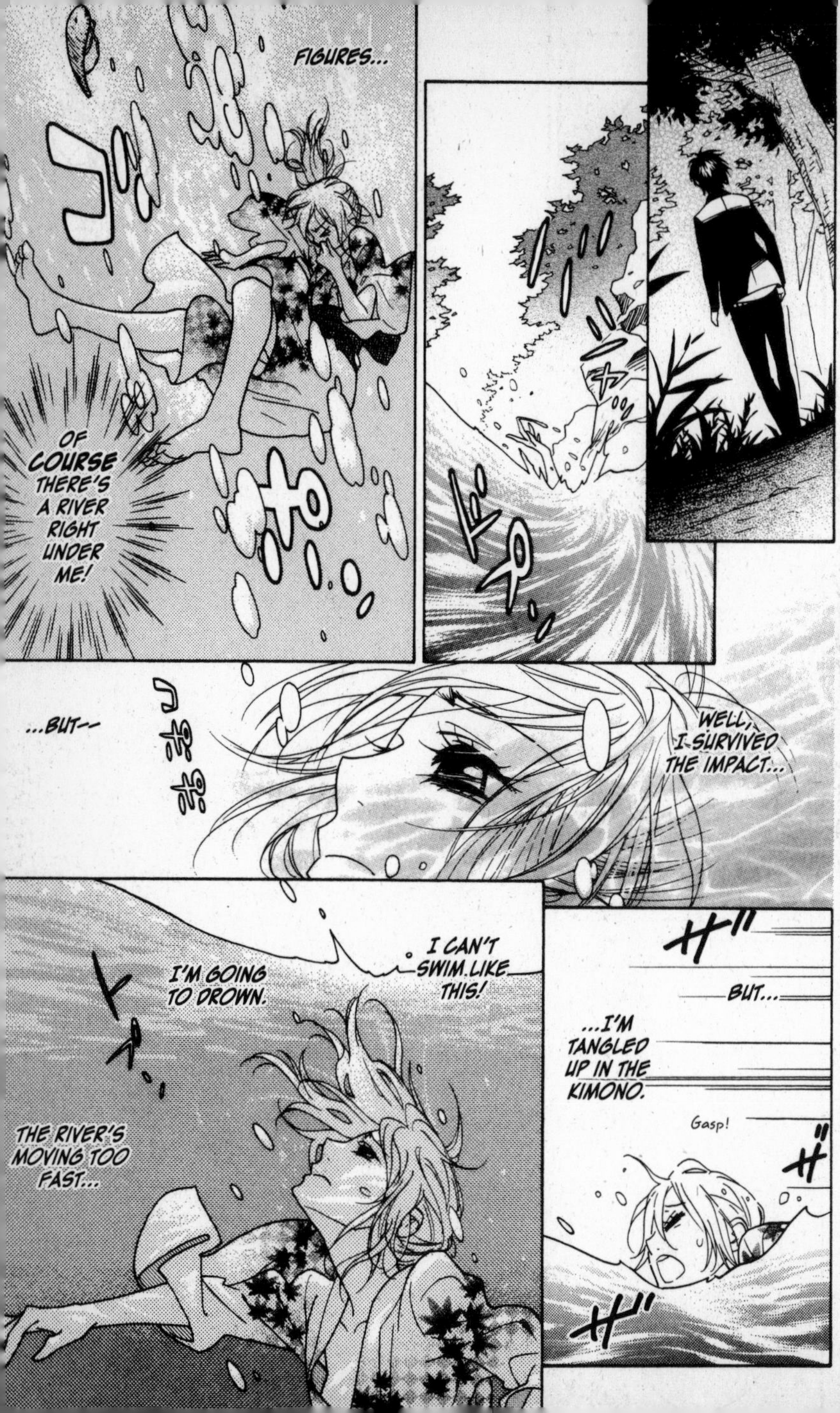
FIGURES...
OF COURSE THERE'S A RIVER RIGHT UNDER ME!
WELL, I SURVIVED THE IMPACT...
...BUT--
BUT...
...I'M TANGLED UP IN THE KIMONO.
Gasp!
I CAN'T SWIM LIKE THIS!
I'M GOING TO DROWN.
THE RIVER'S MOVING TOO FAST...

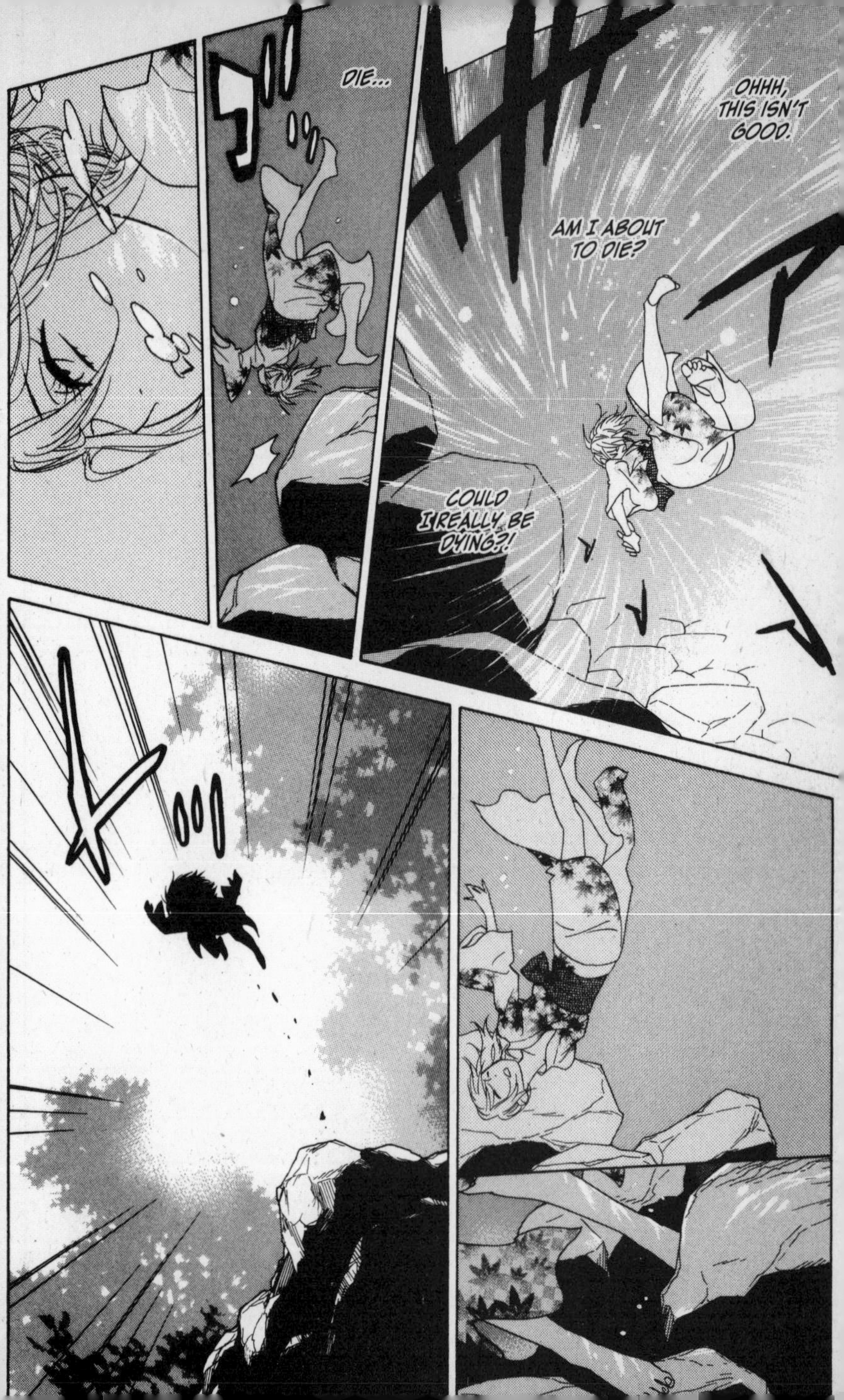
OHHH, THIS ISN'T GOOD.
AM I ABOUT TO DIE?
COULD I REALLY BE DYING?!
DIE...

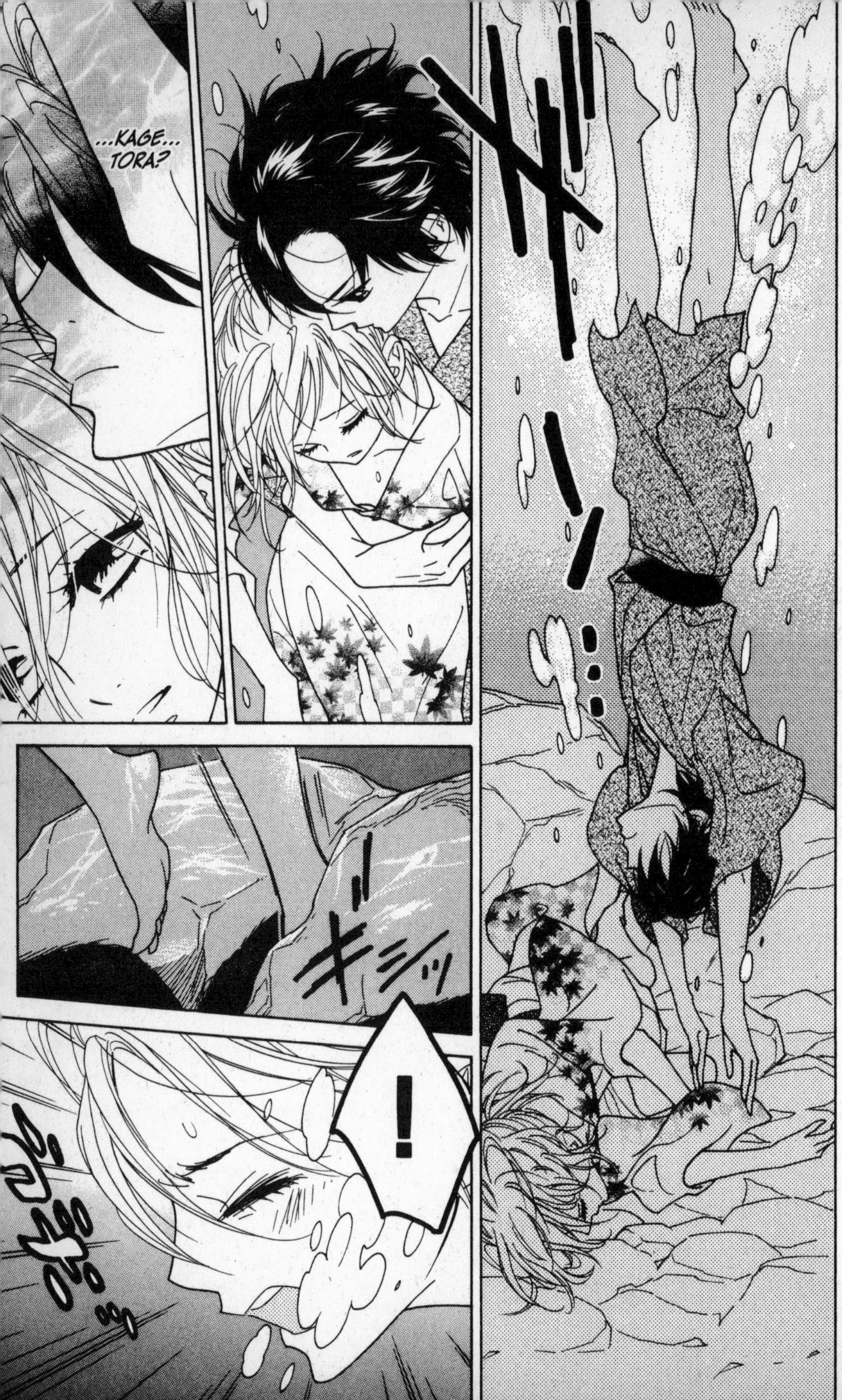
...KAGE... TORA?
ギシッ
!

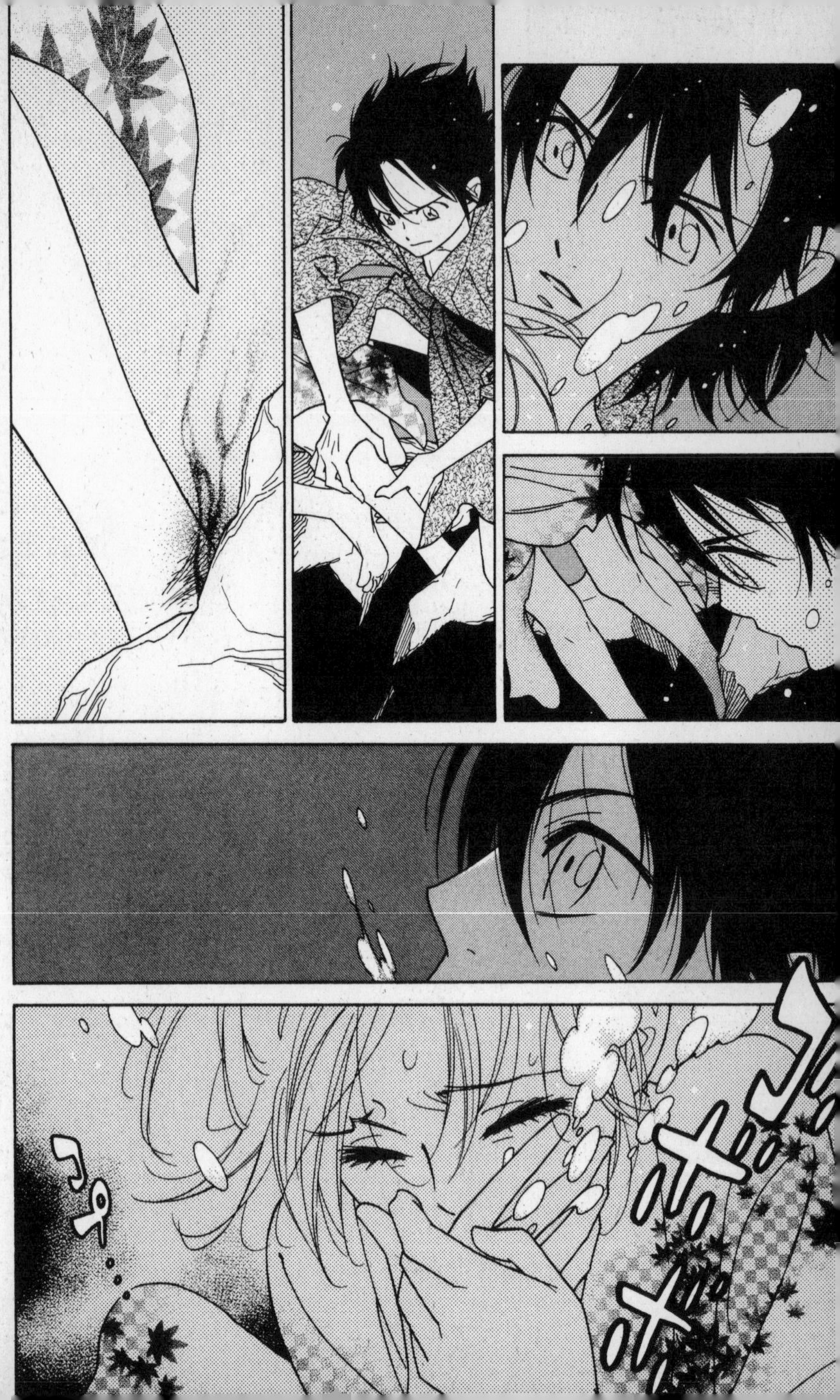
ゴボッ
ボッ
コプ…

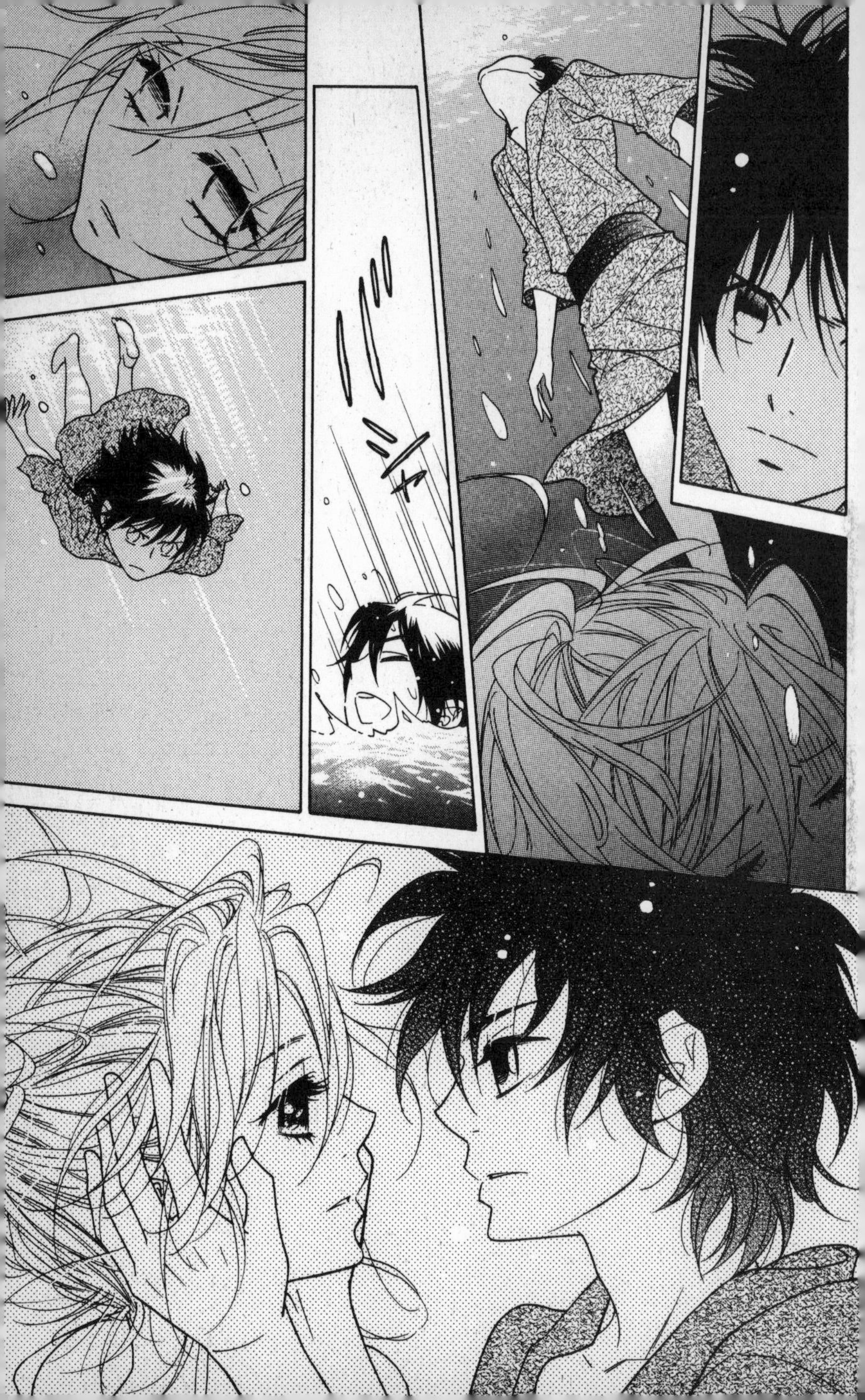

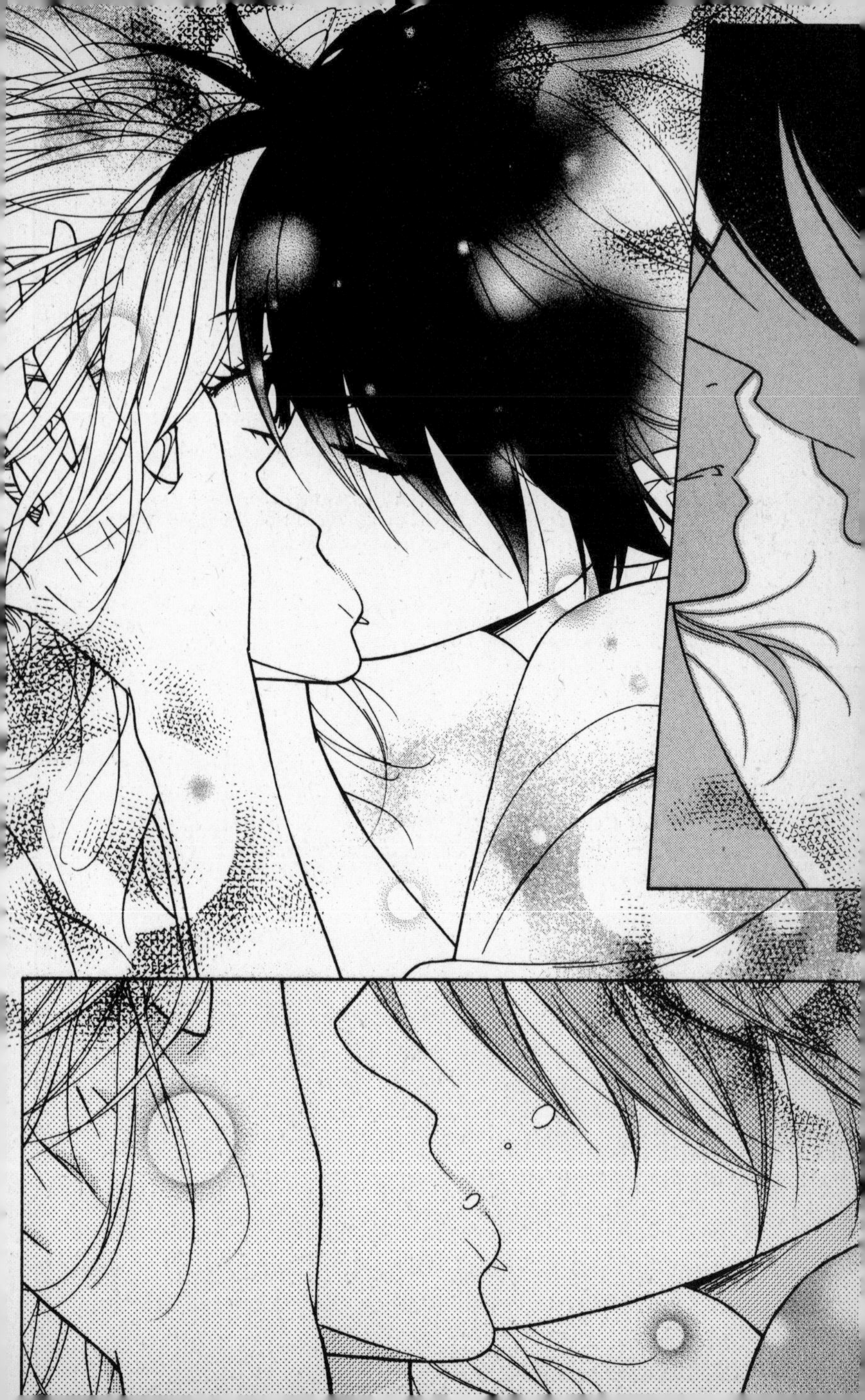

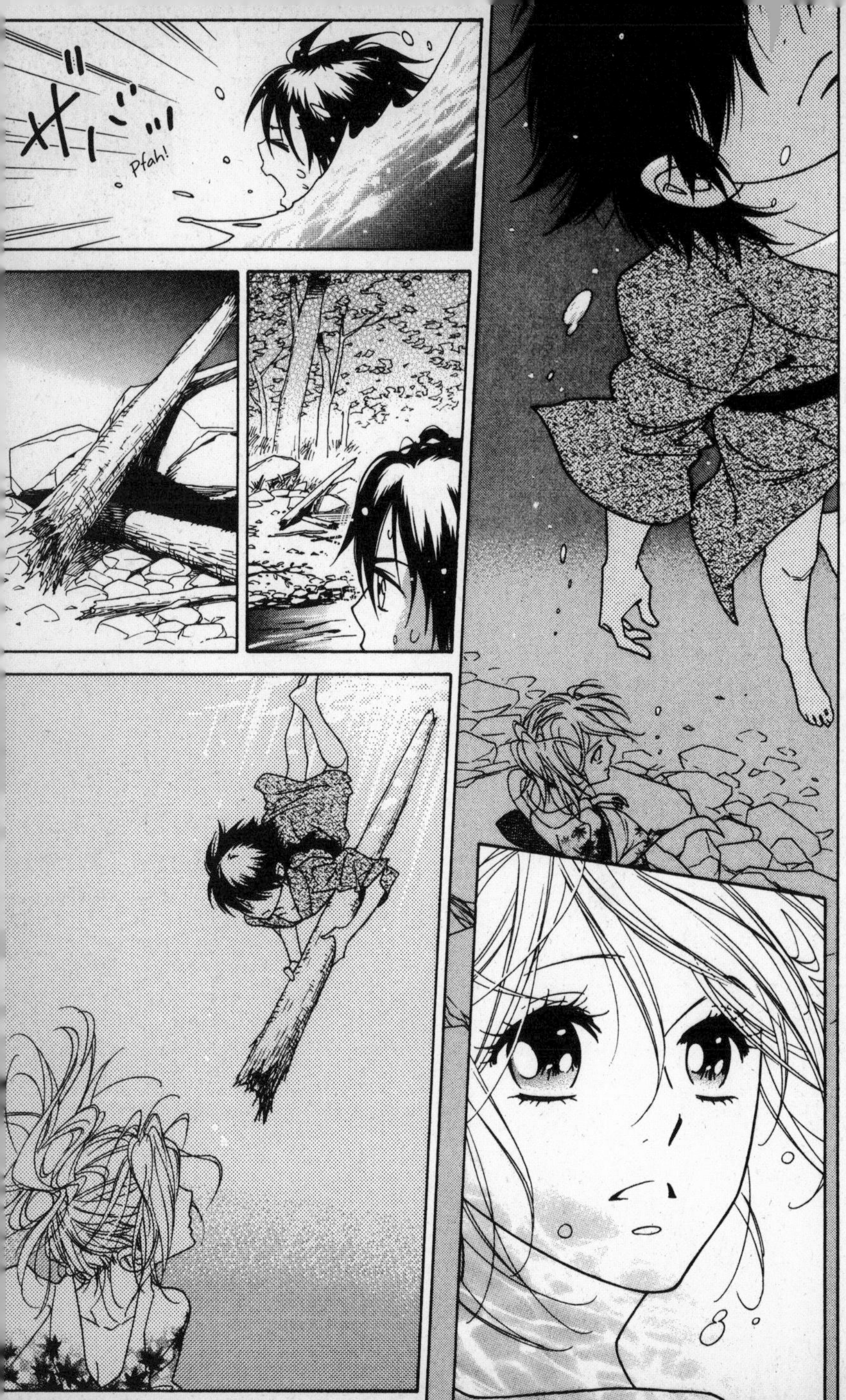
Pfah!

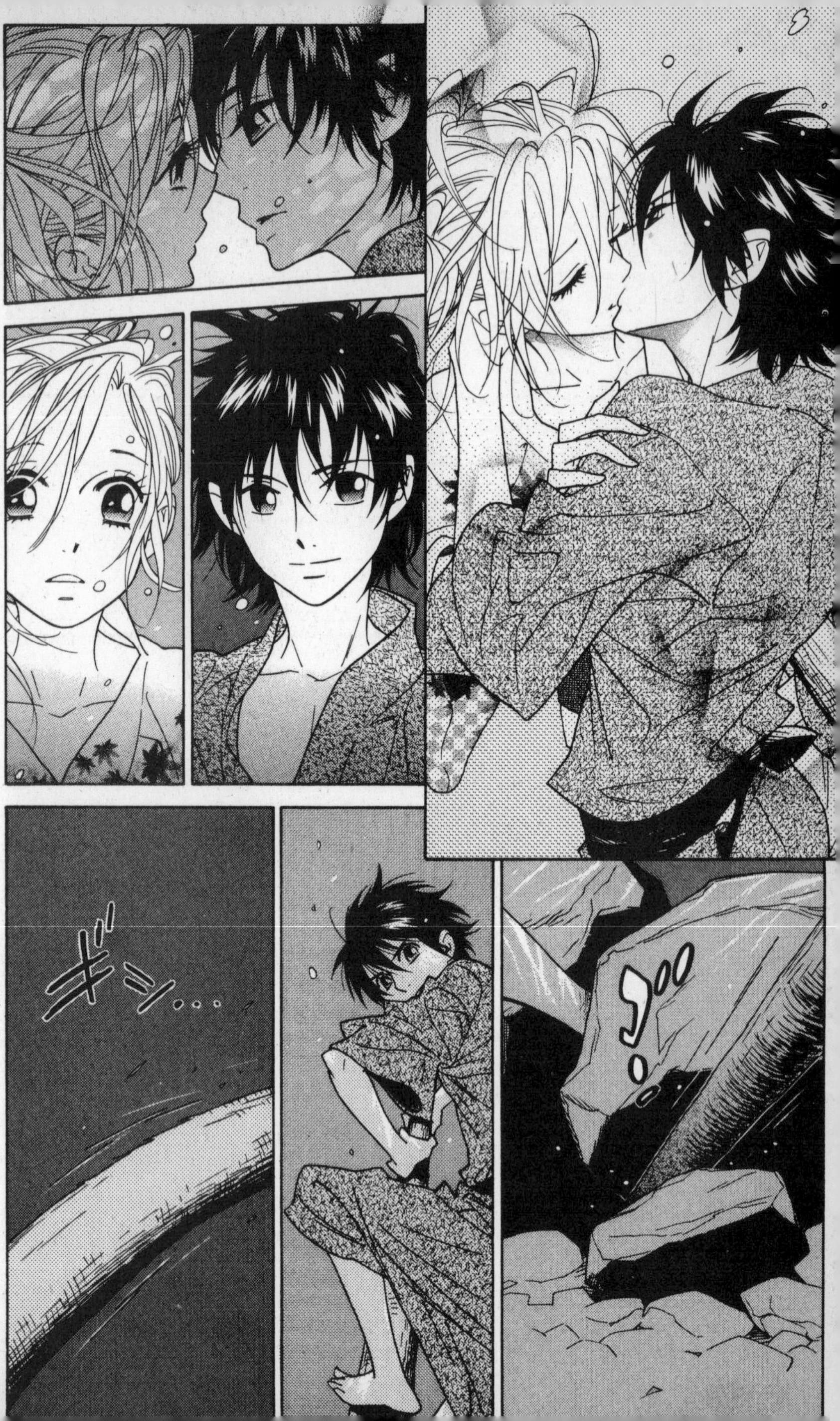
ゴ..
ギシ...

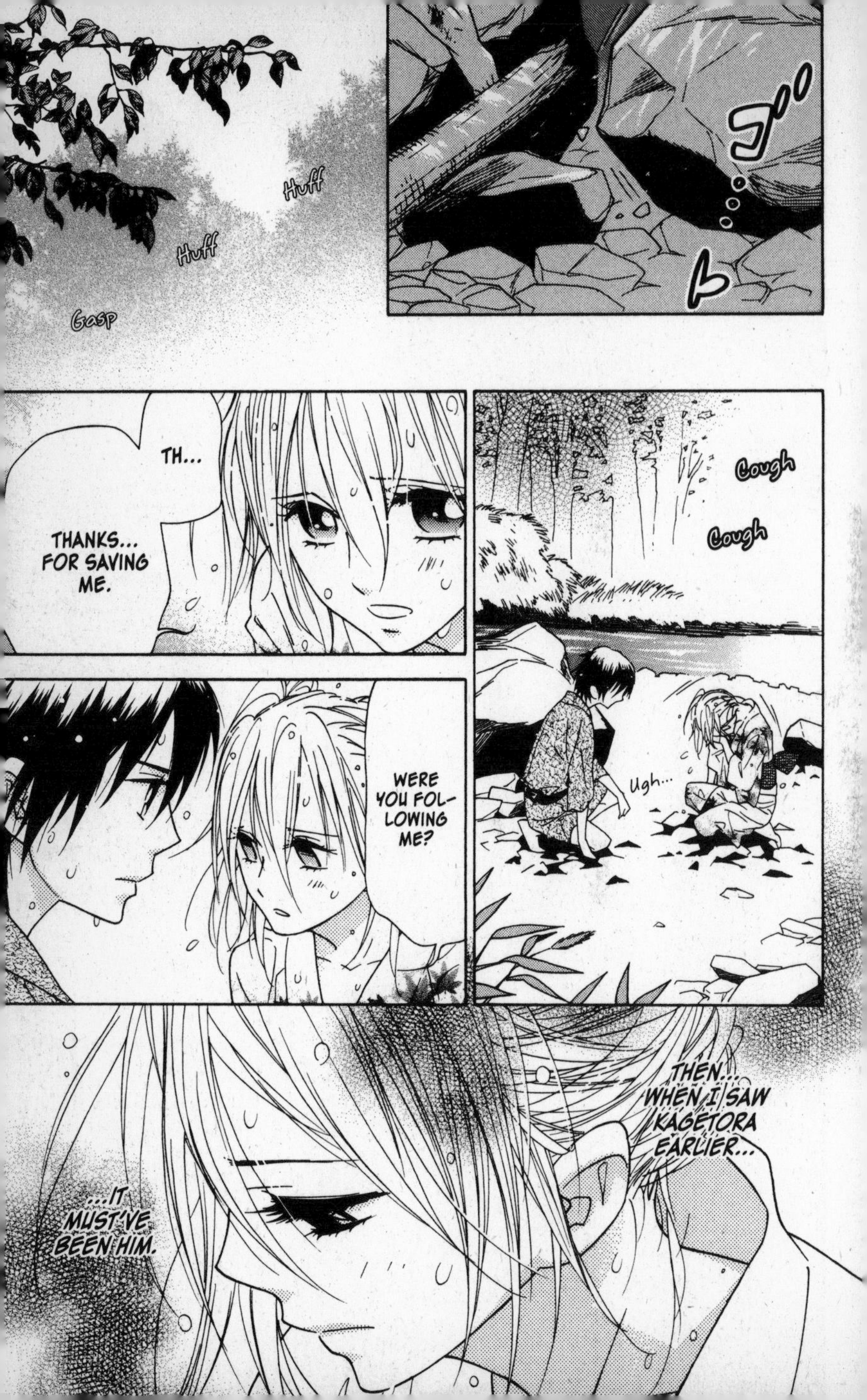
Huff
Huff
Gasp
Cough
Cough
Ugh...
TH...
THANKS... FOR SAVING ME.
WERE YOU FOL-LOWING ME?
THEN... WHEN I SAW KAGETORA EARLIER...
...IT MUST'VE BEEN HIM.

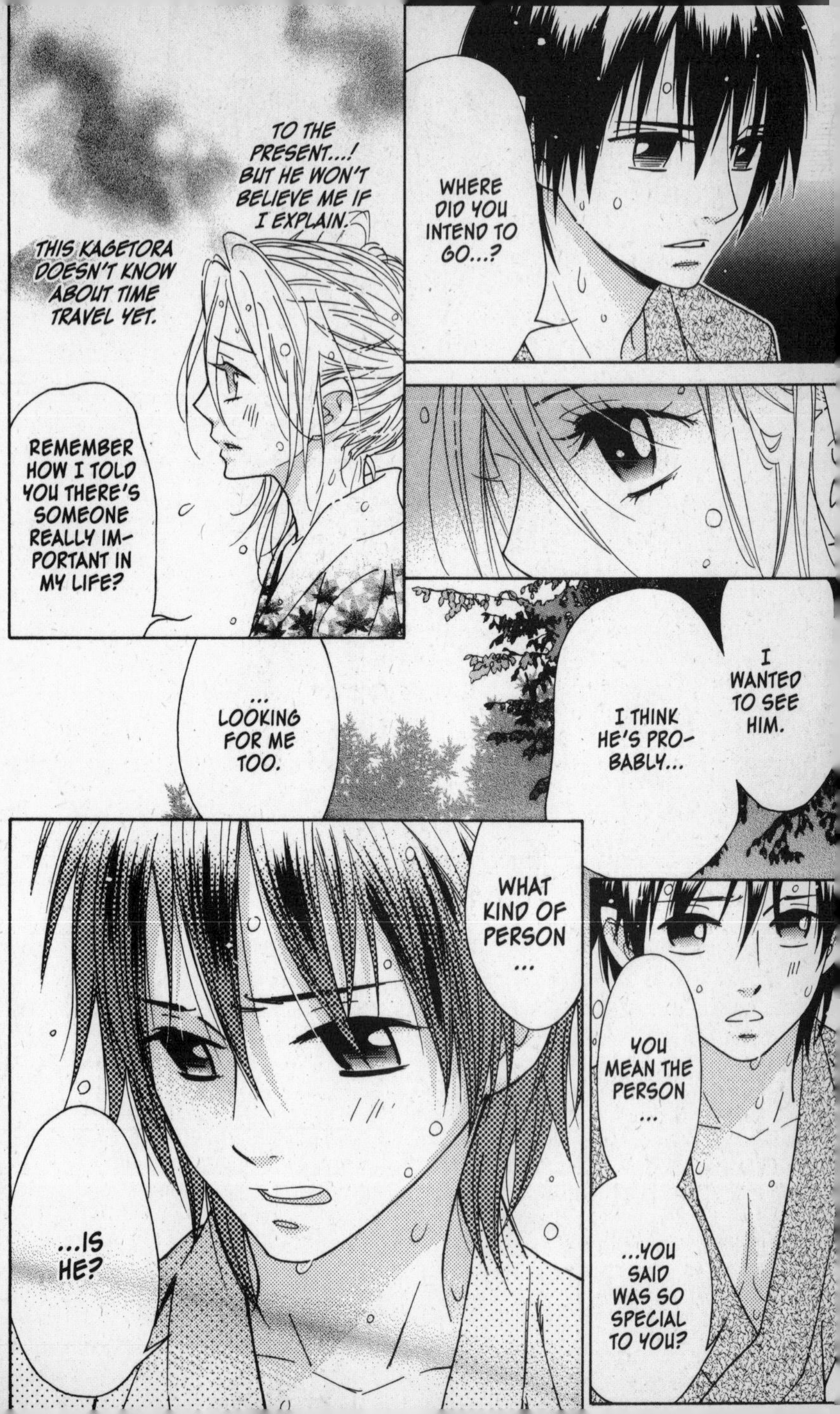
WHERE DID YOU INTEND TO GO...?
TO THE PRESENT...! BUT HE WON'T BELIEVE ME IF I EXPLAIN.
THIS KAGETORA DOESN'T KNOW ABOUT TIME TRAVEL YET.
REMEMBER HOW I TOLD YOU THERE'S SOMEONE REALLY IM-PORTANT IN MY LIFE?
I WANTED TO SEE HIM.
I THINK HE'S PRO-BABLY...
...LOOKING FOR ME TOO.
YOU MEAN THE PERSON...
...YOU SAID WAS SO SPECIAL TO YOU?
WHAT KIND OF PERSON...
...IS HE?

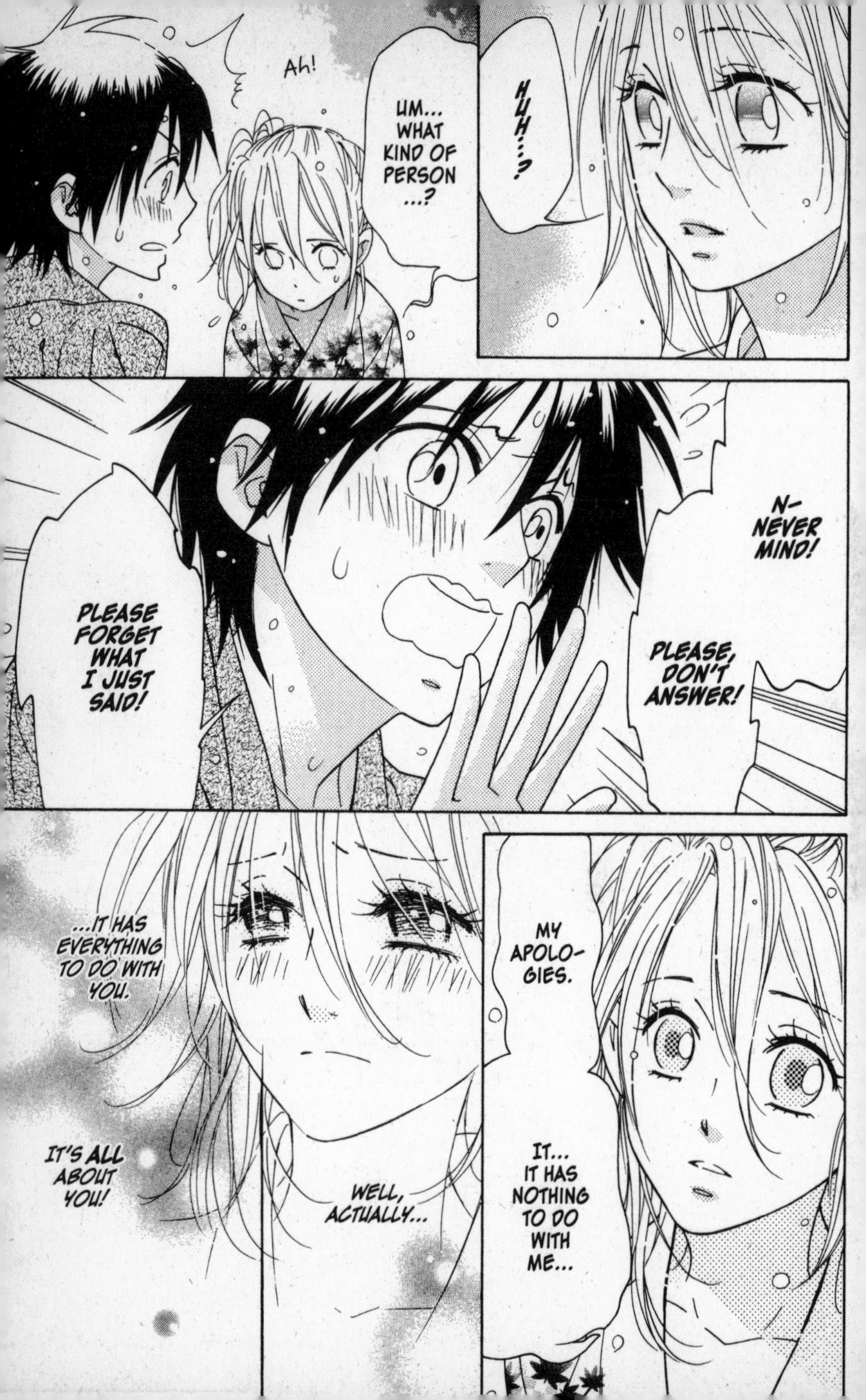
HUH...?
UM... WHAT KIND OF PERSON ...?
Ah!
N-NEVER MIND!
PLEASE, DON'T ANSWER!
PLEASE FORGET WHAT I JUST SAID!
MY APOLOGIES.
IT... IT HAS NOTHING TO DO WITH ME...
WELL, ACTUALLY...
...IT HAS EVERYTHING TO DO WITH YOU.
IT'S ALL ABOUT YOU!

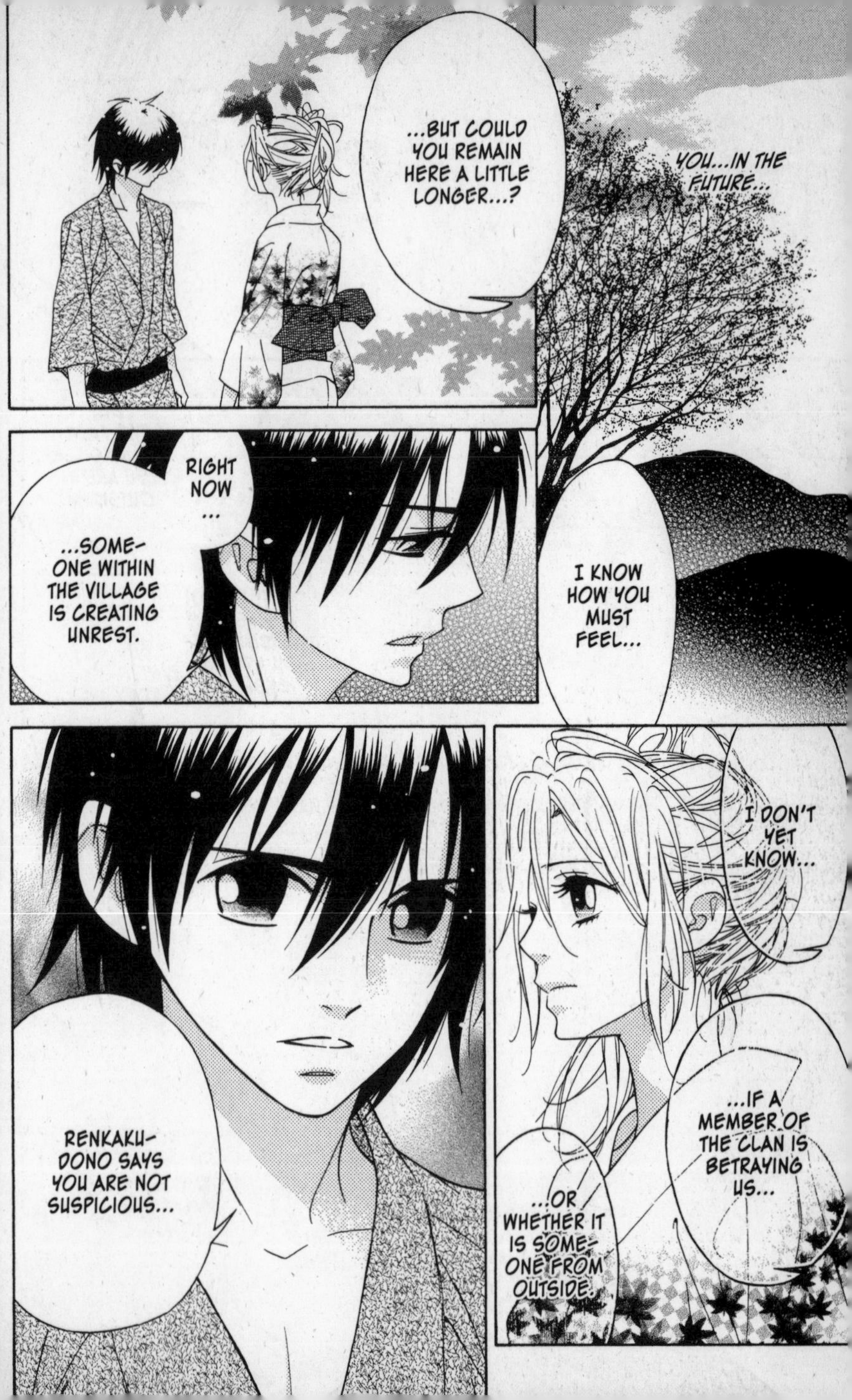
YOU...IN THE FUTURE...
...BUT COULD YOU REMAIN HERE A LITTLE LONGER...?
I KNOW HOW YOU MUST FEEL...
RIGHT NOW...
...SOME-ONE WITHIN THE VILLAGE IS CREATING UNREST.
I DON'T YET KNOW...
...IF A MEMBER OF THE CLAN IS BETRAYING US...
...OR WHETHER IT IS SOME-ONE FROM OUTSIDE.
RENKAKU-DONO SAYS YOU ARE NOT SUSPICIOUS...

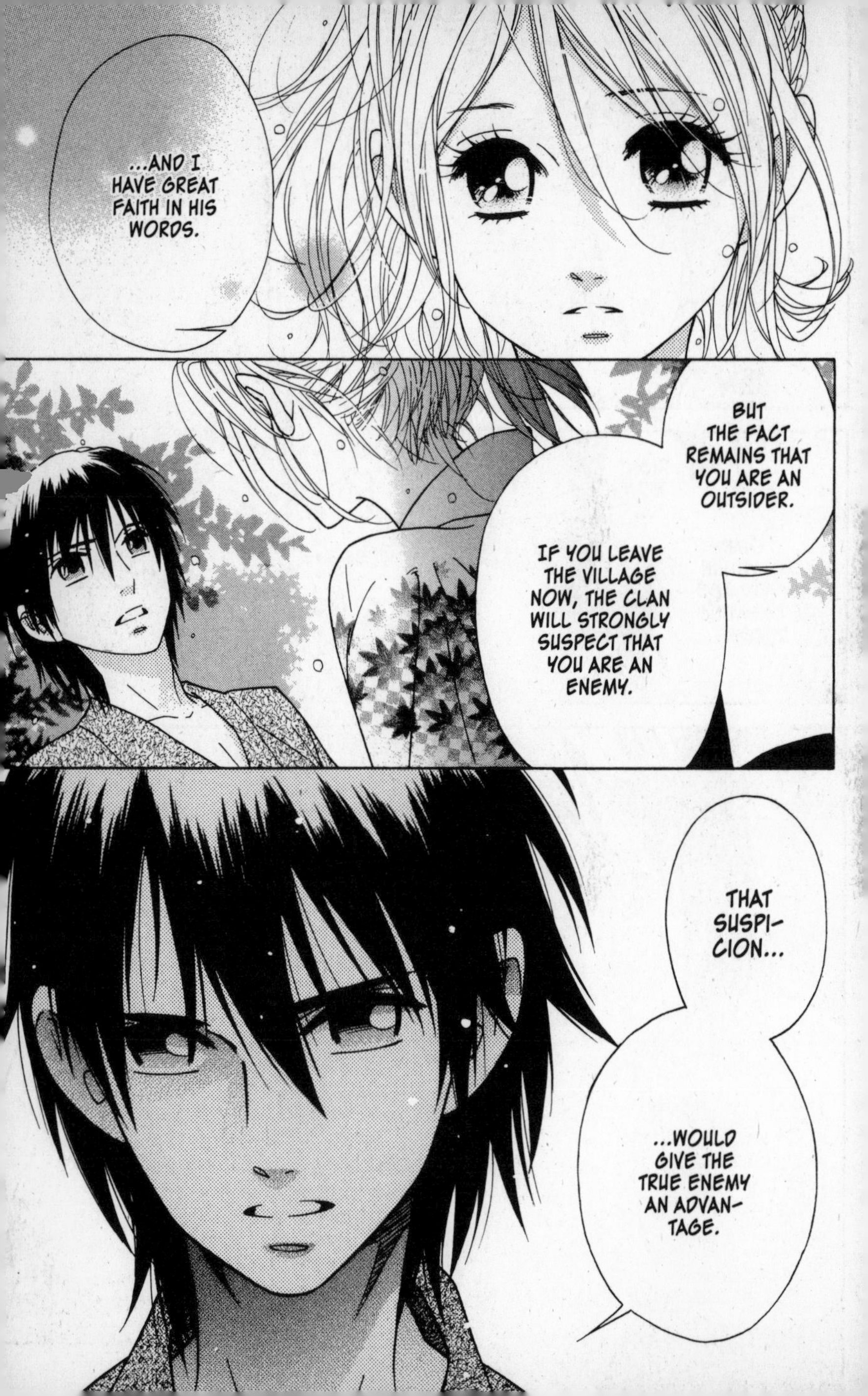
...AND I HAVE GREAT FAITH IN HIS WORDS.
BUT THE FACT REMAINS THAT YOU ARE AN OUTSIDER.
IF YOU LEAVE THE VILLAGE NOW, THE CLAN WILL STRONGLY SUSPECT THAT YOU ARE AN ENEMY.
THAT SUSPI-CION...
...WOULD GIVE THE TRUE ENEMY AN ADVAN-TAGE.

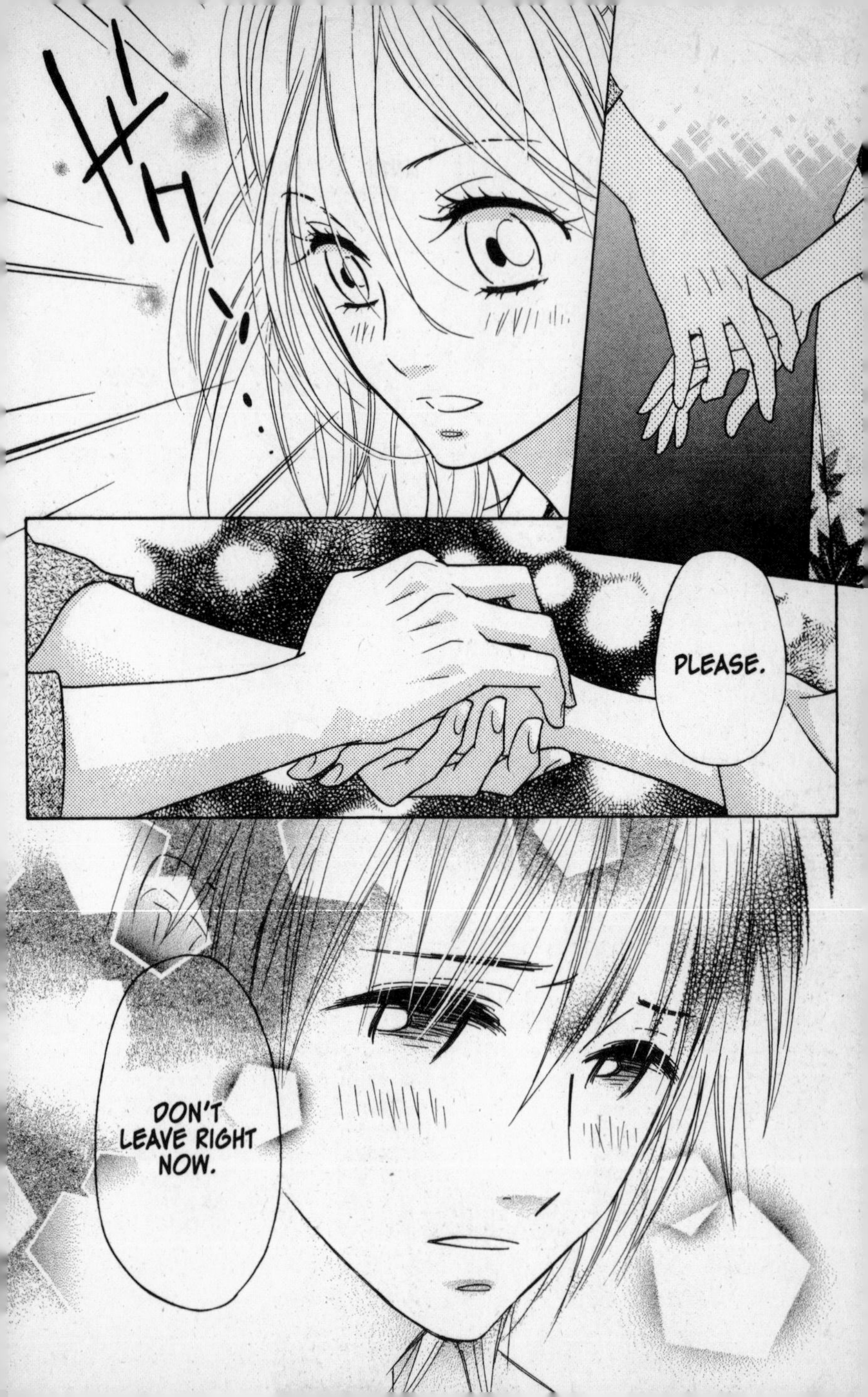
PLEASE.
DON'T LEAVE RIGHT NOW.

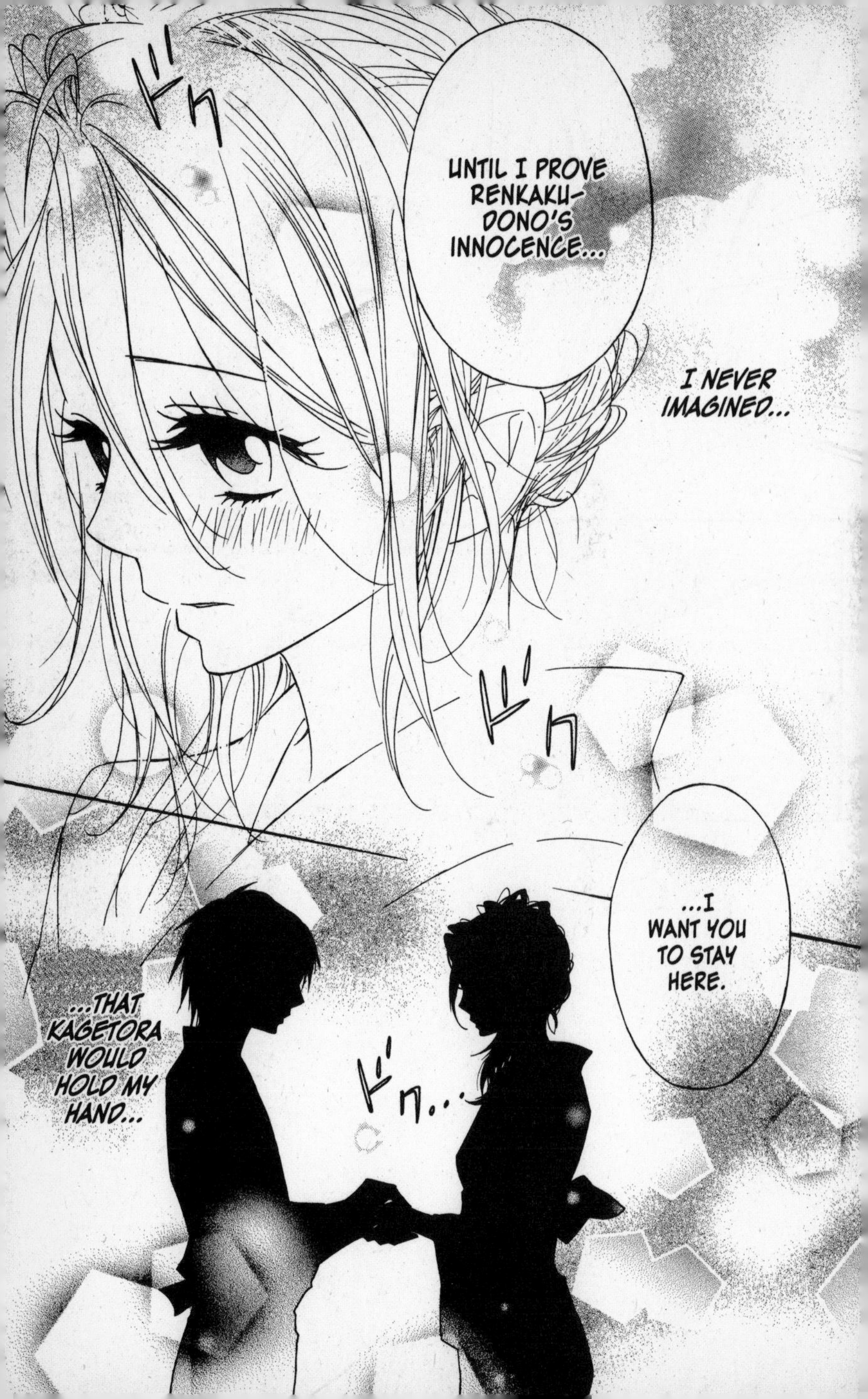
UNTIL I PROVE RENKAKU-DONO'S INNOCENCE...
ドク
I NEVER IMAGINED...
ドク
...I WANT YOU TO STAY HERE.
...THAT KAGETORA WOULD HOLD MY HAND...
ドク...

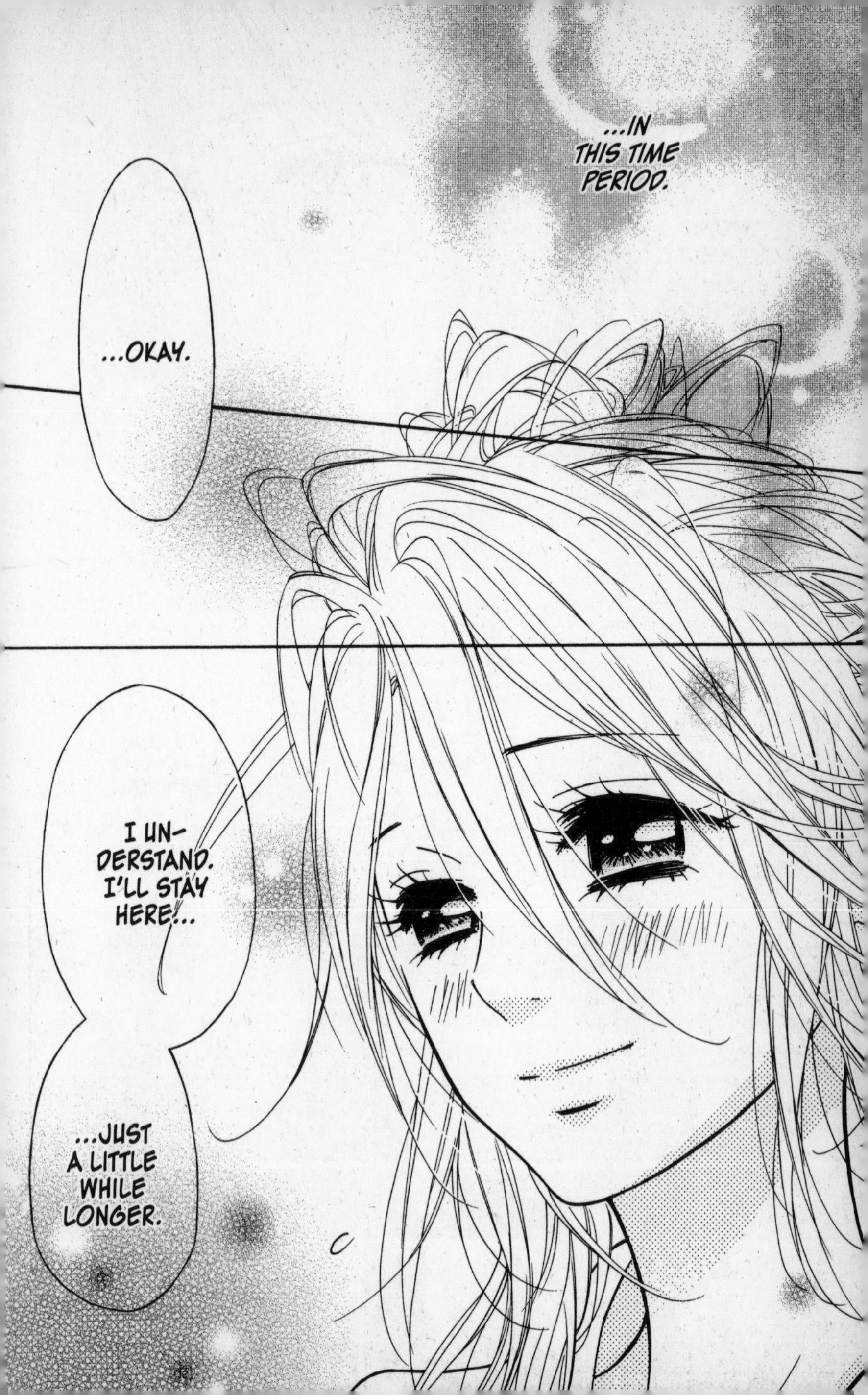
...IN THIS TIME PERIOD.
...OKAY.
I UNDERSTAND. I'LL STAY HERE...
...JUST A LITTLE WHILE LONGER.

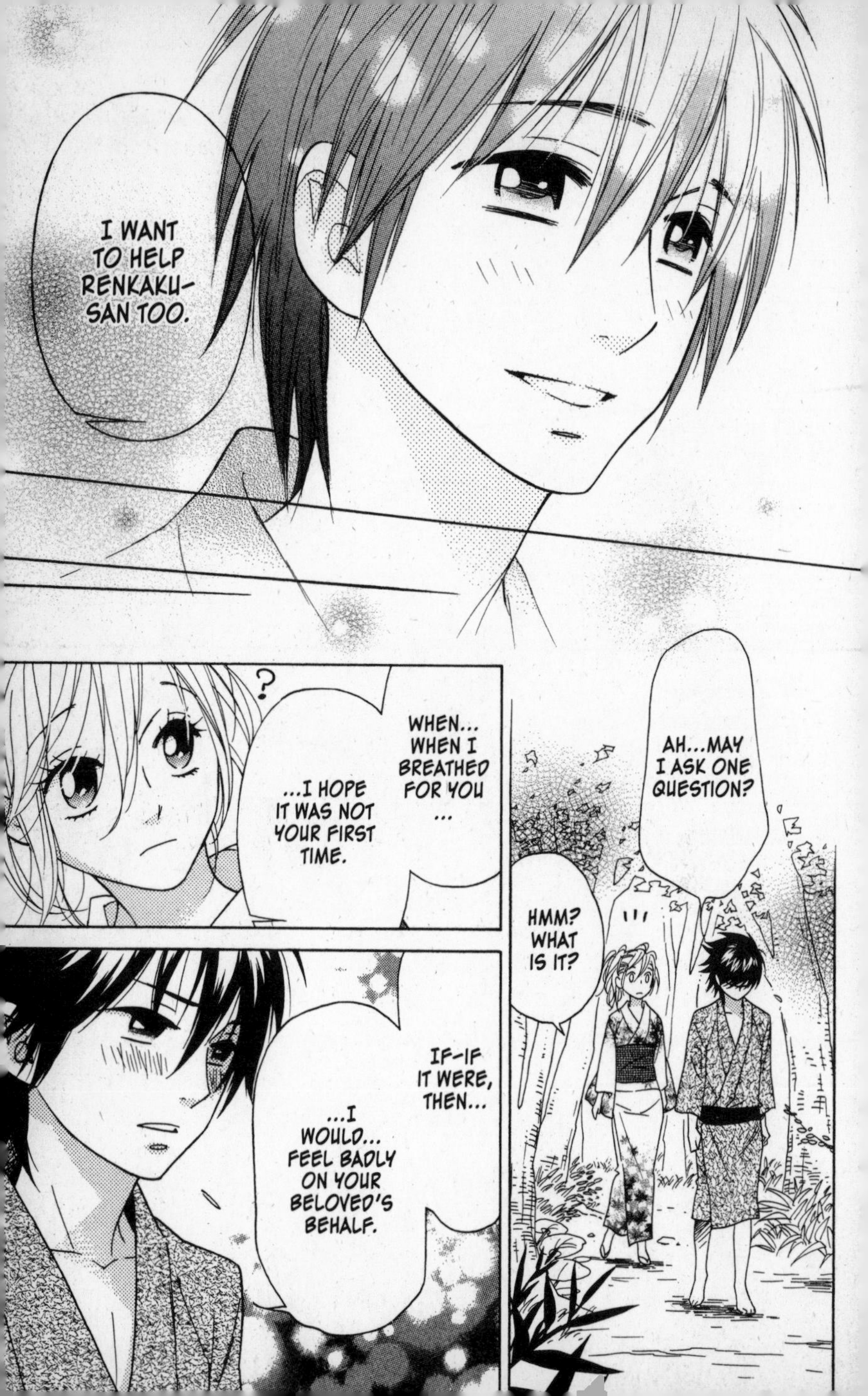
I WANT TO HELP RENKAKU-SAN TOO.
AH...MAY I ASK ONE QUESTION?
HMM? WHAT IS IT?
WHEN... WHEN I BREATHED FOR YOU ...
...I HOPE IT WAS NOT YOUR FIRST TIME.
IF-IF IT WERE, THEN...
...I WOULD... FEEL BADLY ON YOUR BELOVED'S BEHALF.

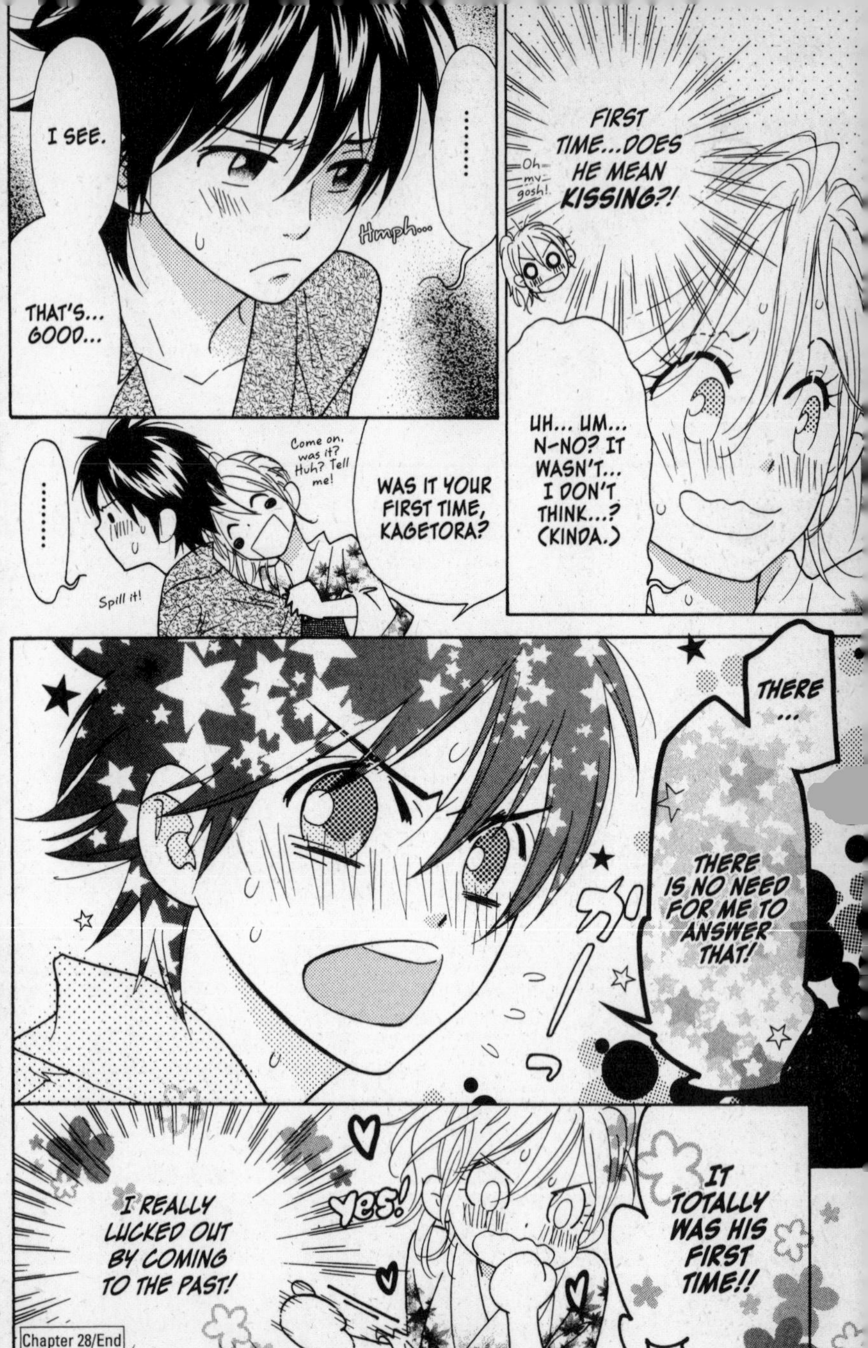
FIRST TIME...DOES HE MEAN KISSING?!
Oh my gosh!
UH... UM... N-NO? IT WASN'T... I DON'T THINK...? (KINDA.)
......
Hmph...
I SEE.
THAT'S... GOOD...
WAS IT YOUR FIRST TIME, KAGETORA?
Come on, was it? Huh? Tell me!
Spill it!
......
THERE...
THERE IS NO NEED FOR ME TO ANSWER THAT!
IT TOTALLY WAS HIS FIRST TIME!!
YES!
I REALLY LUCKED OUT BY COMING TO THE PAST!
Chapter 28/End

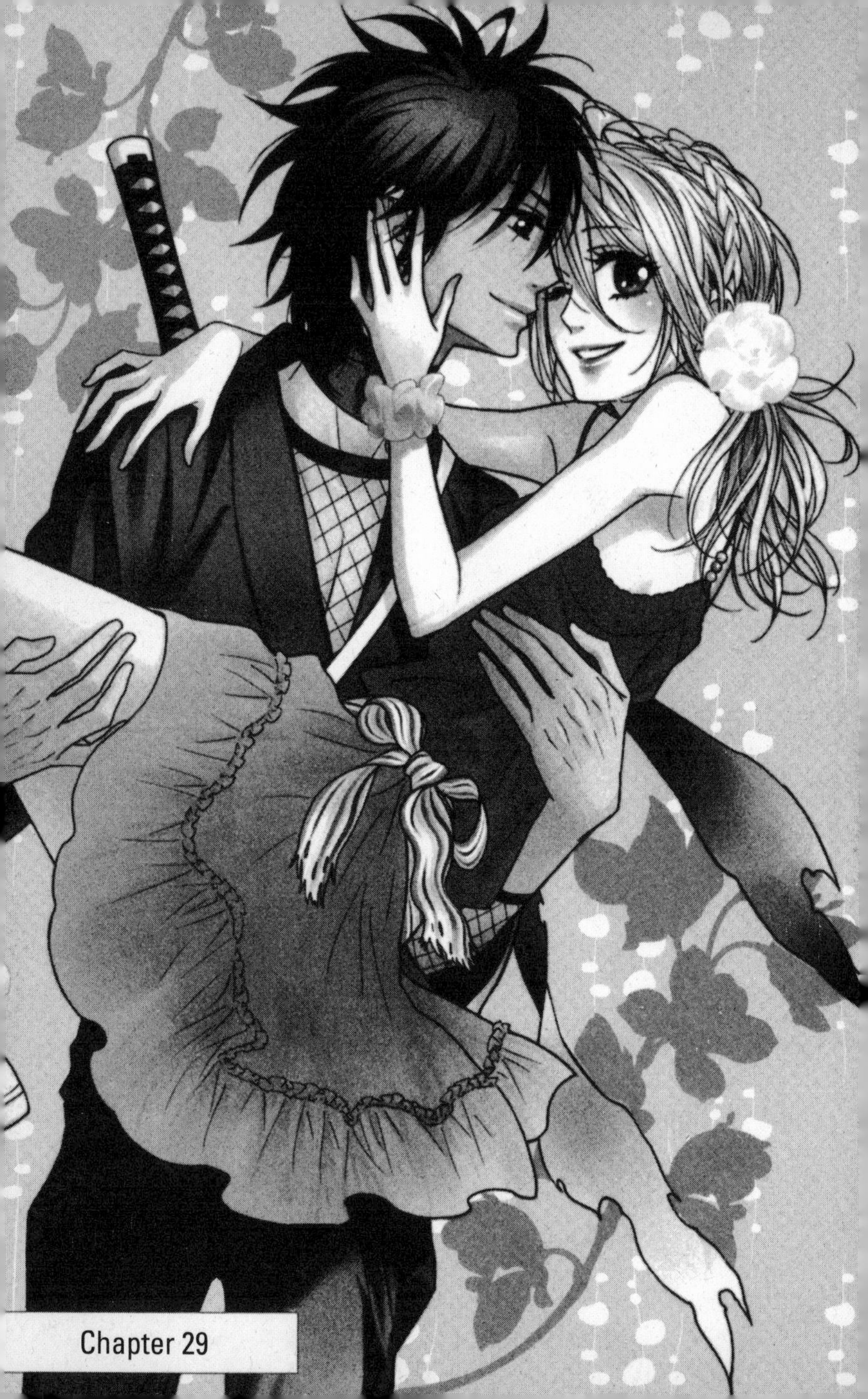

Chapter 29

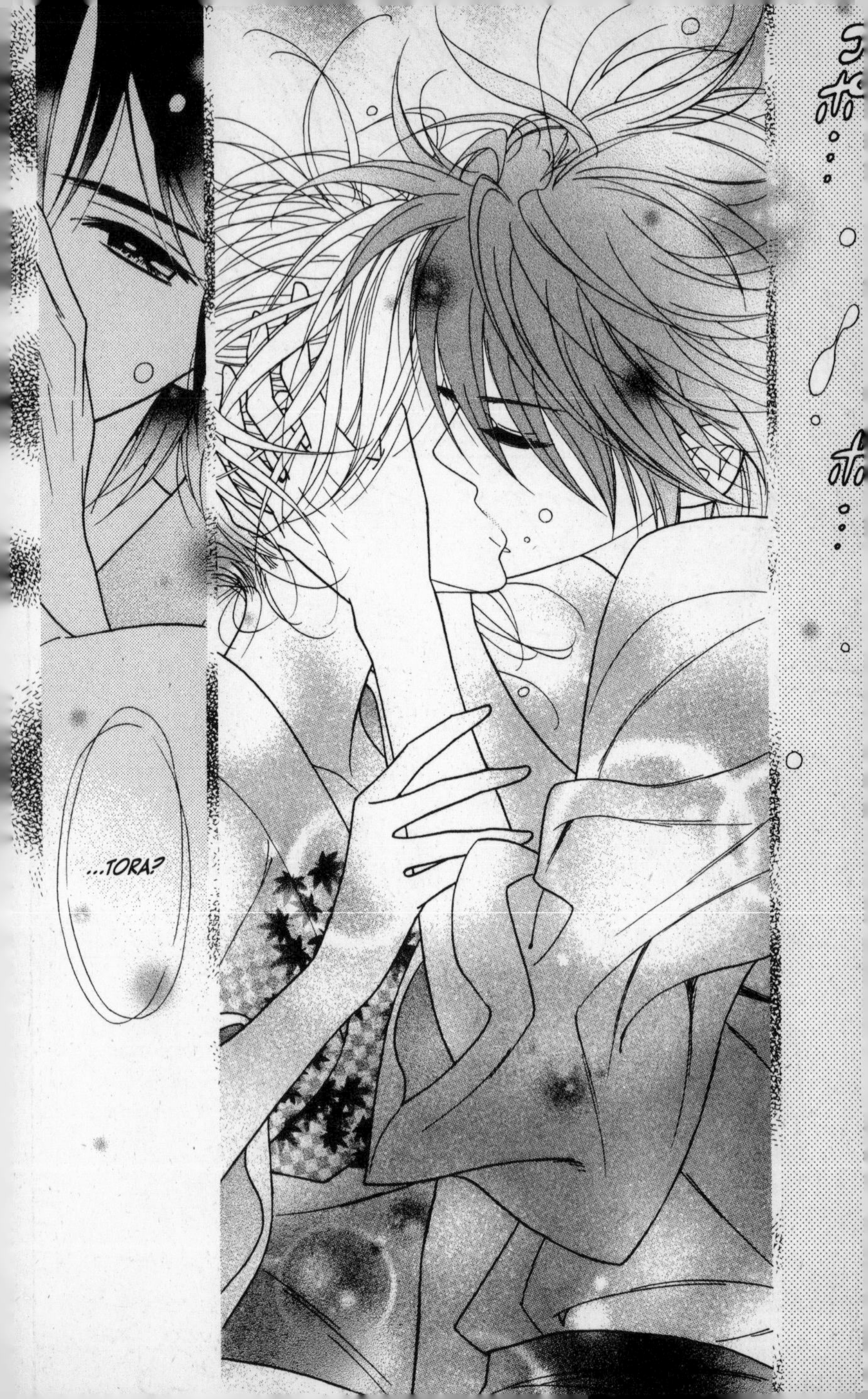
...TORA?

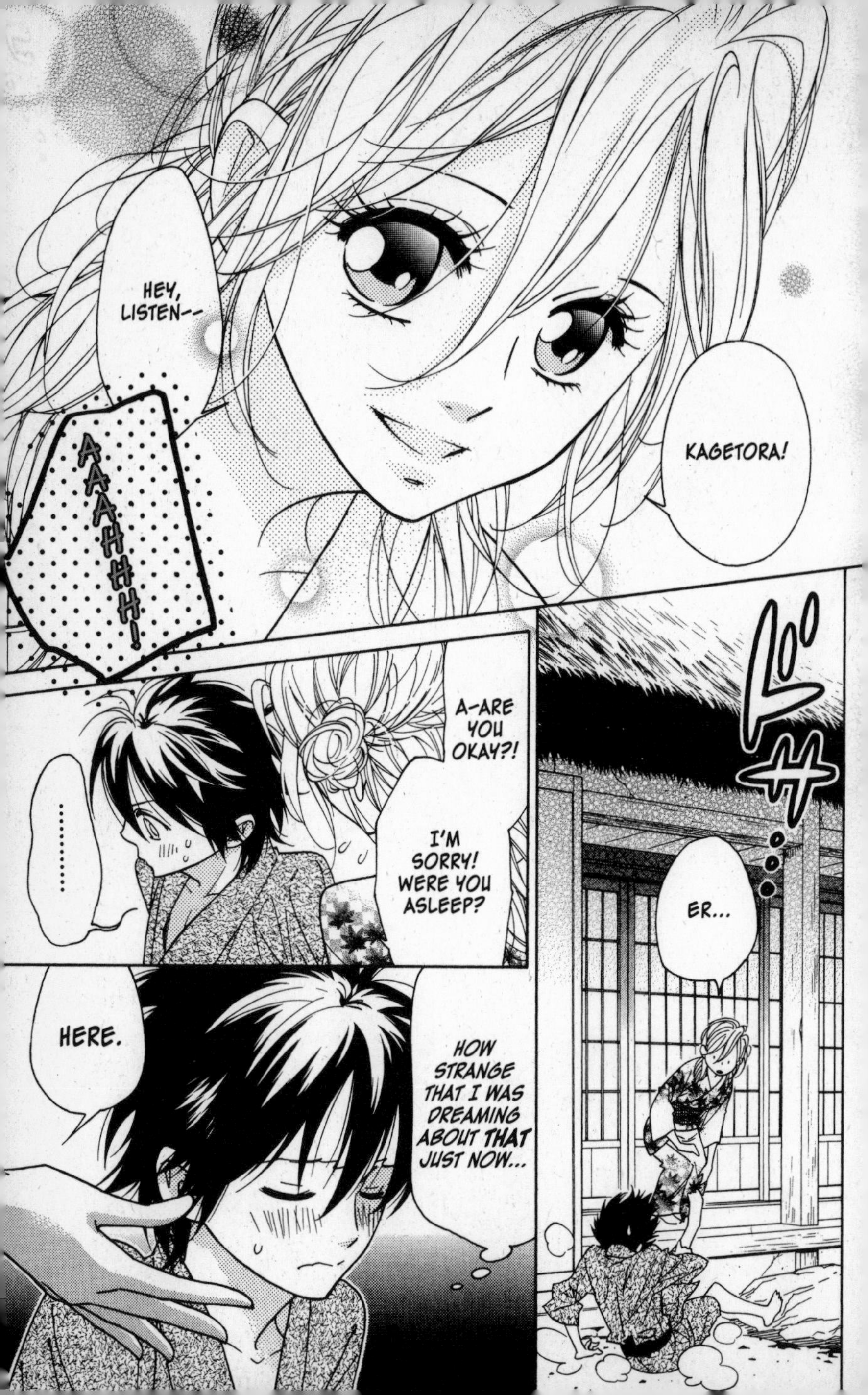
KAGETORA!
HEY, LISTEN--
AAAHHHH!
ER...
A-ARE YOU OKAY?!
I'M SORRY! WERE YOU ASLEEP?
......
HOW STRANGE THAT I WAS DREAMING ABOUT THAT JUST NOW...
HERE.

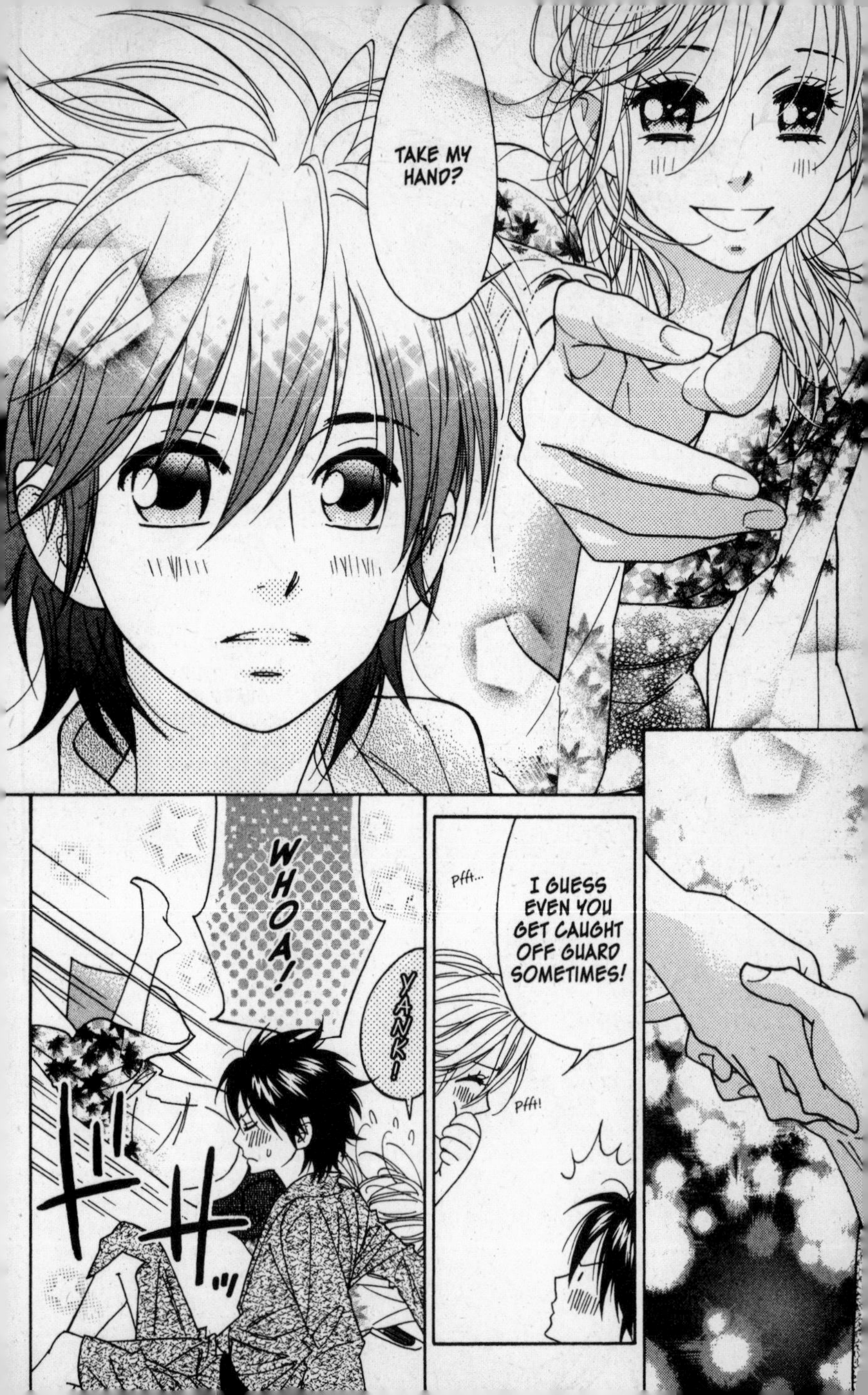
TAKE MY HAND?
Pfft...
I GUESS EVEN YOU GET CAUGHT OFF GUARD SOMETIMES!
Pfft!
WHOA!
YANK!

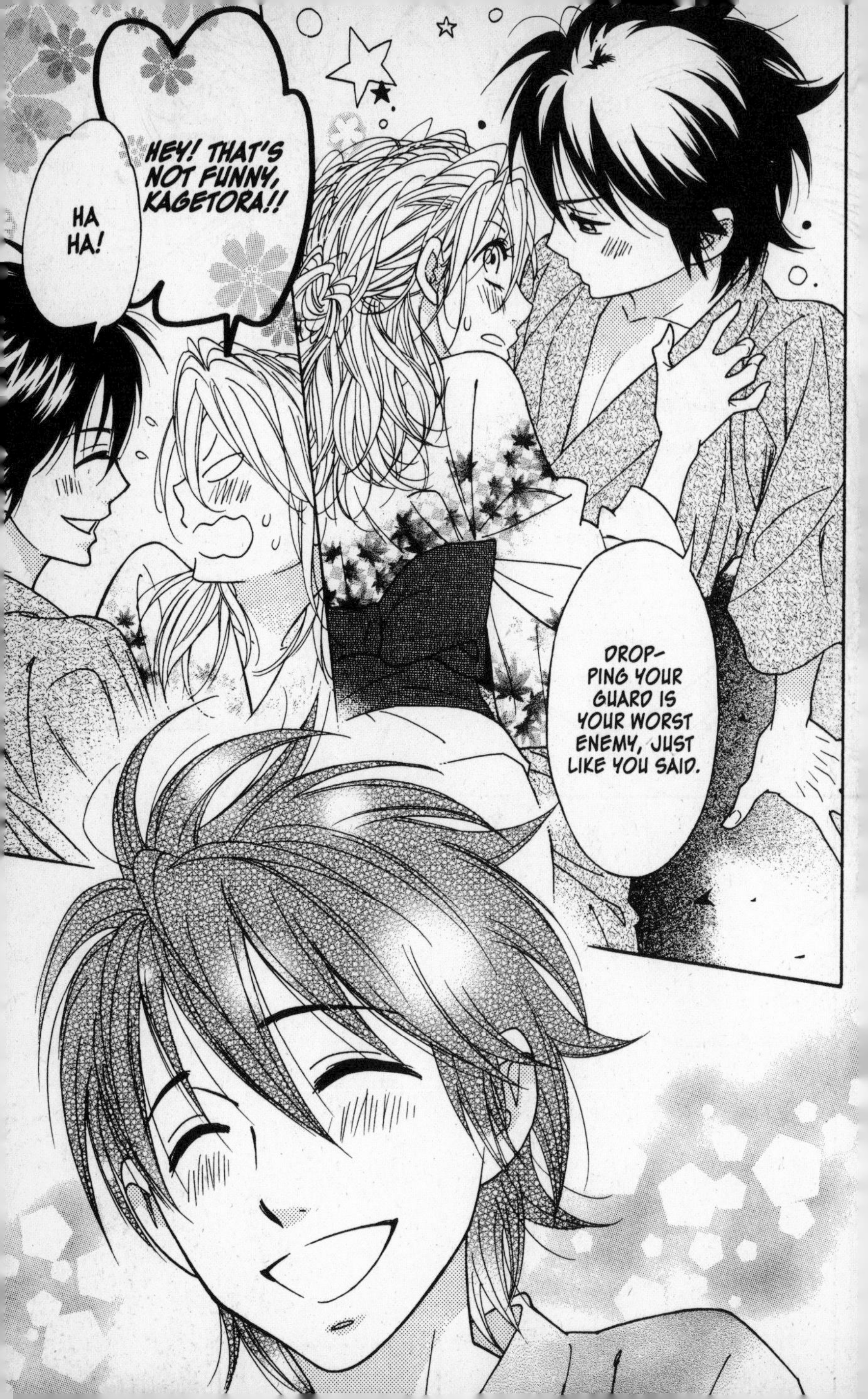
DROPPING YOUR GUARD IS YOUR WORST ENEMY, JUST LIKE YOU SAID.
HEY! THAT'S NOT FUNNY, KAGETORA!!
HA HA!

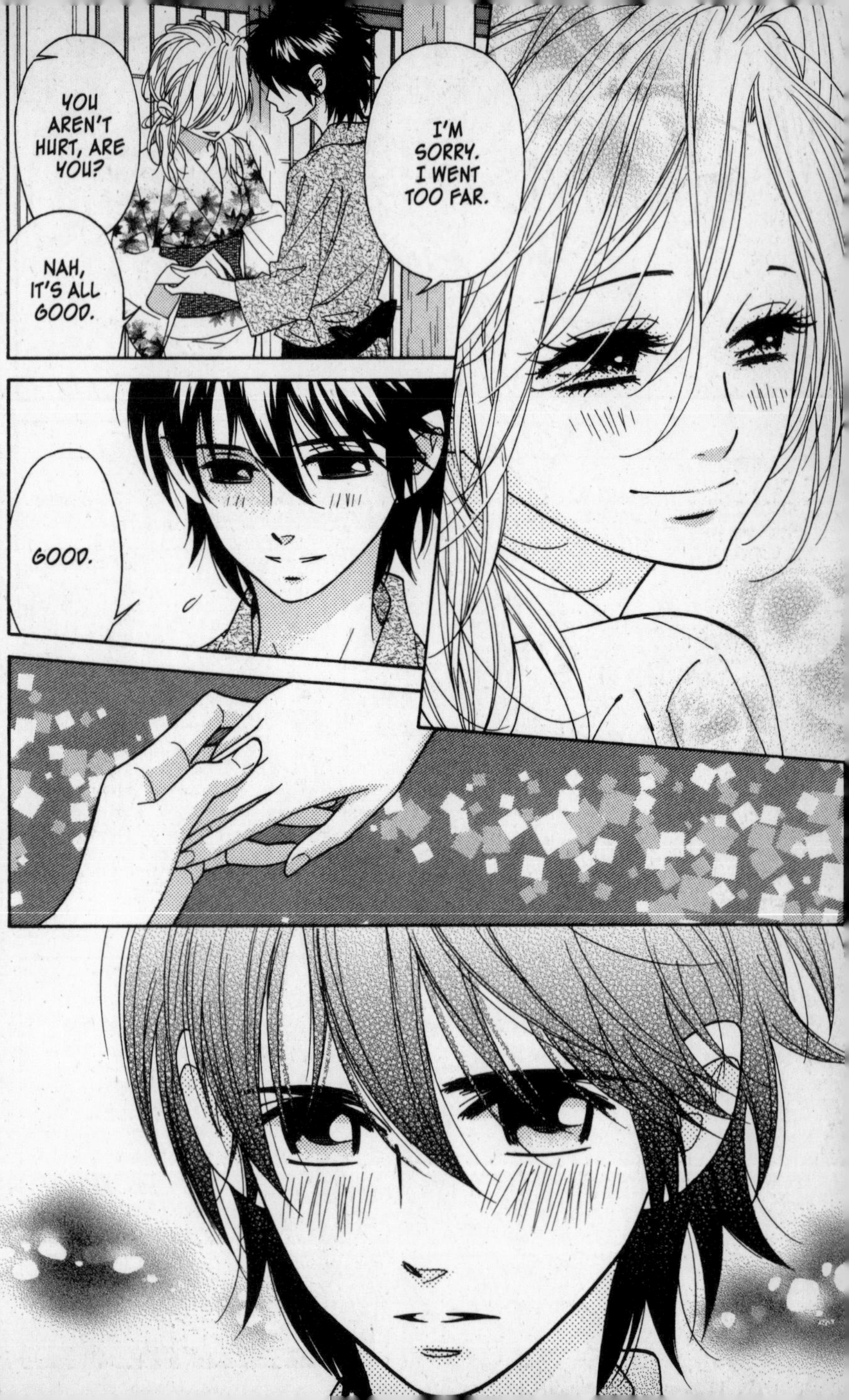
I'M SORRY. I WENT TOO FAR.
YOU AREN'T HURT, ARE YOU?
NAH, IT'S ALL GOOD.
GOOD.

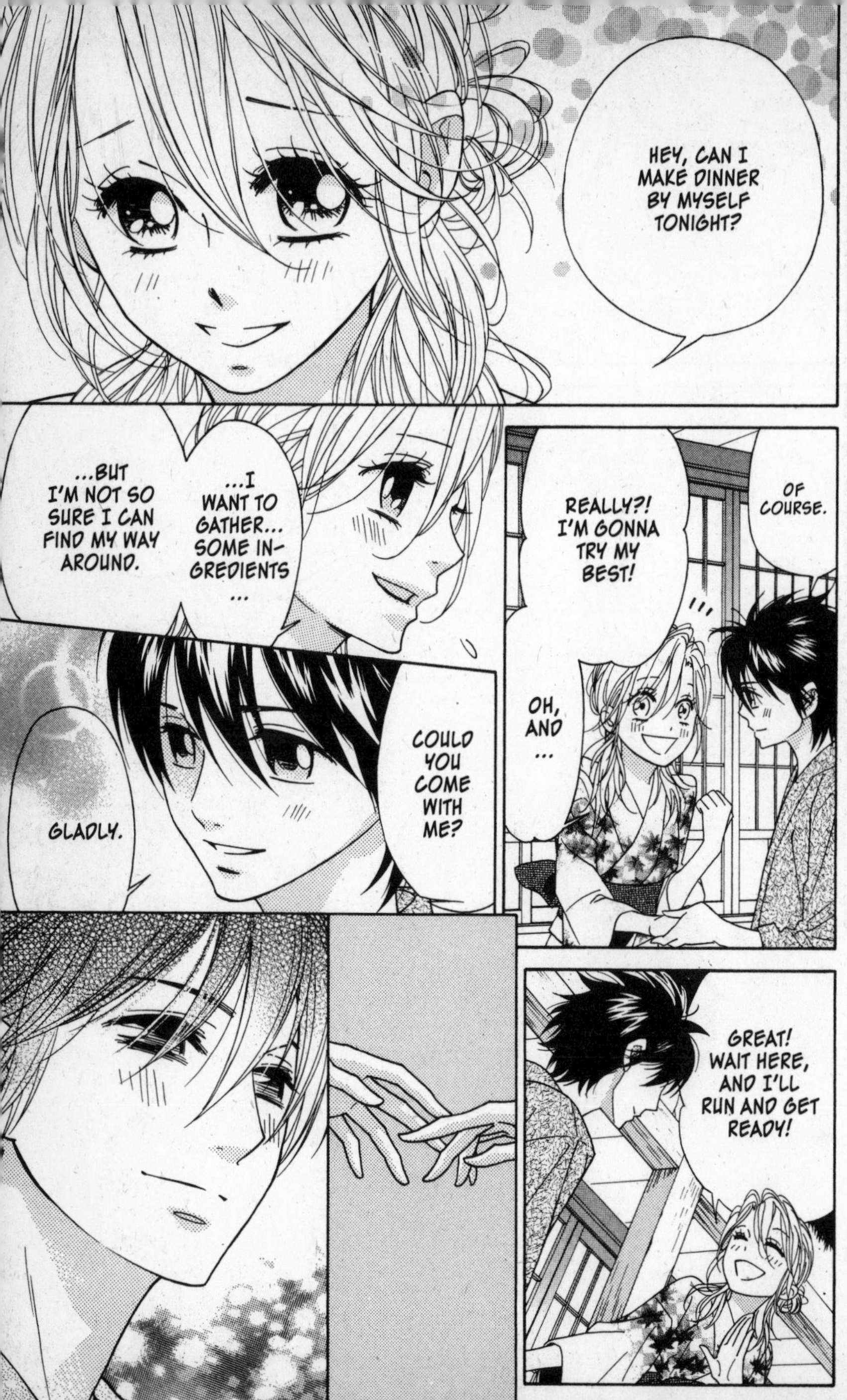
HEY, CAN I MAKE DINNER BY MYSELF TONIGHT?
OF COURSE.
REALLY?! I'M GONNA TRY MY BEST!
OH, AND ...
...I WANT TO GATHER... SOME INGREDIENTS ...
...BUT I'M NOT SO SURE I CAN FIND MY WAY AROUND.
COULD YOU COME WITH ME?
GLADLY.
GREAT! WAIT HERE, AND I'LL RUN AND GET READY!

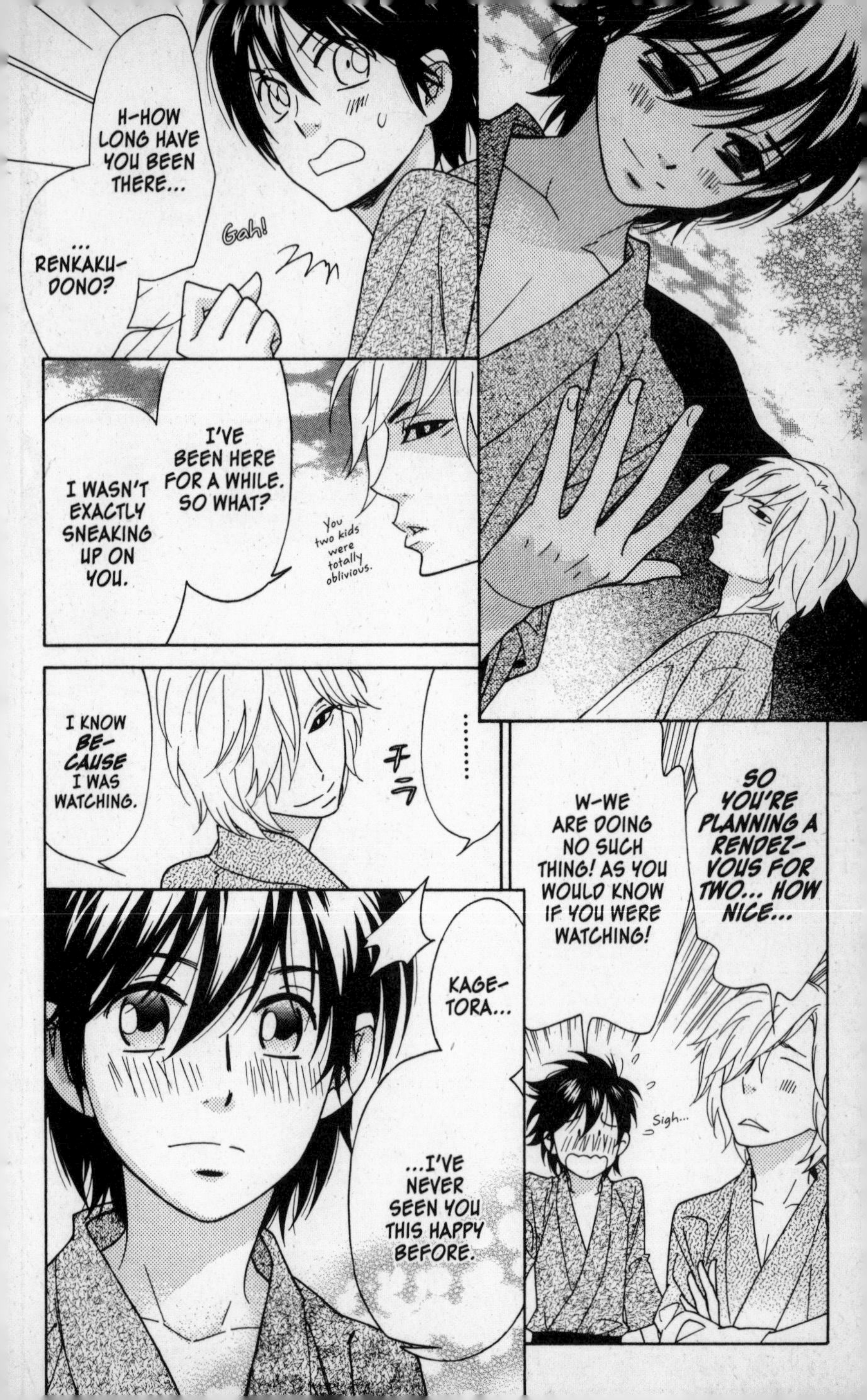
H-HOW LONG HAVE YOU BEEN THERE...
...RENKAKU-DONO?
Gah!
I'VE BEEN HERE FOR A WHILE. SO WHAT?
I WASN'T EXACTLY SNEAKING UP ON YOU.
You two kids were totally oblivious.
SO YOU'RE PLANNING A RENDEZ-VOUS FOR TWO... HOW NICE...
W-WE ARE DOING NO SUCH THING! AS YOU WOULD KNOW IF YOU WERE WATCHING!
Sigh...
....
I KNOW BE-CAUSE I WAS WATCHING.
KAGE-TORA...
...I'VE NEVER SEEN YOU THIS HAPPY BEFORE.

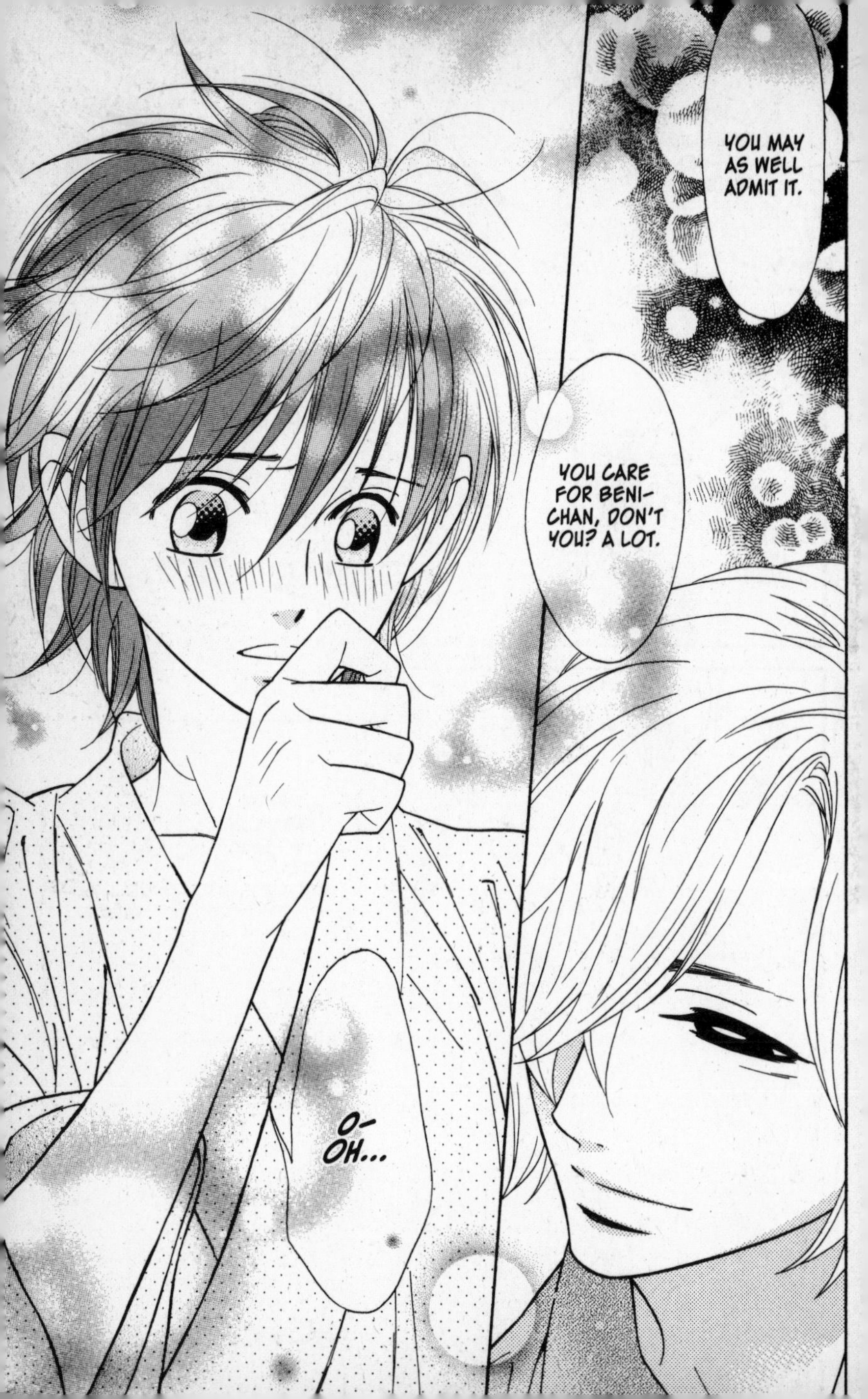
YOU MAY AS WELL ADMIT IT.
YOU CARE FOR BENI-CHAN, DON'T YOU? A LOT.
O-OH...

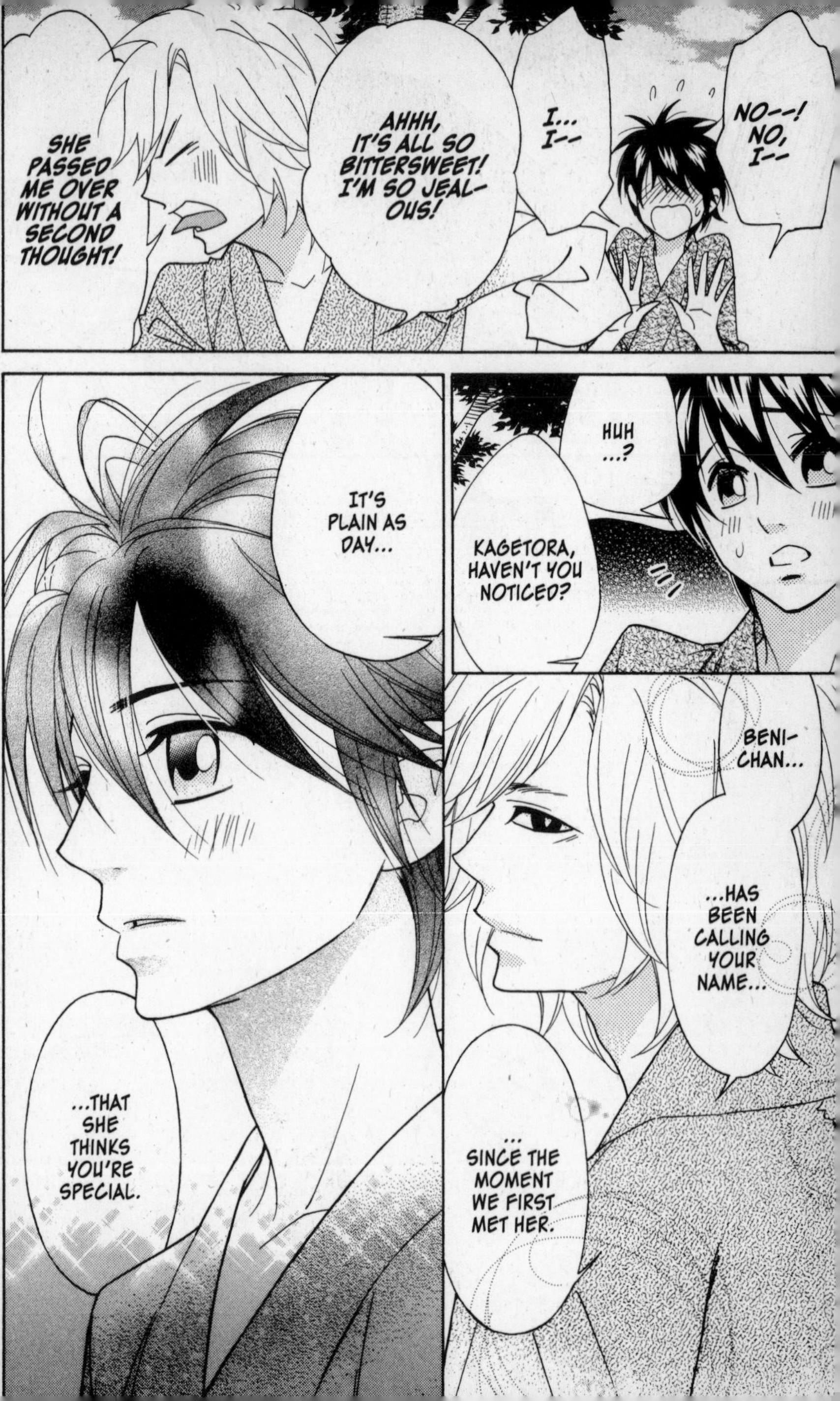
NO--! NO, I--
I... I--
AHHH, IT'S ALL SO BITTERSWEET! I'M SO JEAL-OUS!
SHE PASSED ME OVER WITHOUT A SECOND THOUGHT!
HUH ...?
KAGETORA, HAVEN'T YOU NOTICED?
BENI-CHAN...
...HAS BEEN CALLING YOUR NAME...
... SINCE THE MOMENT WE FIRST MET HER.
IT'S PLAIN AS DAY...
...THAT SHE THINKS YOU'RE SPECIAL.

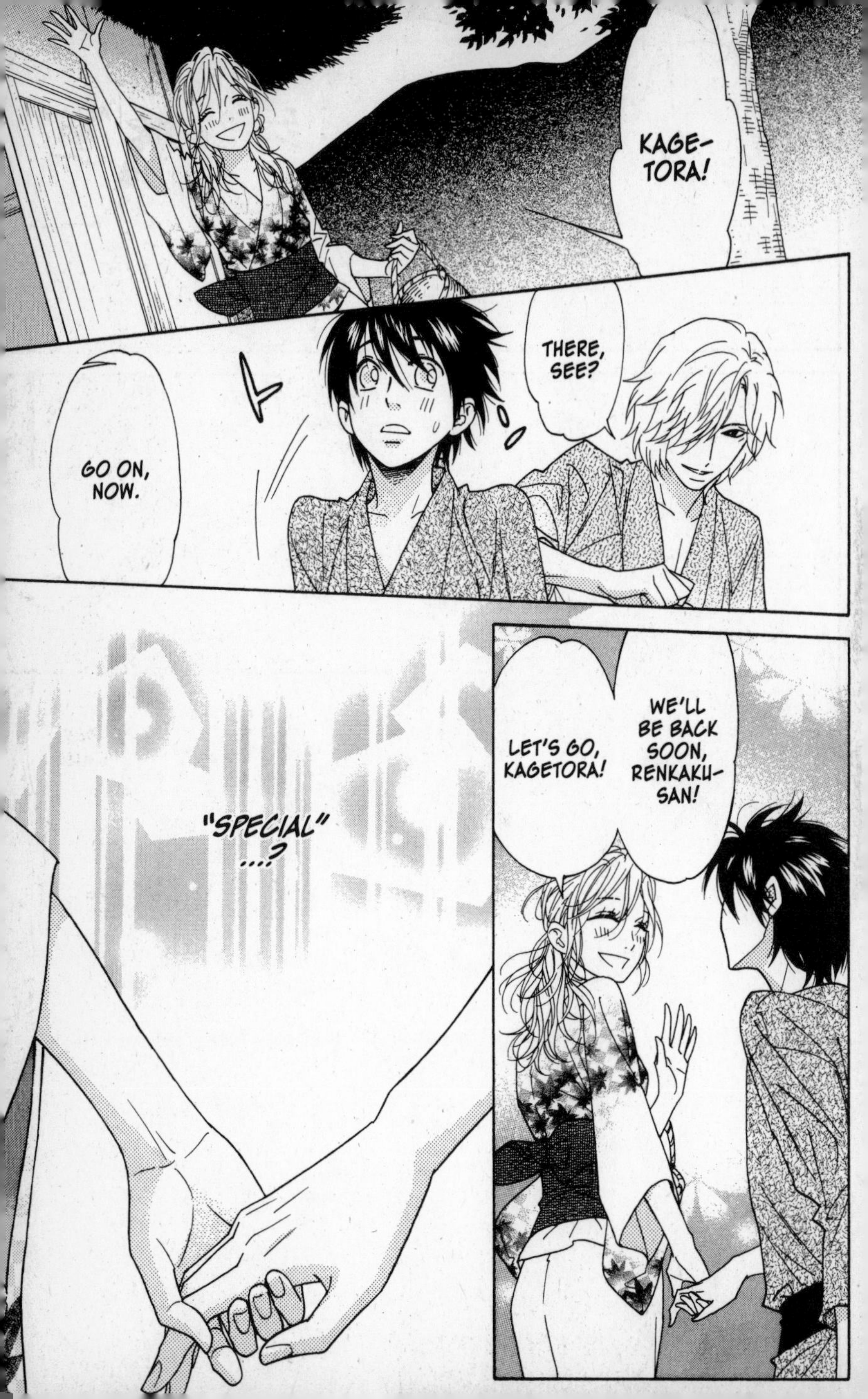
KAGE-TORA!
THERE, SEE?
GO ON, NOW.
WE'LL BE BACK SOON, RENKAKU-SAN!
LET'S GO, KAGETORA!
"SPECIAL" ...?

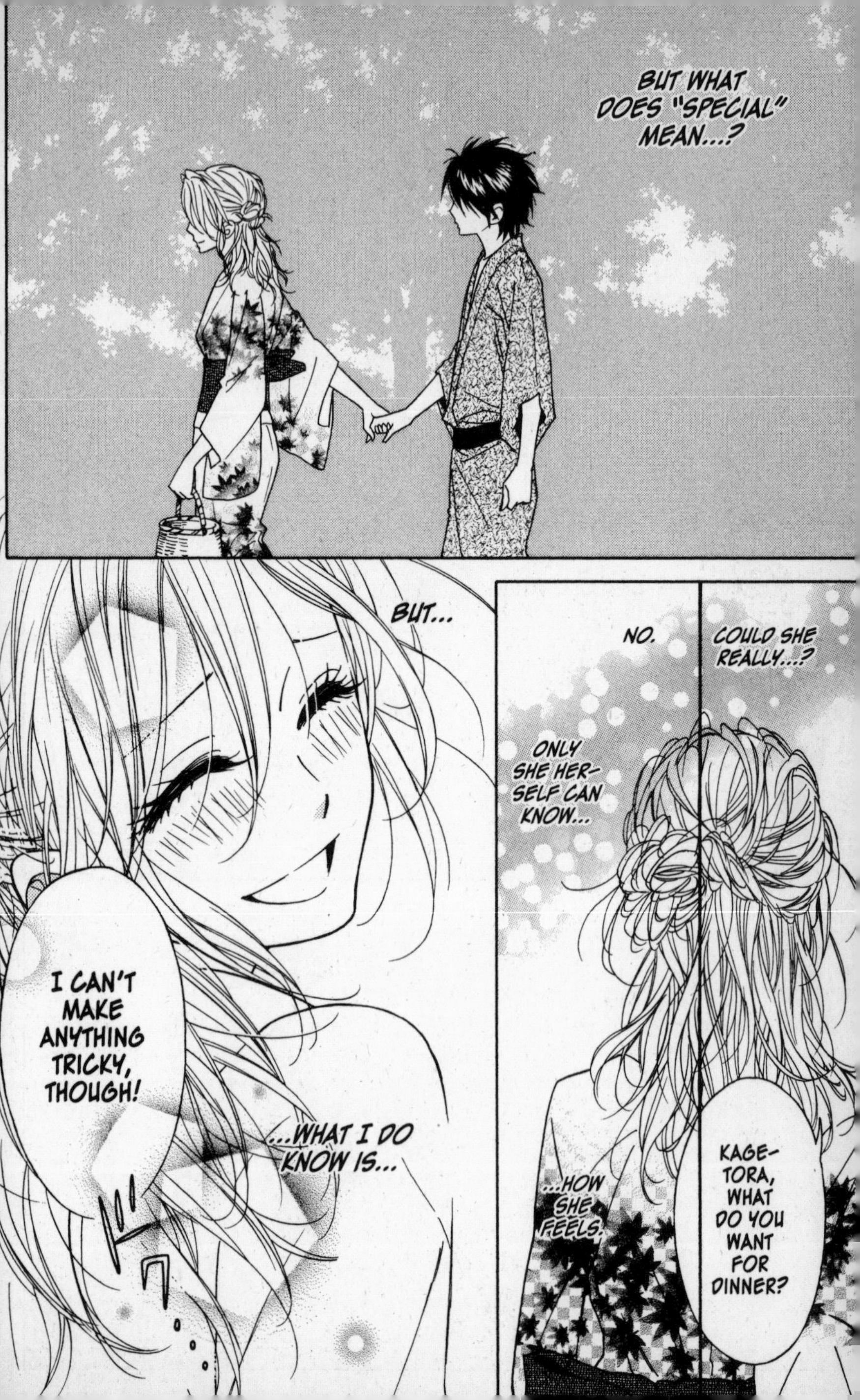
BUT WHAT DOES "SPECIAL" MEAN...?
COULD SHE REALLY...?
NO.
ONLY SHE HER-SELF CAN KNOW...
...HOW SHE FEELS.
KAGE-TORA, WHAT DO YOU WANT FOR DINNER?
BUT...
...WHAT I DO KNOW IS...
I CAN'T MAKE ANYTHING TRICKY, THOUGH!

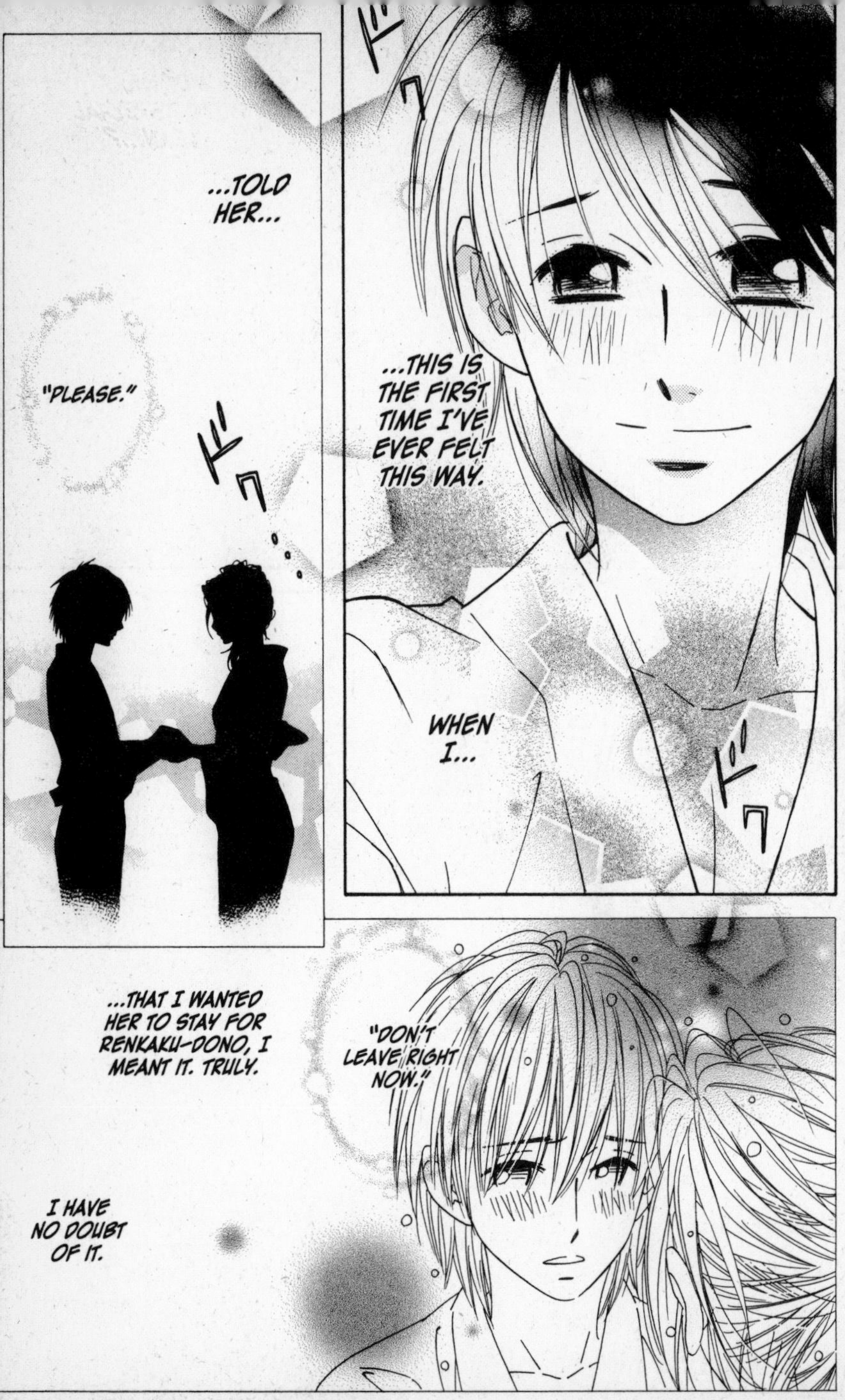
...THIS IS THE FIRST TIME I'VE EVER FELT THIS WAY.
WHEN I...
...TOLD HER...
"PLEASE."
"DON'T LEAVE RIGHT NOW."
...THAT I WANTED HER TO STAY FOR RENKAKU-DONO, I MEANT IT. TRULY.
I HAVE NO DOUBT OF IT.

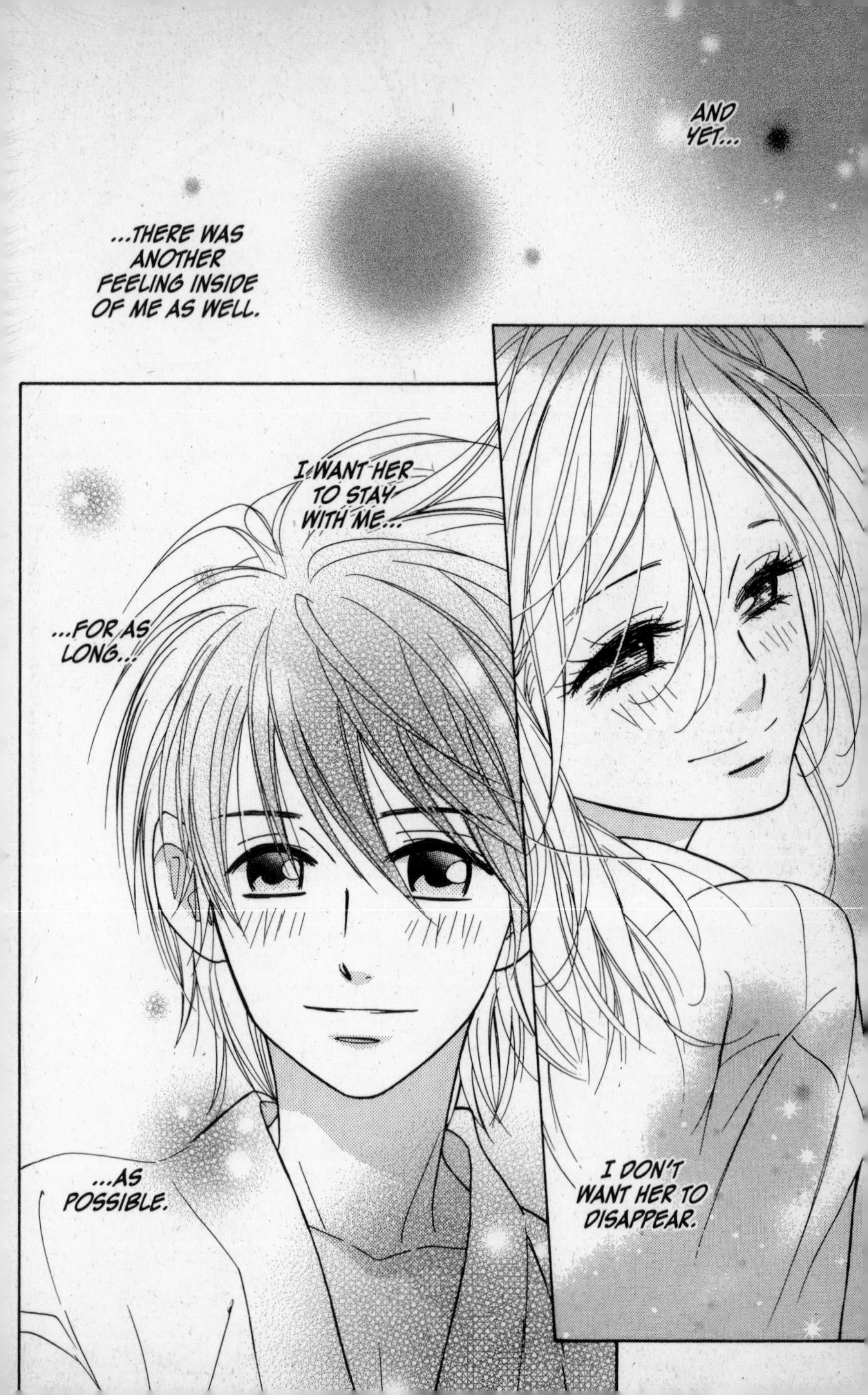

AND YET...
...THERE WAS ANOTHER FEELING INSIDE OF ME AS WELL.
I DON'T WANT HER TO DISAPPEAR.
I WANT HER TO STAY WITH ME...
...FOR AS LONG...
...AS POSSIBLE.

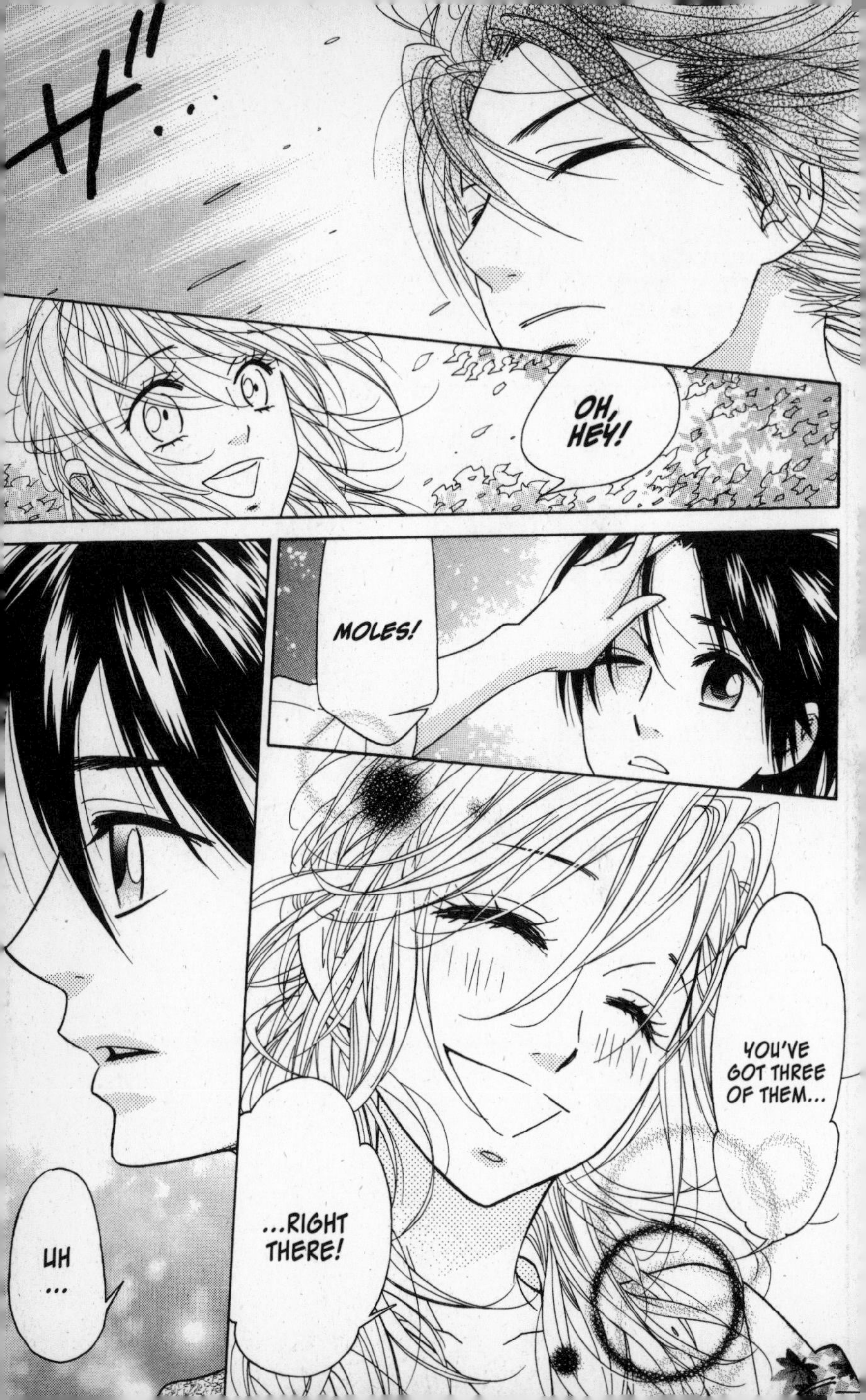
ザ…
OH, HEY!
MOLES!
YOU'VE GOT THREE OF THEM...
...RIGHT THERE!
UH ...

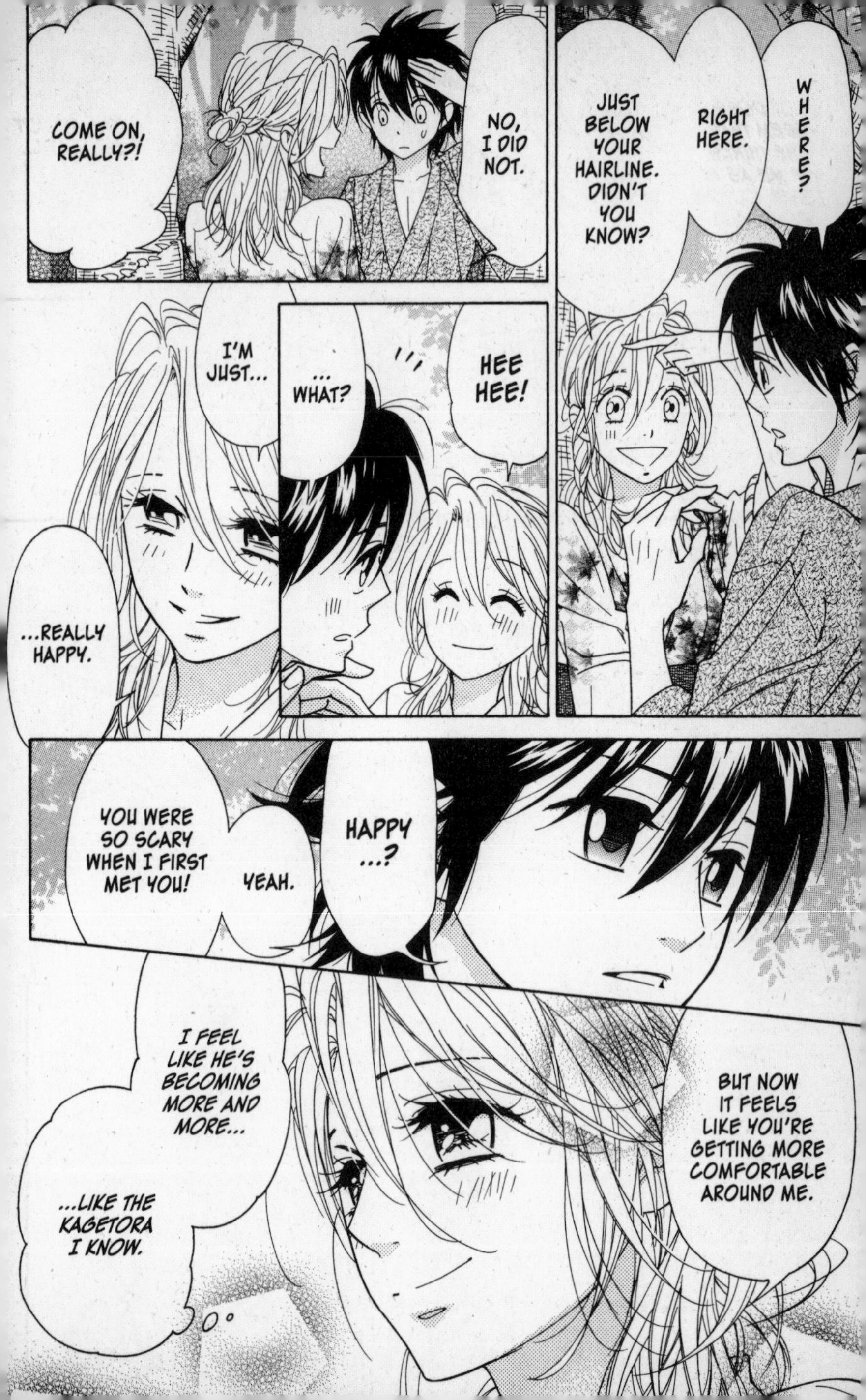
WHERE?
RIGHT HERE.
JUST BELOW YOUR HAIRLINE. DIDN'T YOU KNOW?
NO, I DID NOT.
COME ON, REALLY?!
HEE HEE!
... WHAT?
I'M JUST...
...REALLY HAPPY.
HAPPY ...?
YEAH.
YOU WERE SO SCARY WHEN I FIRST MET YOU!
BUT NOW IT FEELS LIKE YOU'RE GETTING MORE COMFORTABLE AROUND ME.
I FEEL LIKE HE'S BECOMING MORE AND MORE...
...LIKE THE KAGETORA I KNOW.

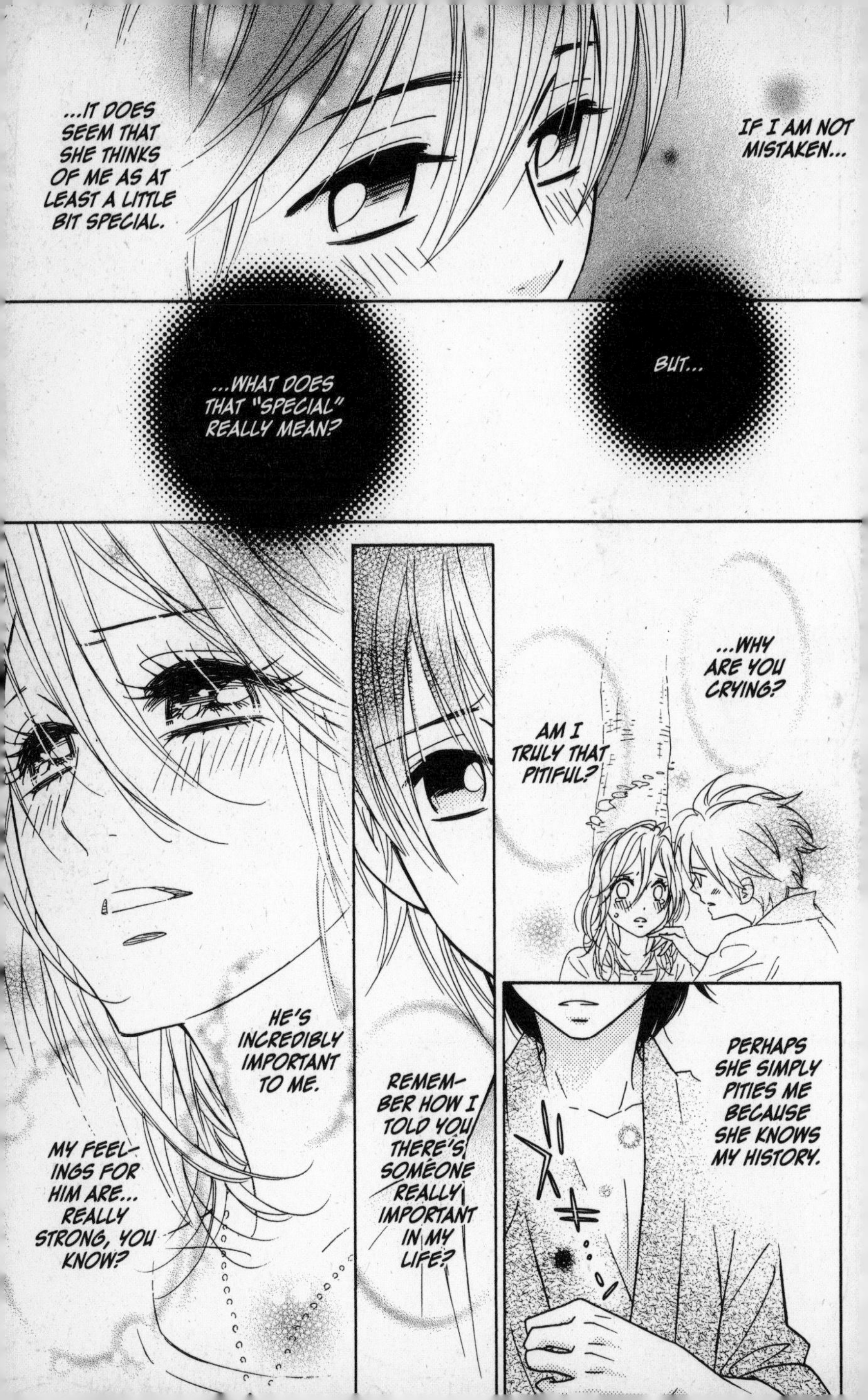

IF I AM NOT MISTAKEN...
...IT DOES SEEM THAT SHE THINKS OF ME AS AT LEAST A LITTLE BIT SPECIAL.
BUT...
...WHAT DOES THAT "SPECIAL" REALLY MEAN?
...WHY ARE YOU CRYING?
AM I TRULY THAT PITIFUL?
PERHAPS SHE SIMPLY PITIES ME BECAUSE SHE KNOWS MY HISTORY.
REMEM-BER HOW I TOLD YOU THERE'S SOMEONE REALLY IMPORTANT IN MY LIFE?
HE'S INCREDIBLY IMPORTANT TO ME.
MY FEEL-INGS FOR HIM ARE... REALLY STRONG, YOU KNOW?

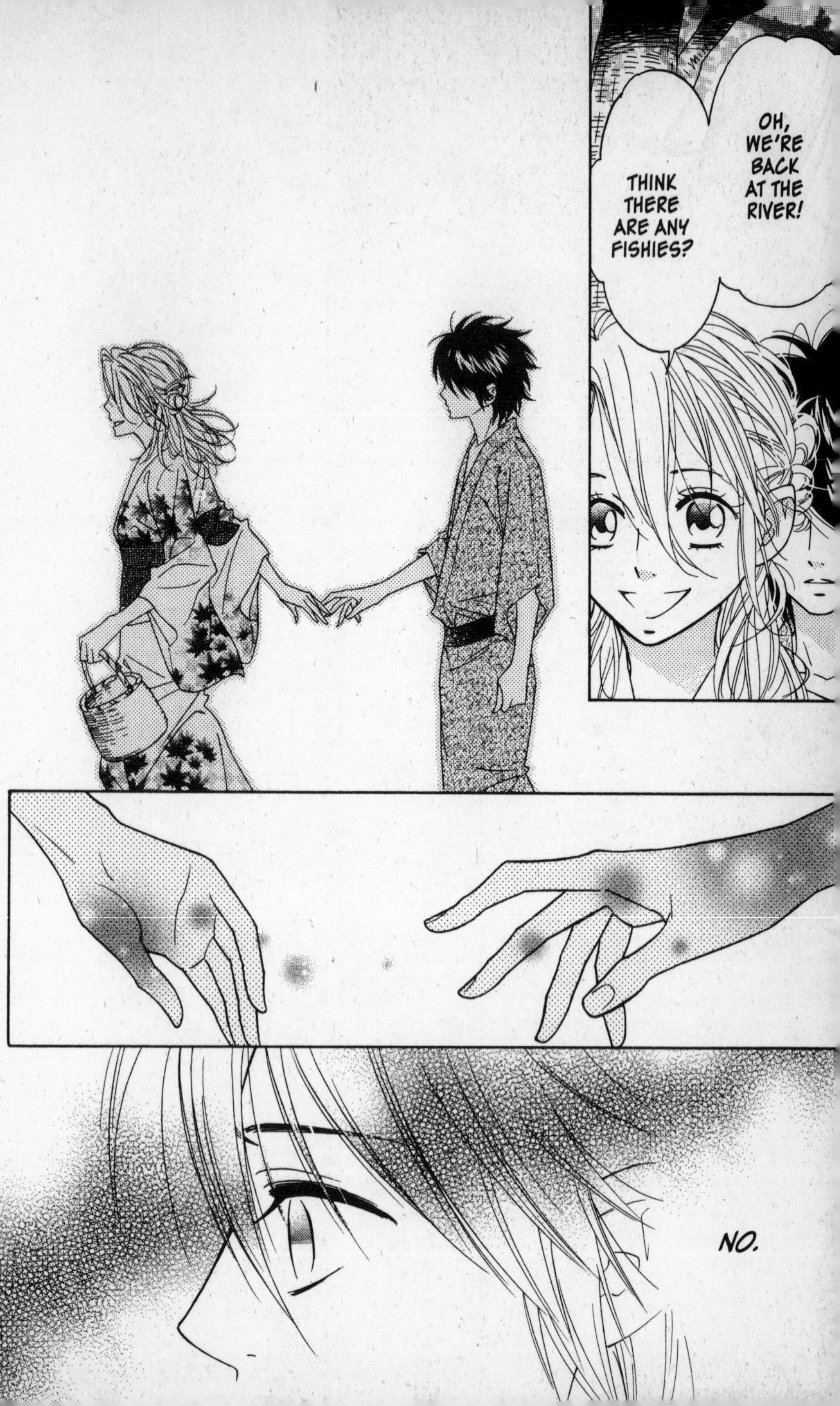
OH, WE'RE BACK AT THE RIVER!
THINK THERE ARE ANY FISHIES?
NO.

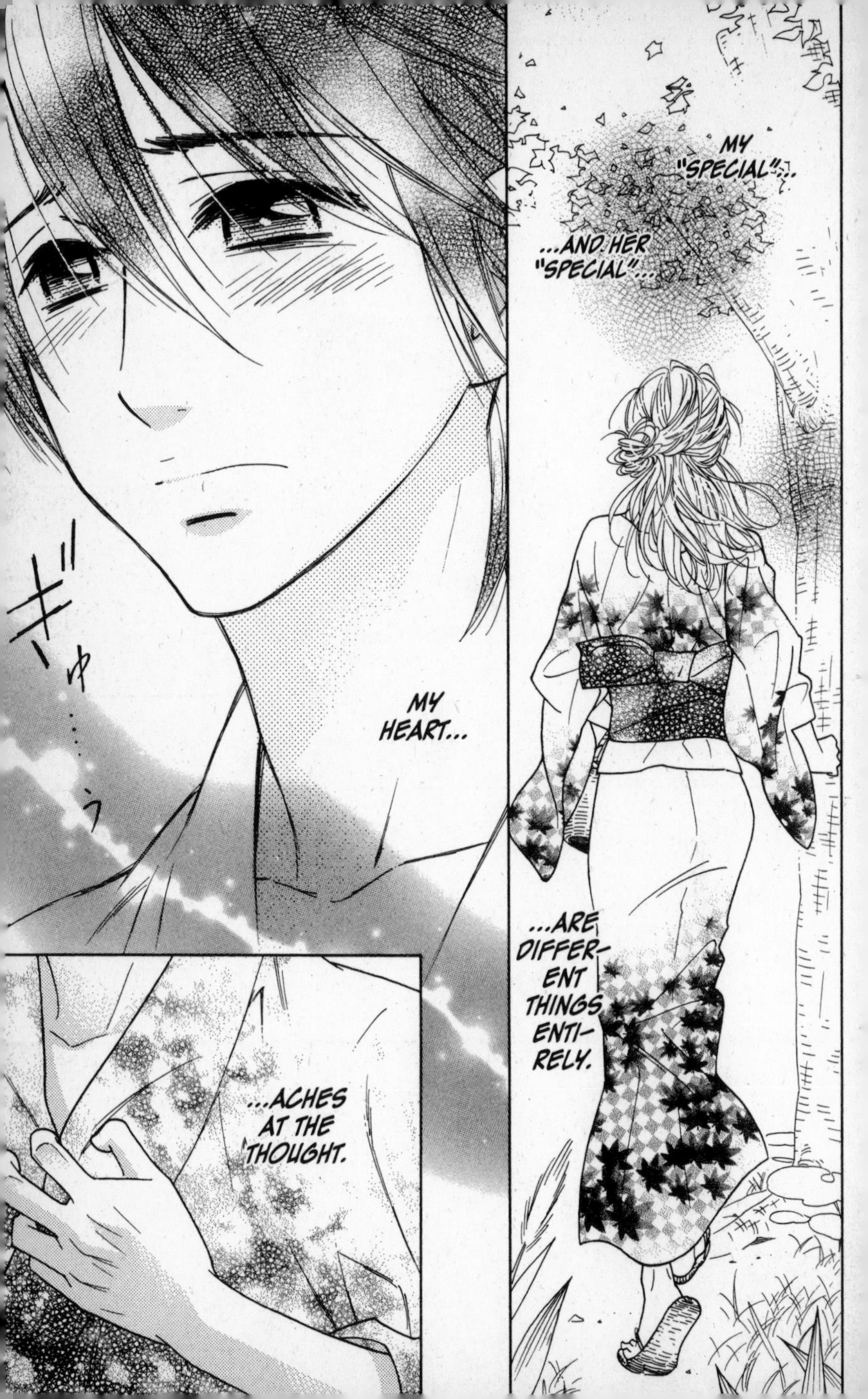

MY "SPECIAL"...
...AND HER "SPECIAL"...
...ARE DIFFERENT THINGS ENTIRELY.
MY HEART...
...ACHES AT THE THOUGHT.

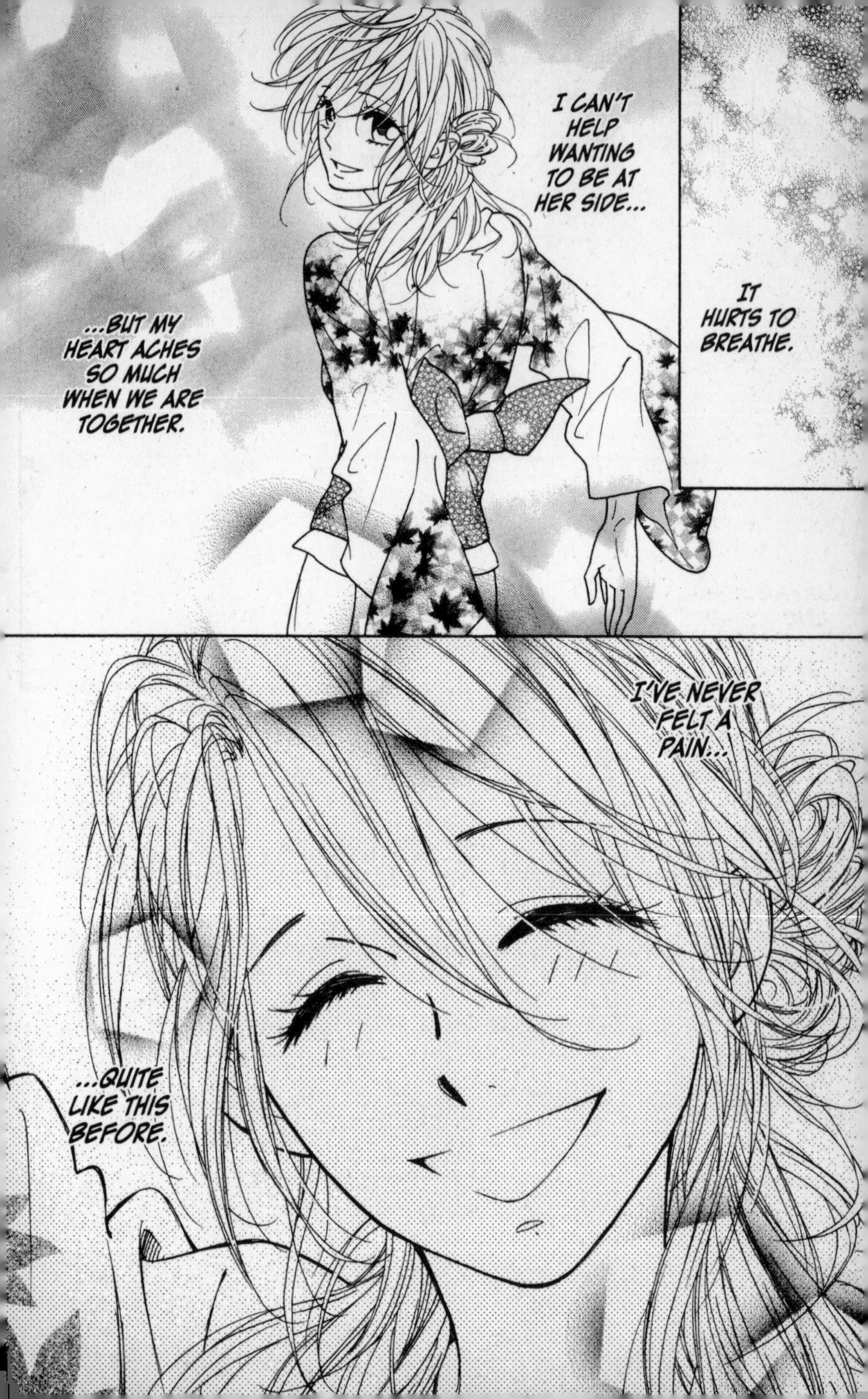
I CAN'T HELP WANTING TO BE AT HER SIDE...
...BUT MY HEART ACHES SO MUCH WHEN WE ARE TOGETHER.
IT HURTS TO BREATHE.
I'VE NEVER FELT A PAIN...
...QUITE LIKE THIS BEFORE.

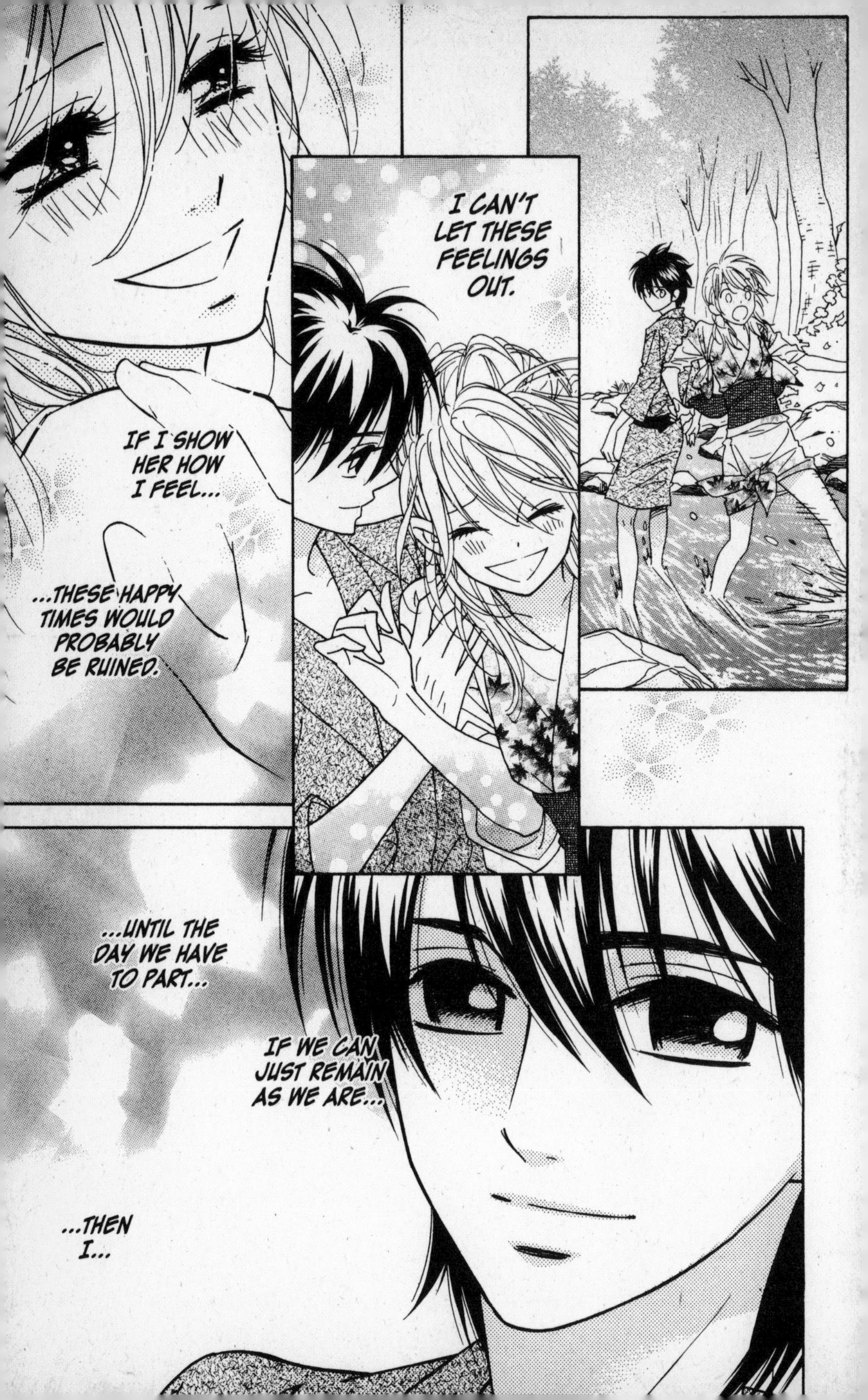
I CAN'T LET THESE FEELINGS OUT.
IF I SHOW HER HOW I FEEL...
...THESE HAPPY TIMES WOULD PROBABLY BE RUINED.
IF WE CAN JUST REMAIN AS WE ARE...
...UNTIL THE DAY WE HAVE TO PART...
...THEN I...

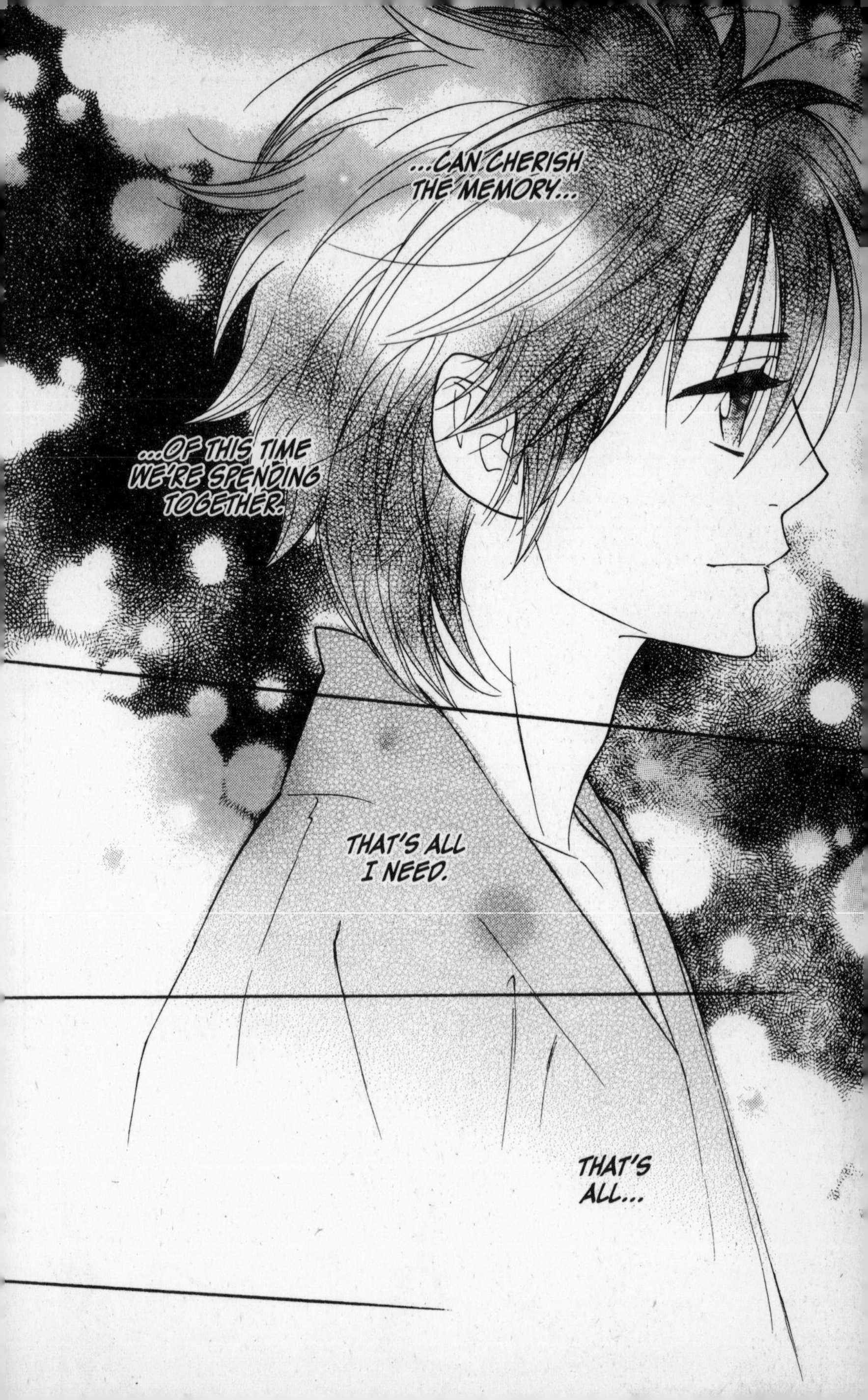
...CAN CHERISH THE MEMORY...
...OF THIS TIME WE'RE SPENDING TOGETHER.
THAT'S ALL I NEED.
THAT'S ALL...

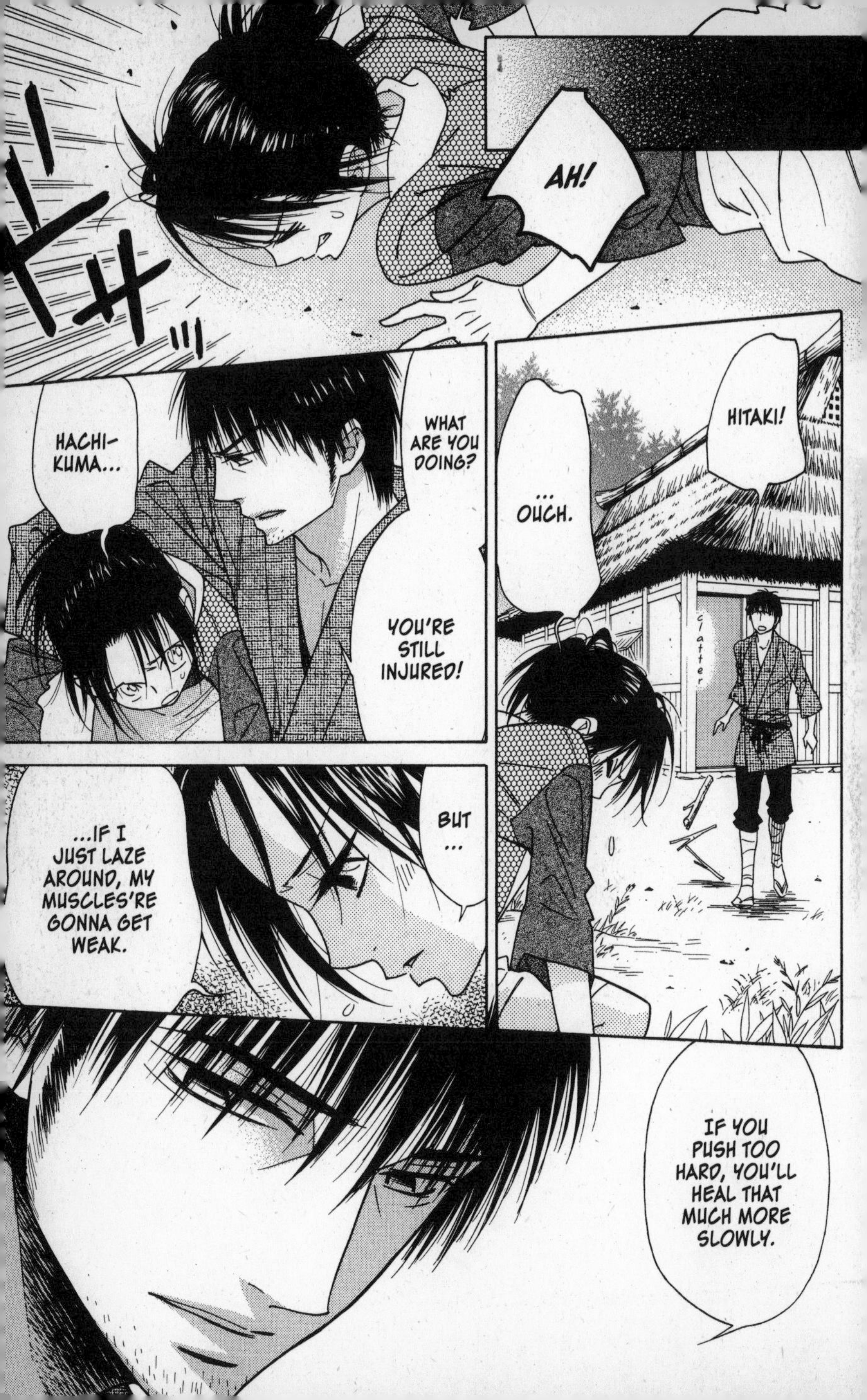

AH!
HITAKI!
clatter
... OUCH.
WHAT ARE YOU DOING?
HACHI-KUMA...
YOU'RE STILL INJURED!
BUT ...
...IF I JUST LAZE AROUND, MY MUSCLES'RE GONNA GET WEAK.
IF YOU PUSH TOO HARD, YOU'LL HEAL THAT MUCH MORE SLOWLY.

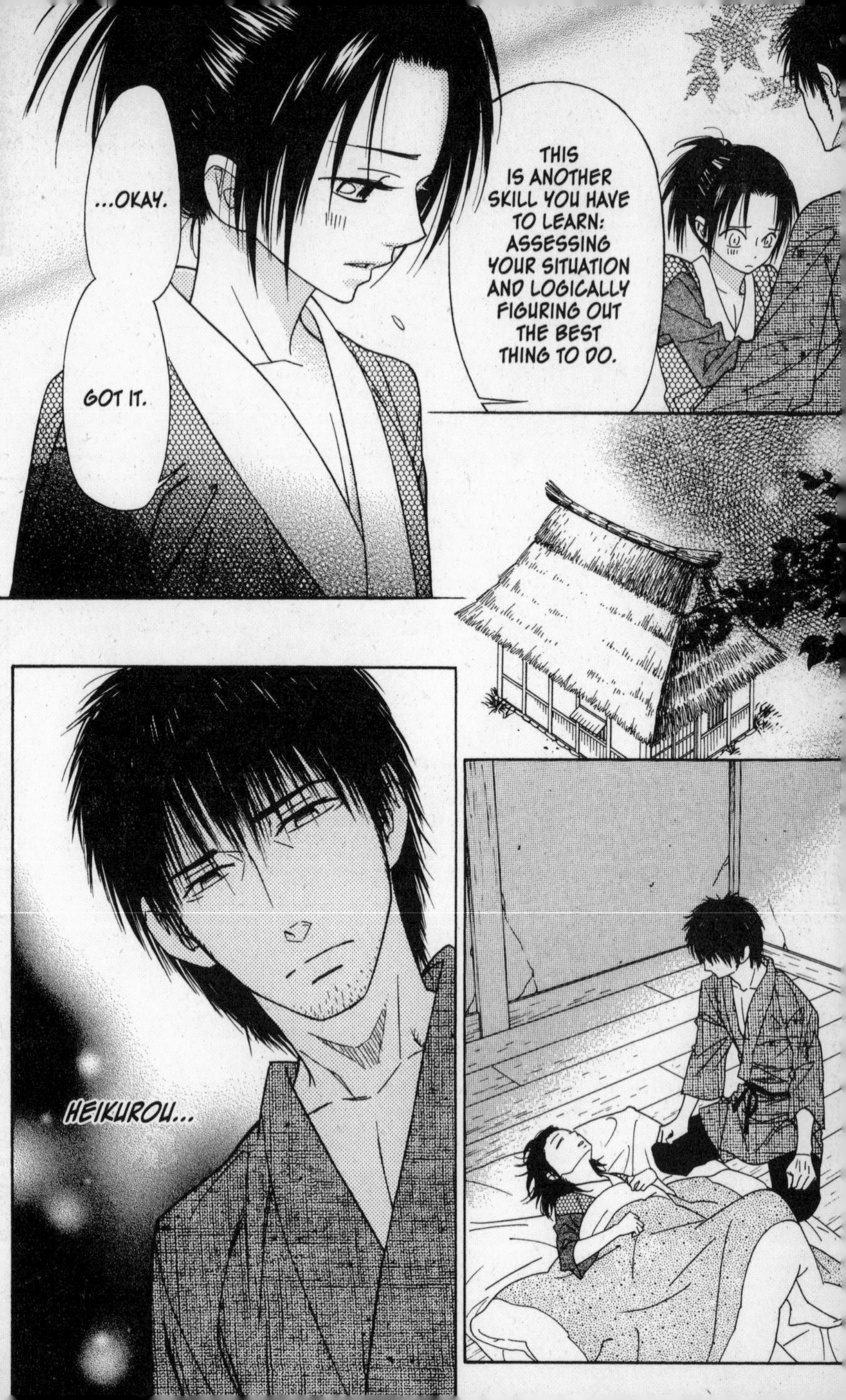
THIS IS ANOTHER SKILL YOU HAVE TO LEARN: ASSESSING YOUR SITUATION AND LOGICALLY FIGURING OUT THE BEST THING TO DO.
...OKAY.
GOT IT.
HEIKUROU...

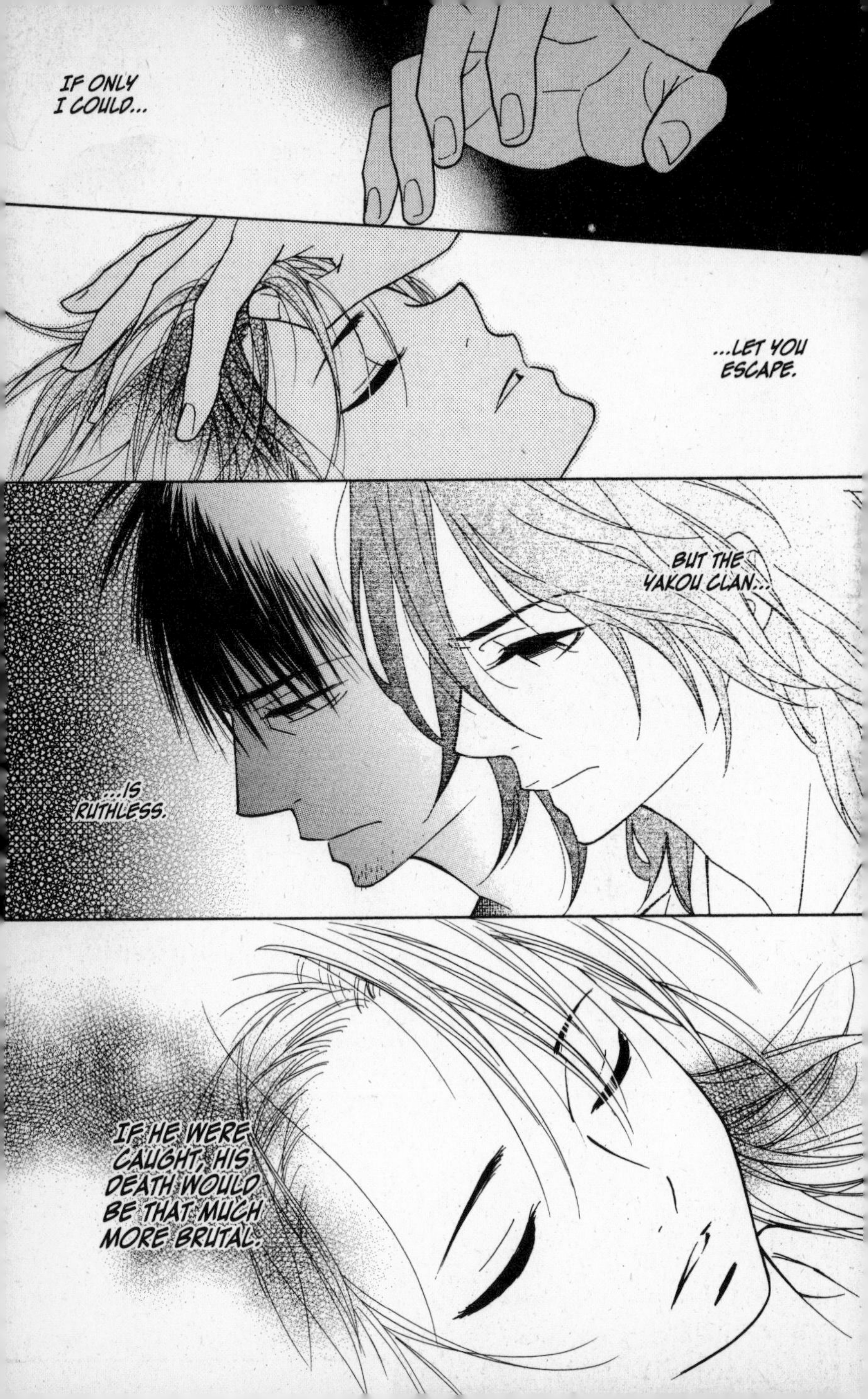
IF ONLY I COULD...
...LET YOU ESCAPE.
BUT THE YAKOU CLAN...
...IS RUTHLESS.
IF HE WERE CAUGHT, HIS DEATH WOULD BE THAT MUCH MORE BRUTAL.

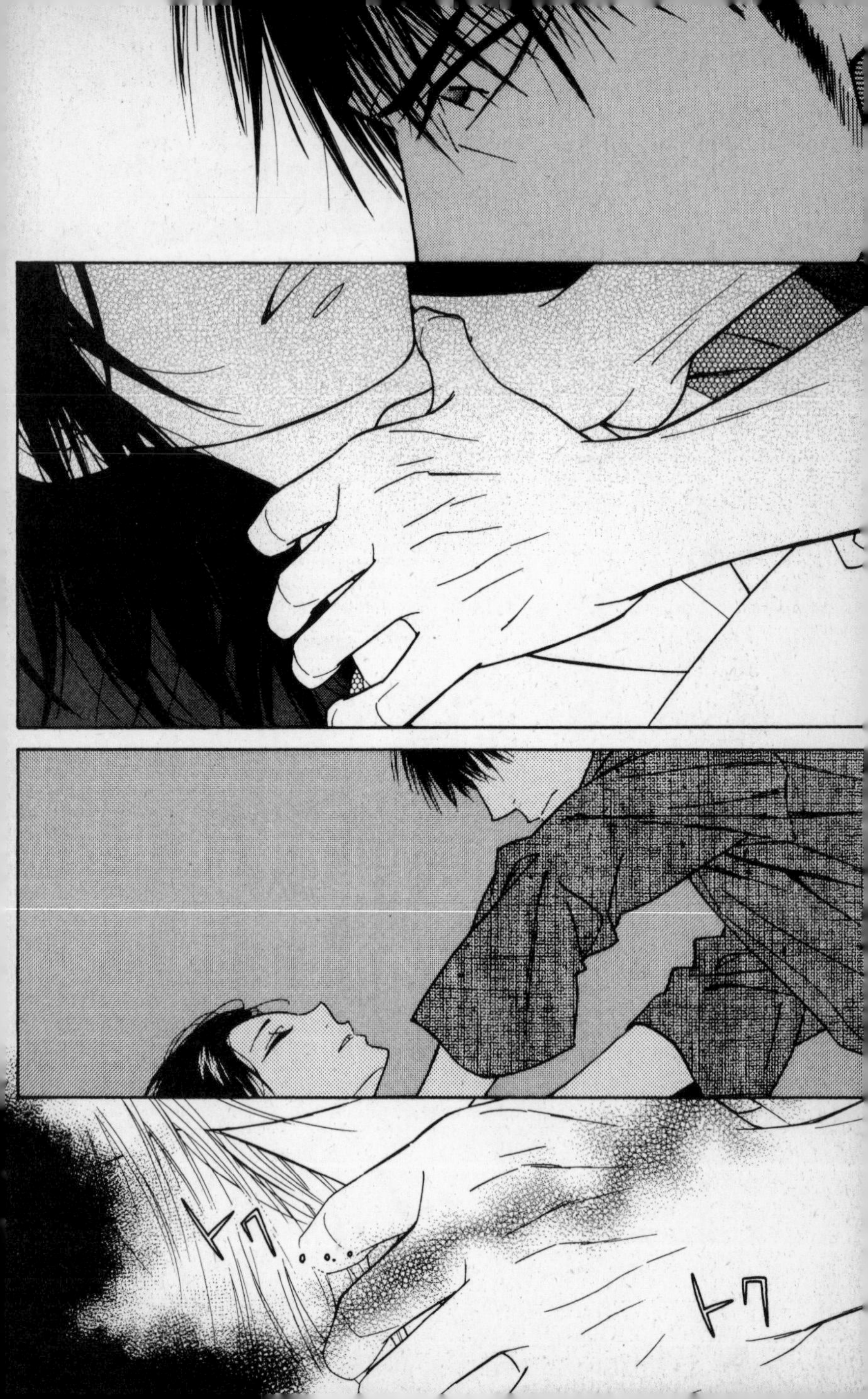
トク...
トク

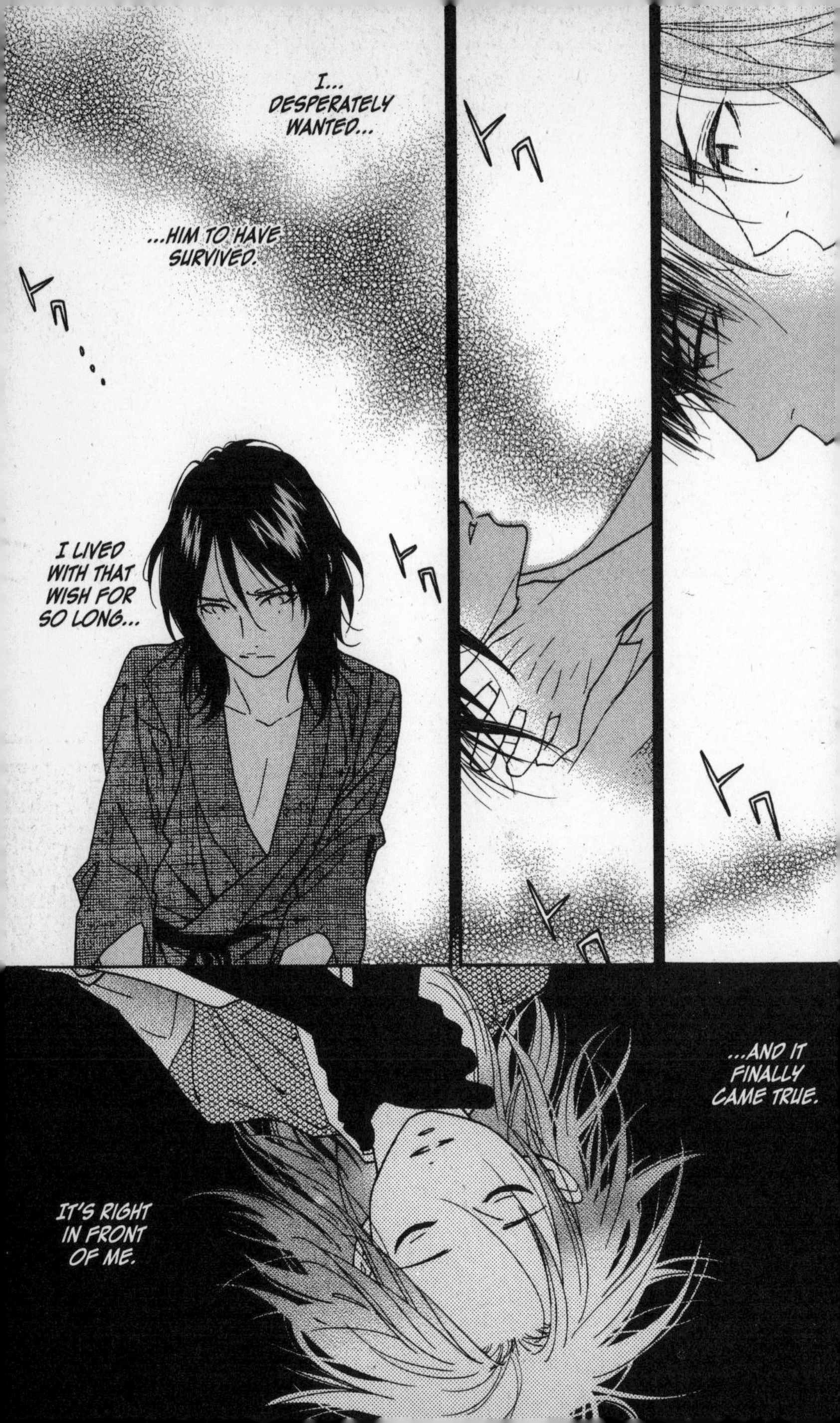
I... DESPERATELY WANTED...
...HIM TO HAVE SURVIVED.
I LIVED WITH THAT WISH FOR SO LONG...
...AND IT FINALLY CAME TRUE.
IT'S RIGHT IN FRONT OF ME.

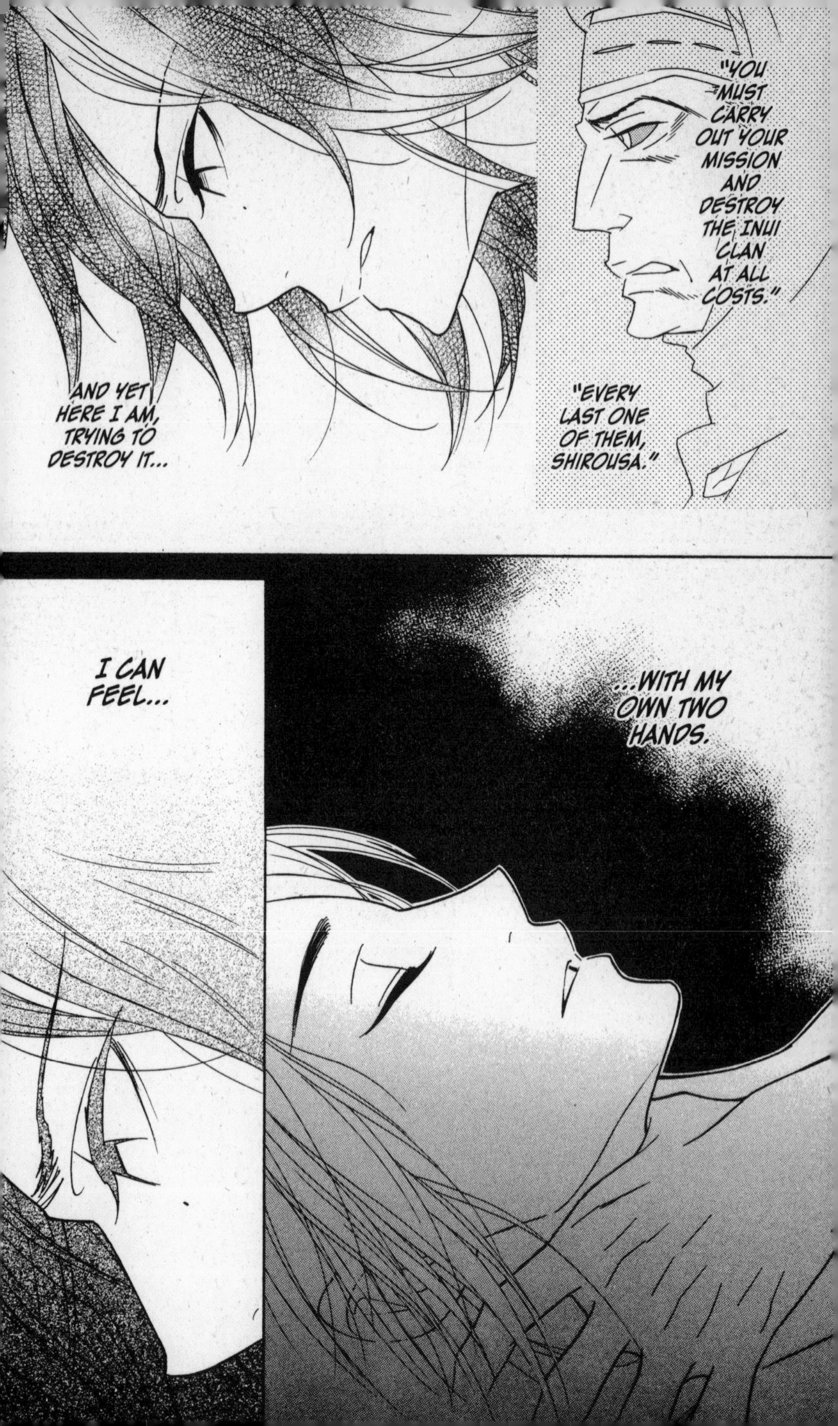
"YOU MUST CARRY OUT YOUR MISSION AND DESTROY THE INUI CLAN AT ALL COSTS."
"EVERY LAST ONE OF THEM, SHIROUSA."
AND YET HERE I AM, TRYING TO DESTROY IT...
...WITH MY OWN TWO HANDS.
I CAN FEEL...

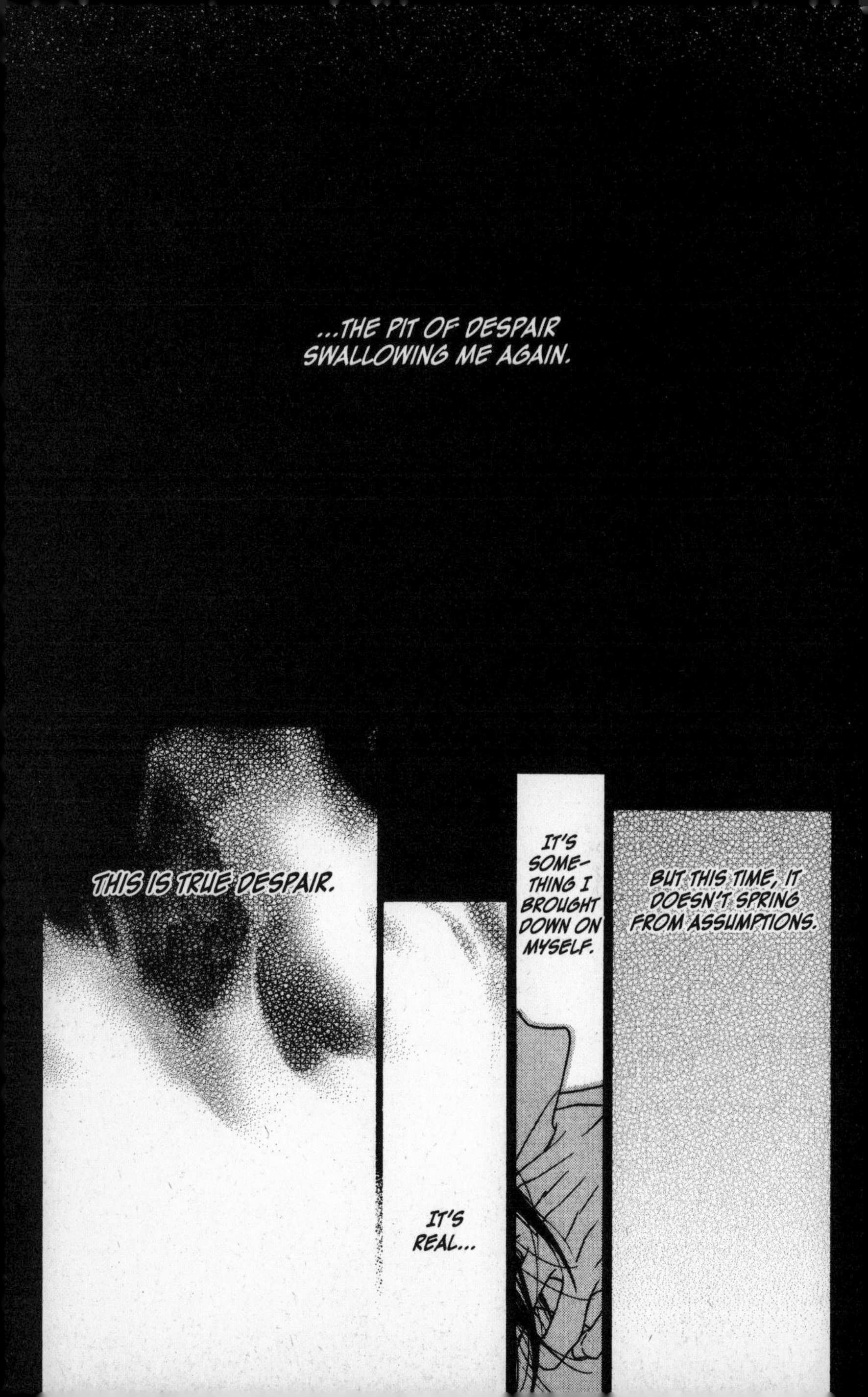
...THE PIT OF DESPAIR SWALLOWING ME AGAIN.
BUT THIS TIME, IT DOESN'T SPRING FROM ASSUMPTIONS.
IT'S SOME-THING I BROUGHT DOWN ON MYSELF.
IT'S REAL...
THIS IS TRUE DESPAIR.

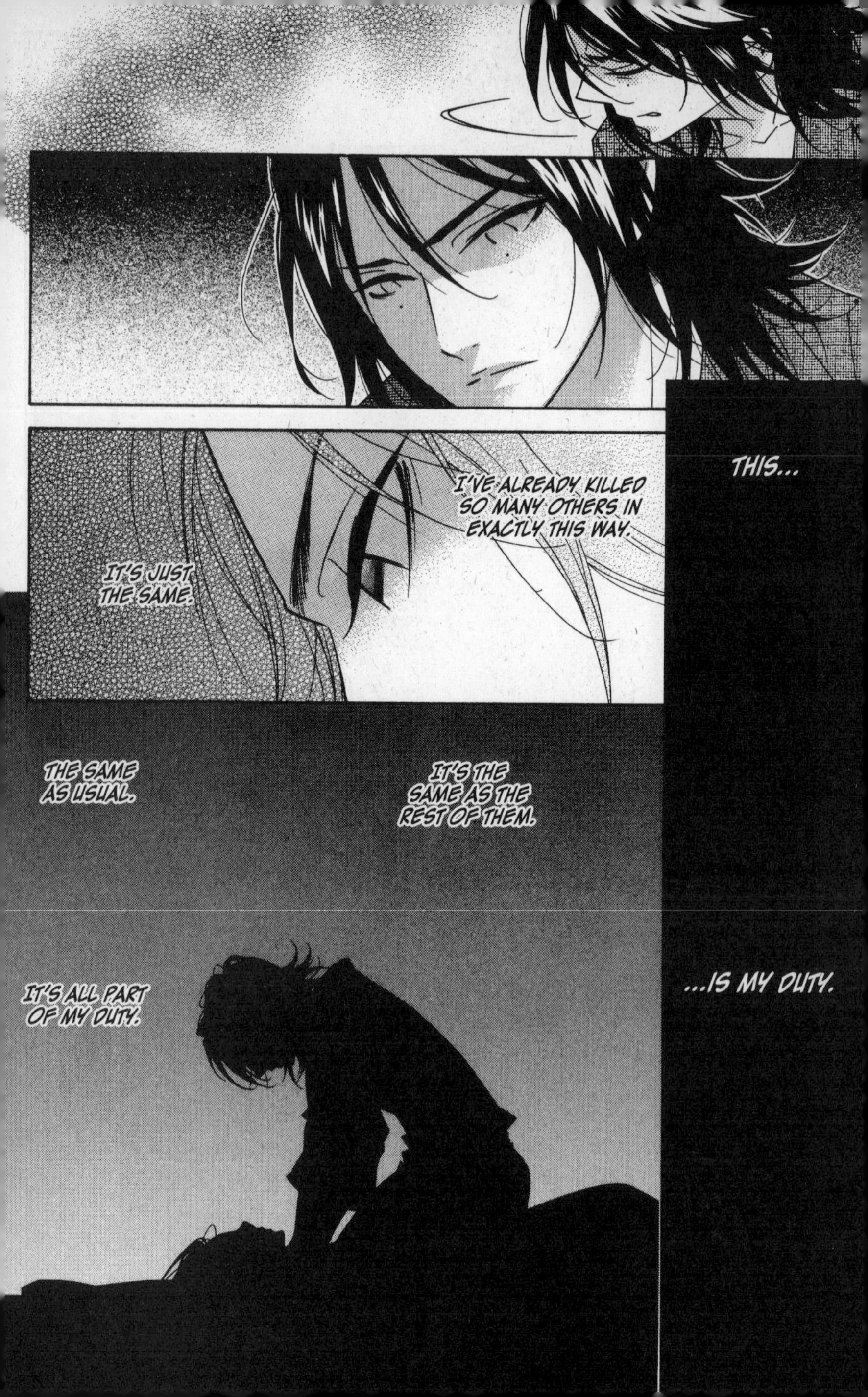
THIS...
I'VE ALREADY KILLED SO MANY OTHERS IN EXACTLY THIS WAY.
IT'S JUST THE SAME.
IT'S THE SAME AS THE REST OF THEM.
THE SAME AS USUAL.
...IS MY DUTY.
IT'S ALL PART OF MY DUTY.

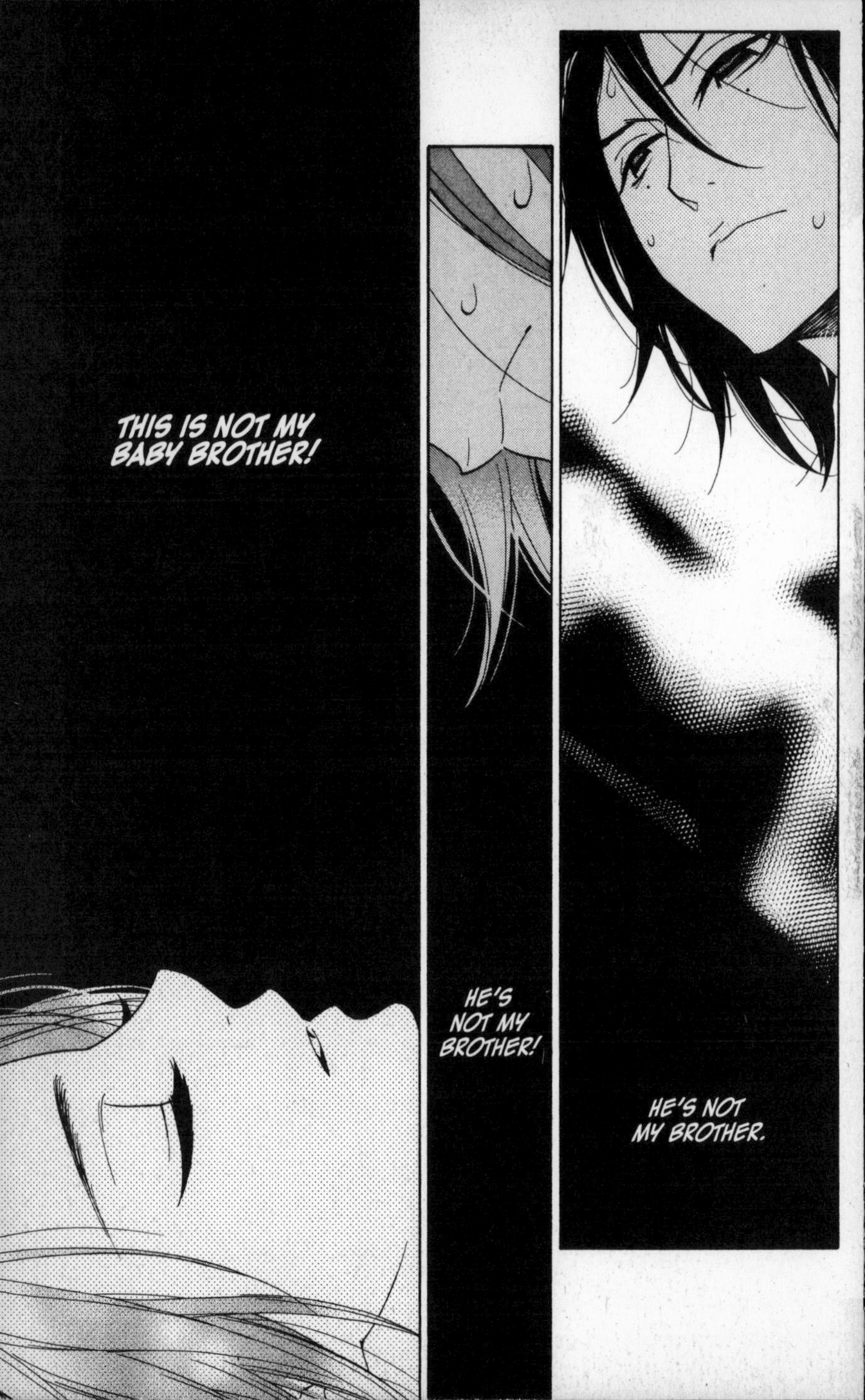
HE'S NOT
MY BROTHER.
HE'S
NOT MY
BROTHER!
THIS IS NOT MY
BABY BROTHER!

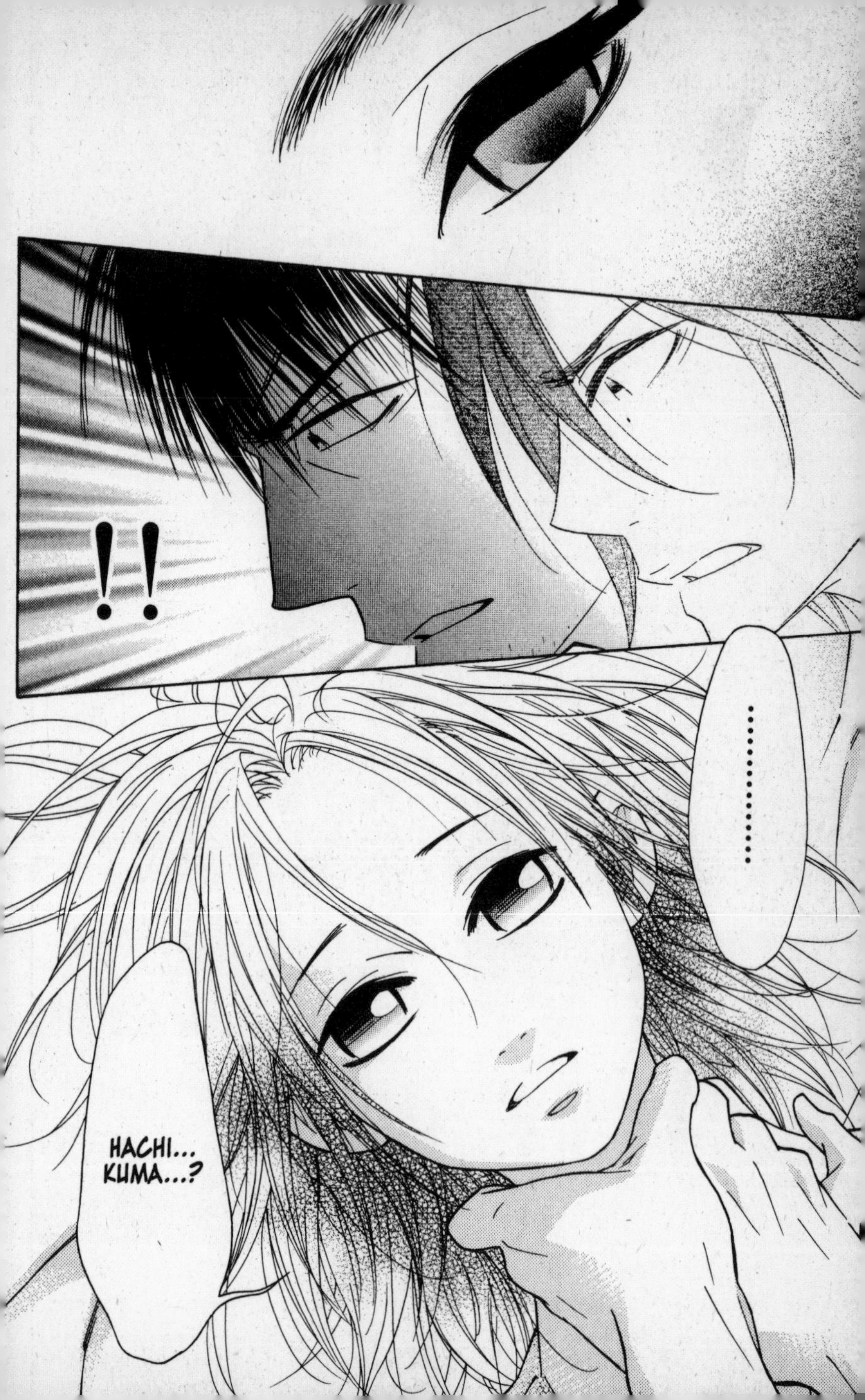
!!
....
HACHI... KUMA...?

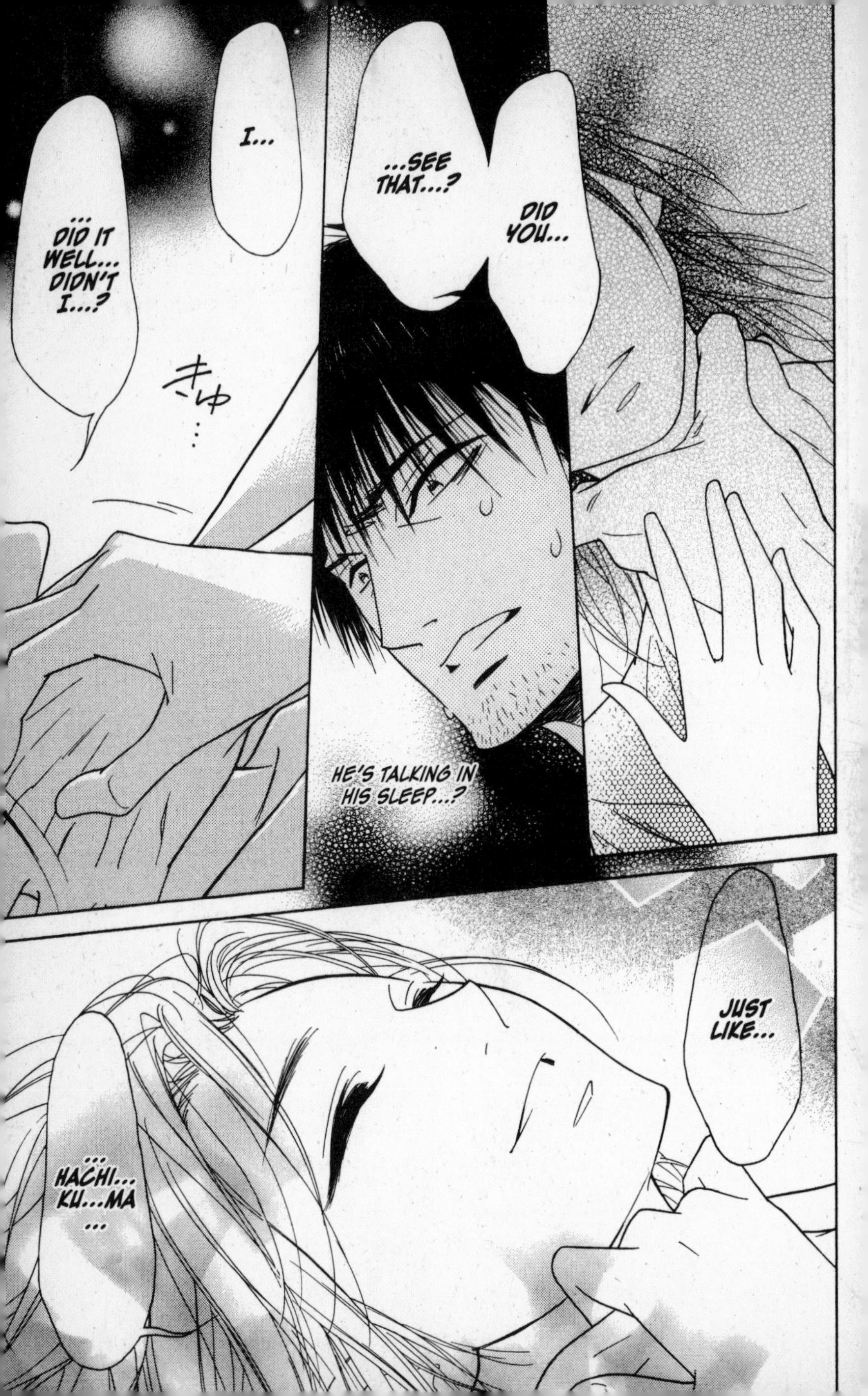
DID YOU...
...SEE THAT...?
I...
...DID IT WELL... DIDN'T I...?
きゅ…
HE'S TALKING IN HIS SLEEP...?
JUST LIKE...
...HACHI...KU...MA...

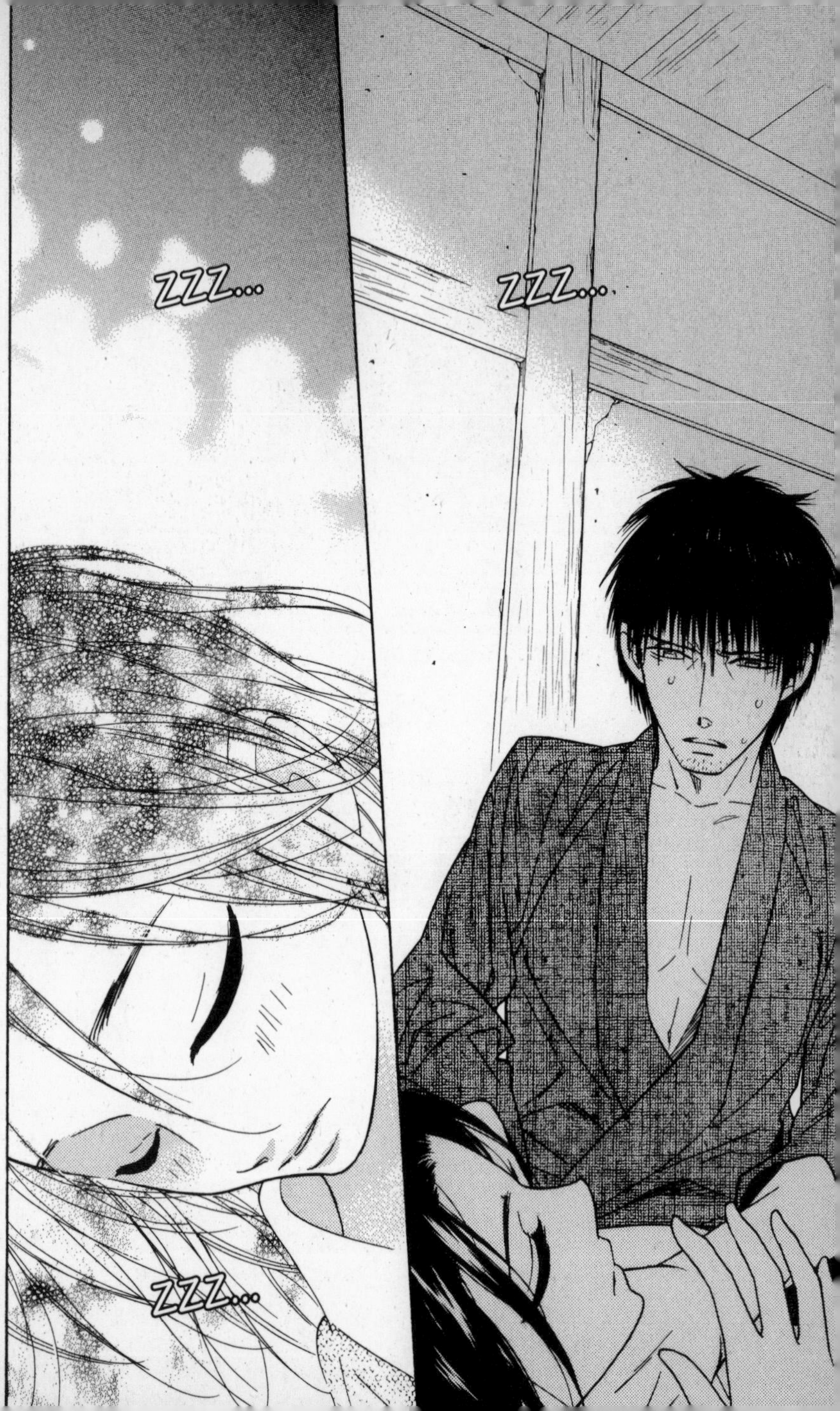
ZZZ...
ZZZ...
ZZZ...

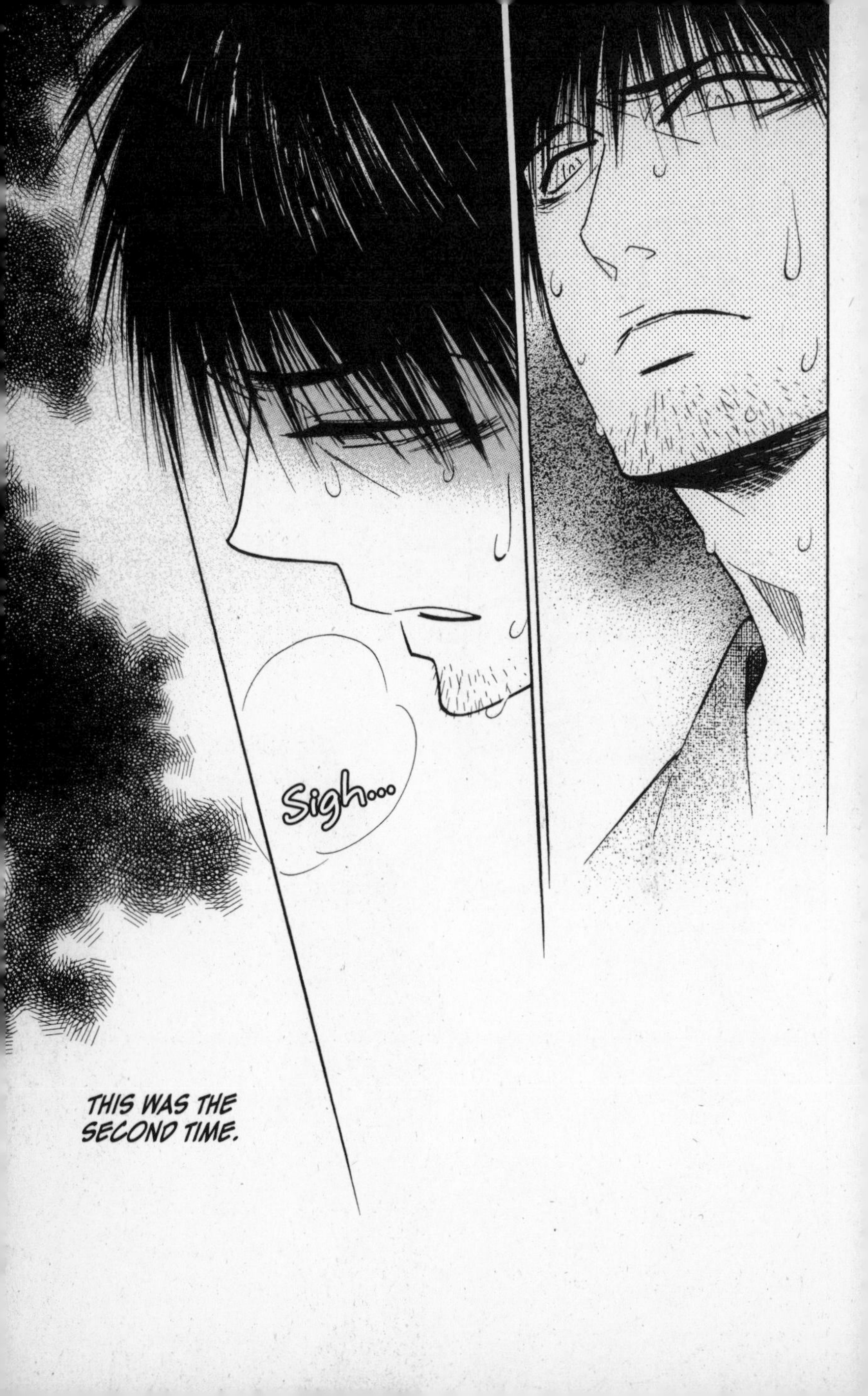
Sigh...
THIS WAS THE SECOND TIME.

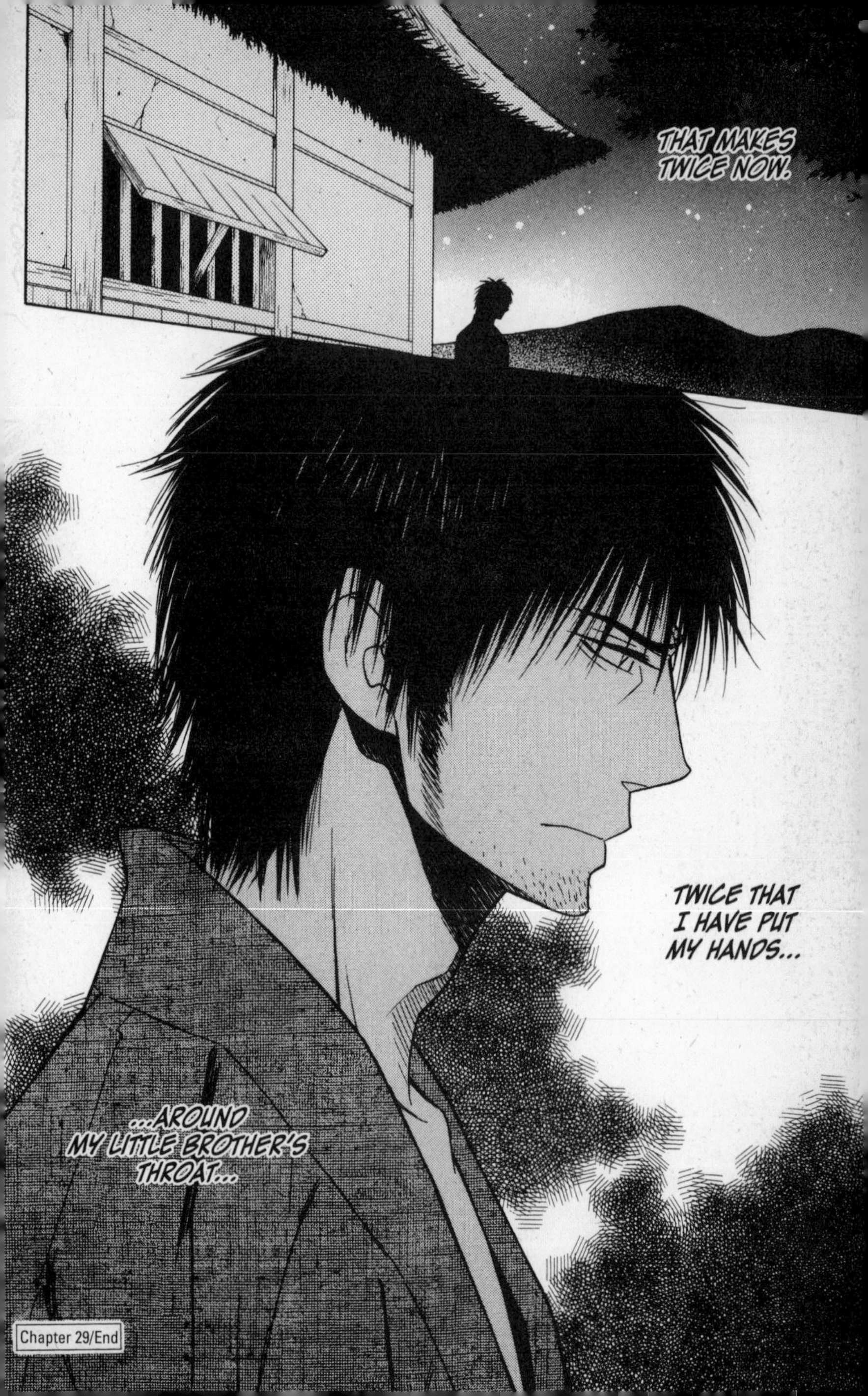
THAT MAKES TWICE NOW.
TWICE THAT I HAVE PUT MY HANDS...
...AROUND MY LITTLE BROTHER'S THROAT...
Chapter 29/End

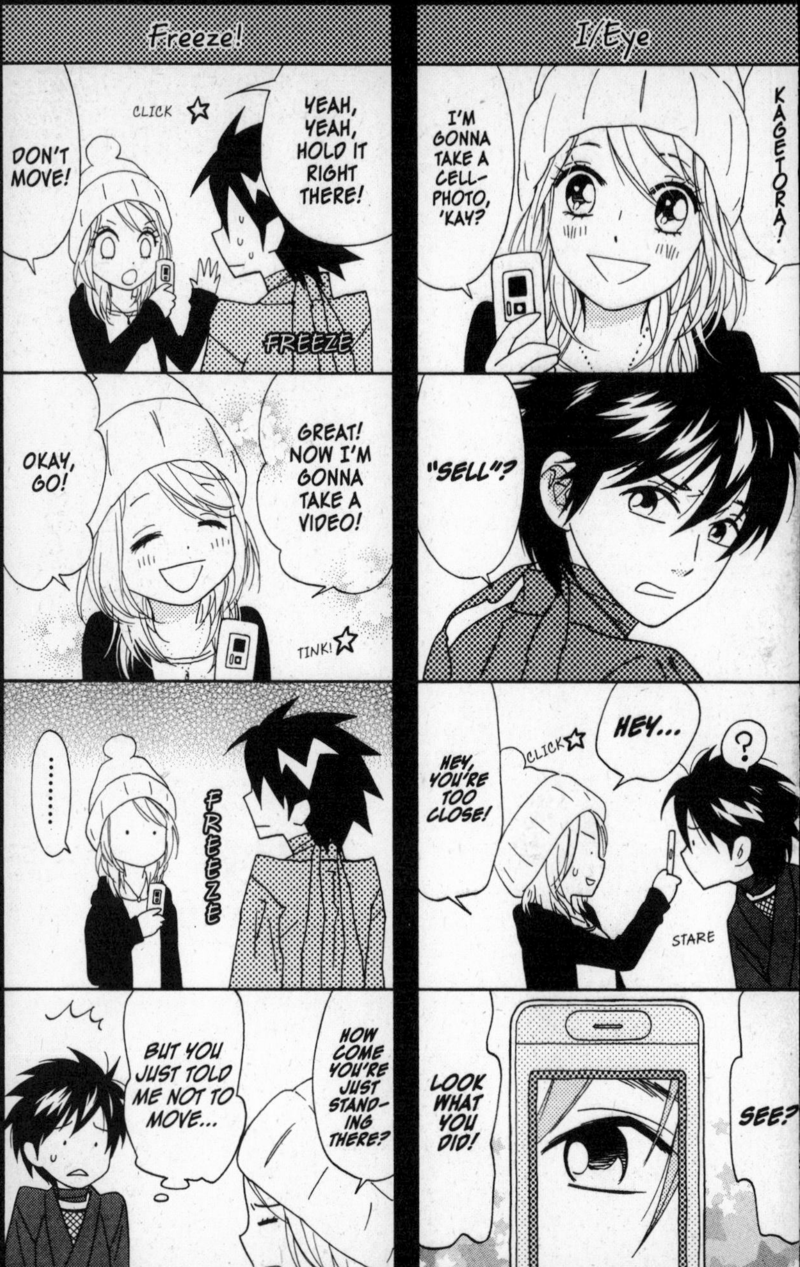
I/Eye
KAGETORA!
I'M GONNA TAKE A CELL-PHOTO, 'KAY?
"SELL"?
HEY...
CLICK
HEY, YOU'RE TOO CLOSE!
?
STARE
SEE?
LOOK WHAT YOU DID!
Freeze!
YEAH, YEAH, HOLD IT RIGHT THERE!
CLICK
DON'T MOVE!
FREEZE
GREAT! NOW I'M GONNA TAKE A VIDEO!
OKAY, GO!
TINK!
FREEZE
......
HOW COME YOU'RE JUST STANDING THERE?
BUT YOU JUST TOLD ME NOT TO MOVE...

No, not me...

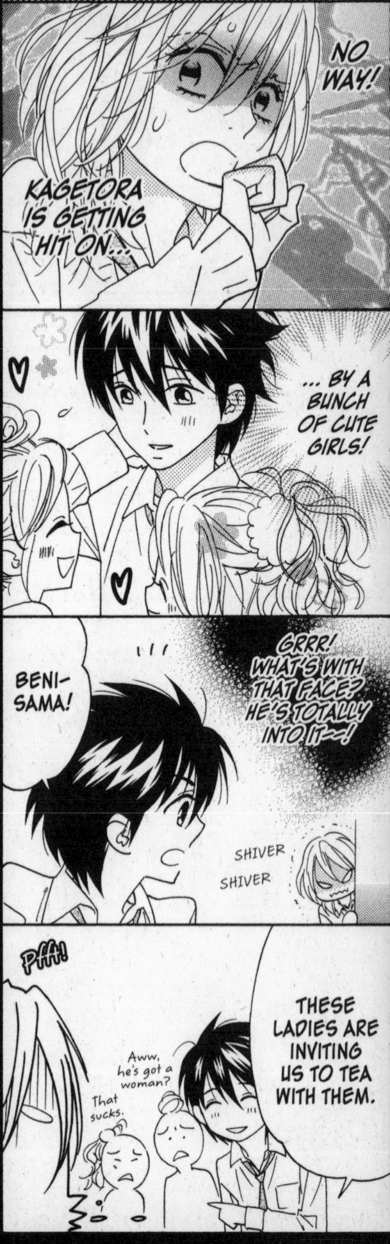
NO WAY!
KAGETORA IS GETTING HIT ON...
... BY A BUNCH OF CUTE GIRLS!
BENI-SAMA!
GRRR! WHAT'S WITH THAT FACE? HE'S TOTALLY INTO IT--!
SHIVER
SHIVER
Pfft!
THESE LADIES ARE INVITING US TO TEA WITH THEM.
Aww, he's got a woman?
That sucks.

Is that...slang?

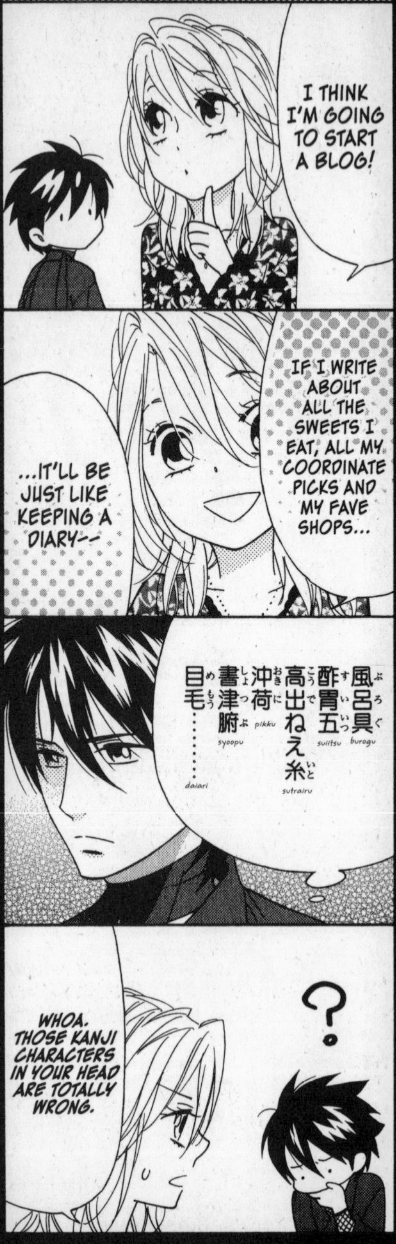
I THINK I'M GOING TO START A BLOG!
IF I WRITE ABOUT ALL THE SWEETS I EAT, ALL MY COORDINATE PICKS AND MY FAVE SHOPS...
...IT'LL BE JUST LIKE KEEPING A DIARY--
風呂具 burogu
酢胃五 suiitsu
高出ねえ糸 sutrairu
沖荷 pikku
書津腑 syoopu
目毛…… daiari
WHOA. THOSE KANJI CHARACTERS IN YOUR HEAD ARE TOTALLY WRONG.
?

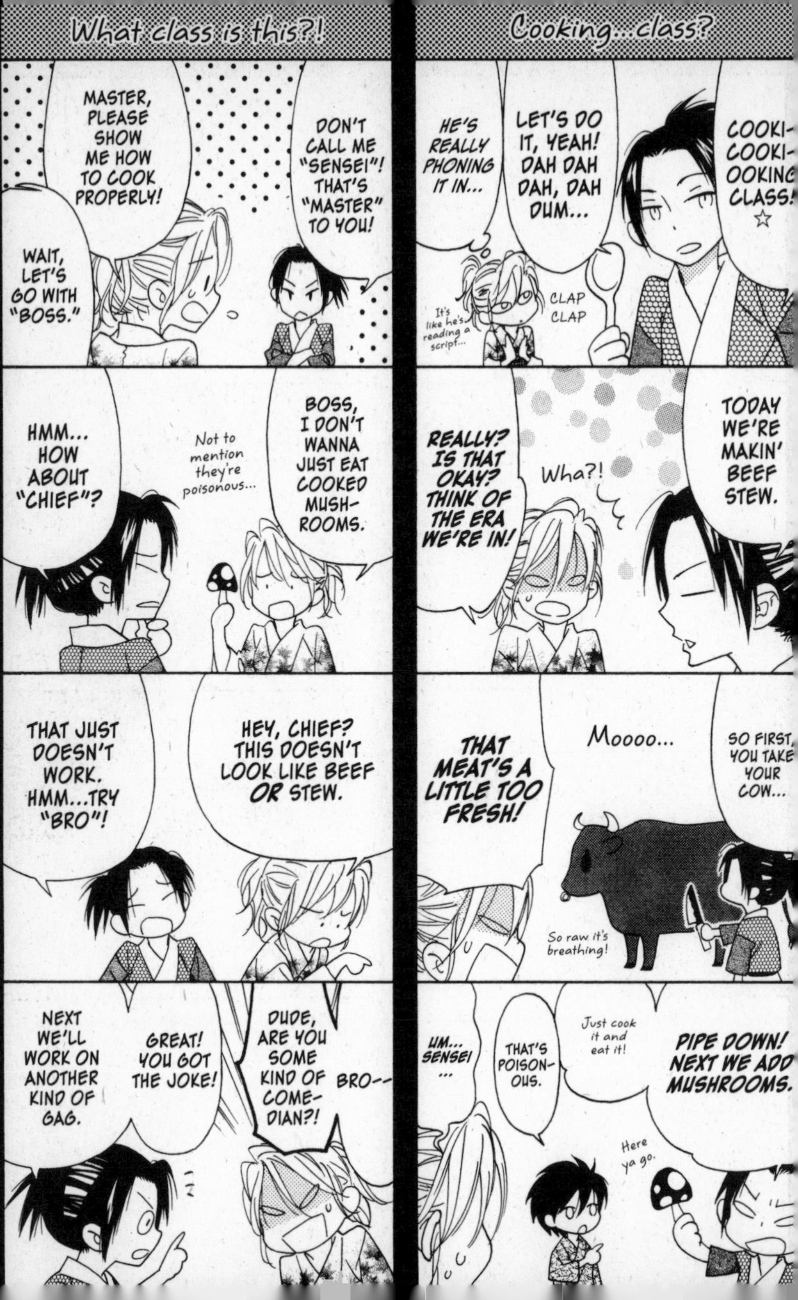
Cooking...class?
COOKI-COOKI-OOKING CLASS! ☆
LET'S DO IT, YEAH! DAH DAH DAH, DAH DUM...
HE'S REALLY PHONING IT IN...
CLAP CLAP
It's like he's reading a script...
TODAY WE'RE MAKIN' BEEF STEW.
Wha?!
REALLY? IS THAT OKAY? THINK OF THE ERA WE'RE IN!
SO FIRST, YOU TAKE YOUR COW...
Moooo...
THAT MEAT'S A LITTLE TOO FRESH!
So raw it's breathing!
PIPE DOWN! NEXT WE ADD MUSHROOMS.
Just cook it and eat it!
THAT'S POISON-OUS.
UM... SENSEI...
Here ya go.
What class is this?!
DON'T CALL ME "SENSEI"! THAT'S "MASTER" TO YOU!
MASTER, PLEASE SHOW ME HOW TO COOK PROPERLY!
WAIT, LET'S GO WITH "BOSS."
BOSS, I DON'T WANNA JUST EAT COOKED MUSH-ROOMS.
Not to mention they're poisonous...
HMM... HOW ABOUT "CHIEF"?
HEY, CHIEF? THIS DOESN'T LOOK LIKE BEEF OR STEW.
THAT JUST DOESN'T WORK. HMM...TRY "BRO"!
BRO--
DUDE, ARE YOU SOME KIND OF COME-DIAN?!
GREAT! YOU GOT THE JOKE!
NEXT WE'LL WORK ON ANOTHER KIND OF GAG.

In the next volume of

"HACHIKUMA" TRIES TO DEEPEN THE INUI CLAN'S SUSPICION OF RENKAKU, BUT RENKAKU IS ON TO HIM... OR IS HE JUST ON TO THE FACT THAT HIS BELOVED EIJI HAS A CRUSH ON HACHIKUMA? MEANWHILE, BENI STRUGGLES WITH HER GROWING FEELINGS FOR YOUNG KAGETORA. WILL CONFESSING HER FEELINGS FOR HIM NOW AFFECT THEIR FEELINGS FAR IN THE FUTURE? AND BIG KAGETORA STUMBLES INTO A NEW TIME PERIOD, IN BETWEEN HIS PAST AND BENI'S PRESENT, AND BOY IS HE SURPRISED BY WHO HE FINDS THERE!

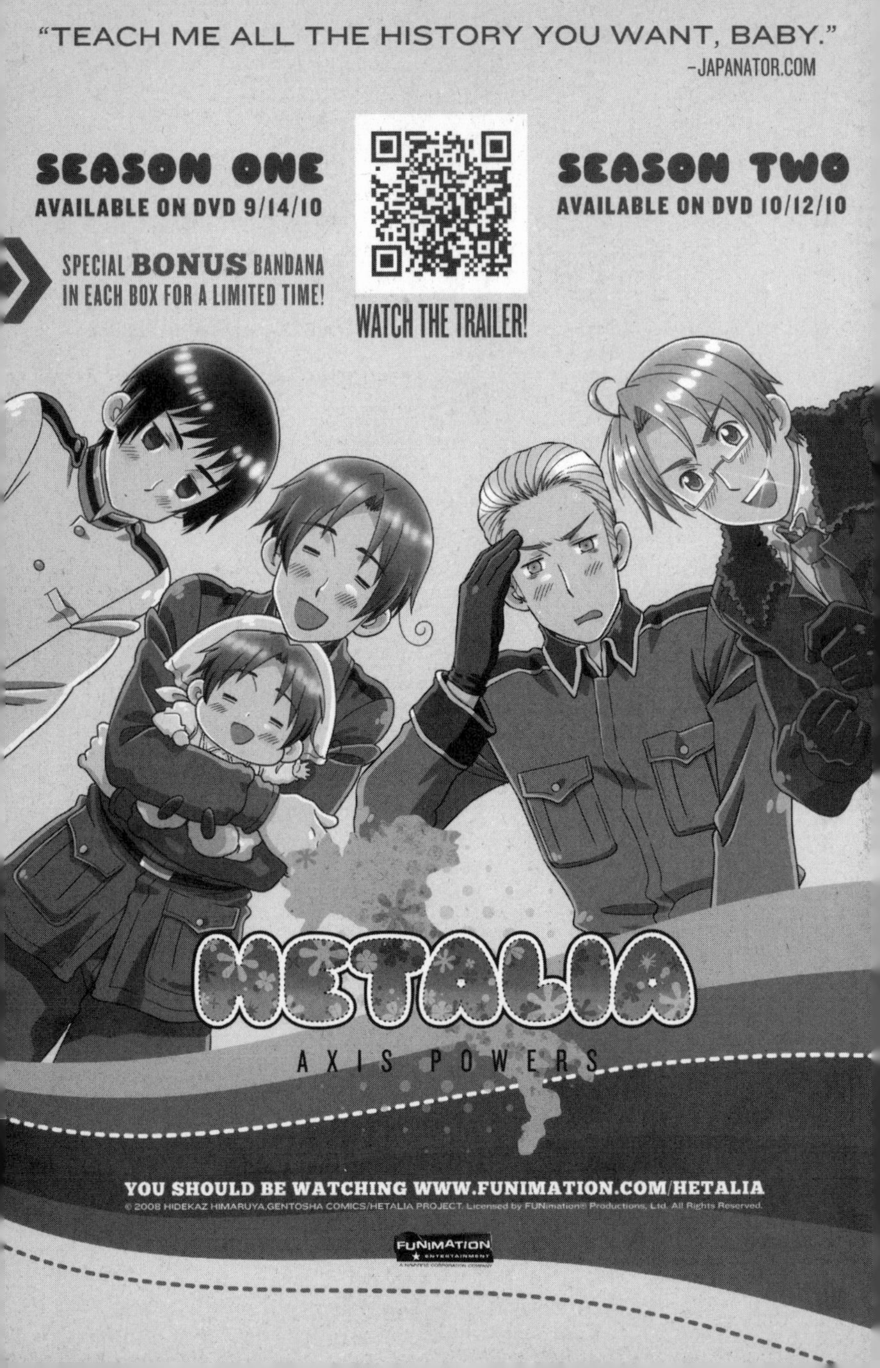

"TEACH ME ALL THE HISTORY YOU WANT, BABY."
–JAPANATOR.COM
SEASON ONE
AVAILABLE ON DVD 9/14/10
SPECIAL BONUS BANDANA IN EACH BOX FOR A LIMITED TIME!
WATCH THE TRAILER!
SEASON TWO
AVAILABLE ON DVD 10/12/10
HETALIA
AXIS POWERS
YOU SHOULD BE WATCHING WWW.FUNIMATION.COM/HETALIA
© 2008 HIDEKAZ HIMARUYA,GENTOSHA COMICS/HETALIA PROJECT. Licensed by FUNimation® Productions, Ltd. All Rights Reserved.
FUNIMATION ENTERTAINMENT

Great Empires,
A Fight to the Finish...and PASTA?

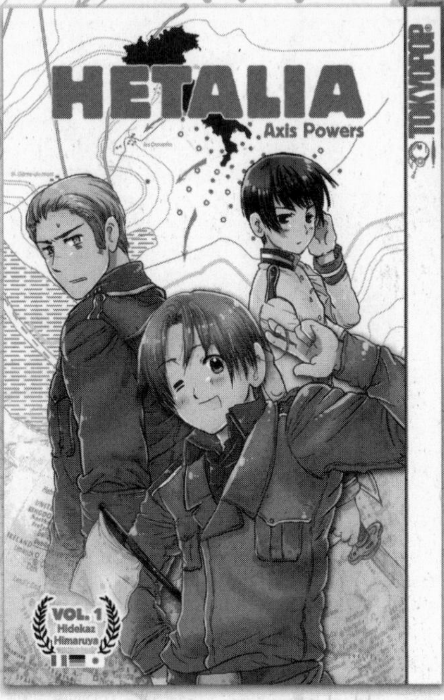
HETALIA
Axis Powers
TOKYOPOP
VOL. 1
Hidekaz
Himaruya

Manga available October 2010!!

Get ready to brush up on world history with these handsome and hysterical personifications of the Axis Powers as they meet, become friends and form one of the most powerful alliances the world has ever seen!

It all begins when tough soldier Germany stumbles upon Italy, who, despite being the descendant of the greatest empire in history, is found hiding in a tomato box. In another twist of fate around a rather lovely kotatsu, Japan hops on board and the Axis Powers are forged! What trials and tribulations will this mighty trio face?

COMEDY

OT OLDER TEEN AGE 16+

LIKE US ON FACEBOOK.COM/TOKYOPOP

Happy CAFE

Enjoy VOL 4

Our strong and sweet heroine continues to spread happiness at Café Bonheur . . .

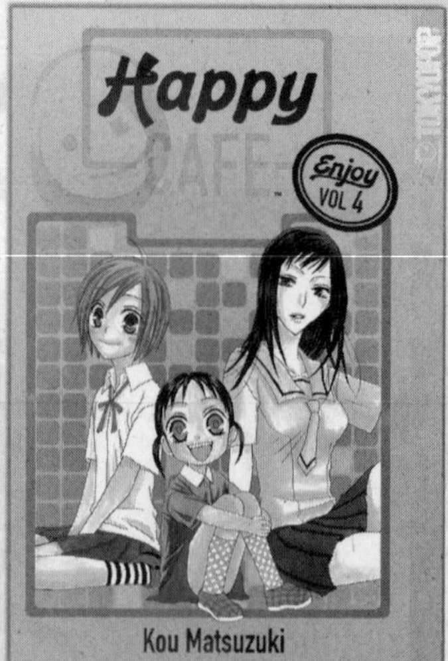
Happy
CAFE
Enjoy
VOL 4
TOKYOPOP
Kou Matsuzuki

Uru finds herself stuck in Shindo's apartment during a blackout. As the evening wears on, she accidentally falls asleep on his shoulder, keeping him up all night and eventually getting him sick! Can Uru help cure his ills?

If you like Me and My Brothers, you'll definitely enjoy Happy Café!

BE SURE TO VISIT WWW.TOKYOPOP.COM/SHOP FOR EVERYTHING YOU COULD EVER WANT!

The second epic trilogy continues!

Princess Ai: The Prism of Midnight Dawn

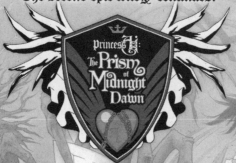

Ai fights to escape the clutches of her mysterious and malevolent captors, not knowing whether Kent, left behind on the Other Side, is even still alive. A frantic rescue mission commences, and in the end, even Ai's magical voice may not be enough to protect her from the trials of the Black Forest.

Dark secrets are revealed, and Ai must use all her strength and courage to face off against the new threat to Ai-Land. But will she ever see Kent again...?

Princess Ai
The Prism of Midnight Dawn
2

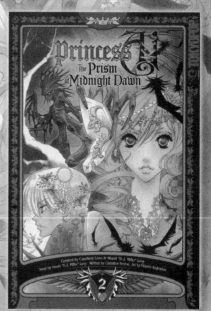

"A very intriguing read that will satisfy old fans and create new fans, too."
– *Bookloons*

Maid Sama!™

The class president has a little secret she's keeping from the sexy bad boy in school...

"It's hard to deny this guilty pleasure when it looks like it's having so much fun."
–About.com

The rogue hypnotist strikes again, this time planting the suggestion in Misaki that if she falls asleep, she'll wake up hating Usui! Well, hating him more than usual... So it's up to Usui to preserve their relationship (such as it is) by keeping Misaki awake as long as possible!

ROMANCE

T TEEN AGE 13+

Maid Sama!
Hiro Fujiwara
TOKYOPOP
4

BE SURE TO VISIT WWW.TOKYOPOP.COM/SHOP FOR EVERYTHING YOU COULD EVER WANT!

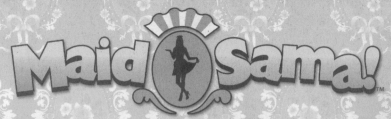

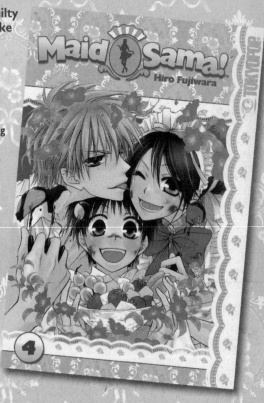